THE CULT OF THE NATION
IN FRANCE

The Cult of the Nation in France

Inventing Nationalism, 1680–1800

DAVID A. BELL

HARVARD UNIVERSITY PRESS

Cambridge, Massachusetts

London, England

First Harvard University Press paperback edition, 2003

Second printing, 2003

Library of Congress Cataloging-in-Publication Data

Bell, David Avrom.
The cult of the nation in France : inventing nationalism,
1680–1800 / David A. Bell.
p. cm.
Includes bibliographical references and index.
ISBN 0-674-00447-7 (cloth)
ISBN 0-674-01237-2 (paper)
1. Nationalism—France—History.
2. France—Politics and government—17th century.
3. France—Politics and government—18th century.
4. French language—Political aspects.
5. National characteristics, French.
I. Title.
DC121.3 .B45 2001
320.54′0944′09033—dc21   2001024695

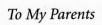

To My Parents

Contents

List of Illustrations

Preface

This project has been long in the making. In some ways, I can trace it back to the first kindling of my enthusiasm for history nearly thirty years ago, when, looking through a historical atlas, I found that the national boundaries I was learning about in grade school were not timeless and immutable. Instead, they had flowed back and forth across the European continent like tides, raising up and then again submerging countries with exotic names like Lotharingia and Montenegro, Lombardy and Moldavia. I wondered about visiting these places, about crossing the Austrian-Ottoman frontier, and about what the map might look like if there were, for instance, a North and South France alongside West and East Germany.

I was therefore delighted, during college, to see a draft article by Patrice Higonnet with a linguistic map of France in 1789—a map that carved the familiar territory into exotic quasi-nations like Brittany, Flanders, Occitania, and the Basque Country. It was delicious to realize that even in the relatively recent past, crossing the Loire River could seem in some respects like crossing an international border.

Later, a book by Michel de Certeau, Dominique Julia, and Jacques Revel, *Une politique de la langue,* gave me further insight into the linguistic situation in France at the time of the Revolution and provided samples of revolutionary-era Occitan writing. The book remained vividly in my mind two years later when, in graduate school at Princeton, I made language and nation-building in eighteenth-century Alsace the subject of my first extended research paper.

Nationalism and language in the meantime were becoming prominent topics, thanks to the collapse of communism, the newest reshuffling of European borders, the apparent revival of nationalism throughout the world (including national movements in Lombardy, Montenegro, and Moldavia, if not yet in Lotharingia), and a much ballyhooed crisis of national identity in France itself.

I have now been working on the topic for several years, and this book is the result. In the process I have had a considerable amount of assistance, which it is my pleasure to acknowledge here. Needless to say, the flaws which remain are my responsibility alone.

Financially, I enjoyed especially generous support from the Morse Fellowships of Yale University, the National Endowment for the Humanities, and the Woodrow Wilson International Center for Scholars. The first of these allowed me to take a year off from teaching to do research in France, and the other two gave me the chance to take a second year off and write this book in the comfortable surroundings of the Wilson Center in Washington. Additional financial support, which permitted me to take further research trips to France, came from the Whitney Humanities Center of Yale University, the Griswold Research Funds of Yale University, the East-West Seminar of the International Society for Eighteenth-Century Studies, the Krieger School of Arts and Sciences of the Johns Hopkins University, and the History Department of the Johns Hopkins University.

Research for this project was carried out above all at the old Bibliothèque Nationale of the rue de Richelieu in Paris. My thanks to its staff and to the staffs of the Archives Nationales, the Bibliothèque de la Société de Port-Royal, the Bibliothèque Mazarine, the Bibliothèque Municipale de Toulouse, and the Bibliothèque Nationale et Universitaire de Strasbourg. My thanks as well to Darrin McMahon, Matthew Lauzon, Alec Meredith, and Matthew Stephenson for valuable research assistance. I am in the debt of the cheerful and efficient staffs of the History Department at Johns Hopkins (especially Shirley Hipley, Sharon Widomski, and Lisa Enders), and the Wilson Center (especially Lindsay Collins) for making the experience of working in these places so pleasant and hassle-free.

I have had the opportunity to present aspects of this project to numerous professional gatherings. My thanks to all of the following, and to the audiences that attended: the Departments of History of the University of California at Irvine, Brown University, Cornell University, Catholic University, Emory University, the University of Maryland, and the Johns Hopkins University; the Modern French Study Groups at the University of Pennsylvania and the University of Chicago; the Washington-Baltimore Old Regime French History Group; the Center for European Studies of

Harvard University; the Whitney Humanities Center of Yale University; the work-in-progress group at the Woodrow Wilson Center; the Davis Center of Princeton University; the research seminars of Roger Chartier at the Ecole des Hautes Etudes en Sciences Sociales, Bernard Cottret at the Université de Paris-IV and Jean-Pierre Jessenne at the Université de Rouen; the East-West Seminar of the International Society for Eighteenth-Century Studies; the conference on "Language and Nationalism" at the Whitney Center at Yale; the conference on "The Abbé Grégoire and His Causes" at the Clark Library; the conference on "France: History and Story" at the University of Birmingham; the conference on "Patriotism in the Atlantic World" at the Université de Versailles-Saint-Quentin; the conference on "The Tercentenary of the Bourbons" at the Universidad Autónoma de Madrid; the American Historical Association; the Society for French Historical Studies; the Western Society for French History; the Western Society for Eighteenth-Century Studies; the Society for the History of the Early American Republic; and the North American Society for Legal History. My special thanks to Anthony Grafton and my graduate adviser, Robert Darnton, for hosting me so warmly at the Davis Center.

Many friends and colleagues have read and responded to various parts of this project and provided valuable criticism, suggestions, and encouragement. My deep thanks to Keith Michael Baker, Doron Ben-Atar, Philip Benedict, Ann Blair, Gail Bossenga, Gregory Brown, Jack Censer, Roger Chartier, Paul Cohen, Linda Colley, Robert Darnton, Steven Englund, Joël Félix, Paul Friedland, Rita Hermon-Belot, Carla Hesse, Patrice Higonnet, Michael Holquist, Lynn Hunt, Colin Jones, Richard Kagan, Steven Kaplan, Michael Kazin, Sarah Maza, John Merriman, Robert Morrissey, John Pocock, Jeremy Popkin, Jeffrey Ravel, Sophia Rosenfeld, Robert Schneider, Alyssa Sepinwall, William Sewell, Gabrielle Spiegel, David Stebenne, Donald Sutherland, Timothy Tackett, and Judith Walkowitz. I am particularly grateful for the extensive, detailed comments I received on draft chapters from Daniel Gordon, Darrin McMahon (again), Orest Ranum, Peter Sahlins, and Dale Van Kley, and for the careful and sympathetic reading of the manuscript for Harvard University Press by Joan Landes and an anonymous reader. Dror Wahrman's comments, suggestions, friendship, and intellectual companionship have been invaluable. My colleagues in the History Departments at Yale and Johns Hopkins provided indispensable support. I am grateful to Hélène Dupuy for giving me a copy of her *mémoire de doctorat*. At Harvard University Press, my heartfelt thanks to Aida Donald, Kathleen McDermott, Elizabeth Suttell, and Anita Safran.

Some material in Chapter 6 is adapted from my essay "Lingua Populi, Lingua Dei: Language, Religion and the Origins of French Revolutionary Nationalism," in *American Historical Review* C/5 (1995). Some material in Chapter 3 is adapted from my essay "Jumonville's Death: Nation and Race in Eighteenth-century France," in Colin Jones and Dror Wahrman, eds., *The Age of Cultural Revolutions: Britain and France, 1750–1820* (Berkeley: University of California Press, 2001). Copyright © 2001, The Regents of the University of California.

My debt to Donna Lynn Farber is more personal, and the greatest of all. She and our children, Elana and Joseph, have filled the years I have worked on this book with great happiness.

This book is dedicated to Daniel and Pearl Kazin Bell: loving and supportive parents, intellectuals in the best sense of the word, examples that I will always try to follow. *L'dor va-dor.*

THE CULT OF THE NATION
IN FRANCE

Constructing the Nation

The time has come to write about nations.
—FRANÇOIS-IGNACE D'ESPIARD DE LA BORDE,
L'ESPRIT DES NATIONS (1752)

December 21, 1792. In the drafty, makeshift meeting hall of the National Convention in Paris, the rulers of France are drunk on history. Just four years before, they were ordinary, forgettable men, pursuing ordinary, forgettable careers. Now they know, for a certainty, that posterity will record their names alongside those of the classical heroes they adore. In four years, they have overthrown a monarchy that had lasted for more than a thousand, and—so they believe—have opened the door to an era of universal happiness, if only the truths they uphold can prevail over ignorance and egotism. To defend these truths, they are preparing to sit in judgment over their former king, to hold him responsible for his actions, and to demand of him the ultimate penalty. As Maximilien Robespierre declared in this same hall three weeks previously, fully aware of his words' importance to history: "Louis must die because the *patrie* must live."[1]

But even at this grave moment, the Convention has other work to do, and so Jean-Paul Rabaut de Saint-Etienne rises to speak on the subject of education. In this newly elected, radical assembly, Rabaut is very much yesterday's man. An eloquent representative of France's persecuted Protestants under the old regime, and thus an exemplary victim of "despotism," his career as a revolutionary bloomed early and easily. Now, in the eyes of radical leaders like Robespierre, it has wilted, and gives off the disagreeable, decaying odor of moderation. Rabaut has objected to putting the king on trial and has denounced the rising tide of revolutionary violence. In response, radical demagogues have heaped insult after vituperative insult on him. Already, perhaps, Rabaut can see the path that will take him, in less than a year, to the guillotine.[2] Yet he does nothing today to appease the advocates of violence, for even while laying out his program for national

1

education, he cannot resist taking a sharp jibe at them. Education, he declares, not only inspires the "sweet sentiment" of fraternity, but offers an alternative to "the gloomy terror which is enfolding us, and that dark behavior in which frightened onlookers believe they can see signs of an approaching storm."[3]

Apart from this dark warning, however, Rabaut's speech betrays few signs of historical fatigue or doubt. He still speaks in the same accents of infinite confidence in which he proclaimed, in 1789, that the French nation was "made, not to follow examples, but to give them."[4] A good theory of education, this Calvinist pastor-turned-man-of-the-Enlightenment now explains, should begin with nothing less than the assumption "that man is capable of indefinite perfection, and that this perfection depends on the enlightenment he receives." Millions of individuals can be, and urgently need to be, reshaped like a gigantic piece of clay through the sheer application of political will. "We must, absolutely, renew the present generation, while forging the generation to come," he declares. "We must make of the French a new people." And to do this, he demands "an infallible means of transmitting, constantly and immediately, to all the French at once, the same uniform ideas."[5]

When Rabaut speaks of education, he actually means indoctrination, at least to begin with, for France's needs are too pressing to rely on the slow, steady progress of what he calls *les lumières*—enlightenment. Reshaping the French people in a single generation demands a program of overwhelming force, a second "revolution in heads and hearts" parallel to the one already accomplished in government and society. It must use every available means: "the senses, the imagination, memory, reasoning, all the faculties that man possesses." In practice, it entails subjecting the French to a long list of obligatory civic functions, including physical exercises, parades, festivals, "morality lessons," the reading and memorization of key political texts, and the singing of patriotic songs. Rabaut stresses the need to bewitch the people, if necessary. Education must be "likeable, seductive, and entrancing."[6]

What models does Rabaut offer for this vastly ambitious project of patriotic education? Predictably, for a participant in this most classical of revolutions, he evokes the regimented societies of ancient Sparta and Crete. Yet he quickly adds that enormous differences separate these "children of nature" from modern "agricultural and commercial peoples."[7] He spends far more time discussing another model, and his words on the subject are worth quoting at length:

> The secret was well known to the priests, who, with their catechisms, their processions . . . their ceremonies, sermons, hymns, missions, pilgrimages, patron saints, paintings, and all that nature placed at their disposal, infallibly led men to the goal they designated. They took hold of a man at birth, grasped him again in childhood, adolescence and adulthood, when he married and had children, in his moments of grief and remorse, in the sanctum of his conscience . . . in sickness and at death. In this way they managed to cast many far-flung nations, differing in their customs, languages, laws, color and physical makeup, into the same mold, and to give them the same opinions. O cunning lawgivers, who speak to us in the name of heaven, should we not do in the name of truth and freedom, what you so often did in the name of error and slavery?[8]

Driving the point home, Rabaut does not hesitate to adopt an explicitly religious vocabulary for his proposed civic functions. Each canton will stage its ceremonies in National Temples, or, pending their construction, in churches. The people will sing "hymns" and learn "catechisms." The bulk of the activities will take place on Sundays. It seems a program designed to please a Jesuit more than a Jacobin.

For the moment, though, the Jacobins *are* pleased. According to the newspaper *Le Moniteur*, the Convention interrupts Rabaut's speech several times with applause, and approves his proposals unanimously.[9] Despite the deep shadow cast by the king's trial, the "gloomy terror" of this tense winter momentarily recedes, and Rabaut de Saint-Etienne stands in harmony with his future executioners. His words, which he will soon publish under the title *Project of National Education*, have become official policy for the French state.[10]

Lost in the torrents of French revolutionary politics, Rabaut's speech has received little subsequent attention.[11] Yet it marks, as well as any single event can, the historical moment at which it becomes possible to speak of nationalism in France. It is hardly the first example of French national *sentiment*, a phenomenon whose history extends back to the Middle Ages.[12] But national *sentiment* and national*ism* are by no means the same thing, even if modern theorists frequently conflate them.[13] More than a sentiment, nationalism is a political program which has as its goal not merely to praise, or defend, or strengthen a nation, but actively to construct one, casting its human raw material into a fundamentally new form. Long before the current fashion for treating all social and cultural phenomena

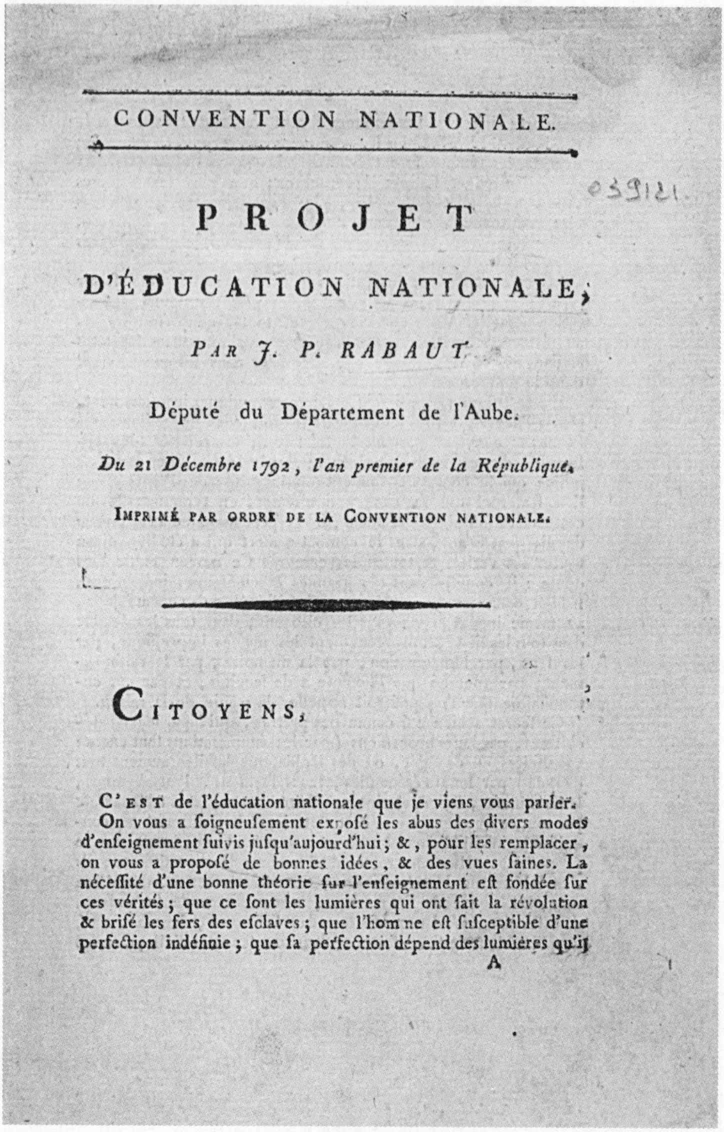

CONVENTION NATIONALE.

PROJET

D'ÉDUCATION NATIONALE;

PAR J. P. RABAUT

Député du Département de l'Aube.

Du 21 Décembre 1792, l'an premier de la République.

IMPRIMÉ PAR ORDRE DE LA CONVENTION NATIONALE.

CITOYENS,

C'EST de l'éducation nationale que je viens vous parler. On vous a ſoigneuſement expoſé les abus des divers modes d'enſeignement ſuivis juſqu'aujourd'hui; &, pour les remplacer, on vous a propoſé de bonnes idées, & des vues ſaines. La néceſſité d'une bonne théorie ſur l'enſeignement eſt fondée ſur ces vérités; que ce ſont les lumières qui ont fait la révolution & briſé les fers des eſclaves; que l'homme eſt ſuſceptible d'une perfection indéfinie; que ſa perfection dépend des lumières qu'il

A

Figure 1. Title page from Jean-Paul Rabaut de Saint-Etienne, *Projet d'éducation nationale* (Project of National Education), Paris, 1792. Rabaut's project, first sketched out in a speech to France's National Convention, aimed at giving all the French "the same, uniform ideas."

as constructions, nationalists quite consciously saw their nations in this manner.

This point has not been generally recognized because nationalists have so often obscured it by invoking their nation's primordial essence, linked to its blood, or language, or historical territory. Such invocations come naturally to them, for only by presenting a nation as something whose existence and rights are beyond question can they justify the large political claims they tend to make on its behalf. Nationalism almost irresistibly calls forth images of immemorial pasts, of lengthy and unbroken lineages, of deep bonds between particular peoples and particular lands. New constructions therefore tend to be presented as acts of *reconstruction*, recovery, and regeneration.[14] Yet even the nationalists most convinced of their nation's immemorial rights still also acknowledge that large-scale political action is necessary to complete and perfect the national entity, so as to forge a truly cohesive body. Relevant measures have included education, the strengthening of common symbols and loyalties, the rectification of political borders, and the suppression or expulsion of minorities within those borders.[15] Even in the time and place—nineteenth-century Germany—perhaps most closely associated with lyrical invocations of a primordial national essence, these tasks were still deemed vital. As Geoff Eley has concisely remarked about the early days of the newly united Second Reich: "Unification entailed a subsequent process of cultural coalescence which in theory it had already presupposed."[16] In other words, no matter how urgently it invokes the past, nationalism has something inescapably paradoxical about it. It makes political claims which take the nation's existence wholly for granted, yet it proposes programs which treat the nation as something yet unbuilt.

Today, the concept of nation-building seems so natural that the fact of its relatively recent origins has gone virtually unnoticed, despite the recent efflorescence of works on nationalism. The word "nation" itself has a long lineage, as does the idea that the human race is naturally divided into nations. Yet until the eighteenth-century age of revolutions, the idea of actively *constructing* a nation through political action lay beyond the mental horizons of Western Europeans.[17] In European usage, nations were facts of nature: they signified basic divisions of the human species, not products of human will.[18] From 1140, when a Norman bishop described the Welsh *natio* to the pope as a group distinct in "language, laws, habits, modes of judgment and customs," to 1694, when the first dictionary of the Académie

Française defined *nation* as "the inhabitants of a common country, who live under the same laws and use the same language," the meaning changed relatively little.[19] Europeans of course believed that nations could have founders, and celebrated such figures in their national literatures, much as Virgil had celebrated the founder of Rome in his *Aeneid*. They also appreciated the importance of a nation's nobility sharing the language and manners of its monarch. The great cardinal-ministers of seventeenth-century France, Richelieu and Mazarin, both hoped to found schools where young nobles of newly annexed provinces could learn how to be French.[20]

None of this, however, amounted to nation-building in the modern sense. Neither Virgil nor Richelieu or Mazarin envisioned taking entire populations—from elegant courtiers to impoverished sharecroppers, from well-polished intellectuals to urban beggars—and forging them all, in their millions, into a single nation, transforming everything from language to manners to the most intimate ideas. They did not imagine programs of national education of the sort sketched out by Rabaut, or massive political action to reduce regional differences, or laws demarcating national citizens from foreigners. Programs this breathtakingly ambitious, programs which deserve the name of "nationalist," arose only in the eighteenth century. It is this fact which makes nationalism, if not national sentiment, a peculiarly modern phenomenon.[21] It is no coincidence that the word "nationalism" itself was coined in the late 1790s, precisely as overwhelmed observers were struggling to make sense of the political deluge they had just witnessed in France.[22]

This book is about the way in which the French came to think of their nation as a political construction and, furthermore, came to see the process of construction itself as a central task of political life. The pages that follow will offer a reinterpretation both of the origins of nationalism, and of an important aspect of modern French history. In the first case, I want to argue that nationalism was invented in the eighteenth century, and to offer a new explanation for why that was so. In the second case, I want to show just how much the political and cultural landscape of France itself changed in the process. For as the French began to think like nationalists, they came to understand many aspects of the world around them in radically new ways.

In one sense, the French began to think like nationalists over a very short period of time: immediately before and during the French Revolution of 1789, less than the space of a single generation. Yet the transformation cannot be properly understood without setting it in a deeper context: it represented the culmination of a process that had begun a century earlier. In this book I will show that in the decades around 1700, two intimately related concepts gained a political salience and centrality they had previously lacked. These were the concepts of the nation itself, and that of the *patrie,* or fatherland. Both referred to the entity known as France, but the first signified above all a group of people sharing certain important, binding qualities, while the second was used in the sense of a territory commanding a person's emotional attachment and ultimate political loyalty (I will have much more to say about these definitions). Their political and cultural importance only increased over the course of the eighteenth century, and by its end they had both come to possess a talismanic power. A cult of the nation had come into being.

Much of the book will be concerned with this pre-revolutionary change. I will emphasize that it was intellectually violent, involving anxious and heated debates over the nature and condition of the French nation and *patrie.* But it was not intellectually unproductive, for the violence ultimately brought about the conditions for the invention of nationalism itself in the revolutionary period. Over the course of the century, thanks to the anxieties the debates generated, a widespread conviction arose that a true nation and a true *patrie* did not yet exist in France. From this conviction, in turn, emerged the sense that these entities needed, desperately, to be constructed. The book, having established this point, will then proceed to explore the French revolutionaries' proposed solutions to the problem: their conscious programs of nation-building and patriotic instruction, such as the one sketched out by Rabaut de Saint-Etienne. Finally, I will trace the consequences of the story for the history of modern France, down to the present day.

I will also argue that the dynamics that governed this story and made nationalism thinkable were principally cultural and religious in nature. Nationalism in France arose simultaneously out of, and in opposition to, Christian systems of belief.[23] The rise of the concepts of nation and *patrie* initially took place as Europeans came to perceive a radical separation between God and the world, searched for ways to discern and maintain terrestrial order in the face of God's absence, and struggled to relegate religion to a newly defined private sphere of human endeavor, separate from politics. It was only when the French ceased to see themselves as part of a great hierarchy uniting heaven and earth, the two linked by an apostolic church and a divinely ordained king, that they could start to see themselves as equal members of a distinct, uniform, and sovereign nation.

Yet despite this desire to find explicitly nonreligious means of binding men and women into a greater whole, early French nationalism remained powerfully shaped by the heritage of Christianity. When the leaders of revolutionary France confronted the task of converting a largely peasant population of twenty-eight million to new, national norms, they ironically found themselves reaching back to an older, clerical model of evangelization. Even Louis XIV, the most ambitious of France's kings, had shown little concern for molding his subjects into a single national body. It was enough that they obeyed his laws, paid his taxes, and demonstrated their loyalty to his government.[24] The precedents for revolutionary nationalism lay, rather, in the great efforts made by Catholic and Protestant churches to convert a peasantry they perceived as still largely pagan and savage to their competing visions of true Christianity. Only the churches, in their long, patient efforts to send missionaries into the villages, to root out superstition and error, and effectively to impose a new culture and new morality on the populations of Western Europe, matched the ambitions of modern nationalists.[25] Rabaut Saint-Etienne recognized this precedent when he spoke of how the priesthood had managed "to cast many far-flung nations, differing in their customs, languages, laws, color and physical makeup, into the same mold." But France now had to invent a secular version of the same process, not to mold different nations together into a single church, but to mold different regions and classes together into a single nation.

Although this is a book about France, I do not wish to claim that the French deserve particular credit for inventing nationalism. French nationalism emerged as part of a general religious and cultural transformation that reached across Europe, from powerful monarchies such as Great Britain to peripheral areas like Greece and Corsica.[26] But France *was* distinguished by the self-consciousness with which the issues were discussed, the unusually strong emphasis on political will as the foundation stone of the nation (as opposed to language or blood or history), and the amazing suddenness and strength with which a coherent nationalist program crystallized during the French Revolution. Moreover, French nationalism has been an almost unparalleled success story. The fascination of scholars and journalists with tiny present-day French regionalist movements, not to mention recent squawks of anxiety over a supposed "crisis of French national identity," has done much to obscure the fact that for two centuries France has been the most strongly cohesive national unit in Europe.[27] France, almost alone among all major European nations, can make the striking claim that in modern times, despite episodes of violent civil war, it has experienced no serious threat of regional secession (not counting Germany's forcible, temporary annexation of Alsace-Lorraine). If the French were not the sole inventors of nationalism, they have been perhaps its principal model.

A general survey of the origins of nationalism in France is by now long overdue. Despite the significance of the French story, and the fact that nearly every general history and theoretical study of nationalism makes copious reference to it, readers still have nothing comparable to the works of Linda Colley for Great Britain, or Eugen Weber for late-nineteenth-century French national identity.[28] This is partly because of an assumption which long went unchallenged among social scientists and social historians, namely that nationalism only emerged hand-in-hand with an industrial, capitalist "modernity."[29] It is also partly because nationalist and patriotic passions flared up so intensely during the French Revolution that scholars have had difficulty believing they had meaningful roots in the *ancien régime*, still less religious roots. It has often seemed that these passions must have sprung forth fully grown in 1789 from the revolutionary process itself. As Giacomo Casanova, usually a keen observer of human impulses, wrote in 1797: "This people has become a worshipper of its *patrie*, without ever having known, before the Revolution, what a *patrie* was, or even the word itself."[30]

Only recently have conditions become more favorable for a study of the sort I am undertaking. On the one hand, social scientists have begun effectively to challenge the necessary association of nationalism with industrial capitalism—although mostly without sufficient recognition of the importance of religion.[31] And on the other, historians of France have set to work exploring the richness and dynamism of pre-revolutionary French political culture, showing that revolutionary ideologies had origins that went well beyond the circles of the *philosophes* and amounted to more than the simple reflection of changing social conditions.[32] Thanks to these studies, and to important new work on related subjects, it has become both necessary and possible to trace the great eighteenth-century ferment around the concepts of *nation* and *patrie*.[33]

The subject matter for such a study is copious and remarkably varied. Yet much of it remains poorly known, and so a brief overview may be useful at this point. What distinguishes this material is not simply the fact that the concepts of nation and *patrie* appear frequently in it, but that they are the objects of sustained—even obsessive—reflection and debate. It is precisely this quality which separates the eighteenth century from earlier periods and reveals its importance to the history of nationalism in France. The words "nation" and *patrie* themselves were, of course, in common usage long before the eighteenth century. *Patrie* served intermittently as a political rallying cry, particularly during the Wars of Religion of the sixteenth century, when Protestants and moderate Catholics found it useful to place loyalty to France above loyalty to any particular confession.[34] But before the late seventeenth century, the French did not write treatises about the meanings of the words or debate these meanings in political pamphlets. They did not speak of either entity as an authority superior to the king or even as clearly distinct from him.[35] It was only in 1683 that the Jansenist cleric Jean Soanen preached a sermon on "Love of the *Patrie*," perhaps the first extended exploration of the theme in French.[36] In the 1710s and 1720s, *nation* and *patrie* both began to feature prominently in criticisms of the absolute monarchy and to appear more frequently in many other sorts of texts.

Then, in 1743, in a turning point of sorts, a little known priest and magistrate from Dijon named François-Ignace d'Espiard de la Borde published a remarkable and unjustly ignored book entitled *Essais sur le génie et le caractère des nations* (*Essays on the Genius and Character of Nations*).[37] Probably because of its muddy style, in a century which treasured French prose for its clarity and wit, the book sank with little trace (although a later version, entitled *The Spirit of the Nations* in obvious imitation of Montesquieu's *The Spirit of the Laws*, did enjoy moderate success).[38] But it was perhaps the first book to make nations the subject of extended scholarly inquiry, and it powerfully foreshadowed subsequent discussions, both in its attention to the role of climate and history in shaping "national character" and in its musings about whether political action could alter this character.[39] D'Espiard even speculated about what it would have taken to "remove the vices contrary to the nature of a free state" from France and create a true French republic, although he nervously insisted he was making this "most singular supposition" purely as a scholarly hypothesis.[40]

Within a decade, more famous figures had begun to examine the same issues. In 1748, Montesquieu made what he called "the general spirit of nations" central to his masterpiece, *L'esprit des lois,* and a few years after that, Voltaire published his vast comparative history of nations, whose full title read *Histoire générale et essai sur les moeurs et l'esprit des nations.*[41] Rousseau, meanwhile, was developing his idea that only a people whose souls had a "national physiognomy" formed by "national institutions" could resist the lure of "vain precepts" and the fate of blending into a vapid European sameness.[42] Rousseau, who has a key place in the development of the idea of the nation as a political construction, pondered, more deeply than any other eighteenth-century thinker, the connections between national and religious sentiments.

Beyond these rarefied intellectual precincts, the great official institutions which dominated French cultural life were also increasingly defining themselves in relation to the *nation.* In 1758, the Académie Française made "the great men of the nation" the theme of its prestigious annual oratorical competitions.[43] Soon afterwards, the Comédie Française began producing a series of stage plays celebrating famous episodes in French national history. They enjoyed enormous popularity, despite Voltaire's mordant quip that audiences would eventually prefer being entertained to being praised for their choice of nationality.[44] France's recalcitrant *parlements* (sovereign courts) evoked "the rights of the nation" in their long-standing quarrel with France's kings over the limits of royal authority, and, as the temperature of political conflict increased, so did use of the phrase.[45] Already in 1754 the Marquis d'Argenson wrote in his journal that "the words *nation* and *state* have never been repeated as often as they are today." By 1789, one historical work reported that "the epithet 'national' is in everyone's mouth . . . A fruit merchant the other day cried out in the street, selling her merchandise: 'national plums, national apples.'"[46]

Voluminous writings likewise celebrated and attempted to stimulate love of the French *patrie.* Indeed, in the decades after 1750 it often seemed as if the French were gorging themselves on things patriotic. They made patriotic addresses and proposed the foundation of patriotic orders, staged patriotic festivals and even ate what one young lawyer, in the heady autumn of 1788, called "properly patriotic suppers."[47] Under Louis XVI, the crown commissioned paintings and sculptures specifically to stimulate patriotic sentiment. Several series of overtly patriotic engravings appeared, including Antoine-François Sergent's melodramatic riposte to Benjamin West's *The Death of General Wolfe:* his rendition of the death of the Marquis de Montcalm, at British hands, in 1759 (the cover illustration for this book).[48] During the century's many wars against Britain, the crown also sponsored a torrent of self-consciously patriotic war literature whose volume and violence surpassed anything seen since the sixteenth century. In it, contemporary military heroes and victims of English atrocities became nothing less than the successors to the flower of French chivalry (as in the fanciful engravings, for an epic poem about the Seven Years' Wars).[49] Writers echoing the eulogists of the Académie invented a virtual "cult of great men," while admirers of the patriotic stage plays gushed endlessly about the moral lessons these could impart. "True patriots can be confirmed in their sentiments," wrote one. "People can say: 'Why can I not do what this person has done? He was French; I am as well.'"[50] Pamphlets appeared with titles like "The Patriotic Merchant," "Patriotic Proposal on Vines, Wines and Ciders," and even "Patriotic Notice Concerning People Suffocated by Coal Vapors."[51] As an aspiring economist wrote in 1764, "from all directions I hear nothing but cries in favor of the *Patrie,* and see nothing but Works that recommend patriotism."[52]

Two relatively crude but nonetheless large-scale measurements confirm the growing importance of the concepts of *nation* and the *patrie* over the last century of the old regime. The catalogue of the French National Library lists no fewer than 895 French-language works published between 1700 and 1789 with the words "nation" or "national" in their title, and another 277 with the words "patrie," "patriote," "patriotique" or "patriotisme," as opposed to only 105 and 16 before 1700. The largest database of French writings similarly reveals a more than fourfold increase in the frequency with which French authors used the words "nation" and "patrie" over the course of the century.[53]

In short, by the late 1780s the words had come to possess awesome symbolic power and taken their place as central organizing concepts of French political culture. For a significant part of the French population, "the nation" now represented the source of all legitimate authority—to the extent that they were willing, in its name, to overthrow a political system which had lasted for centuries, and which was ordained, its apologists insisted, by God himself. It is no accident that if the first great battle of the French Revolution was won on July 14, 1789, the first great challenge to the old order had come earlier, on June 17, when the commoner deputies to the Estates General unilaterally declared themselves a *National* Assembly. Soon enough, this new assembly would formally declare that "the source of all

Figure 2. The killing of French officer Joseph Coulon de Jumonville, in a skirmish with Virginia militia and Indian auxiliaries in the Ohio Valley in 1754, became a favorite topic of French publicists during the Seven Years' War. The engraving, from Antoine-Léonard Thomas, *Jumonville*, Paris, 1759, allegorically compares Jumonville's arrival in North America to the arrival of Crusaders in the Middle East.

sovereignty resides essentially in the nation." Its successor, the Legislative Assembly, would decree in 1792 that "in all communes an altar to the *Patrie* shall be erected, on which shall be engraved the Declaration of Rights, along with the inscription, 'the citizen is born, lives and dies for the *patrie*.'"[54] It was a rare speech, newspaper, pamphlet, or book published in the years after 1789 that did *not* invoke the icons of nation and *patrie*.

Yet even as the concepts reached their apotheosis, they were simultaneously being radically destabilized. The more they were invoked, the more they were discussed and debated, the less the French agreed about what the words actually meant, or indeed whether the things they signified actually existed. This process of destabilization, which took place as traditional constitutional politics collapsed, and a classical republican critique of French institutions and society arose, reached its logical conclusion on the eve of the Revolution. As the French stared into a political void, many writers made the sudden and singular discovery that, contrary to previous assumptions, France was actually *not* a nation. In December of 1788, for instance, the anonymous author of a book purporting to give an Englishman's reaction to events in France wrote that the French "perceive quite well that they are not a nation; they want to become one."[55] A political pamphlet from the same year claimed that "this people, assembled out of a multitude of small, different nations, do not amount to a national body."[56] Soon afterwards, the great orator Mirabeau called France "nothing but an unconstituted aggregate of disunited peoples," while his colleague in Revolution, the abbé Emmanuel Sieyès, spoke of the need to make "all the parts of France a single body, and all the peoples who divide it into a single Nation."[57] A year later, the journalist Pierre-Nicolas Chantreau conceded that France *was* a nation, but said it had "really been" so only since the Revolution itself.[58] In November 1793, in the midst of the Terror, the playwright Marie-Joseph Chénier would put the point even more clearly: "What is our duty in organizing public instruction?" he asked in the Convention. "It is to form republicans; and even more so, to form Frenchmen, to endow the nation with its own, unique physiognomy."[59] Thus was posed the great nationalist paradox: political leaders making wholly unprecedented demands on behalf of "the nation" and justifying their actions by reference to its sovereignty, but simultaneously acknowledging that the nation did not yet exist.

This destabilization brought about an epic shift in the way the French saw themselves. Aspects of their society and culture which they had previously taken for granted, as facts of nature with little significance for France's existence as a nation, now began to appear as intolerable obstacles to its *becoming* a nation. For instance, the "national character," which had aroused such curiosity and celebration in previous decades, became an object of deep, visceral loathing; a supposedly natural French penchant for refinement, frivolity, and intensive sociability was now judged a species of "degeneracy" utterly unsuited to a properly national life. Similarly, France's tremendous regional diversity—from the privileges and the law codes that prevailed in the different provinces to the very languages spoken by the common people—now appeared as a towering barrier to the nation. Previously, it had not seemed particularly strange to most observers that most subjects of the French king spoke Occitan, German, Basque, Breton, Catalan, Italian, Yiddish, or distinct French dialects, rather than standard French. Such diversity was the rule, not the exception, in most of Europe at the time.[60] The radical Jacobins, however, now saw it a fatal hindrance to "national" unity.

In short, the meaning of "nation" itself was changing, from a fact of nature to a product of political will. And as it changed, the most radical revolutionary leaders became convinced that for the Revolution to fulfill its promise, a nation had to be built where none had previously existed. As the abbé Henri Grégoire somewhat chillingly put it on more than one occasion, all citizens had to be "melted into the national mass."[61] Particularly under the Terror, in 1793–94, plans proliferated for reeducating the French, providing them with what we would now call a common national culture, and also making French the single, universal language of the republic (many took inspiration from Rabaut's *Project of National Education*).[62] For the most part, these programs did not come to fruition. A Jacobin state engaged in desperate fighting against external and internal enemies alike, not to mention economic collapse, had few resources available for nation-building on such an ambitious scale. With the fall of the Jacobins in 1794, the programs were in large measure abandoned. Nonetheless, they prefigured the extensive and ambitious nation-building programs undertaken by later French regimes, particularly the Third Republic of 1871–1940, and have served as a model for other countries' efforts as well.[63]

In the chapters that follow I will not analyze this material in strictly chronological fashion. Chapter 1 will lay out the theoretical foundation for the argument about religion and focus on the decades around 1700. The next

Figure 3. The languages of France in 1789. The dialects today referred to as Occitan are branches of a distinct Romance language closely related to Catalan.

three chapters will relegate the religious issues more to the background, as they trace the deployment of and debates over the concepts of the *nation* and the *patrie* before 1789. These chapters will proceed thematically, look-ing at French constitutional politics, international warfare and the percep-tion of foreigners, and French national memory as expressed in the eigh-teenth-century "cult of great men." In the last two chapters I will again engage directly with the religious issue in the course of examining the be-ginnings of the Revolution, the subsequent attempts at "nation-building" (particularly in regard to the question of French multilingualism), and the way these attempts followed from the earlier evangelizing efforts of the Reformation-era clergy.

Throughout, I will necessarily focus on France's educated elites and the printed matter which circulated among them. Determining the attitudes and ideas of other social groups toward the nation and *patrie* may well be possible, but to do so would require research methods fundamentally different from what I have undertaken here.[64] Furthermore, as I will argue in the conclusion, it is the ideas of the eighteenth-century elites which gave the dominant current of French nationalism the shape it would keep for more than two centuries. Only in the last two decades has this current of thought arguably changed beyond recognition, and even today, much of France's cultural leadership continues to militate for a return to an idealized republican past.

In discussing the religious issues, I will not deal systematically with the theological and ecclesiastical controversies that raged in France during the eighteenth century. These controversies did turn in part around the autonomy enjoyed within Roman Catholicism by the Gallican (French) Church. Yet this autonomy was rarely, if ever, construed in what we would call cultural terms. It was a matter of jurisdiction: of the specific rights possessed by French prelates and the French monarchy vis-à-vis the pope. It was not associated with a specifically French national character, or a specifically French set of beliefs. In the minds of jurists and the clergy, "Gallican liberties" were certainly related to French national sentiment. But Gallicanism did not contribute significantly to the invention of nationalism, which derived, I will argue, less from controversies within the religious sphere than from new understandings of the overall role of religion in society. In exploring these new understandings, I will place great stress on the austere and difficult, but enormously influential current of Catholic thought known as Jansenism, whose persecution by the combined forces of the Roman church and French state dominated the eighteenth-century controversies. But if Jansenism has contributed to the history of nationalism, it is not because there was a specifically Jansenist concept of the nation. It is rather because Jansenism encouraged radically new ways of imagining the relationship between the heavenly and terrestrial cities, allowing, in turn, for new ways of imagining the nation.[65]

Before proceeding with this story, two common misconceptions about the history of French nationalism and French national sentiment need to be addressed. The origins of French nationalism may not have received a comprehensive, systematic overview, but they have nonetheless attracted the attention of many scholars, and while much of the resulting work has been invaluable, some of it has also been misleading.

The first widely held misconception is that French nationalism has solely political origins. Ironically, this misconception is cast in two, mutually opposing forms: that nationalism arose at the hands of the French state, continuously, since the Middle Ages; conversely, that it arose in opposition *to* the state. Thus, on the one hand, Pierre Nora has written eloquently that "other countries may owe the sinews of their cohesion and the secret of their togetherness to economics, religion, language, social or ethnic community, or to culture itself; France has owed them to the voluntary and continuous action of the State."[66] On the other hand, the sociologist Liah Greenfeld and certain historians have located the origins of French nationalism in a purported early eighteenth-century effort by frustrated nobles to present themselves as true leaders of a "nation" which predated and took precedence over the monarchy.[67]

As we will see, critics have already done much to overturn the first of these assumptions; the evidence does not support the second, either. But more generally, any interpretation that reduces nationalism to a political strategy and to a series of claims about political sovereignty is fundamentally mistaken.[68] To be sure, in the eighteenth century the idea of sovereignty embodied in the whole nation challenged and ultimately prevailed over the idea of sovereignty embodied in a single man. Opponents of the monarchy deployed "the nation" as a political rallying cry both before and during the revolution. But simply tracking this shift and the strategic deployment of the concept does not explain why the French developed the ability to imagine the nation as a sovereign entity. Earlier opponents of the monarchy had not challenged the king in the name of the nation. What made the eighteenth century different? To answer this question, we must first recognize, as the advocates of the political approach do not, that the concept of the nation was used in many different discursive arenas in the eighteenth century, not just that of constitutional politics. Moreover, the changes in its usage occurred *across* these different arenas, making it difficult to attribute them to political strategy alone. To understand them, we must not only use linguistic analysis to excavate the way different political forces deployed different terms, but also explore the evolving religious and cultural background against which the terms could acquire radically new meanings.[69]

The political approach also obscures the important point that for nationalists, common membership in the nation precedes and transcends political relationships. They define this membership not by the vertical bonds that join the ruler to the ruled, the sovereign to the citizen, but rather by the horizontal, affective bonds that join citizens to each other. This is precisely why metaphors of the family are so often used to describe nations and fatherlands. "The Frenchman . . . sees the entire nation as his own family"; "In France, the nation practically forms a great family"; "The *patrie* is . . . a second, vast family whose members are linked by a sort of civil fraternity"; "France is no longer composed of anything but a single family of brothers and equals"; "All the French are brothers and make up but a single family." These citations from eighteenth-century France could be multiplied endlessly.[70]

In light of this evidence, the family itself might seem a more promising point of departure for interpreting nationalism. The problem here is simply that family metaphors are ubiquitous—nationalists have no special monopoly on them. Most forms of human community have been likened to families, and never more than when a writer has wished to insist upon their affective, nonpolitical nature. The absolute monarchs spoke of France as a family. So did the constitutional monarchists of 1789-1792. So did the radical republicans of 1792–1794. So did Napoleon. Lynn Hunt has brilliantly explored the shifting *forms* of family metaphor employed in French political language in the era of the Revolution.[71] But for the purposes of my argument, the self-representation of the French as brothers in the great family of the *patrie* is less important for itself than for the fact that their previous self-characterizations as "brothers" and "sisters" took place above all in a religious context—penitential "confraternities," monastic orders, and the words of French bishops' pastoral instructions: "My very dear brothers . . ." It is obviously significant that the *patrie* was consistently perceived as a community of brothers, not brothers and sisters, with women essentially absent.[72] I will address this problem, however, in my discussions of the gendering of the *patrie* and nation in French republican thought.

A second misconception that needs to be overturned is one that plagues even much of the best writing on nations and nationalism: namely, that it is at all possible to write the history of a single, relatively stable "national identity." In fact, this project is akin to trying to chain down the sea. "Identity" is, notoriously, a thing whose apparent unity and simplicity breaks down rapidly under close investigation. As the philosopher W. V. Quine has pithily written: "to say of anything that it is identical with itself is trivial, and to say that it is identical with anything else is absurd. What, then, is the use of identity?"[73] Even to the extent that identity is defined simply as a subjective perception, it remains hugely unstable, constantly sliding between the many things people think they are (and think they are not), say they are (and say they are not), what others say they are (and say they are not), and what they think, say, and do despite all of the above. Identities change not only over time, but also according to where one is, and what one is doing. This book is not a history of national identity, but rather of the extraordinary historical moment when *having* a national identity started to be seen as indispensable to a person's existence, and became the focus of unprecedented political efforts and ambitions.[74] One of the things that distinguishes my approach from that of Eugen Weber and Linda Colley (to both of whom I remain indebted) is that their works sometimes take polemical or programmatic statements for expressions of a general national identity, and play down the extent to which the national question could divide, as well as unite. In contrast, as I have indicated, I will treat the nation primarily as what Kathleen Wilson has nicely called a "continually contested terrain."[75] That is to say, I will trace the different things that the *nation* and *patrie* meant to educated French people during the eighteenth century, and the extraordinary actions they took to try and make the world conform to their ideal visions.[76]

Given such close attention to language, it is worth underscoring that I am deliberately using the terms "patriotism" and "nationalism" themselves anachronistically (*patriotisme* only made its entry into the French lexicon in the middle of the eighteenth century, and *nationalisme* did not follow until its very end).[77] But the words are too germane to the subject material to avoid. By "patriotism" I mean an emotional attachment to a place thought of as "home," and more specifically (so as to distinguish it from "local" patriotism) to that territorial entity whose rulers possess final coercive authority over the persons living within it: in this case, the kingdom and then the republic of France. By "nationalism" I mean a program to build a sovereign political community grouping together people who have enough in common—whether language, customs, beliefs, traditions, or some combination of these—to allow them to act as a homogeneous, collective person.[78]

As a foreigner to France, I have had the (sometimes questionable) luxury of standing at a remove from ongoing French debates about the nation. But of course my own beliefs have still informed and influenced my thoughts on the subject, and so, to conclude this introduction, a few general remarks about these beliefs. The sort of nationalism that took shape in the Revolution often seems to have very few defenders in France today, and the most vociferous among them do considerably more harm than good to its image.[79] French nationalism has been attacked by regionalist militants as imperialist, and by neoliberals as collectivist and even proto-totalitarian.[80] These attacks fit in with the general distaste Western intellectuals have long manifested towards nationalism in general.

This general distaste is understandable, given the human price paid for national self-determination over the last two centuries. Objections to specifically French varieties of nationalism must be taken seriously as well. As someone who learned to read Occitan for this project and now counts Pèire Godolin of Toulouse among the finer early modern poets, I would argue that the cultural uniformity advocated by most republicans, from Grégoire onwards, has caused a real degree of French cultural impoverishment. Yet for all this, the architects of nationalism in eighteenth-century France were attempting, in a serious way, to address one of the great problems of modernity: how to keep their community from tearing itself apart without surrendering moral authority to priests who would impose on the earth an order supposedly grounded in divine revelation. The early nationalists sought to create a new form of civic harmony and, in the course of a period marked by vertigo-inducing change, concluded that the solution lay in giving a large and disparate community what we would call a shared culture—common language, customs, beliefs, traditions. Under the Terror they proceeded far too strongly and too rigidly towards what Mona Ozouf has strikingly called "the homogenization of mankind."[81] Yet the problem they addressed remains, and it is not at all clear that there was a realistic alternative to the general direction they took.[82] This book is therefore written out of sympathy—although, I hope, a detached, skeptical sympathy—with their endeavors.

CHAPTER 1

The National and
the Sacred

*Moses formed and executed the astonishing enterprise of shaping
into a national Body a swarm of unhappy fugitives . . . and . . . gave
it this durable form, . . . which even today retains all its strength.*
—JEAN-JACQUES ROUSSEAU (1772)

The nation is prior to everything. It is the source of everything.
—EMMANUEL SIEYÈS (1789)

Historically, Western nationalism, patriotism, and religion have twisted
around each other like sinuous vines. They have each offered sources of
meaning that stretch beyond individual lives, and that have even been
deemed worth giving up lives for. (*Dulce et decorum est pro patria mori.*)[1]
And they have employed the same sorts of symbolic practices, both as aids
to belief and commitment and as a means of delineating what is sacred
and beyond criticism from what is corruptible and profane. Flags, holy
days, parades, processions, shrines, and pilgrimages: all belong to nationalist and patriotic movements, and to religions alike. Rabaut de Saint-
Etienne's 1792 speech to the National Convention was not the first document to expound on these connections, and it would not be the last.

It is therefore surprising that few modern scholars have explored the
connections in a satisfactory manner. It is not that they have failed to
connect nationalism and religion—to the contrary. From Carlton Hayes's
post-World War I essay "Nationalism as a Religion" to Josep Llobera's recent *The God of Modernity,* the tendency has been not simply to connect,
but to *equate* the two. Many prominent authors have done so in one way or
another.[2] Liah Greenfeld rightly remarks that "to say that nationalism is
the modern religion has become a cliché."[3] Yet equating nationalism and
religion ultimately means taking neither one seriously. It is an approach
that most often reduces these two complex intellectual phenomena to

22

nothing but the symbolic practices they share: the flags, processions, and so forth. It takes for granted that the two address identical, timeless, universal spiritual longings. It also assumes that the one rushes in to supplant the other, despite the fact that nationalism has so often flourished most ostentatiously precisely where religious observance has remained most intense.

Religion most often serves these writers principally as a convenient, uncomplicated symbol for something else. It can stand for irrational fanaticism and thereby express frustration at the fact that nationalism apparently leads modern men and women to act so blindly, so emotionally, so much like religious zealots (those writers concerned primarily with Nazi Germany lean hard in this direction). Or it can stand for spiritual comfort and certainty, and thereby express a Romantic nostalgia for older, disappearing forms of spiritual community. It is no coincidence that one of the first—and incomparably the most eloquent—expositions of the comparison between nationalism and religion came not from a modern theorist but from the greatest of Romantic historians, Jules Michelet, in 1831: "My noble country, you must take the place of the God who escapes us, that you may fill within us the immeasurable abyss which extinct Christianity has left there. You owe us the equivalent of the infinite."[4]

In neither schema, however, does religion have much complexity or history, or do much of anything except vent its sound and fury and then, as modernity dawns, be heard no more. Thus even Benedict Anderson, perhaps the most thoughtful advocate of the comparison, ultimately gives little sustained attention to the dynamics of religious history. Early on in his book *Imagined Communities,* he makes an important and suggestive remark: "What I am proposing is that nationalism has to be understood by aligning it, not with self-consciously held political ideologies, but with the large [religious] cultural systems that preceded it, out of which—as well as against which—it came into being."[5] Yet Anderson does not elaborate on the insight. Indeed, he never really abandons a simple functionalism which holds religion and nationalism commensurate because each, in its way, helps people cope with "the overwhelming burden of human suffering." He, too, sees religion "ebbing" in the eighteenth century, thereby "requiring" something to replace it.[6] Moreover, the nationalist *deus ex machina* itself arises, in Anderson's theory, thanks to a wholly secular dynamic, which he traces principally to print capitalism and early modern imperial administrative practices.

Is it, then, worth pursuing the connection between religion and nationalism? Absolutely. Nationalism in France, at least, cannot begin to be understood properly without reference to religion. The way to start, however, is not to define nationalism as a religion itself. The concepts of nation and *patrie* did not acquire their power because the French saw them as deities taking the place of the Christian God. Rather, I will argue in this chapter, it was in large part because the French came to see the Christian God himself in a new manner. Early French nationalists certainly borrowed wholesale from Christianity's symbolic repertory, just as Rabaut de Saint-Etienne urged them to do. Indeed, one of the purposes of this chapter will be to show just how "Catholic" the French cult of the nation remained in key respects, particularly in comparison with its counterpart in Protestant Great Britain. But the borrowings from Catholicism cast a deceptive aura of similarity over phenomena of a fundamentally different order. The cult of the nation did not arise as a replacement for Christianity, and it did not have as its purpose to orient believers towards any sort of heavenly city. It arose as the French came to perceive a new relation between the divine and human spheres, and it had as its purpose to reorder the latter, at precisely the moment when modern concepts of the "secular" came into being.

Foundational Concepts

What was the background against which the concepts of the nation and the *patrie* acquired their talismanic power in the eighteenth century? The most convincing accounts to date have mostly found an answer in the alleged rise of noble opposition to royal absolutism, after the domineering Louis XIV gave way to successors who lacked a certain rigidity in the spinal column.[7] Their historical microscope has above all sought out anti-absolutist figures like the grumpy racialist Henri de Boulainvilliers, who rummaged through the ancient history of the Gauls and Franks, tendentiously and inaccurately, to discover the supposedly original and still-binding rights of the French "nation" over its kings.[8] Of course, these writers intended the exercise of these immemorial rights to remain firmly in the hands of the noble descendants of the Frankish conquerors, or of the sovereign courts (*parlements*) which had supposedly succeeded their general assemblies. Several historians have argued that such anti-absolutist writings served as the key source for the later, revolutionary "ideology" of the nation.[9]

Boulainvilliers—whose ideas were shaped not only by his status as a noble but by his membership in "libertine" religious circles—does have a real importance in the story of French nationalism, as we will see. Overall, however, the "anti-absolutist" approach takes writers like him out of several historical contexts. First, while these thinkers may have used the word "nation," they nonetheless had more in common with sixteenth-century constitutionalist predecessors like François Hotman than with the French revolutionaries.[10] They did not equate the nation with the French population as a whole, or assert that it had any right to change France's ancient constitution and hierarchical, corporate social order, or grant it any right of resistance against tyranny, far less ground such a right in any notion of a social contract. If they used the phrase "the rights of the nation," they most often meant not natural rights but positive rights—rights defined by French law and history, whose use belonged not to the nation as a whole but to the modern French institutions that had inherited the authority of the nation's original assemblies, those imagined gatherings of the triumphant Franks in their thousands on the Champ de Mars next to conquered Roman Lutèce.[11] The actual political changes they demanded, as in the case of the earlier constitutionalists, consisted mostly of a shift in power from the crown to its traditional, corporate, noble rivals.[12] Nor did they treat the nation as a political artifact in need of construction, as the French revolutionaries would later do. DISMISSES A-ABSOL APPROACH

Second, the "anti-absolutist" approach privileges one particular political use of the terms "nation" and *patrie,* ignoring the fact that their efflorescence in the eighteenth century occurred across a wide cultural front, ranging from travel writing to literary depictions of foreigners, from treatises on civic duty to paeans to the reigning monarch, and to wartime propaganda. Did these other works simply follow in the anti-absolutists' awkward footsteps? Given the widely different political opinions they expressed, this is unlikely. Did these other uses of the terms have no lasting significance? The evidence presented in this book will suggest they did.

It is crucial to recognize that the rise of these terms represented only a part of a larger shift in the language the French used to talk about themselves and their community in the eighteenth century.[13] In taking a new, more prominent place in French public discourse, the words *nation* and *patrie* had a great deal of company. Half a century ago, historians noted the origins of the modern concept of "civilization" in the mid-eighteenth century.[14] More recently, others have explored the redefinition of *société* as what Keith Michael Baker calls "an autonomous ground of human existence" in the earlier part of the century, and charted its vastly more prominent usage thereafter.[15] As for *public* and *opinion publique,* a virtual cottage industry has recently arisen to explore the way they came to signify a sort of supreme tribunal in matters both aesthetic and political.[16] The concepts of *moeurs* (very roughly translatable as "manners") and *peuple* underwent similar processes of redefinition, contestation, and expanding usage, while royal officials transformed the hard-to-translate concept of *police* (roughly, "public order") so that it came to signify the enlightened exercise of centralized authority.[17] These shifts, which in turn relate to changing understandings of politeness, urbanity, commerce, and citizenship, point to a fundamental transformation in what might be called the vocabulary of human relations during this period.[18]

The new or redefined concepts had much more in common than simple novelty. Five of them in particular—*société, nation, patrie, civilisation,* and *public*—stand out as being especially close and especially illuminating of the overall phenomenon. Each described an entity which did not owe its existence to any religious or political authority or indeed to any principle external to itself. If anything, each was conceived as something that existed prior to both politics and organized religion and that delineated elementary forms of human relations.[19] Each could also appear, depending on the observer's perspective, as *the* fundamental ground against which to measure all other forms of communal life (leading to disagreements among modern scholars, who have variously claimed that one or another was considered *most* fundamental).[20] They can usefully be called "foundational concepts," and their history in this period needs to be understood as a broad shift in the way the French imagined the world around them: from a perspective in which the human terrestrial order was seen as subordinated to exterior (particularly divine) determinations, to one in which it was seen as autonomous and self-regulating. It was this shift which would, by the end of the eighteenth century, make it possible for the French to hold up the nation, rather than God or the king, as the source of all legitimate authority. It also made them see the thing being conceptualized as a product of human will, and therefore, potentially, as a malleable artifact.

A comprehensive history of nationalism must therefore deal with this general shift, which began in the decades around the year 1700. In this spirit, I would like to propose, in necessarily schematic form, a broad explanatory framework which draws, somewhat eclectically, on several theorists and historians who have helped transform our understandings of the origins of religious and political modernity: above all Marcel Gauchet, Reinhart Koselleck, and Jürgen Habermas.[21] Their works are very different, indeed often at odds with each other, but they help illuminate different facets of a complex process that did not obey any single logic or stem from any single cause.

Religion has a key place in this process, but it would be a mistake to attribute everything to this single factor. Historical change is never so simple. Rather, the process can usefully be thought of as having occurred in two distinct, if connected, realms. They can be called the realm of religious thought and the realm of material organization.[22] The first refers to the array of thinking about religion in France, on the part of official defenders of orthodoxy, influential religious dissenters such as the Jansenists, Erastian defenders of the state's religious authority, and also the philosophical skeptics often treated as opponents of religion. By the second realm I mean the way the French imagined the physical space of France, and attempted to organize it, particularly for the purposes of administration and commerce.

The Realm of Religious Thought

In this first realm, the decades around 1700 have always been regarded as crucial. But for what reason? For one still influential school of intellectual history, exemplified by Paul Hazard's stirring work, Europe in this period witnessed nothing less than a blazing intellectual war. On the one side stood intrepid, aggressive rationalists; on the other, "ardent souls" desperately defending their faiths. The armies clashed, loudly and heroically, and the rationalists swept the field. In a single generation, Europeans went from "thinking like Bossuet" to "thinking like Voltaire."[23]

While this interpretation of the period certainly reflects the perceptions of many contemporaries and has provided a heroic genealogy for subsequent generations of professed secularists, it also effectively conceals the similarities between the two "armies" and obscures the way both participated in a profound, long-term change in the relationship between God and the world in European thought. To grasp the contours of this overall change, it is more useful to turn to the work of the contemporary French philosopher Marcel Gauchet. In his ambitious book *The Disenchantment of the World* (which uses the term "disenchantment" in a very different sense from Max Weber), Gauchet argues that the long-term historical "trajectory" of Christianity has consisted of a steady intensification of the per-

ceived separation between the human and the divine.[24] By the end of the
seventeenth century ("the point . . . where specifically Christian history
comes to a halt"), at least for the most advanced Christian thinkers, God
had become an absolute, wholly alien Other, entirely apart and withdrawn
from the human world.[25] This vision of a "hidden God" could lead to
an enormous, crushing, despairing sense of solitude—yet, paradoxically,
Gauchet argues, it also offered liberation, for by virtue of the absolute separation from the divine, the human world gained a form of autonomy. In
early polytheistic religions, humanity had existed in "a position of absolute
dependence" on a mythical, divine past. "The underlying belief is that we
owe everything we have . . . to Ancestors, Heroes or Gods. All we can do is
follow, imitate and repeat."[26] But by the endpoint of Christian evolution
(which Gauchet considers, in a sense, the end of religion itself), the world
had become a place which could be apprehended on its own terms and
also, crucially, transformed on human terms, allowing mankind to develop new forms of knowledge, a new relationship with nature, and—especially—a new politics.[27] "God's difference," Gauchet writes, "leaves the
human community completely to itself," with the result that, ultimately, all
power now has to derive legitimacy *from* that community.[28] The familiar
modern distinction between "religious" and "secular" was being born.

In these reflections on God's "withdrawal" from the world, Gauchet
clearly has in mind Calvinism and even more so, the current of early modern Catholic thought called Jansenism, which emphasized the radical contrast between God's infinite goodness and the corrupt, concupiscent state
of humanity.[29] In its purest form, Jansenism flourished only in limited clerical circles, but its overall influence was vast, touching such key seventeenth-century figures as Racine and Pascal, and leaving its mark on the
eighteenth-century *philosophes* as well. It was arguably the most powerful
force in French intellectual life in the decades around 1700, precisely the
point where Gauchet locates the end of Christian history.[30] The particular
originality of Gauchet's interpretation, however, is that it goes beyond any
single movement and challenges the reader to consider pious Calvinists
and Jansenists, on the one hand, and the great early modern natural and
skeptical philosophers, on the other hand, as two sides of the same fundamental process. In his vision, which accords with much recent scholarship
on the period, Newton searching for order in the natural world, Locke de-
riving the legitimacy of power from the consent of the governed, or Bayle
challenging superstition and intolerance achieved as much as they did not

despite the efforts of Christian theologians, but in part *because* of the efforts of those theologians to delineate an autonomous and malleable terrestrial sphere possessing its own knowable laws.[31]

To illustrate the argument, consider one of the earliest French writings that entirely concerned itself with "love of country": the 1683 sermon by Jean Soanen, a future leader of French Jansenism. Preached in wartime, it mostly consisted of stern reminders about just how seriously the French needed to take their rendering unto Caesar, coupled with praise for France's current Caesar, Louis XIV. But on the first page, Soanen also laid out a set of remarkable reflections on the *patrie* in relation to things human and divine:

> The Lord, in creating these globes of fire that revolve over our heads; in drawing the flowers and fruits in which our eyes rejoice from the bowels of the earth; in commanding the sun to follow its course without interruption; in tracing the paths which the stars and planets must follow without deviation, has wished to teach us just what order and harmony are, and to lead us to imitate such a beautiful arrangement and such a beautiful plan in our own behavior. Every creature stays in its place; every being fulfills its function. Only man troubles and disturbs the universe. Only man, carrying out only those duties which please him, raises up a chaos in his own heart, insults God himself, and disfigures society.[32]

Here, beautifully and economically expressed, is a vision of a world which God has created and then left to its own devices, with natural objects obeying strict laws that human observation can presumably uncover. "Only man" disturbs the order God has established, and to recover this order man cannot rely on God but must establish a human equivalent to it. The first step in this direction, Soanen then proceeds to argue, is for "citizens" to devote themselves to their *patrie*.[33]

Gauchet's work not only helps understand Soanen's sermon but suggests why the priest wanted his listeners to make the concept of *patrie* central to their lives. The intellectual achievements of the late seventeenth and early eighteenth centuries, by so clearly delineating the terrestrial sphere, also demanded a new vocabulary to describe it and to help human beings discern and maintain order and stability in the face of the terrifying absence of God. Keith Baker, drawing on Gauchet's work, has recently made just such an argument about the transformation of the term *société* in the late seventeenth century.[34] I would argue, however, that *société* was just one of a number of potentially competing concepts which Europeans reached for to meet this need (Gauchet himself, interestingly, has elsewhere put particular emphasis on the concept of "nation").[35]

Going beyond Gauchet, I would also argue that the new concern with a purely terrestrial order did not take shape in the philosophical and theological arenas alone. Whatever its ultimate roots in the religious *longue durée,* in the context of seventeenth- and eighteenth-century France it also derived from a terror that was far more tangible than the idea of an absent deity: religious warfare. Throughout Europe, the memories of Protestant-Catholic conflict, and its attendant horrors, remained so burningly vivid in the eighteenth century that J. G. A. Pocock has recently ventured to define the Enlightenment itself as "a series of programs for strengthening civil sovereignty and putting an end to the Wars of Religion."[36] In France, echoes of the horrific religious butchery of 1569–1594, which provoked Agrippa d'Aubigné's haunting lament "O France désolée! O terre sanguinaire, / Non pas terre, mais cendre," resonated long after Henri IV finally brought it to an end with his famous Parisian mass.[37] In the eighteenth century, the wars inspired a virtual cult of Henri IV, and obsessed the *philosophes.* Voltaire, for instance, made the events the subject of his most ambitious epic, *La Henriade,* which dwelt at length on the grisly horrors (blood steaming in the streets of Paris, children dashed to their deaths against flagstones). He returned to them in many other works as well.[38] Diderot wrote memorably of "one half of the nation bathing itself, out of piety, in the blood of the other half."[39] The wars also provided subject material for some of the most explosive stage dramas of the eighteenth century, notably Marie-Joseph Chénier's *Charles IX.*[40] Political pamphleteers routinely evoked the days when "the *patrie*'s own children tore open its entrails," and royal ministers especially dreaded any return to the days in which two successive monarchs fell victim to assassins' knives.[41] The reformer Turgot sternly instructed the young Louis XVI about the sixteenth century's terrible spirit, "which put daggers in the hands of kings to butcher the people, and in the hands of the people to butcher kings. Here, Sire, is a great subject for reflection which princes should have constantly present in their thoughts."[42] Even in 1789, Camille Desmoulins roused the crowds at the Palais-Royal by warning about a Saint Bartholomew's Day Massacre of patriots.[43] In short, just as the memory of the French Revolution dominated and helped structure French politics for long after 1789, so these wars remained perhaps the most basic political reference point during the last two centuries of the old regime.

From the start, French writers and statesmen drew one basic lesson from the wars: if religious passions were not excluded from all but certain carefully delineated spheres of human activity, suicidal strife would follow. As Voltaire would later put it: "C'est la religion dont le zèle inhumain / Met à tous les Français les armes à la main."[44] From Michel de l'Hôpital in the sixteenth century to André-Hercule de Fleury and Henri-François d'Aguesseau in the eighteenth, royal officials struggled to contain such excess zeal and lived in terror of its divisive effects.[45] And as early as the sixteenth century itself, figures like de l'Hôpital (an influential lord chancellor) argued that the solution to confessional strife might lie in strengthening devotion to a common *patrie*. The period of the wars thus saw a flourishing of patriotic language in France (including the invention of the word "patriote" itself in the 1560s), accompanied by fierce denunciations of foreign enemies, especially on the part of the moderate, royalist Catholic faction known as the *politiques*.[46]

This early enthusiasm for the *patrie*, however, remained limited in comparison with the broader conceptual shift of the late seventeenth and early eighteenth centuries. Indeed, when the *politiques* and Henri IV emerged victorious from the wars, the notion of the *patrie* lost something of its necessity. Religious warfare no longer threatened to rip the country apart, and the French now had a popular—and Catholic—king who not only served as a focal point for allegiance in his own right, but could stand as the great link between the terrestrial and heavenly cities, binding them together into what was still conceived of as one grand hierarchy. For the royal ministers of the seventeenth century, the solution to the problem of preventing religious warfare lay not in patriotic enthusiasm, but in conceding absolute, uncontested authority to the monarchical state as the guarantor of justice and order and the source of harmonious, polite human relations. In their view, as Reinhart Koselleck has argued, the state and the king were the axes around which the community should revolve.[47]

As the wars retreated in time, many writers came to see the state itself as part of the problem.[48] Voltaire, Diderot, and Chénier, for instance, equated religious strife less with anarchy than with fanaticism and the violation of private conscience and rejected unquestioning obedience to authority in favor of the institution of toleration. Indeed, they condemned royal power as fanaticism's handmaiden, citing such events as King Charles IX's complicity in the Saint Bartholomew's Day Massacre and, more recently, King Louis XIV's revocation of toleration for Protestants. In the same vein, late-eighteenth-century stage plays like Mercier's *La destruction de la ligue*, and still more, Chénier's ferocious *Charles IX,* directly attacked the monarchy for encouraging religious violence. By 1789, the popular poet Ecouchard Lebrun could write fiercely of Charles IX: "O Charles! Il est temps que le crime s'expie / De ce tombeau royal, sors, sors, cadavre impie!"[49] To those who remembered the Wars of Religion in this manner, it now followed that the state could not provide the basic framework of terrestrial order any more than organized religion could. And so there then arose, in this context as well, a need for the new conceptual tools.

The Realm of Material Organization

In the sort of historical writing that seeks to understand the evolution of concepts like "nation," "society," and "civilization," explanations that invoke social and economic factors are presently almost entirely out of fashion. Yet until quite recently most scholars treated the formation of national consciousness as an almost literal process of construction, involving bricks and mortar, iron track and copper wire. Uniting men and women scattered across a large territory, it was argued, demands a high degree of communications and mobility, combined with a cohesive state and economy. Nations need roads, canals, and eventually railroads; postal services and eventually the telegraph; widespread publishing and eventually newspapers; public schools and perhaps conscription.[50] This point of view particularly appealed to French writers, who also tended to give the story a hero: the state, maker of the nation.

The current generation of cultural and intellectual historians tends to view these accounts with deep suspicion. First, they quite correctly scold, it is a fallacy to assume any direct, automatic, relation between social and technological change and changes in consciousness. The languages in which we attribute meanings to things have their own histories and their own dynamics. These languages do not simply respond, passively, to "deeper" structural changes, like so many loose stones on the slopes of a volcano. As for the more specifically French fixation on the state as the maker of the nation, critics have pointed out that it anachronistically projects the attitudes of post-revolutionary officials overtly concerned with nation-building back into a very different monarchical past, making of "the state" an eternal, unchanging presence in French life.[51] It has been convincingly demonstrated that old regime policies supposedly aimed at forging "national" unity had more to do with concern for the majesty of the king and the efficiency of the royal administration.[52] While the French state, in the revolutionary period, became an *instrument* of nation-building, it is a mistake to imagine the state as an impersonal force that has striven since the Middle Ages to forge a nation around itself.

Still, acknowledging these points should not imply relegating all that brick, wire, and track, not to mention newspapers and administrative circulars, to history's dustbin. The progress of transport and communication, of administrative and commercial practices, and the dissemination of printed matter may not by themselves have led ineluctably to the development of new conceptual means of discerning and ordering the world, including the redefined concepts of "nation" and *patrie*. They did, however, lead contemporaries to pose questions, demand explanations, and reexamine concepts that were already in flux. Changes in this realm of material organization had "cultural origins" of their own, of course, yet they were not simply derivative of these origins. They had their own internal dynamics and a relationship to a host of unpredictable and extraneous factors, including especially the vicissitudes of European warfare.

In the realm of material organization, the decades around the year 1700, again, proved especially significant, across a spectrum of activities that ranged from government administration to journalism to forms of voluntary association. To begin with, by the end of the seventeenth century King Louis XIV had achieved a greater control over the use of violent force in his kingdom than did any of his predecessors. His administration, while far from the model of authoritarian efficiency described by Alexis de Tocqueville, had nonetheless become the most powerful in French history, as shown by its success in raising unprecedentedly large armies and tax revenues.[53] Powerful nobles and discontented peasants no longer had the capacity to throw the entire kingdom into turmoil through rebellion. At the same time, foreign warfare was beginning to take a less horrific toll on the French population, civilian and military alike.[54] The *cost* of warfare, however, was spiraling relentlessly upwards, placing extraordinary new fiscal pressures on the monarchy. Louis may have seen himself, quite traditionally, as the first gentleman of the realm, but these pressures forced him to adopt new forms of taxation that overrode privilege and placed rulers and ruled into a new relationship. One historian describes the crucial *capitation* of 1695 and *dixième* of 1710 as follows: "Extending, in principle, from city to city, from southern provinces to northern ones, and from peasants to princes, these two taxes were designed to traverse the boundaries of privilege that divided the geographic, social and legal landscape of France."[55]

Even as Louis's officials carried out these innovations, they also strove for newly systematic ways of observing and measuring France, and reducing its complexities to a set of general propositions. In 1663 Colbert ordered royal officials to carry out a general survey of French territory, and soon afterwards he charged the new Academy of Sciences with the first comprehensive mapping of France. Somewhat later Vauban, an advocate of the new forms of taxation, pioneered the collection of national economic and demographic statistics. By the late 1690s, Bishop Fénelon could instruct Louis XIV's heir on the knowledge needed by a model modern monarch in these terms: "Do you know the number of men who compose your nation; how many women, how many workers, how many merchants . . .? A king must know [his subjects'] principal customs, their liberties, their commerce . . . A king ignorant of these things is but half a king."[56] In response, the administration carried out an even more ambitious overview of the French provinces than Colbert's: the so-called *Etat de la France*. Critics of the state seized on the same new concepts and techniques.[57]

While officials, driven by the ever-desperate need for increased revenues, subjected France to this new sort of gaze, changes in the circulation of printed matter were bringing the country's educated elites into closer contact with each other than ever before. In the 1680s, French-language newspapers from the Netherlands began to circulate in France, providing readers with an alternative to the official, court-centered *Gazette de France*. The same readers soon also had access to official periodicals devoted to the arts and the sciences, and, after 1727, to the wildly successful Jansenist underground paper, the *Nouvelles ecclésiastiques*. While the real flowering of the periodical press in France took place later, already by 1730 readers could find far more regular and varied sources of news and information than fifty years before.[58]

Finally, the years around 1700 marked three milestones in the rise of what Jürgen Habermas, in analyzing forms of communication and association, has termed the "bourgeois public sphere."[59] In the 1690s, the first coffee houses opened in Paris. The 1720s saw the founding of the first French Masonic lodges. And in the same period Mme. de Tencin and the Marquise de Lambert led the way in transforming salons, which had previously functioned principally as schools of aristocratic manners, into serious intellectual forums.[60] Each of these establishments provided a place for educated,

well-off individuals to gather and exchange opinions outside the traditional structures of estates and corporate bodies. Together with the periodicals, they facilitated the emergence of a new public sphere which stretched
across the boundaries of privilege and even geography (lodges belonged to
an international network; coffee houses aimed to provide the same urbane
atmosphere regardless of location). Habermas and his commentators have
argued that the development of this sphere, which lay outside the traditional circuits of authority, allowed "private" individuals to subject all
forms of authority to critical reason.[61]

Taken individually, none of these developments in the realm of material
organization deserves the description "revolutionary." Together, however,
they amounted to a striking shift in the way France's educated elites dealt
with and perceived themselves and their government. The extent of this
shift is particularly apparent from the perspective of provincial cities. Robert Schneider's exemplary study of Toulouse shows that in the late seventeenth and early eighteenth centuries, the concerns of the city's educated
elites underwent a striking change in polarity. First, they had to sacrifice
their municipal autonomy to the central state. At the same time, their own
cultural interests "turned away from local concerns . . . and were focused
instead on language, manners, the ways of Paris."[62] Toulousains began
reading national newspapers, attending Jesuit-sponsored plays that ex-
tolled the progress of French arms, and participating in Parisian-style
academies. Poetry in the local Occitan dialect, which had flourished as late
as the mid-seventeenth century, withered. Schneider has interpreted this
shift primarily in terms of the growing rift between municipal elites and
the poor. Yet the new orientation of Toulouse's elites toward national cultural and administrative networks is just as significant. It marks the con-
solidation of France's diverse provinces, at least from the point of view of
their most literate, well-off citizens, into a newly uniform and homogeneous space. More broadly, it suggests that the traditional vocabulary of estates and orders, sanctioned by the king and ultimately modeled on the celestial hierarchy, was becoming less and less relevant to their terrestrial
experience.

God on Earth

The changes in the material and spiritual realms suggest why the French of
the eighteenth century found it so attractive to describe the world around
them using the new or newly redefined foundational concepts of *société*,

civilization, patrie, nation, and *public.* Each allowed them to imagine an arena of harmonious human coexistence whose principles did not ultimately derive from the dictates of an (increasingly absent) God—a God, moreover, whose worship had led, in recent memory, to desperately traumatic strife. Contemporary observers perceived this turn from God quite clearly. The radical journalist Jean-François Sobry, whose controversial 1786 book *Le mode françois* was suppressed by the royal ministry, wrote with particular sharpness that "societies of men are founded on one of two principles: love of the *patrie* or attachment to an exclusive religion," and saw France moving from the latter to the former.[63] Rousseau, famously, also defined patriotism as distinct from and perhaps wholly opposed to religious devotion. Defenders of the old religious order perceived the shift too, as in this comment from the Jesuit *Dictionnaire de Trévoux:* "Some modern moralists dare to suggest that all man's duties emanate from the principle of society, which is to say that if we lived apart from society, we would have no duties. What a detestable doctrine."[64] In addition to removing religious dependence, each of the foundational concepts referred to a form of human community free from symbolic subjection to a king who was increasingly perceived as having abetted persecution and perpetuated strife. Finally, each concept helped officials and educated elites make sense of the new administrative practices and the new forms of communication and sociability that were cutting across the traditional boundaries between estates, orders, and provinces.

These concepts were central to an even broader shift in the vocabulary of human relations, involving changing ideas of politeness, *moeurs, police,* and commerce. As early modern writers often suggested, following codes of polite conduct, having good *moeurs,* being properly "policed," and engaging in mutually profitable commerce all offered men and women means of avoiding destructive civil strife without resorting to a morality dependent on divine revelation.[65] In this sense, these concepts resembled the "foundational" ones just discussed. They were different, however, insofar as they referred to the *forms* of human interaction and did not invoke the same sense of physical space and collectivity. Furthermore, in France, at least until the last decades of the old regime, *police* and politeness in particular remained heavily dependent on the figure of the divine-right monarch, who stood as the ultimate arbiter of proper behavior.

Conversely, the foundational concepts just discussed helped lead to new concepts of citizenship which defined the condition of individual membership—especially in the nation. As Peter Sahlins has shown, it was in the 1760s that a French monarchy, consciously attempting to render the kingdom better "policed," began to create clear distinctions between French nationals and foreigners, even as men of letters and jurists were revivifying classical ideas of participatory citizenship.[66] In this sense, the concepts not only gave French elites new ways of understanding the world around them, but also helped them imagine new roles for themselves in it: as active agents, rather than passive subjects of divine or monarchical will. At the same time, the shift opened the way for far-reaching controversies (which, for the most part, must remain outside the scope of this book) over the limits of inclusion in such entities as the nation, the *patrie,* or the public.

It is tempting to interpret the emergence of these new ways of discerning and ordering the world as a process of de-Christianization—tempting, but also misleading. First of all, neither a perception of God's distance from the world nor an insistence on purely terrestrial forms of order implies anything about the *existence* of God or the continuing duty of people to worship him. Historians have found evidence for the decline of formal religious observance in the eighteenth century, but they have not managed to establish any corresponding decline in belief as such or a commensurate rise in atheism.[67] It seems more likely that there occurred what Bernard Groethuysen long ago called a "shrinkage or contraction of faith": a loss of belief in miracles and other manifestations of Divine Providence in the world, permitting the Christian "to confine himself in his everyday life to altogether secular attitudes . . . looking exclusively to the rules of prudence and good sense to regulate the details of his life."[68] In other words, the shift in language reflects not so much secularization as what might be called the interiorization of religious belief—its relegation to the private consciences of individual believers.[69] Rousseau evoked precisely this idea in *The Social Contract,* in his contrast of the "religion of man" to the "religion of the citizen." He noted that the "religion of man," which he identified with the "holy, sublime and true religion" of the Gospel, had "no particular connection with the body politic, leaves the laws only the force they themselves possess, adding nothing to them; and hence one of the chief bonds holding any particular society together is lacking." Rousseau concluded, "I know nothing more contrary to the social spirit." The passage, while purporting to describe an ancient, pristine Christianity, perfectly captured the changes in the religious sphere taking place in Rousseau's own day, and pointed to the direction in which Christianity would henceforth evolve.[70]

If the new and redefined concepts represented purely terrestrial ways of ordering the world, they nonetheless retained crucial similarities to their religious counterparts. The very sense of harmony they evoked inescapably recalled earlier visions of the heavenly city. Furthermore, each not only described something which supposedly existed prior to politics and to organized religion, and which could be taken for a fundamental ground of human existence, but also something beyond all possible criticism and therefore, in an important sense, something sacred. It has been shown that eighteenth-century discussions of how individuals came together in *société* rarely failed to invoke religion, even if the theorists increasingly demoted religion to a mere adjunct and aid to supposedly natural human sociability.[71] Indeed, these writers, in praising *société*, frequently adopted the sort of metaphorical religious language long employed for describing France's divinely ordained kings. To give just one example, the *Encyclopédie* article entitled *"Philosophe"* declared that *"société civile* is, so to speak, a divinity on earth."[72]

This same sense of sacrality was invested with even greater strength in the concept of *patrie*. The Latin noun *patria* had strong religious connotations from the start, and after the fall of Rome, it survived mostly in religious usage: the Christian's true *patria* lay in the Kingdom of Heaven. In the high Middle Ages, secular rulers began to adopt the word for their own purposes, but "the main contents of the veneration of *patria* were derived from a world of thought which was religious in a broad sense." The secular kingdom was imagined on the model of the *corpus mysticum* of the Church, headed by Jesus.[73] French writers continued to employ the analogy in the era of Henri IV, when both the *politique* Lord Chancellor De Thou and the ultra-Catholic Guillaume Des Autelz could call the *patrie* "a second divinity" or "a second deity."[74] As for the eighteenth century, descriptions of the *patrie* as a "God," "divinity," or something "sacred," and of patriotism as "a vast chain linked to Divinity" or a "sacred love," were utterly commonplace.[75] During the Revolution, the 1792 Petition of Agitators to the Legislative Assembly declared that "the image of the *patrie* is the sole divinity it is permissible to worship."[76]

It was the Calvinist, Geneva-born Rousseau who, even while exploring the consequences of the world's "disenchantment," speculated most profoundly upon the continuing place of the sacred in the foundation of human communities. (It is tempting to conclude that Calvinism, and the sense of distance between the heavenly and terrestrial cities it instilled, may have helped Rousseau, and later Rabaut, to imagine secular counterparts to the bonds religion instills between believers.) Thus in *The Social Contract* Rousseau insisted that a properly constituted polity requires not merely the consent and participation of the people, but a Lawgiver who invokes divine authority for his laws and a "civil religion" which inspires people to love their duties.[77] He returned to the theme even more powerfully in his 1772 *Considerations on the Government of Poland*, in a section which turned both Jewish and Roman histories on their heads. First, he took the historical sense of national purpose and unity that the Jews themselves attributed to their covenant with God, and removed it from the religious context entirely. Moses "formed and executed," he wrote,

> the astonishing enterprise of shaping into a national Body a swarm of unhappy fugitives, bereft of arts, weapons, talents, virtues and courage, and who, not having a single square inch of land for their own, passed for a foreign band on all the face of the earth. Moses dared turn this wandering and servile band into a political Body, a free people; and while it wandered in the wilderness without even a stone to rest on, he gave it this durable form, resistant to time, fate and conquerors, which five thousand years have not been able to destroy or even alter, and which even today retains all its strength, although the national Body itself no longer exists.[78]

As for Rome, Rousseau argued that its real founder was not Romulus, who had merely "assembled brigands," but his successor Numa, the codifier of Roman paganism. Numa made the Romans into an "indissoluble body by transforming them into Citizens, less by laws, which their rustic poverty hardly needed yet, than by gentle institutions which attached them to each other, and to their land, by making their city sacred to them through these apparently frivolous and superstitious rites."[79]

These remarkable passages, which for perhaps the first time in history clearly articulated the idea of the nation as a political construction, illustrate better than any other text the way that nationalism arose both out of and against a religious system of belief. In his treatment of the Jews Rousseau jarringly rewrote sacred history as a secular story of nation-building, something only conceivable in an at least partially "disenchanted" world. He replaced a transcendent vision in which human existence derived its structure and purpose from external, supernatural forces with a political vision in which this structure and purpose arose out of humanity itself. In the Roman case he injected the sacred back into a story conventionally seen as secular, emphasizing the dependence of nation-building on religion—but a civil religion that oriented citizens toward the terrestrial city, not a transcendent one that turned them away from it. Rousseau therefore showed that nationalism borrows from religious practices but also fundamentally transforms them; it is not, so to speak, communion wine poured into a new bottle.

Boundaries and Time

The emergence of these new ways of discerning and ordering the world represents only the starting point for understanding the cultural and religious framework of French nationalism. Foundational concepts like *patrie*, *nation*, and *société* had crucial roles to play in the great constitutional and intellectual movements and conflicts of eighteenth-century France, and were themselves significantly transformed in the process. The following chapters will explore these transformations and their consequences for the emergence of nationalism itself at the time of the Revolution. First, however, it is important to sketch out some of the differences and contradictions that existed *within* the new semantic field throughout the eighteenth century.

The most important distinction is that between the concepts of *patrie* and *civilisation*. To be sure, neither had a fixed and uniform meaning.[80] Voltaire himself called *patrie* a variable and contradictory term. Yet Voltaire was a self-professed enemy of patriotism ("the *philosophe* belongs to no country") who ridiculed Joan of Arc and called his own country a "land of monkeys and tigers."[81] He had every reason to deny any fixed, intrinsic meaning to *patrie*. Yet for most eighteenth-century French writers, even before Rousseau seized on the word and made it central to the great debate he provoked over human progress, *patrie* did have one very clear set of associations: with the ancient Greek and Roman republics. French writers throughout the century may have argued bitterly over the place the *patrie* should hold in the modern world. Many expended vast mental effort and even more ink to prove love of *patrie* compatible with monarchy, and from the 1750s it is possible to talk of a concerted program of "royal patriotism." Yet their almost pathetic eagerness on this score itself underlined the *patrie's* fundamental association with a different form of government. It was Montesquieu who expressed the traditional point of view when he identified love of the *patrie* with republican virtue and stated that in monarchies the state could exist without it.[82]

Insofar as it retained this association with the classical republics, *patrie* had two particularly distinctive characteristics within the semantic field that emerged in the early eighteenth century. First, it denoted a community that was essentially closed. Citizens belonged to the *patrie*, literally the land of their fathers, by birth, and owed their exclusive allegiance to it. Those outside the magic circle were excluded, deserving indifference at best and perhaps suspicion or outright hostility. Secondly, the term implied a particular vision of the passage of time: a *patrie* did not progress but declined. It possessed a pristine past but faced a perilous future, filled with the dangers of corruption, of decay, of the insidious poison of self-interest leeching away the precious fluid of republican virtue and leaving the community vulnerable to conquest and destruction.[83] If the future of the *patrie* held any promise at all, it lay in the possibility of a return to its original state (at least in this sense, the *patrie* was considered a political construction from the very beginning).

The neologism *civilisation*, by contrast, had almost precisely the opposite characteristics, which is why Rousseau's opponents embraced it so readily.[84] Civilization was, by definition, open and inclusive, ready to welcome any "civilized" person. It stretched across many different countries, but did not necessarily include everyone within those countries. Furthermore, it implied a vision of historical progress in which mankind evolved (unequally, it is true) toward civilization from earlier stages, labeled "savage" or "barbarian." If the future of the *patrie* held innumerable perils, the future of civilization held great promise, as expressed most memorably in Condorcet's vision of steady, rational historical progress. "We have seen human reason slowly shape itself," he wrote, "through the natural progress of civilization."[85] The radical republicanism which arose at the end of the old regime and enjoyed its apotheosis in 1793–94 expressed an adoration of the *patrie* and an abhorrence of *civilisation*.

The other new and redefined concepts did not fall so easily at one end or another of the axis defined by these two, but French writers deployed them in the same debates. Thus for Voltaire and d'Holbach, the term *société* implied something that, like *civilisation*, stretched across political boundaries and carried with it a sense of historical progress. Other writers, however, used *société* as a virtual synonym for *patrie*, complete with its resonances of decline.[86] Similarly, for Voltaire, especially in his great historical essays, *moeurs* developed slowly over the centuries, turning increasingly "gentle" and refined (at least in the proper conditions). For Rousseau, however, *moeurs* sprang fully developed from the hands of the all-powerful Legislators who founded properly constituted states, and thereafter could rot and decay as easily as the most delicate blossom.

The concept of "nation" presents the most complicated case. Like *patrie*, it referred to an essentially closed community, one defined by common origins (even if the occasional foreigner might join it, thereby "naturalizing"—literally changing his or her nature—in the process).[87] In the eighteenth century, however, the word lacked the resonances of intense belonging and fatality associated with *patrie*, not to mention the exaltation of place and ethnicity and "the mystique of the language, people and common origin" characteristic of nineteenth-century nationalism.[88] Nor did *nation* have a particular association with classical republics (dictionary and encyclopedia articles on *patrie* almost always invoked Greece and Rome, articles on *nation* hardly ever did).[89] Yet if writers did not assume that nations *necessarily* fell into decay, nonetheless, as we will see in the next chapter, three important groups of French writers—*parlementaire*, physiocratic, and republican—agreed that the French nation in particular *had* fallen into decay, and urgently required "regeneration."

It was the Marquis de Mirabeau, one of the strangest and least remembered of major eighteenth-century French thinkers, who best expressed the tension that ran between the concepts of *patrie* and *civilisation*.[90] Mirabeau's unconventional, ungainly prose earned him derision from the gatekeepers of French prose "clarity," but also allowed him unusual freedom to experiment with language. He adored neologisms, and among the words to which he gave currency in his masterpiece, *L'ami des hommes*, were both "civilization" and "regeneration," that future centerpiece of republican patriotic rhetoric.[91] In fact, Mirabeau's entire, large, lumbering work can be read as an attempt to reconcile classical republicanism with the ideas of civilization and historical progress, particularly in the realm of political economy. Thus he devoted a long section to love of *patrie* and exalted it in republican language worthy of Rousseau (although he argued for the compatibility of patriotism and monarchy). Yet he also defended the progress of the arts and sciences.[92] Mirabeau ultimately attempted to bring decline and progress together by devising a cyclical interpretation of history, in which "regeneration" provided a bridge between one cycle of growth and decay and the next.[93] His work's great vogue in the 1750s and

1760s indicates that readers found his attempts at conciliation intriguing, although ultimately less convincing than Rousseau's argument that patriotism brooked no compromise with other loyalties.

Overall, then, not only did the use of "nation" and *"patrie"* develop as part of a larger shift in the language that the French used to describe forms of human coexistence; it also occupied a distinctive place *within* this language, pointing to a more sharply bounded type of community and a more pessimistic view of the passage of time. It is necessary to keep in mind, however, that this shift in language took place against a very significant backdrop. Whatever the continuing, overwhelming presence of classical antiquity in early modern Europe, which led a young Rousseau to gorge himself on Plutarch and a generation of Revolutionaries to read Polybius and Tacitus as user's manuals for democratic politics, France of course remained a deeply Catholic country. Formal education remained largely in the hands of the clergy, and the Church preserved the power to censor and condemn irreligious writings. Furthermore, whatever the changes within the religious sphere that took place in France in the late seventeenth and eighteenth centuries, the practices and opinions of the Church hardly became irrelevant but continued to exert an enormous influence on the manner in which discussions of the nation developed. The sense of sacrality invested in the concept of the *patrie* only enhanced the Church's influence, for the French approached this terrestrial object of adoration in what can only be called a deeply Catholic manner. The extent to which this was the case can be shown most easily in a brief comparison between Catholic France and Protestant England.

Catholics and Protestants, French and English

In 1759, at the height of the Seven Years' War, Robert-Martin Lesuire published a ferocious novel about the English with the expressive title of *Les sauvages de l'Europe*. It is the story of a naïve young couple who travel to England thinking it the land of advanced philosophy, only to receive a series of rude shocks worthy of *Candide* at the hands of the frightful inhabitants, including first-hand experiences of English riots, highways, hangings, kidnappings, prisons, and insane asylums, not to mention the dreadful cuisine ("English fierceness comes from the still-bloody flesh they devour").[94] What seemed to bother Lesuire most about these savages, however, was their lack of respect for France. Wherever his heroes turn, they stumble upon the crudest xenophobia. Passers-by exclaim "Goddamn!" on hearing French spoken, while dramatists and theatrical audiences seem to do little other than mock things Gallic. The couple see a man executed for "having shown humanity to two Frenchmen," and indeed meet only one Englishman who "heard the word French pronounced without going into convulsions."[95]

Such amazed horror at the Francophobia and excessive patriotism of the English was a leitmotif in French writing about that country in the eighteenth century. Few portraits of the English failed to mention their "excessive principles of patriotic honor," "inveterate hatred of the French," "silly idea of their own excellence," and "puerile relentlessness in mocking our fashions," not to mention their alleged tendency to label all foreigners "French dog," regardless of nationality. "They hate us and will always hate us," the Parisian lawyer Edmond Barbier wrote in his diary.[96]

It would be easy to write these opinions off as mere hypocrisy, as if the French had never stooped to vilify perfidious Albion in their turn. Yet they actually point to a significant difference between French and English varieties of patriotic and national sentiment. In fact, vilification of national enemies and assertions of France's superiority had very narrow applications under the old regime—far narrower than in the Revolution or the nineteenth century. The French did not define themselves primarily by "othering" foreigners. Attempting any precise measurement of xenophobia of course makes little sense, given the state of the evidence: except in a very few cases, we do not know how widely any particular text circulated, let alone how readers responded to it. But several studies of French attitudes towards England have concluded that hostility and admiration balanced each other, indeed that the two existed in a sort of symbiotic relationship.[97] Nor did xenophobic writings necessarily reflect widespread opinions. The mass of Anglophobic works printed during the wars of 1756–1763 and 1778–1783 owed their existence to concerted propaganda campaigns on the part of France's foreign ministry.[98]

Even overtly patriotic writing was usually quite compatible with the sort of cosmopolitan (indeed Anglophilic) literature most famously represented by Voltaire's *Philosophical Letters* and Montesquieu's *The Spirit of the Laws*.[99] Writers who exalted patriotism in one sentence frequently used the next to denounce "national hatreds and odious rivalries," "fatal prejudices," "atrocious insults," and other examples of xenophobia that only an "overexcited populace" or "true fools" could believe.[100] The abbé Mably in the *Entretiens sur Phocion*, the Chevalier de Jaucourt in the article "Patrie" for the *Encyclopédie*, and Montesquieu in his *Cahiers*, all stressed that love of country and love of humanity were not mutually exclusive.[101] In fact, the great mass of overtly patriotic writing did not mention foreign countries at all but equated love of the *patrie* simply with concern for the common good. To quote a typical definition, written by Jean-François Sobry in 1786, "he who loves his *patrie* takes pleasure in being a good father, good son, good husband, good master, good servant, good friend, good counselor, in a word, a good citizen." Sobry called love of *patrie* the "first social principle."[102] Others called it "the continuous practice of political virtues," the "secret spring which maintains constant order in the State," and the "bond without which every Society decomposes," while claiming that it "shapes the heart" and filled a "void in the soul."[103]

Even the works of literature that historians most often held up as examples of eighteenth-century French nationalism and Anglophobia can prove, on close examination, surprisingly sympathetic toward foreigners. Pierre Buirette de Belloy's phenomenally popular *Le siège de Calais*, a 1765 melodrama about the Hundred Years' War, contained favorable English characters, called the English "rivals more than enemies," and praised "the fraternal bond between all humans."[104] The play's villain, England's Edward III, himself acknowledged the error of his ways at the end of the play, as did the truculent protagonist of Charles-Simon Favart's successful 1765 comedy, *L'Anglois à Bordeaux*, usually described as an exemplary piece of Anglophobia.[105] Even Lesuire's *Les sauvages de l'Europe* included favorable English characters (not to mention an admirable Chinese sage), and it concluded that the savage islanders might yet redeem themselves.[106] Most significant of all, Anglophobic works in the eighteenth century almost never invoked the religious differences between the two countries, despite the hostility toward Protestantism that still permeated French society, particularly in the south. If pamphleteers of the sixteenth century had excoriated the English as heretics ruled by a modern Jezebel, their eighteenth-century successors resolutely refrained from such inflammatory tactics.[107]

National and patriotic sentiment in England did have some similarities to the French variety, reflecting the countries' common classical heritage and their close intellectual ties. In England, too, a current of writing flourished that equated patriotism with love of the common good. Its single most important example, Bolingbroke's *Idea of a Patriot King*, came close enough in spirit to its French counterparts to become something of a bestseller in French translation.[108] England boasted its own small tribe of self-proclaimed cosmopolitans, and they were just as susceptible as the rest of Western Europe to a French cultural influence then reaching its zenith.[109]

Nonetheless, recent work has made clear that this cosmopolitanism and Francophilia paled before what Linda Colley calls "a vast superstructure of prejudice throughout eighteenth-century Britain" directed particularly at the French and at Catholics, with origins that can be traced back at least to the Reformation.[110] These studies confirm not only the (admittedly partial) complaints of the French themselves, but also the more even-handed judgments of third parties, as to the astonishing strength of xenophobia in eighteenth-century English culture (in the words of a Swiss writer, for example, "no people on earth hates another as much as the English hate the French").[111] Printmakers from William Hogarth on down mocked the French as lecherous, cowardly, filthy, ruthless, and untrustworthy, in an iconographic tradition which had no French counterpart at all until the Revolution. Novelists, dramatists, and moralists railed against insidious, effeminate French influences, and organizations such as the Laudable Association of Anti-Gallicans, founded in 1745, even urged consumers to boycott French goods. British victories in the field over France touched off spontaneous, nationwide celebrations.[112] A recent comparison of British and French colonial policies in North America, which shows that an exclusionary Britain set up much stricter boundaries than France did between white settlers and Indians and made it far more difficult for Indians to integrate into colonial society, adds further substance to the picture.[113] Religious prejudice formed an integral element of the British national idiom in a way that had no French equivalent. Almanacs, holidays like Guy Fawkes Day, and pious works like John Foxe's gruesome martyrology kept the memory of Catholic atrocities vivid. Preachers railed against "papists," and poets celebrated England as a second Israel, a chosen people.[114]

This view of the outside world both spurred, and drew strength from, a virtual cultural revolution aimed at "rediscovering" a native English tradition and cleansing it of impure foreign accretions. A mere thirty-year period, 1750–1780, saw the chartering of the Society of Antiquaries, the preparation of Johnson's *Dictionary,* the *Biographia Britannica* and the *Encyclopedia Britannica,* the opening of the British Museum, and the publication of the first histories of English painting, music, and poetry. The formation of an English literary canon took place in the same period, as did the rise of a nationalist historiography. Furthermore, this quest to uncover a national essence proceeded under the aegis of what Gerald Newman calls "rampant racialism," based on the exaltation of the native "Teutonic" stock.[115] While France also experienced something of a "medievalist" revival in this period, it lacked both the institutional strength and the racial emphasis of its English equivalent.[116]

These French and English examples show just how differently the concept of *patrie* could function in practice.[117] In France, an important current of writing tended to minimize the connotations of exclusivity and fatality that had been associated with the concept of *patrie* from antiquity, and to make it more compatible with the new concept of *civilisation*. Hence the lesser importance in French culture of fears of foreign corruption, and the writers' tendency to describe even the worst enemies as "savages" who might yet eventually improve themselves enough to join a civilized world community. Not all writers subscribed to these beliefs, and enormous debate took place among those who did. Still, the comparison with England is instructive. In England, the eighteenth century saw the logic of exclusivity and fatality associated with the concept of "love of country" taken to an extreme.[118] The calls to recover native traditions and cleanse the country of foreign influence, and the strong emphasis on England's racial distinctiveness, all bespoke an anxious desire to keep the national community as exclusive as possible. The ubiquitous warnings against corruption, associated with the adoption of foreign ways, echoed the classical lament that all polities eventually fall prey to the weak flesh and spirit of their citizens. Again, these concepts did not prevail to the exclusion of all others, and remained subject to lively debate. Yet the contours of the debate in the two countries remained strikingly different.

Needless to say, no single factor can explain this contrast. Any really thorough explanation would have to consider everything from the heritage of Roman imperialism in England and France to the persistence of serious threats to internal security (far worse in Britain, which Bonnie Prince Charlie came so close to conquering in 1745). Still, the different religious backgrounds have particular importance. I would argue that despite the tendency of many eighteenth-century French writers to contrast patriotic and religious devotion, their efforts to minimize the classical connotations of *patrie*—to make patriotism compatible not merely with monarchy but with love of humanity and human progress—nonetheless reflected the Catholic commitment to a universal human community, and the Catholic belief in the freedom of all sinners to achieve salvation. Even if these writers believed patriotism and the nation should inherit the role religious dogma had once held in maintaining terrestrial order, their vision of this order retained a strongly Catholic sensibility.

In Protestant England, by contrast, the choice between God and fatherland presented itself much less starkly, and religious universalism had far less resonance. The Church was a state church headed by the English king, not a foreign pope. Furthermore, preachers in England, like those in New England, the Netherlands, South Africa, and many other Protestant communities, tended to identify the cause of their people with the cause of God, through the Old Testament metaphor of England or Britain as a "second Israel."[119] This metaphor needs to be read with care, for the preachers did not equate the population of England with God's elect (even Israel had its share of sinners), and the more Calvinistic among them in particular had a strong commitment to Protestantism as an international movement. Foxe's martyrs were not all English, and his book actually says little about England itself.[120] Yet Protestantism and the classical republican concept of *patria* nonetheless reinforced each other in powerful ways. Both the Protestant promise of a return to a primitive and pristine form of Christianity and the ubiquitous Protestant image of an erring Israel succumbing to temptation paralleled the classical theme of the inevitable erosion of republican virtue. The Protestant (and particularly the Calvinist) sense of a terrible and impassable boundary between the elect and the damned paralleled the classical republican theme of the radical difference between citizens and foreigners. This all made it easy for the Protestants to borrow from the language of classical patriotism in describing God's elect, and to borrow from the language of divine election in describing their fatherland. The consequence, from the sixteenth century onward, was the facilitation of a powerful, exclusionary, and xenophobic patriotic tradition that had no real parallel in France.[121] Montesquieu recognized something of this dynamic when he wrote "that the Catholic religion better suits a monarchy and that the Protestant religion is better adapted to a republic."[122]

The influence of Catholicism in France was not so great as to flatten out all distinctions and to produce a single, uniform, static view of the nation. In reality, it left room for enormous disagreement and debate. While a line can certainly be traced from the *philosophes* and pamphleteers of the mid-century to Rabaut Saint-Etienne and his injunction to follow the example of the priesthood, it was an exceptionally tortuous one. In fact, as the next chapter will begin to explore, nothing *divided* the French so much as their membership in a common *nation* and *patrie.*

The comparison of Britain with France also shows that for all the differences and debates, these developments can be shown to form part of a broad European movement. It was not just in France that, by the early eighteenth century, the concepts of "nation" and *patrie* acquired such a fundamental sense of authority that participants in the great political and cultural movements and conflicts of the day instinctively reached for them to support their points of view. The processes of "disenchantment" and material change sketched out above went far beyond France's borders, and so did the cult of nation and country. Dour French magistrates and radical British pamphleteers, Francophilic British ministers and Catholic French priests decrying blasphemy, propagandists in the service of Europe's foreign ministries and *philosophes* of all nationalities, the virtuous and the scoundrels: all were patriots now, in the first and last resort. All would soon be nationalists as well.

CHAPTER 2

The Politics of Patriotism and National Sentiment

L'état et le monarque, à nos yeux confondus
N'ont jamais divisé nos voeux et nos tribus.
De là cet amour et cette idôlatrie
Qui dans le souverain adore la patrie.
[The state and the monarch, mixed together in our eyes,
have never divided our wishes and our tribes.
Thence this love and this idolatry,
Which, in the sovereign, worships the patrie.]

—PIERRE BUIRETTE DE BELLOY, *LE SIÈGE DE CALAIS* (1765)

There is *no* patrie *where there are courtiers and eaters of pensions,* *no* patrie *where there are Bastilles, no* patrie *where there are prelates and parlements.*

—PIERRE-NICOLAS CHANTREAU, *DICTIONNAIRE NATIONAL ET ANECDOTIQUE* (1790)

The ceremony that took place on November 15, 1715, in the Palace of Justice in Paris, was anything but revolutionary. The noble magistrates of the highest court in the kingdom, the *Parlement* of Paris, marched in procession, accompanied by solemn music and swathed in heavy robes whose bright scarlet symbolized the undying royal majesty of which they partook, into a courtroom chamber sparkling with gold fleur-de-lis. Here, seated so that each man's position in the ensemble spelled out his location within the greater hierarchy of the kingdom, the Society of Orders incarnate, they listened to a series of invocations and orations reminding them of their duties and preparing them for the coming term of dispensing the king's justice. Everything about the ceremony expressed veneration for tradition, for authority both divine and terrestrial, for order and hierarchy, and for the institutions of the French state.

Yet one of the orations delivered on this occasion, by Lord Chancellor Henri-François d'Aguesseau, on the theme of "love of country" ("amour de la patrie"), appears with hindsight to have clashed mightily with the setting. D'Aguesseau spoke not of subjects and *parlements* but of "citizens" and "senates." He obliquely criticized the newly-deceased Louis XIV and even praised the republican form of government. In republics, he declared, "every Citizen, from the earliest age, practically from birth, grows used to seeing the fate of the State as his own. This perfect equality, and this sort of civil fraternity, which makes all Citizens like a single family, interests them all equally in the fortunes and misfortunes of the *Patrie*." In monarchical soil, by contrast, love of country was "like a strange plant."[1] Alphonse Aulard, late nineteenth-century official historian of the French Revolution, found d'Aguesseau's language to be "not just of 1789, but of a patriot of the Year II [i.e. the height of the Terror]."[2]

In some ways, Aulard's enthusiasm got the better of him: D'Aguesseau was no forerunner of Robespierre.[3] Throughout his long career, the chancellor maintained a deep and abiding loyalty to France's absolute monarchy, and acted firmly to squelch dissenting murmurs within the world of the law.[4] In the oration itself, the criticism of Louis XIV was muted and discreet.[5] As for the words "citizen" and "senate," and the admiration for the moral life of the ancient republics, these things were utterly commonplace among early modern French judges and lawyers, who considered themselves latter-day colleagues of Demosthenes and Cicero—and not so unusual in the broader culture, either, drenched as it was in the Greek and Roman classics. The oration expressed a resolutely moralistic, but nonetheless thoroughly depoliticized republicanism: a call for men to act as if they were Roman citizens while living under a Christian absolute monarchy. REPUBLICANISM - PATRIOTISM

All the same, d'Aguesseau's oration did represent something new in French political life. Unlike earlier authors, who had simply invoked the *patrie* in a sentence or two, he turned it into a subject of systematic reflection. Furthermore, he presented it both as a fundamental category of political life and as an object of allegiance and affection distinct from the king.[6] The *patrie*, for d'Aguesseau, was the body of "citizens" who ideally enjoyed "perfect equality" and "civil fraternity."[7] Love of the *patrie* meant love of the common good, not love of the monarch, and the strength of that love constituted the ultimate measure of a political community's worth. "What a strange spectacle for the zeal of the public man," d'Aguesseau mused, in an obvious, pointed criticism of France in 1715. "A great kingdom, but no *patrie*; a numerous people, but hardly any more citizens."[8] Such language had some precedents in Renaissance Italy and seventeenth-century England, where classical republican ideas had flourished, but not in monarchical France.[9]

The fact that a prominent French political figure departed from tradition in this manner in 1715 is significant. By this date, the processes of "disenchantment" and material change discussed above had gone far. On the one hand, the sense that God had withdrawn from the world, leaving it to function according to its own knowable laws, and on the other, the growing cohesion of the French state, coupled with dramatic advancements in forms of communication and association, were leading the French to develop a new conceptual framework with which to discern and maintain terrestrial order. More immediately, the death of Louis XIV earlier in the year, after a reign of more than seven decades, had produced a startling sense of disorientation. Precisely because of the strengthening of the state in previous decades, the yawning chaos and violence that had characterized every other royal succession since 1560 did not take place. But the brief regency of Duke Philippe d'Orléans (1715–1722) during Louis XV's childhood quickly turned into a period of unprecedented experimentation in peaceful, contestatory public politics. Within three years, the duke had briefly put much of France's formidable government machinery under the control of the high aristocracy, restored the *parlements* to their traditional, obstructionist political role (Louis XIV had succeeded in muzzling them), and presided over drastic reforms in the state finances. Emmanuel Le Roy Ladurie justly calls the regency "a quite stunning political phase."[10] In short, conditions were ripe for the French to experiment with new visions of the polity in which the figures of the *patrie* and the nation occupied central positions, inspiring forms of adoration akin to religious devotion.

D'Aguesseau himself, not coincidentally, stood in the forefront of all these changes: religious, material, and political. His religious sympathies lay with Jansenism, which had gone to unprecedented lengths in its stress on the radical separation of God from a corrupt, concupiscent humanity, and whose adherents had undergone severe persecution as a result.[11] In this sense d'Aguesseau was close to the more openly Jansenist Jean Soanen, one of the few other figures of the period to take the *patrie* as his central theme. Meanwhile, as the son of an *intendant* (the chief official of a prov-

ince) and a high servant of the monarchy himself, d'Aguesseau had participated in the construction of a more powerful, cohesive state, and was also
keenly aware of the power of printed words and the power of the public
which read them.[12] He would later write in a private note, provoked by the
publication and wide distribution of an inflammatory legal brief: "The
king does not rule over the opinions of men: he judges individuals, and the
public judges him . . . There is no power whose principal instrument is not
some sort of persuasion."[13] Finally, d'Aguesseau belonged to the milieu
of the *parlements,* which traditionally considered themselves an indispensable restraint on royal authority. In his 1715 oration, he defined the
parlementaire magistrate as nothing less than the "voice of the *patrie,*" and
"akin to the depository of public interests." Referring obliquely to the re-
gent's restoration of the *parlements'* full "right of remonstrance" (the de-
vice which allowed them to obstruct, although not to veto, royal legislation) he said it had created "something akin to a new *patrie,* which seems
to bear on its forehead the certain foreshadowing of public happiness."[14]

For these reasons, d'Aguesseau's oration signaled the beginning of a new
era in French political culture and cultural politics: an era of increasingly
open, public debate, taking place in a relatively stable, peaceful, and cohesive national framework, aided by a rapidly expanding market for the
printed word, in which the basic organizing concepts were the "foundational" ones discussed above. That is to say, the French increasingly defined
themselves not as Catholics, or subjects, but as members of a *société, public,
nation,* or *patrie* (and soon, *civilisation*)—forms of association that were
not structured from without, by God or a king, but arose from supposedly
natural human qualities such as "sociability" or "patriotism." Moreover,
nation and *patrie* in particular came to be seen as holding unquestioned
sway over people's emotions and even their lives, in return giving even the
humblest of the French the dignity and pride of calling themselves *citizens.*
Fervent royalists partook of these changes equally with opponents of the
crown, and indeed, the period saw the emergence of a powerful program
of what could be called "royal patriotism." Over the course of the seventy-
four years that separated d'Aguesseau's oration from the start of the Revolution, the concepts of *nation* and *patrie* came to occupy a central position
in French political culture.

This centrality is obvious to anyone who has ever taken even a small
taste of the great, bubbling stew of political writing the French produced
at the end of the 1780s. Yet the manner in which the concepts *became* cen-

tral remains obscure. Several historians have examined uses of the words themselves during the eighteenth century, but few have given serious consideration to the larger contexts which shaped the evolution of meanings.[15] Edmond Dziembowski's recent study of French patriotism between 1750 and 1770 makes for a noteworthy exception. Yet it attributes the rise of a new patriotic language in France almost entirely to the single factor of Franco-British rivalry, and mostly disregards the effects of two other, simultaneous, and equally weighty internal developments: an extended constitutional crisis, and the rise of new sensibilities associated with the Enlightenment.[16] This chapter will consider the politics, while the next two will reexamine the issues of warfare and cultural change.

The Old Regime Style of Politics

Politics in the old regime differed so radically from what we understand by the word today that it almost makes sense to use a different word to describe it. Men and women competed, as always, for power, position, status, and jurisdiction, and argued incessantly over these things, but they generally did so under the pretense of wishing only to restore or maintain a state of affairs that dated from time immemorial, in a complex and delicate hierarchy presided over by God's anointed king. They also did so in the knowledge that at any time, in the name of that same king, they might find themselves summarily stripped of power, position, status, jurisdiction, and indeed all freedom. France was not a totalitarian state, and a great deal of what might be called semi-free debate did take place, particularly among persons who enjoyed one form or another of institutional protection. But neither was the Bastille a myth, and the threat it represented made France a place where the most radical and destabilizing arguments tended to come cloaked in thick layers of flattery and deceptive orthodoxy.

The details of eighteenth-century political conflict do not need retelling here. The *parlements*, which presented themselves as the repositories and defenders of traditional liberties, engaged in almost continuous squabbling with the crown over issues which ranged from religion to taxation to judicial reform to the structure of the state itself. The story mostly took the form of a hugely complex and exquisitely choreographed ballet of "respectful remonstrance" and considered response that could go on for months or years before breaking down into well-calculated acts of defiance and authority: judicial strikes on the one side, and on the other, forcible "registration" of laws, the exiling of the recalcitrant magistrates, and short-lived attempts to restructure the court system. Alongside the official statements, each camp and its supporters generated a steady flow of illegal and intemperate pamphlets and periodicals.[17] Meanwhile, from the 1750s onwards, other, less well-defined currents of opposition arose that were broadly associated with the *philosophes* of the Enlightenment. Finding their principal forms of expression in periodicals, pamphlets, and legal briefs filed by sympathetic lawyers and then printed and sold to the general public, these critics tended to mobilize above all on issues of perceived misconduct of justice, such as the Calas Affair (the case of a Protestant executed on trumped-up charges in 1762, which Voltaire transformed into a *cause célèbre*).[18] Throughout the century, the number of books, pamphlets, and newspapers engaged in and reporting on all these issues expanded vertiginously, as did the number of places, from coffee houses to literary societies to lending libraries, where people could gather to discuss them.[19]

Despite the outpouring of so much ink, it is easy to downplay the significance of the debates. In the case of the *parlements*, nearly every crisis was also accompanied by long negotiation and an intense search for honorable compromise (marked by wrangling over the wording and even the punctuation of official statements). In nearly every case both sides eventually found it best to return to something approaching the *status quo ante*, and as a result, in 1789, the *parlements* still occupied much the same institutional and legal position they had done in 1715.[20] As for the *philosophes*, until the collapse of the French state in the 1780s, the impact of their writings on political issues other than judicial reform and religious toleration remained distinctly limited. Rousseau's *Social Contract*, by nearly every account the most "revolutionary" work of the Enlightenment, had relatively little success for years after its publication in 1762.[21]

Yet the appearance of continuity is, in the end, deceptive. At three decisive moments the nature of political debate changed and intensified, with massive consequences for the future of French patriotic and national sentiment. The first moment was the regency of Philippe d'Orléans (1715–1722). Then, between 1748 and 1756, a *parlementaire* crisis that began with quarrels over taxation and Jansenism soon came to include the question of the courts' right to impede royal legislation, and culminated in a year-long exile for the *Parlement* of Paris. As these tensions escalated, the high courts and their supporters not only made bolder claims than ever before, but self-consciously chose to put their arguments before the "tribunal of public opinion." To this end they produced an unprecedentedly large volume of pamphlets, newspapers, legal briefs, and broadsides, which they counted on to reach readers both directly, and in coffeehouses, reading societies, and other new arteries for the circulation of printed matter. Crucially, in response to this offensive, the crown decided it had to compete in kind. Royal ministers had always sponsored their own pamphlet literature, but in the 1750s they systematized their previously erratic operations by engaging Jacob-Nicolas Moreau to serve, in effect, as their chief propagandist in matters both foreign and domestic. Moreau, an ambitious Parisian lawyer with a knack for ingratiating himself with the powerful, insisted that every *parlementaire* declaration meet with a royal response. "If bad citizens speak so loudly, it is because good citizens don't speak enough," he wrote in a newspaper he founded precisely to respond to critics of the government.[22] In changing tack in this manner, the crown went a long way toward legitimizing political debate itself.[23] It also attempted to appropriate the concept of the *patrie* for its own benefit, in a concerted campaign of royal patriotism.

Third, in 1771, King Louis XV and his Lord Chancellor Maupeou, at the end of a particularly convoluted and drawn-out battle with the *parlements,* abruptly ended the long-running dance of remonstrance and reply with a brutal show of force. They arrested and exiled the magistrates, stripped them of their offices, and replaced them with the crown's own, pliant nominees. In doing what even the authoritarian Louis XIV had never done, they provoked the greatest institutional crisis in France since the Fronde of the mid-seventeenth century, and prompted the formation of a broad-based opposition movement which included devotees of the *philosophes* as well as supporters of the *parlements.* This movement called itself, significantly, the *parti patriote.* During the crisis, the amount of printed matter again rose sharply and its polemical content grew notably sharper.[24]

At each of these moments, the uses of *patrie* and *nation* shifted noticeably. Before 1750, a few authors did seize on them as central concepts, but they still had a limited place in overall political debate. Opponents of the theoretically absolute monarchy mostly still restricted themselves to venerable strategies of French opposition and rebellion: invoking the king's duty to God, or his need to respect the laws laid down by his predecessors, or his subordination to certain "fundamental laws" of the kingdom. Between 1750 and 1771, the concepts gained a much larger place in debate, along with *public* and *opinion publique* (*societé, civilisation,* and *peuple* remained

more tangential, although in the last case only until 1789).[25] Yet even opponents of the crown did not invoke them to propose drastic changes in the
form of French government. Only after 1771, when large numbers of the
French started to take seriously the possibility of such a change, did the political debate generate the ideological elements out of which the French
revolutionaries could create new and stunningly powerful national and
patriotic doctrines. Only then did the construction of the nation, and the
defense of a *patrie* distinct from the king, come to appear at once the most
pressing and the most sacred of political tasks.

Law and the Uses of the Nation (1715–1771)

Start with the concept of *nation*. Even as Louis XIV lay dying, the reaction-
ary nobleman Henri, Comte de Boulainvilliers, was putting the final
touches on his unwieldy compilation *L'état de la France,* which included a
provocative essay on the "state of the French nation" at its earliest moments, after the Germanic tribe of the Franks took over the crumbling Roman Empire's province of Gaul.[26] Boulainvilliers, like d'Aguesseau, both
analyzed and stood at the forefront of the religious, material, and political
changes discussed in the previous chapter.[27] He was no conventional Catholic but a free-thinking skeptic, who wrote extensively and sympathetically
on Spinoza in works which circulated in manuscript because they never
would have passed the French censor. He participated in the administrative
survey of France sponsored by his patron the Duke of Burgundy, and indeed intended the *Etat* as a summary of this enterprise. He was also one of
the sharpest critics of Louis XIV's monarchy, going far beyond the modest
aristocratic reform aspirations of other members of the Burgundy circle.
In the *Etat,* he claimed with more passion than historical accuracy that the
Franks had come to decisions collectively and chosen their first kings by
election. The French nobility of the eighteenth century, he further postu-
lated, could trace its direct descent to this original Frankish nation, and so
by right retained all its original privileges. A biographer has commented
that "one finds Boulainvilliers constituting as his object of study a French
'nation' independent of the crown, indeed, 'antagonistic' to the crown."[28]
And just as d'Aguesseau identified the *patrie* with the noble *parlements,*
Boulainvilliers identified the nation with another particular group: the nobility as a whole.

Boulainvilliers's importance to the pre-history of French nationalism should not be exaggerated. As already pointed out, he belonged to a long-standing tradition of French constitutionalism, and did not treat the nation as a political construction. Yet his arguments, which he continued to develop in the years before his death in 1722, still have significance. Simply by using the word *nation,* rather than asserting the rights of an ancient corporate institution like the Estates General (France's principal representative body, which did not meet between 1615 and 1789), he gave it political salience it had previously lacked. He also associated traditional constitutionalist claims with it, even as he was revivifying these claims. He therefore touched off decades of clotted but passionate controversies over the French nation's nature and history, in which half-forgotten (and sometimes mythical) figures like Clothaire, Childebert, and Pharamond loomed up out of the Dark Ages and for a time seemed to have as much importance in French political discussion as recent kings and ministers. Antiquarians searched through dusty archives for lost capitularies with the intensity of knights chasing the grail, in the hope of finding the missing links of a chain connecting the Frankish assemblies with contemporary institutions. The *philosophes* Mably and Montesquieu were only the most prominent writers to contribute to the controversies. And from all these discussions a sort of political competition arose. Who had originally constituted the nation? Who were their modern descendants? Who had the right to speak for them?[29]

The questions were inflammatory, but before 1770 the answers remained largely framed within traditional constitutionalist terms. Even the most radical critics of the monarchy proceeded by arguing that the nation was endowed with certain particular "rights" from its earliest existence, and that just like other particular, positive "rights" and "privileges" (the two terms were practically synonymous under the old regime), these passed from one generation to the next like forms of property. Hence in the eighteenth century the nation still possessed the same rights it had first acquired at its foundation in the fifth, allowing it by law to check or even overrule the actions of the monarchy. Historical and legal research was of course required to prove the point, with the result that most political discussions of the nation from this period took the form of legal history.[30] From Boulainvilliers this sort of critical legalism passed into the writings of the more extreme Jansenist constitutionalists, who as early as 1730 were calling the *parlements* "the Senate of the nation" and labeling the king somewhat dismissively as "the nation's chief."[31] Spurred by the crisis of the

1750s, members of the *parlements* themselves, guided by the Parisian law-yer Adrien-Louis Le Paige, began to insert claims about "the right of the nation," "the rights and privileges of the nation," "the rights, liberties and franchises of the nation," and even "the sacred right of the nation" into their published remonstrances. The texts circulated widely, and independent newspapers like the *Gazette de Leyde* reprinted the most important ones along with the king's responses.[32] Le Paige further buttressed the claims in massively erudite, clandestinely published, best-selling works of legal history.[33]

In response, supporters of the monarchy did not deny the existence of a French "nation," but they insisted that it could only express itself through the person of the monarch. Bossuet had already made the point in his late-seventeenth-century defense of absolute royal authority: "Thus the sovereign magistrate has in his hands all the strength of the nation, which submits to, and obeys him."[34] Boulainvilliers's critic, the *abbé* Dubos, added the historical argument that it was the monarchy which had founded the nation, rather than the reverse.[35] Eighteenth-century royalists did little more than repeat these points and scold the *parlements* for disputing their self-evident truth. Thus Lord Chancellor Lamoignon, in a 1759 reply to remonstrances of the *Parlement* of Paris: "The right of the Nation is spoken of, as if was distinct from the laws, of which the King is the source and the principle."[36] Thus the angry words of the king himself to the *Parlement* of Paris in 1766, in what became known as the "session of the flagellation": "the rights and interests of the nation, which some dare to regard as a separate body from the monarch, are necessarily united with my rights and interests, and repose only in my hands."[37] Toward the end of the old regime, apologists for the crown echoed Louis's words in virtually everything they wrote.[38]

These debates succeeded, by the 1760s, in making the concept of the nation central to French political culture. Yet simple assertions about the nation's rights left open the key questions of how those rights could be expressed and represented. The monarchists—including Louis XV during the "flagellation" session—painted their opponents in broad strokes as dangerous "republicans" who not only put the nation above the king, but would give the nation free choice to decide the form of its government. But in the 1750s and 1760s, this amounted to a scare tactic. For Le Paige and the *parlementaires,* the rights of the nation remained positive rights, defined by French law, and they belonged not to the nation as a whole, whatever form it might take, but to the institutional descendants of the ancient assemblies. Le Paige did not grant "the nation" any clear right of resistance against the king, and to him its "rights" did not signify anything terribly different from the traditional "fundamental laws" of the kingdom. Furthermore, while the *parlements* claimed powers of "representation," they did not thereby mean that the nation had freely chosen them to act in its place. As Keith Baker and Paul Friedland have pointed out, this quintessentially modern concept of representation only triumphed with the Revolution. In most pre-revolutionary works, "representation" meant something quite different and much closer to what we would call incarnation. For Le Paige, the *parlements* did not simply speak *for* the nation; they actually *were* the nation. They embodied it, in a quasi-miraculous manner that bore a resemblance to transubstantiation.[39] The nation could only take shape in them. Montesquieu, in *The Spirit of the Laws,* had similarly written that in the early Middle Ages "one often assembled the nation, that is, the lords and bishops."[40] When the king replied to the *parlements* in 1766, he claimed that he himself *was* the nation, again in the sense of incarnating or embodying it, as opposed to being its chosen deputy.

Morality and the Uses of the *Patrie* (1715–1771)

Arguments about the *patrie* proceeded in a very different manner. Unlike the *nation,* the *patrie* was not thought to possess an active will. It also lacked the specific "rights" and the detailed history which the *nation* had in such abundance (although the history of "patriotic actions" could be catalogued *ad infinitum*). While the *nation* was seen as a fact of nature, the *patrie* was presented as endlessly fragile, subject to deterioration, corruption, and destruction, and therefore in need of stout guardians—all in keeping with the classical tradition discussed in Chapter 1. Indeed, the noun *patrie* was rarely followed by an active verb, unless it was something on the order of "lose," "receive," or "suffer." All in all, the *patrie* was considered less a physical space than a state of mind: the product of *amour de la patrie,* or *patriotisme,* that quasi-sacred, pre-political impulse that allowed humans to avoid killing each other and to act for the common good. Talking about the *patrie* was a way of making moral judgments about the attitudes of the French toward the common good and the way that political actions affected these attitudes.[41] A few authors dared to present the *patrie* as something separate from the king, and a very few—notably the

Chevalier de Jaucourt in the *Encyclopédie*'s article "Patrie"—even placed it above him. "[The *patrie*] is a power superior to all the powers it establishes within it: archons, sufetes, ephors, consuls or kings" (the flannel of classical erudition carefully muffled the sentence's true radicalism).[42] Yet the inability of the *patrie* to express itself in any specific, constitutional manner or to claim specific "rights" limited the utility and the popularity of this argument.[43]

Between 1715 and 1750, despite the precedent of d'Aguesseau's oration, the *patrie* still appeared infrequently in the remonstrances and polemical literature generated by the quarrels between the crown and the *parlements*. A few orations and treatises on the theme of "amour de la patrie" did appear, but they tended to present it solely as a general civic ethic and avoided even the muted political comment that d'Aguesseau had permitted himself.[44] As the examples of Soanen and d'Aguesseau would suggest, it was mostly Jansenists who invoked the *patrie* as a source of political authority. Seized with a burning sense of God's withdrawal from the world, doubting the Church's claim to temporal powers, and harshly persecuted by both Church and state, they employed language which would not appear in mainstream political debate for decades. Thus, for example, the Jansenist lawyer Louis Chevalier, in a printed and widely distributed legal argument from 1716 that defended the state's right to overrule decisions of clerical courts: "Is there a French heart which would dare argue the contrary? We defy him to appear. He would have to renounce the *patrie*, relinquish the inner sentiments which arise in the soul at birth, tear out his French heart and degenerate wholly from his ancestors."[45] Jansenist pamphlets praised allies of their desperate cause as "voices of the *patrie*."[46]

After 1750, with the intensification of political conflict and the crown's implicit legitimization of debate, the situation changed. While the *patrie* continued to feature prominently in many contexts far removed from political dispute (and could refer to regions or towns, as well as to all of France), polemical writers now attempted to appropriate both it and "patriotism" for political uses. Loud clashes took place over the terms, particularly in regard to the fraught relationship between the *patrie* and the king.

These clashes mostly flared on the question of whether patriotism, and thus a *patrie*, even existed in France. In 1755, for instance, a journeyman purveyor of Enlightenment, the gadfly priest Gabriel-François Coyer, bewailed the disappearance of the very word *patrie* from the French language. It was, he claimed, no longer heard, "in either the country or the cities, the provinces or the capital, and still less at court." Coyer saw in this absence the sign of a dangerous decline of civic spirit and the triumph of crass self-interest.[47] Jaucourt echoed his complaint, sometimes word for word, in the *Encyclopédie*, and so did Rousseau (he did not say the word itself had disappeared, but rather that it had lost its meaning thanks to the disappearance of true patriotic sentiment).[48] Others, however, asserted just the reverse: "Patriotism in France has today reached the highest point of perfection"; "This sentiment is more alive and more generous in the French citizen than it was in the most Patriotic Roman"; "no people is more distinguished in the love of country than the French."[49]

The question of the *patrie's* existence may seem too abstract to have generated significant political passion, but in fact the political stakes behind it were huge. In the seventeenth century, Jean de la Bruyère had reiterated classical republican assumptions in a famous dictum: "there is no *patrie* at all under despotism." Many others echoed him, from d'Aguesseau and Montesquieu down to the journalist Pierre-Nicolas Chantreau's brilliant 1790 diatribe, quoted at the start of this chapter.[50] Lamenting the absence of the *patrie*, in other words, served as a coded but unsubtle means of accusing the monarchy of despotic tendencies. As a 1787 commentator on things patriotic explained quite clearly: "It has long been complained of that this generous sentiment has died out in France, and this complaint . . . has more than once served to accuse the form of Monarchical Government and its constitution, as suitable only for weakening, even annihilating, love of the *patrie*."[51] The author was probably thinking of Coyer, who had made his own political sympathies clear enough by remarking that the word *patrie* survived among only two groups: the "depositories of the law," meaning the *parlements*, and "men of letters."[52] The *parlements* themselves occasionally reached the point of warning that if the crown attacked them, "the stability of the laws and the existence of the *patrie* will be destroyed, and then will commence the reign of universal slavery" (to quote a 1765 remonstrance of the *Parlement* of Rouen).[53] The radical *parlementaire* lawyer Edme-François Darigrand similarly asked, in an inflammatory 1763 pamphlet that earned him a stay in the Bastille: "will the peoples . . . have to abandon their unhappy *patrie*, bathed as it is in their tears and blood?"[54] Before 1771, however, the *parlements* made more systematic use of the language of the nation. The polemicists who did most to make *patrie* a central category in French political culture, and indeed to create a cult of it, owed their allegiance not to the high courts but to Versailles.

Royal Patriotism

Between 1750 and 1789, the kings of France became patriots. That is to say, their apologists not only insisted, loudly and frequently, that France was indeed a *patrie* and brimmed with patriotic sentiment; they gave the credit entirely to the king himself.[55] "The name of the *patrie* can still be pronounced," the author of a 1762 speech to the Academy of Lyon insisted, again probably in response to Coyer. "The King and the *patrie* are two objects that are united, incorporated together . . . in the hearts of the nation, as in the national constitution."[56] Many others argued the same case, including Coyer's critic the Chevalier d'Arcq, a self-proclaimed defender of the military nobility, who claimed "I cannot distinguish the Prince from the *patrie*," and a certain Beausobre, who wrote: "He who doesn't love his master, doesn't love his *patrie*; in vain can we distinguish these two things, they are inseparable."[57] A lawyer named Rossel dilated on the subject *ad nauseam* in a *History of French Patriotism* that highlighted the devotion of the French to the monarchy in eight long volumes. So did the contestants in a 1787 essay contest sponsored by the Academy of Châlons-sur-Marne, on the subject of how to foster patriotism in monarchies. Entry after entry denied the republican idea that patriotism only existed in republics, and found patriotic love flourishing nowhere so strongly as in France.[58] In a similar vein, the painter Pierre-Alexandre Wille chose to represent *French Patriotism* (1785) in the figure of a father gesturing towards a bust of Louis XVI at the moment of his son's departure for military service. Similar visual language appeared in Antoine-François Sergent's *Mémorial pittoresque de la France,* and in the many late eighteenth-century images of the "great men of the *patrie*," which often depicted their subjects as an honor guard surrounding the monarch.[59]

Most famously, Buirette de Belloy's phenomenally popular 1765 play, the *Siege of Calais,* made the intensity of French patriotism and its indistinguishability from love of the king its principal theme, as in the passage quoted at the start of this chapter. In case later readers failed to get the point, Belloy's eulogist gushed (in a lavish 1779 edition of his works) that Belloy had "taught the French that patriotism does not belong to Republics alone, and that they too . . . bore in their hearts this virtuous sentiment."[60] The royal ministry, which had encouraged Belloy from the start, showed a grateful vigor in promoting the play, sponsoring free performances at the Comédie Française and at garrisons around the country.[61]

PATRIE I LOVE OF KING
INSEPARABLE

Figure 4. A classic example of royal patriotism, the painting shows a young military officer departing for war as his father gestures toward a bust of King Louis XVI. Pierre-Alexandre Wille, *Le patriotisme français, ou le départ* (French Patriotism, or the Departure), 1785.

Like nearly all of the authors quoted above, Belloy also paused to take a good swipe or two at cosmopolitan *philosophes*—"those hearts frozen and dead to their country," as he put it.[62]

Although many of these patriotic works were produced for officially supervised institutions such as the Comédie Française, the Académie Française, and provincial academies, it is uncertain how many had direct sponsorship from the ministry. Nonetheless, such a large volume of material all expressing the same officially sanctioned point of view can only be considered the result of a concerted campaign of royal patriotism, produced in reaction to *parlementaire* and enlightened critiques of Louis XV's rule. Certainly the crown's opponents themselves perceived it in this manner. The generally pro-*parlementaire* journalist Louis-Sébastien Mercier, in his utopian 1772 novel *The Year 2440*, went so far as to call patriotism "a fanaticism invented by the kings and deadly to the universe."[63] Louis Petit de Bachaumont's newsletter, *Mémoires secrets,* commented tartly on the crown's promotion of the *Siege of Calais:* "In this way the present government has profited from Monsieur de Belloy's mania for writing tragedies with French heroes to engender a supposed fanaticism of the nation towards its kings, and to make it serve as a vehicle for the introduction of despotism."[64] The use of the word "fanaticism" underscored the connection these critics perceived between the campaign and efforts to stir religious passions.

As we will see in more detail in the next chapter (and as Dziembowski has exhaustively demonstrated), the campaign derived not only from the metaphorical warfare taking place in palaces and courtrooms, but from the very real Seven Years' War against England in the 1750s and 1760s.[65] During this period, the ministry made unprecedented efforts to stimulate and publicize public expressions of patriotism, promoting plays like Belloy's, soliciting ostentatious donations to the war effort, and encouraging the publication of violently Anglophobic pamphlets and poetry. Yet even at the height of the war, officials never lost sight of the internal political stakes, and seized on the potent language of patriotism to discredit *parlementaire* and *philosophique* opponents alike. It is hardly a coincidence that they chose as their chief propagandist against Britain a man who had already proved to be their most effective writer against both domestic enemies: the caustic and slippery Jacob-Nicolas Moreau (he wrote the virulent anti-*philosophe* play *Les cacouacs,* as well as of some of the most important pieces of anti-*parlementaire* propaganda). Moreau himself recounted that the royal minister who recruited him in 1755 to write against the British lumped foreign and domestic operations together quite openly.[66] In 1759–60, Moreau ceased publication of an anti-English broadsheet and launched his new, short-lived newspaper devoted to the praise of French patriotism and to the excoriation of *parlements* and *philosophes: Le Moniteur françois* (The French Monitor).[67] The voluminous anti-Enlightenment literature of this period routinely conflated the *philosophes* with the national enemy across the Channel and equated cosmopolitan indifference to the *patrie* with treason, pure and simple.[68] "Fanaticism for the *patrie* is legitimate zeal," a royalist poet from 1767 strikingly declared. And he continued, in anticipation of Saint-Just: "Il faut pour la Patrie une chaleur sublime / Un amour qui soit passion; / Que l'indifférence est un crime / La tiédeur une trahison" [For the *Patrie*, a sublime heat is needed, a love that is a passion; Here indifference is a crime, lack of enthusiasm amounts to treason].[69]

This royal patriotism, which overshadowed all other use of patriotic language in France before 1771, was a remarkable phenomenon. In one sense, it harked back to late medieval and Renaissance traditions of glorifying both France and the king, of merging the two within a single, sacred aura.[70] But in several critical ways it would have been inconceivable without the intellectual and material transformations described in the last chapter. Consider, for instance, the crown's use of print to reach "public opinion." Organized print campaigns had precedents, of course, but now the crown was conceiving its interventions not as something exceptional, a strategy suited for moments of national crisis (such as the Wars of Religion or the Fronde), but as a normal, permanent feature of political life. Rather than just sponsor pamphlets to intervene on particular topics, the royalists now also funded periodicals such as Moreau's *Moniteur françois,* which aimed to have a continuous and permanent effect. As Moreau himself remarked in the first issue, he saw his task less as political argument than political education: "The instruction of men is one of the principles of all political governments. Why should it be neglected in the case of a people over whom opinion itself has so much power?"[71] Secondly, in citing the extent of French patriotism as a justification for royal authority, the royal apologists implicitly accepted the argument, enunciated by d'Aguesseau and others, that patriotism constituted a measure of a regime's moral worth. Just like its opponents, the crown was treating the *patrie* as a foundational concept, a fundamental ground against which to measure other forms of human coexistence.

Finally, royalist literature consistently identified "patriotism" not with a political principle, but with an emotion: the love of the French for their kings, as in Belloy's lines about the "adoration" of the king or Beausobre's equation of love for the *patrie* and love for one's master. In 1749, a year of bitter conflict between Louis XV and the *Parlement* of Paris, the Académie Française made "the love of the French for their kings" the subject of its annual poetry competition, and the entries sang inflated paeans to the intertwined figures of king and country.[72] Down to the end of the old regime, the idea that "the Patriotism of the French [is] principally founded on their love for their kings" (to cite an exemplary 1762 speech by the lawyer Basset de la Marelle) appeared incessantly, like a leitmotif.[73] As Thomas Kaiser has shown, the theme of the mutual love of king and subjects became a mainstay of royal ideology under Louis XIV and dominated the propaganda of his successor, who ostentatiously adopted the title "The Well-Beloved" after the demonstrative (if stage-managed) public relief at his recovery from illness in 1744.[74] Kaiser argues that royal apologists first adopted the concept to counter images of Louis XIV as a warrior king who cared more for conquest than for his subjects' welfare.

But the appeal to love needs to be situated not only in relation to the monarchy's immediate political strategies, but to the broader intellectual context of "disenchantment," philosophical skepticism, and suspicion of organized religion. In the eighteenth century, it was becoming more and more difficult to justify absolute monarchy by God's will alone, as royal apologists like Bossuet had tried to do (with an insistence that hinted at desperation). The traditional rituals and rhetoric designed to render the monarchy sacred were losing their effect.[75] Yet replacing scriptural justification with one grounded in secular ideas of natural law and a social contract, even in Hobbes's absolutist version, raised the unacceptable prospect of the people demanding the contract's renegotiation ("would the nation not have the right to say that it had not entered into any contract?" mused d'Aguesseau in private reflections in 1730).[76] Until the end of the old regime, the crown firmly eschewed any resort to contract theory and natural law. A language of love, accompanied by the predictable family metaphors (the king as "father of the people"), provided a way of sidestepping this dilemma and, in a sense, potentially resacralizing the monarchy. It presented the bond between king and subject as something that preceded and transcended mere politics, as something unbreakable and above criticism: as an object, in Belloy's words, of "idolatry." And in the mid-eighteenth century, it was a natural step for royal apologists to try and strengthen this language further by uniting it with the concept of the *patrie,* which had itself emerged transformed out of the same turn-of-the-century intellectual crucible and still possessed its strong religious connotations.

The Pre-Revolutionary Synthesis

Despite the importance of royal patriotism, until the last two decades of the old regime both *patrie* and nation still had distinctly limited meanings. The crown made use of these terms for the conservative purpose of defending the royal prerogative and silencing its critics. But even the critics invoked them principally to help restore France to an earlier and presumably superior state. With *nation,* they called for the restoration of legal arrangements which gave to particular institutions or legal groups a preeminent position within the French polity. With *patrie,* they called for the restoration of a moral community in which individuals worked for the common good. In each case, the practical aim was to alter the balance of power among existing political institutions. The notion that the nation might, through an act of free will, choose to dispense with these institutions altogether arose only in the nightmares of the absolutists. Before 1771, it was arguably the term "public opinion" which had a more radical effect in French political debate than either *patrie* or nation. Public opinion lacked the comforting classical familiarity of the one, and the associations with venerable French constitutional arrangements of the other. It referred instead to a new social reality that many of the French found deeply disturbing. Public opinion did not find its embodiment in the person of the king or in familiar institutions like *parlements* or Estates, but in the new, diffuse realm of newspapers, pamphlets, coffee houses, salons, academies, and other forums which allowed the French to take part in ongoing conversation without much consideration of their formal place in the corporate hierarchy of the kingdom.

These equations changed, however, when Louis XV and Lord Chancellor Maupeou broke the *parlements,* restructuring age-old French institutions in a way that lacked any precedent in French history and law. The so-called coup of 1771 demonstrated not only to the magistrates and their supporters, but also to a wide spectrum of French readers, that the crown itself no longer respected either the grand principles of French law or the wishes of the public; neither could therefore act as an effective restraint on royal power to prevent monarchical authority from degenerating into despotism. From now on, opposition to the crown would have to search for different sources of legitimization.

In the Maupeou crisis, the *parlements* turned to the concept of *patrie* as a key weapon in their conceptual armory. They began to refer to themselves as the *parti patriote* and lamented, as Coyer had done, the apparent extinction of the *patrie* and patriotic sentiment alike at the king's hands.[77] Thus an anonymous *parlementaire* pamphleteer complained in 1771, echoing Coyer, that "the word *patrie* is scarcely known."[78] Other supporters of the high courts referred to the "misfortunes" and "suffering" of the *patrie* and hailed the magistrates as the "guardians," even the "guardian angels" of this fragile and abused entity.[79] They repeatedly emphasized their own "patriotic sentiments," taking advantage of the enormously wider currency that the vocabulary had acquired as a result of the program of royal patriotism (in this sense, at least, the program can be said to have rather spectacularly backfired).[80]

The rise in the use of the words "patriote" and "patriotique" was particularly dramatic and significant—in the French texts available in the principal electronic database, their use increased nearly fourfold between 1765–1769 and 1770–1774.[81] Just as the birth of the adjective "revolutionary" after 1789 signified a new conception of "revolution" itself as an active process, driven by human will, rather than as something beyond human control (the sense in which the word had formerly been used), so the use of "patriote" and "patriotique" suggested that the fatal corruption and decline of the *patrie* was not merely something to be lamented, but something that could be fought against and even reversed through political action.[82] The *patriotes* rejected the royal claims that France already was a *patrie*, but, they claimed, it could still *become* one. And they therefore held out the prospect that this form of sacred, ideal human community, in which affective and moral ties bound individuals together into a single family, could be created on this earth. In this promise of a new birth of patriotism they rejected the classical republican tenet that the *patrie* could only decline, not progress. The *patrie*, always treated as a political artifact because of its close association with republics, was now also perceived as something whose reconstruction was still a possible and indeed an urgent task.

Meanwhile, in their discussions of the nation, these dissident writers began to consider political options from outside their well-worn legal play-book, and some started to embrace a full-blown theory of absolute na-tional sovereignty in which the nation could indeed freely choose its form of government. "It is the nation which is sovereign," wrote the Comte de Lauragais in one of the most popular pamphlets of the crisis. "It is so by its power, and by the nature of things."[83] The anonymous *L'inauguration de Pharamond* (referring to a mythical king of the Franks) added that "The Nation has the right to convoke itself."[84] Even an innately conservative and consensus-seeking lawyer like Le Paige belatedly acknowledged that the *parlements* could not take the place of the Estates General, whose convoca-tion after more than 150 years he suddenly deemed desirable.[85] His more adventurous Jansenist colleagues Claude Mey, Gabriel-Nicolas Maultrot, and Armand-Gaston Camus started to draw on natural law as well as on classical republican ideas in their hugely influential 1772 *Maximes du droit public françois.*[86]

Going even further than these Jansenists, some particularly radical law-yers (anticipating the leading role their profession would take in 1789) started infusing the ideas of Jean-Jacques Rousseau's *Social Contract* into the mainstream of French political discussion. In 1775, the young Parisian Jacques-Claude Martin de Mariveaux published *L'ami des lois,* which re-hearsed the familiar potted histories of the Franks and their successors but then went much farther. "Man is born free," declared Martin vigorously if not originally, and added for good measure that "the French Nation has a social contract" that gave it the right to choose whatever form of govern-ment it wished, without reference to any original foundation.[87] In the same year the Bordeaux lawyer Guillaume-Joseph Saige published his influential Rousseauian *Catéchisme du citoyen,* which argued the point even more ex-plicitly: "For there is nothing essential in the political body but the social contract and the exercise of the general will; apart from that, everything is absolutely contingent and depends, for its form as for its existence, on the supreme will of the nation."[88] While Saige also genuflected toward the Franks and ancient French institutions, his defense of absolute national sovereignty made them entirely redundant. If the nation could at any mo-ment choose to structure the political body exactly as it wished, then French history and French law had no necessary claims on it. They no longer seemed to define the essence of the nation, as they had done in the 1750s, and in the shift there lurked a terrifying question: just what, if not history and law, *did* make the French into a nation?

For a brief period it seemed as if the question might go unposed. In

1774 Louis XV died, and his young successor, Louis XVI, recalled the old *parlements*, who returned in gaudy triumph to their palaces of justice. The clock seemed to be moving backwards. But while the move succeeded in its immediate purpose of generating a halo of easy popularity for the new king, there was no return to the *status quo ante*, and the halo soon faded.[89] Indeed, while the self-proclaimed *patriotes* saluted the magistrates, they no longer considered them the nation's eternal guardians but only its best available allies. For a few years an uneasy internal peace prevailed, aided by France's revenge over Britain in the War of American Independence, and the ability of Controller General Jacques Necker to disguise the catastrophic situation of French finances. But by 1786 the French state had started on an inexorable slide toward bankruptcy and political crisis, and the old fissures quickly reopened.

In the years immediately preceding the Revolution, the concepts of *patrie* and *nation* emerged as the principal sources of political legitimacy invoked by nearly all political writers, while "public opinion" fell into something of an eclipse.[90] In the period 1787–1789 alone, the words "patrie" or "nation" appeared in the titles of no fewer than 520 works.[91] An enterprising publisher, reissuing a famous Huguenot diatribe against Louis XIV originally called *Les soupirs de la France esclave* (The Sighs of Enslaved France) retitled it, simply, *Les voeux d'un patriote* (Wishes of a Patriot).[92] With state authority evaporating, *patrie* and *nation* served most effectively to mobilize readers for possible political action. For a time, the traditional juridical forms of argument about the *nation* remained popular. The Franks and Gauls did not disappear from the scene, and "patriots" and supporters of the ministry alike continued to wrestle in the archives of medieval institutions right down to the beginning of 1789, not infrequently choking on the dust they stirred up.[93] Writers continued to use the word "nation" in a narrowly legalistic sense, although often taking the argument to new lengths (Pierre-Jean Agier's *Le jurisconsulte national,* for instance, urged the Estates General to reclaim full power from the king, in the name of the ancient constitution).[94] Others sought to bolster their claims with both natural *and* positive law, in the manner of Martin and Saige. Comte Emmanuel d'Antraigues's enormously popular 1788 *Mémoire sur les Etats-généraux,* for instance, made clear that the French had "other titles to their national liberty than those covered by eight centuries of archival dust," but nonetheless discussed "the precious remains of our first institutions" at length.[95]

Yet even as the form of argument remained familiar, the stakes grew infinitely higher. In the "pre-revolution" of 1786–1789, most "patriotic" writers no longer invoked the "patrie" and the "nation" merely in the hopes of altering the balance of power among existing institutions. With the state collapsing, they did so in order to justify the wholesale transformation of the political system.[96] Significantly, some of them now tried to do away with the very label "patriot" because of its association with the *parlements,* which they no longer considered an essential part of the French constitution, and adopted instead the name of "national." They did so even after Louis XVI, desperate to institute financial reforms, again attempted a draconian restructuring of the *parlements* in May 1788, provoking a virtual revolt on the courts' behalf. The Parisian lawyer Jacques Godard, secretary to one of the leaders of the former "patriot" party, wrote to a cousin soon after this latest "coup" that "there are now in Paris and in the whole of the Kingdom the names of three parties: that of the royalists, that of the *parlementaires* and that of the Nationals. These latter two have made common cause; the Nationals hope that this alliance will be long, and that at its return the *parlement,* instructed by this crisis, will remain attached to good principles."[97] In the summer the *parlements* again returned, and Louis XVI capitulated to the louder and more violent protests and declared he would finally summon the Estates General to meet. But the *Parlement* of Paris, instead of remaining true to what Godard considered "good principles," ruled in September that the Estates should meet "according to the forms of 1614"—that is, clergy, nobility, and commoners would each have the same number of delegates, and each estate would vote separately, condemning the great bulk of the French population to minority status. At this point the *patriote* alliance shattered completely, and its bourgeois members, allied with a good number of liberal nobles, turned their attention away from attacking "royal despotism" to denounce a new and virulent enemy: "aristocracy," embodied first and foremost by the *parlements* themselves.

These decisive events opened the way for a true revolutionary movement claiming to act in the name of the nation. During the eight months that separated the Paris *Parlement's* decision about the form of the Estates from the actual opening of that body in May 1789, a pamphlet debate erupted whose volume and intellectual audacity had no precedent in French history. The king's invitation to his subjects to express themselves, which accompanied his summoning of the Estates, had been taken as a declaration of freedom of the press. At the same time, propertied men came together to elect deputies and formally express their grievances and proposals for reform. In this great blooming of political expression, the party Godard called the Nationals relentlessly advanced the idea that everything depended on the supreme will of the nation. Their most important manifesto was Emmanuel Sieyès's brilliant *What Is the Third Estate?*, which presented the deputies to the Third Estate as the nation's true representatives. Sieyès, more than any other author, set the terms of the early revolutionary debate, firmly establishing the nation not only as the highest authority in France, but as an authority that could act with complete freedom through the intermediary of elected deputies.[98] The stage was now set for the first great act of the Revolution: the Third Estate's momentous arrogation of the title National Assembly, at Sieyès's own instigation, on June 17, 1789.

But what *was* the nation? Could the familiar historical legal and historical definitions still prevail, and if not, what could take their place? In the months before the convocation of the Estates, the questions could not be ignored. Moreover, as the French pondered them, the nation came to seem as fragile, as threatened, and as much in need of construction as the *patrie.* As we have seen, more and more French writers, including Sieyès himself, started to describe the nation as something which did not yet exist.

The problem was exacerbated by the fact that during these same debates, the traditional, juridical means of argument was used not only in reference to France itself, but to individual French provinces, and in a manner which called the existence of the nation itself into question from another direction. In 1788–89, it was feared, widely—and as it turned out, correctly— that the king or the Estates General might take drastic and unprecedented measures against traditional provincial liberties and privileges. In response, self-appointed spokesmen for many provinces asserted the utter inviolability of these liberties, over even the unity of France itself, and they claimed for the provinces the status not just of "nations" (a terminology that was not uncommon in the eighteenth century) but of "nations" equal to France itself. Supporters of two regional *parlements* had first experimented with these arguments during the *coup* of 1771, in pamphlets entitled *Manifesto to the Normans* and *Manifesto to the Bretons.* The first of these asserted that "we [the Norman people] are bound to France by agreements which are no more and no less authentic than . . . all other treaties between nations," while the second similarly stressed the "voluntary" agreement by which Brittany had passed under French domination.[99]

In 1788–89, these pamphlets were reprinted and widely emulated. The nobility of the Norman capital of Rouen, for instance, now referred to Normandy's "national constitution." The magistrates of Pau, in the southwest, described themselves as inhabitants of "a country [*pays*] foreign to France, although ruled by the same king," and talked of the Pyrenean "nations" of Navarre and Béarn. The former mayor of Strasbourg, Johann von Türckheim, asked: "will Lower Alsace have the courage and resolution to withdraw from a French republic . . . to declare that it was subject to the French crown but not the French nation, and intends to preserve its rights and liberties?" Similar claims were made in Provence.[100]

To a certain extent, the language is deceptive. Not only was it not unheard of for French provinces to be called "nations"; what was at issue was not fear of losing irreducibly unique provincial identities, but specific provincial legal privileges. Lest the texts be taken as examples of regional nationalism, consider that despite the vast differences in language, law, historical tradition, and social structure between France's regions at the time, no serious movement for regional independence arose either before or during the Revolution, even at the worst moments of bloody civil war in 1793–94. Even when German-speaking Alsatians were thrown out of office and threatened with mass deportation, no movement for secession arose in Alsace.[101] Yet the pre-revolutionary declarations did explicitly, if briefly, raise the specter of France literally dissolving into smaller units. Moreover, by taking the juridical mode of argument and using it to question the national unity on which the *parlements'* original juridical critique of the crown had been premised, they arguably undercut the credibility of the juridical language in general.

At the same time, as we will see more fully in Chapter 5, French political literature was giving plentiful expression to another powerful image: that of an "exhausted France," of a corrupt, servile, and degenerate nation on its deathbed.[102] This image, whose form owed much to Rousseau's pessimism, also dated its first appearance to the "coup" of 1771, but in 1788–89 it became ubiquitous. "O my Nation! To what degree of abasement have you fallen," wrote the future Jacobin Jérôme Pétion in his exemplary *Avis aux François*.[103] A 1789 address to the Estates General adopted a particularly despairing tone: "Is there a nation more immoral than the French? Is there one that misunderstands and violates the laws with such *légèreté?* . . . When one has grown old in corruption, one can no longer be healed, and when the maladies are at their height, the sick man shudders at the sight of the doctor. So, *messeigneurs,* abandon the present generation." Countless other authors experimented with variations on this dismal theme.[104]

There thus arrived an extraordinary moment in the history of French national sentiment: unprecedented claims on behalf of the *nation* together with unprecedented doubts about it, all in a context in which leaders of the nascent revolutionary movement were also loudly lamenting France's failure to constitute a true *patrie.* It was precisely in this condition of semantic flux that the existence of the *nation* itself could be questioned and that France's regional diversity could come to appear, for the first time, as a significant political problem.[105] At the very moment of the nation's political apotheosis, no one seemed to know what a nation was. A certain Toussaint Guiraudet (in obvious imitation of Sieyès), even made the question the title of a pamphlet: *Qu'est-ce que la nation et qu'est-ce que la France?* (What Is the Nation and What Is France?)[106]

And at this moment when state authority seemed to be disappearing into a vacuum, few of the French felt capable of responding to the question by opening up their creaky volumes of legal history. Childebert and Pharamond were returning to the realms of antiquarianism and myth.[107] In the early months of 1789 invocations of the national past did not disappear, but they now tended to come without their previous legal historical specificity. Disquisitions on the punctuation of Carolingian capitularies were increasingly superseded by Rousseauian celebrations of the centuries of Gaulish or medieval vigor and strength that had supposedly preceded the decadence and lethargy of the absolute monarchy. The national past of antiquarians and lawyers was giving way to the national past of Romantic poets and historians. But this was not to be a simple return to every aspect of the *status quo ante.* While the authors used words like "revival," "restoration," and "recovery," by far the most important term was "regeneration," which implied a new, original creation out of old and degenerate matter.[108] Regeneration was an active process of nation construction, driven by political will.

Already in early 1789, the ongoing debates gave a sense of the different ways the French revolutionaries would attempt to define and construct the nation. In some passages, which reflected the influence of the physiocrats, the process of construction seemed to resemble an engineering problem, with the nation treated as a collection of millions of individual human building blocks.[109] "By a nation," insisted the Parisian lawyer Pierre-Louis de Lacretelle, "can be understood only the sum total of citizens who belong there by permanent residence, by landed property, or through an industry which makes them necessary." Guiraudet similarly insisted that "the nation is not a compound of Orders, but a society of approximately twenty-five million men living under laws that it has given itself . . . France is not a compound of Provinces, but a space of twenty-five thousand square leagues." Most powerfully, Sieyès himself argued that the deputies to the Third Estate were the true representatives of the nation because they represented the vast majority of the population and the most important "social interests."[110] A conception of political representation as the election of deputies on behalf of mathematically delineated constituencies was beginning to challenge the older concept of representation as the embodiment of corporate entities.[111]

Yet if the idea of constructing a nation sometimes drove authors to speak in the accents of the engineer and statistician, it more often drew from them—as it had done from the architects of "royal patriotism"—deliberate echoes of prophecy and the realm of the sacred. The term "regeneration" itself, which was a key word of revolutionary vocabulary from 1789 on, offers a case in point, for it had been used, until shortly before, mostly in theological contexts. Although it occasionally signified the repair of injured bodily tissue, before the mid-century it most often meant baptism or resurrection. It began to pass into political usage with the Marquis de Mirabeau's *L'ami des hommes,* and achieved wide currency in the late 1780s. As Alyssa Sepinwall has written: "Regeneration was becoming a displacement of the Gospels . . . Regenerating was no longer only the province of God, but an operation which could be directed by humans"—although the process remained quasi-miraculous.[112] Similarly, to quote Jean Starobinski: "After having made such a dark and apparently irreversible diagnosis of their age, Rousseau and his disciples could only imagine the liberating change as a sort of miracle, on the religious model: the image of the resurrection, of the second coming, of regeneration, haunted them."[113] At this moment of uncertainty over the very existence of the nation and the future of the polity, French writers, accustomed to ordering the world around them without reference to God, found themselves almost instinctively attempting to touch their readers with words still redolent of Scripture.

In sum, by the time the Estates General actually met in May 1789, the "nation" on behalf of which the deputies would imminently wage a Revolution had been called radically into doubt, but at the same time hopes had been raised that one could still be built. In fact, in the optimistic early years of the Revolution it would be possible to believe that the construction had already, painlessly, almost miraculously taken place. Recall Chantreau's remark that France "really became a nation" in 1789.[114] And by the same token, the early revolutionaries were now willing to admit that France had also, finally, become a true *patrie*. Madame Roland, in 1790, used the phrase "since we acquired a *patrie*," and the University of Paris, in the same year, declared that "the French have sensed that they now have a *patrie*."[115] The *patrie*, too, was the object of regeneration, promised since the 1770s and now apparently accomplished. Revolutionary radicals would soon be disabused of this easy optimism, a disappointment that led them to embrace a far more ambitious and severe program of construction.

These shifts left room for enormous disagreement about both the *patrie* and the *nation*, particularly in regard to the position of the king within them. Throughout the Revolution, forces on what was becoming known as the right would maintain the tenets of the old regime's program of royal patriotism, insisting on the inseparability of king and *patrie*, and king and *nation*.[116] On the left, the king came to appear not only detachable from both, but positively inimical to both. Their survival required nothing less than his death. Meanwhile, the concept of regeneration was ambiguous enough to provoke far more arguments than it resolved. In sum, what had taken place before the Revolution, and particularly since Maupeou's 1771 "coup," was not the development of a single, overriding concept of the *nation* or the *patrie*. Rather, it was the generation of those ideological elements out of which the revolutionaries would forge their own (often clashing) patriotic and nationalist doctrines. These doctrines would often bear more than a tint of millenarianism and would blaze so brightly across Europe that Chantreau and Madame Roland (and Casanova) could be forgiven for thinking that nothing like a nation or a *patrie* had existed in France before.

CHAPTER 3

English Barbarians, French Martyrs

Aux armes, citoyens!

—DENIS-PONCE ECOUCHARD (LEBRUN), "ODE AUX
FRANÇAIS" (ANGERS, 1762)

Va, pour t'entredétruire, armer tes bataillons
Et de ton sang impur abreuver tes sillons.
[Go, to destroy yourself, arm your battalions,
And water your furrows with your impure blood].

—CLAUDE-RIGOBERT LEFEBVRE DE BEAUVRAY, *ADRESSE*
À LA NATION ANGLOISE (1757)

In the early morning of May 28, 1754, in the woods of what is now south-western Pennsylvania, a killing took place. The victims, a thirty-six-year-old French-Canadian officer named Joseph Coulon de Jumonville and nine soldiers under his command, had pitched camp for the night on the way from their base at Fort Duquesne (present-day Pittsburgh) to Britain's Fort Necessity, more than 40 miles to the south. Although supposedly at peace, France and Britain were each building chains of forts to support their rival claims to the great stretches of land between the Appalachians and the Mississippi, in the great game of military chess familiar from the novels of James Fenimore Cooper. Jumonville's mission was to instruct the British to withdraw immediately from what the French considered their territory. At Fort Necessity, however, Seneca Indian scouts had not only in-formed the inexperienced, twenty-two-year-old British commander about Jumonville's approach, but persuaded him it was the prelude to a French attack (the Seneca leader Tanaghrisson, known as the Half King, had a grudge of his own against the French). The commander therefore moved to intercept the French with a detachment of soldiers, and they crept up on Jumonville's encampment at dawn. It is unclear exactly who opened fire, but after a few confused volleys, the French were quickly overcome. Jumonville, wounded but alive, died under the Seneca leader's hatchet. The Senecas took several French scalps, and the newly seasoned British officer wrote boastfully to his brother back home in Virginia: "I heard the bullets whistle, and believe me, there is something charming in the sound."

This incident has long been familiar to North American historians. It marked not only the opening skirmish in what would soon turn into the Seven Years' War, but also a key moment in the career of the cocky young British officer—a man by the name of George Washington. In fact, it nearly brought Washington's career to a premature end. Scarcely a month after Jumonville's death, a large French force—led, dramatically enough, by Jumonville's brother—captured Fort Necessity in a pitched battle with Washington's forces. They then forced Washington to sign a confession that he had "assassinated" an ambassador traveling under a flag of truce. Only Washington's slippery insistence that he had not understood the French text he had signed allowed him to avoid a damaging scandal. His detractors and admirers have argued about the incident ever since.[1]

Jumonville's death, for all its importance to the outbreak of hostilities and to Washington's career, also won a prominent place in a very different theater of operations. During the Seven Years' War, the French and British alike made wide use of printed propaganda, and the French side used Jumonville's death as a *leitmotif,* a perfect illustration of the enemy's treacherous conduct.[2] Pamphlets, songs, journals, and supposedly impartial collections of documents stridently condemned the English and Washington (sometimes misidentified as "Wemcheston"), while enshrining the dead officer as a martyr of the *patrie*.[3] The incident even gave rise to a sixty-page long epic poem, Antoine-Léonard Thomas's ferociously patriotic *Jumonville*. A few lines suffice to give the general flavor:

> Par un plomb homicide indignement percé,
> Aux pieds de ses bourreaux il tombe renversé.
> Trois fois il souleva [sic] sa pesante paupière,
> Trois fois son oeil éteint se ferme à la lumière.
> De la France en mourant le tendre souvenir,
> Vient charmer sa grande âme à son dernier soupir.
> Il meurt: foulés aux pieds d'une troupe inhumaine
> Ses membres déchirés palpitent sur l'arène.
> [Unworthily pierced by a murderous bullet

He falls at the feet of his executioners.
Three times he lifts his heavy eyelid,
Three times his dulled eye closes to the light.
In dying, the tender memory of France
Comes to delight his great soul.
He dies: trampled under the feet of an inhuman band,
His torn members throb on the ground].[4]

The poem launched Thomas on a successful literary career and was singled out in a popular Swiss book on "national pride" as the *nec plus ultra* of French hatred of foreigners.[5] So it is no surprise that as early as 1757, the Jesuit newspaper *Mémoires de Trévoux* could comment that "all the world has learned of the treatment meted out to the Sieur de Jumonville."[6] The unfortunate officer, his undistinguished life now eclipsed by his sensational leaving of it, gained such a posthumous reputation that collective biographies of "great Frenchmen," published in profusion in the waning decades of the *ancien régime,* included him right alongside such icons of French military glory as Bayard and Duguesclin.[7] Some of the poetry lamenting Jumonville's death remained well known enough in 1792 for Rouget de Lisle to crib from it in writing the *Marseillaise* (see, for instance, the epigraphs to this chapter).[8]

To twentieth-century eyes such atrocity literature seems quite unremarkable—indeed, by our woefully jaded standards, rather tame, and so it has been largely ignored.[9] Yet it constituted another arena in which the French seized on the concepts of the *nation* and the *patrie* and put them to new uses. In this instance, they did so in response to the changing demands of warfare, and one effect was to change perceptions and representations of warfare itself. The war literature of the 1750s and 1760s, for the first time in French history, presented an international conflict neither as a duel between royal houses nor as a clash of religions, but as a battle between irreconcilable nations.

As in the case of the constitutional conflicts, on one level this shift illustrates the progressive detachment of French political culture from its former religious context. In contrast to the stridently anti-Catholic propaganda flowing from the other side of the Channel, French war literature rarely mentioned the religious differences between France and England—despite the survival of anti-Protestant bigotry in France, and despite suspicions that some French Protestants may have had illicit contacts with the

Figure 5. Another version of the killing of French officer Jumonville by Virginia militia and their Indian auxiliaries in the Ohio Valley in 1754. Once again, the scene is illustrated allegorically by comparison to combats between Saracens and Crusaders. Antoine-Léonard Thomas, *Jumonville*, Paris, 1759.

English enemy.[10] The French war literature also formed part and parcel of the campaign of royal patriotism, which itself marked so striking a departure from orthodox Catholic justifications of absolute monarchy. Yet just as the pamphleteers of the pre-Revolution found themselves reaching back to the quasi-religious concept of "regeneration" as part of their quest to rebuild the nation, so the propagandists of the Seven Years' War broke with recent predecessors to adopt various ideas and practices from the literature of the Wars of Religion. Paradoxically, this return to the past helped lay the groundwork for the development of modern, racially based forms of nationalism.

There were two great xenophobic moments in eighteenth-century French history: the Seven Years' War that started with Jumonville's death, and the revolutionary wars that started in 1792. The second certainly dwarfed the first in intensity. At the height of the Revolution, Jacobin clubs across France were spitting forth hatred of that "enemy of the human race" William Pitt, and denouncing the English as a "race of cannibals." Bertrand Barère not only called the English "a people foreign to humanity, [who] must disappear," but convinced the Convention to pass a (thankfully little obeyed) motion instructing French commanders in the field to take no English prisoners alive.[11] Yet the two moments have striking similarities. In both cases, the cosmopolitanism so often associated with eighteenth-century French culture abruptly disappeared from books and periodicals, to be replaced by snarling hostility to France's enemies. In both cases, this change occurred thanks above all to the concerted efforts of the French government, which sought to mobilize resources and public opinion behind the war effort. And the revolutionary literature in fact followed models developed in the earlier period, sometimes quite literally, as in the case of the *Marseillaise*. It is impossible to say, given the available evidence, whether the Seven Years' War literature had anything like the popular resonance of its revolutionary counterpart, which helped shape a wave of patriotic mobilization unparalleled in European history. But at the very least—as the revolutionary borrowings themselves demonstrate—this earlier body of work put important ideas and motifs into broad circulation. For this reason, and to continue my exploration of the transformation of patriotism and national sentiment in the last decades of the old regime, I will concentrate here particularly on the Seven Years' War, although I will also look ahead to the Revolution.

Englishmen and Barbarians

In modern accounts, the Seven Years' War is considered important not only for the decisive realignment of European power that it brought about (especially the triumph of Britain and Prussia and the decline of France and Austria), but also because it was a new sort of war. It could almost be called the first world war, for the combatants battled each other in North America, Africa, India, and on every ocean, as well as in Europe. They spent unprecedented sums in the process, and the war hastened the development of several Western European states into vast fiscal-military machines, capable of keeping hundreds of thousands of men in the field and scores of ships of the line on the high seas.[12] It has generally escaped notice, however, that the propaganda efforts (at least on the French side) also represented a considerable novelty. The vilification of national enemies itself was hardly new, of course; the Hundred Years' War and the Wars of Religion offered ample precedent. But the Seven Years' War saw not simply the expression of national antipathies, but their employment in a sustained, intensive print campaign aimed at mobilizing the French nation against an enemy nation. The only precedent for this sort of campaign lay in the history of religious warfare, in such episodes as the Catholic League's frenetic efforts to mobilize its supporters against the Protestant Henri of Navarre, and before that, in the battles between Protestants and Catholics in Luther's Germany.[14]

Consider, first, the sheer volume: at least 80 items per year appeared in France during the Seven Years' War, more than double the amount produced during the recent wars of the Spanish and Austrian Successions (the second of which ended just six years before Jumonville's death).[15] The *Journal encyclopédique* signaled its awareness of this change with a wry quip: "The future will scarcely believe it, but the war between the English and the French has been as lively on paper as on the high seas."[16] Not since the Wars of Religion had French printing presses churned out such quantities of xenophobic polemic. Tracking its distribution is difficult, but we know that at least one item, the issue of Jacob-Nicolas Moreau's newspaper *L'Observateur hollandois* that recounted Jumonville's death, sold 8,000 copies, an impressive figure for the period. The paper was pirated by Dutch, Italian, and German publishers and translated into several languages.[17] The burgeoning European periodical press gave considerable attention to the polemical works, as did the British themselves, who responded in kind.[18] As a result, not only Jumonville's death, but also other major themes of French propaganda had wide diffusion, such as the triumphant early seizure of Port-Mahon in Minorca from the unfortunate Admiral Byng, and the heroic death of the Chevalier d'Assas in the battle of Clostercamp.[19]

The material also represented a new departure in its violence. Although unimpressive by twentieth-century standards, the language reached a level of invective not seen in French war literature since the sixteenth century— certainly not in the thin, almost decorous productions of the recent War of the Austrian Succession.[20] The propaganda portrayed the English as "vultures," a "perjurious race" driven by "blind wrath" and "undying hatred," people who had removed themselves from "that universal Republic, which embraces all nations in its heart."[21] It consistently compared them to the grasping, mercantile Carthaginians, and suggested that England would soon, quite deservedly, share Carthage's hideous fate.[22]

Simply taking note of the numbers and the violence, however, does not advance our understanding very far. The crucial questions are what form the material took, and what strategies the authors employed. Most importantly, rather than tar the English as "heretics," the propaganda tended to stigmatize them as lawbreaking "barbarians" and to contrast them, insistently and unfavorably, to American Indians. Moreau was the first to use this theme. In his 1755 description of Jumonville's death in L'Observateur hollandois, he accused the English of "infamies which have distinguished peoples whom Europeans consider Barbarians," and of "this wild license which previously distinguished the northern Barbarians."[23] He also linked English "barbarism" to the long history of English civil discord and the islanders' proven inability to refrain even from killing one another.[24]

Following Moreau, Antoine-Léonard Thomas virtually structured his epic poem Jumonville around the theme. He began it with a pointed Virgilian epigraph—"What race of men is this? What fatherland is so barbarous as to allow this custom?"—and continued relentlessly in this vein.[25] The Englishman was a "new barbarian" (p. 23) who committed "a barbarian homicide" (p. 4) and showed "a barbarian joy" in it (p. 24). Thomas also asserted no fewer than four times that the Indians themselves, for all their qualities of "ferocity," "cruelty," and "roughness" (p. 44), were shocked and angered by Jumonville's killing (pp. ix, 22, 30, 44). Immediately after the description of Jumonville's death, the poet addressed himself directly to the Indians:

Du moins votre grossière et farouche droiture
Suit les premières Loix de la simple nature.
L'Anglais, nouveau barbare, a traversé les mers
Pour apporter ce crime au fonds de vos déserts.
Allez, du fer tranchant, d'une hâche sanglante
Gravez sur vos rochers cette image effrayante.
[At least your crude and ferocious uprightness
Follows simple nature's first laws.
The Englishman, a new barbarian, has crossed the seas
To bring this crime to the heart of your wilderness.
Go, and engrave on your rocks this horrifying image
Of cutting steel and bloody axe] (pp. 22–23).

For Thomas, both Indians and English behave at a vast remove from European norms of politeness and morality, but the latter even more so. The *Mémoires de Trévoux* grasped the point perfectly in its review of *Jumonville:* "These Englishmen on the Oyo [Ohio River] . . . were more barbarian than the Iroquois and the Hurons. They, at least, shuddered when they heard of the attack on Jumonville."[26]

Other chroniclers of Jumonville's death joined in as well. The poet Lebrun echoed Moreau's words in his indignation at the "barbaric" conqueror who gave lessons in crime to Indians much less deserving of the epithet:

De la Terre et des Mers Dépredateur avare,
Au Huron qu'il dédaigne, et qu'il nomme barbare
Il apprend des Forfaits.
[Greedy despoiler of land and seas,
He teaches infamies to the Huron whom he disdains
    and calls barbarian].[27]

A historically minded abbé named Séran de la Tour, expatiating at book length on the comparison of England to Carthage, devoted two pages to this particular instance of "English barbarism"—and three more to the Indians' horrified reaction.[28] He and others likewise stressed the "discord" that lay at the heart of the English soul.[29]

The incident in the Pennsylvania woods provided the ideal illustration of the theme, but its use permeated nearly all the polemical anti-English literature of the Seven Years' War (most of which did not deal with events in North America). Again and again, French publicists decried turbulent English "barbarians" and compared them unfavorably with non-European peoples. The author of a poem on a wide range of English atrocities asked, for instance, "Dans les antres profonds de la vaste Lybie / Vit-on jamais régner autant de barbarie? [In the deep lairs of vast Libya, did one ever see so much barbarism reign?]"[30] Satirical verses carrying a mock *approbation* from a fictive Royal Academy of Barbary of Tunis put a particularly sharp speech in the mouth of Montcalm, the French general who would soon find defeat and death on the Plains of Abraham:

> . . . amis, vous êtes nés Français.
> N'imitéz point par cet affreux ravage
> La Barbarie et le ton des Anglais,
> Laisséz agir la nation sauvage . . .
> Qu'un Iroquois a bien plus de clémence
> Que ces Milords qu'on fait pour de l'argent.
> . . . friends, you were born French.
> Don't imitate the Barbarism and the tone of the English
> In this horrid depredation.
> Let the savage nation act . . .
> An Iroquois has far more mercy in him
> Than these Milords who buy their titles].[31]

The ministerial publicist Lefebvre de Beauvray told the subjects of his 1757 poetic *Adresse à la nation angloise:* "Oui c'est vous qu'on a vûs, portant dans Votre sein / Toute la cruauté du féroce Africain" [Yes it is you that we have seen, carrying in your breast / All the cruelty of the fierce African].[32] Most insistently, Robert-Martin Lesuire devoted an entire comic novel to the theme: his *Les sauvages de l'Europe.*[33] "The English lie at mid-point between men and beasts," says Lesuire's hero. "All the difference I can see between the English and the Savages of Africa, is that the latter spare the fair sex."[34]

One further point about the theme is worth making. Polemical writing of this sort hardly lent itself to lexical precision, but nonetheless, from the 1750s through the 1790s, the texts mostly distinguished English "barbarians" from non-European "savages" (Lesuire was the principal exception). The latter term, in keeping with its origins in "selvaggi," or forest-dwellers, in the early modern period generally implied creatures without fixed abode, law, or polite customs, possibly even without language—but also without guile or hypocrisy. It most often connoted a greater closeness to nature and man's original state. The more pejorative "barbarian," by contrast, implied a degree of social corruption and willful rejection of polite behavior (particularly respect for the law), and was most often applied to non-European peoples possessed of a high degree of social organization (such as the inhabitants of the Barbary coast).[35] As a concise example of the difference, consider that eighteenth-century authors spoke of "noble savages" but never of "noble barbarians."[36]

Overall, this juxtaposition of the English to non-Europeans served an obvious polemical purpose. Not that it was an entirely new theme for French publicists. During the Wars of Religion, when the Spanish had filled the role of national enemy, Huguenots and *politiques* occasionally denounced *them* as barbarians and gleefully copied into their broadsides Las Casas's accounts of Spanish New World atrocities.[37] Still, the renewed predilection for the theme in the 1750s, like the dimensions of the wartime literature itself, *was* novel and deserves explanation.

Mobilizing the Nation

To find this explanation, the first questions to ask are: who wrote the literature, and what readership did they hope to reach? Many of the texts appeared anonymously, but it is still possible to make one broad generalization: the literature did not simply well up spontaneously from the breasts of inspired patriotic authors. To a very large extent (although just how large remains uncertain), it was directed from above, by the royal ministry. As the hostile satirist Mouffle d'Angerville later wrote, "these writings [were] produced under the auspices of the Ministry, whose secret sponsorship remained hidden, [so that they] seemed nothing but the effusion of a patriotic heart."[38] The literature certainly cannot be read as evidence of widespread and spontaneous outbreaks of patriotic devotion and xenophobia, although some of this doubtless occurred.[39]

The key figure was none other than Moreau, whom the foreign affairs department provided with plentiful funds, the services of a translator and clerk, and confidential papers. Thus supplied, he wrote pamphlets and produced the lion's share of two newspapers: the highly successful *L'Observateur hollandois*, and, later in the war, *Le Moniteur françois*. He also published in book form, in both English and French, papers seized from Washington at Fort Necessity.[40] Considerable textual evidence suggests that the other authors took their source material and their themes directly from Moreau's writings. Some openly admitted as much, while others cribbed lines and quotations from him (Thomas took the preface to *Jumonville* almost verbatim from *L'Observateur hollandois,* and even his Virgilian epigraph had previously appeared in its pages—to paraphrase Dr. Swift, "Get scraps of Virgil from your friends, And have them at your fingers' ends").[41] The ministry employed other official propagandists as well, probably including the prolifical Anglophobic lawyer Lefebvre de Beauvray (who also cooperated with it against the *parlements*). A year after writing *Jumonville,* Thomas became private secretary to Foreign Minister Choiseul.[42] War poetry flooded the pages of official periodicals such as the *Mercure de France,* and it seems likely that many of the more than 150 separate poems, songs, and "fêtes" collected in one 1757 volume had official sponsorship.[43]

At least at the beginning, the ministry's intended audience was not so much French as international. When it hired Moreau in 1755, it did so first and foremost with the goal of keeping the Netherlands neutral in the looming Franco-British conflict, which is why the Parisian lawyer took on the unconvincing persona of a sturdy Dutch burgher (Monsieur Van ***) in his *Observateur hollandois.* His publication of Washington's papers formed something of an unofficial codicil to France's formal declaration of war, a testimony to the justice of France's cause. Yet the newspaper was published in French, and when Moreau boasted of the sensation it caused, he meant the sensation in France itself, not the Netherlands.[44] Reading the paper, it is hard to believe that Moreau did not principally have a French audience in mind. In the issue centered on Jumonville's death, he wrote of the French: "When will this amiable and generous Nation learn to amuse its imagination with objects worthy of occupying its reason? When will the love of the *patrie* which lives in the heart of all Frenchmen convey its heat to those many minds who occupy themselves wholly with arid and frivolous questions?"[45] It was not the sort of passage to stir the blood of Dutch readers.

As the war proceeded, the early French victories turned to ashes and France faced the prospect of massive defeat, including the loss of most of its overseas empire. The principal purpose of the propaganda then became all the more clear: to mobilize French readers behind the crown's war effort. Moreau's *Le Moniteur françois* openly aimed at a domestic audience, and Moreau recounted in his memoirs that a major pamphlet he wrote comparing France and England (whose publication the ministry hastily scotched when negotiators agreed on terms for peace) had as its goal "to bring back the confidence that we needed more than ever, and to raise up our courage." Similarly, in a work entitled *Lettre sur la paix*, "I exhorted the nation to recapture the customs, courage and virtues of its ancestors."[46] At the same time, the ministry attempted to stifle expressions of Anglophilia, which had flourished in print without much constraint during the War of the Austrian Succession, and held up "cosmopolitanism" as a particularly grievous sin.[47] As Edmond Dziembowski has convincingly argued, the French war literature found a model of patriotic fervor in England itself (although this fervor was linked to the turbulent nature of the English and their politics, which supposedly showed through in everything from election riots to the execution of Charles I).[48]

Not surprisingly, the literary propagandists seized on any and all evidence that the French were making unprecedented sacrifices for victory—for instance, in voluntary contributions to the war effort. A contributor to the anti-*philosophe* Elie Fréron's newspaper *L'Année littéraire* had called as early as 1756 for such donations: "We have to engage the nation, or at least the well-off people, to make an effort worthy of true French patriots, in giving voluntarily what they can give without harming their fortune, which is much less than the effort one makes for one's *patrie* in giving up one's life."[49] In 1759 and 1760, with the disastrous state of French finances almost matching the disastrous state of French arms, the crown started encouraging this sort of "voluntary" activity, including the donation of a 74-gun warship by the Estates of Languedoc, and of at least eight other smaller ships (including one baptized the *Citoyen*) by a variety of benefactors.[50] In November of 1759, Controller General of Finances Silhouette issued letters patent calling on the French to bring their silver plate to the mint, either as donations or to be exchanged for promissory notes, and the king set an example with some of his own silver. These contributions had a negligible impact on the overall budgetary situation; their purpose was more symbolic than financial.[51] The letters patent actually generated a great deal of resentment and fear ("this sort of expedient is ordinarily the state's last resort in the face of calamities," noted the caustic Parisian lawyer Edmond Barbier in his diary), but few dared disobey, for fear of belying the image of national unity.[52] A letter from an adviser to a Parisian convent is particularly telling: "I informed [the nuns] that they are in circumstances in which it is essential that they appear patriotic, and ready to obey His Majesty's wishes."[53]

In the shift from a propaganda effort aimed at least partly at an international audience to one designed to stimulate domestic "confidence" and "courage" and to present the image of a united nation, the literature of the Seven Years' War in some respects followed a model first elaborated earlier in the century, during the War of the Spanish Succession. Then, too, although on a noticeably smaller scale, the ministry underwrote pamphlets to persuade neutral foreign observers of the justice of the French cause; especially notable was Jean de la Chapelle's vituperative *Lettres d'un Suisse*.[54] As that war turned more desperate for the French, the crown issued several public letters, supposedly written by the king himself, in which Louis XIV stressed his love for his people and his desire to secure a lasting and honorable peace. One letter addressed to royal governors was read out from church pulpits across the kingdom.[55] Moreau consulted de la Chapelle in writing his *Observateur hollandois,* and several patriotic publications from the mid-century recalled Louis's letter in making their own exhortations to the French.[56]

Yet in fact the difference between the two sets of war literature is enormous. The first presented the war as a war of kings, of royal houses. De la Chapelle consistently attacked the perfidies and infamies of the "House of Austria" and the "Emperor," not of Austrians. Although he used the word "barbarian," it was to describe the "House of Austria's barbarous maxims."[57] When the ministry appealed to the French nation, it did so in the guise of the king speaking to noble governors *about* his "faithful subjects."[58] In contrast, the literature of the Seven Years' War, including a manifesto written by Foreign Minister Choiseul himself, presented the conflict between France and Britain in quite a different manner, as a war of nations.[59] The anonymous contributor to Fréron's newspaper (possibly Fréron himself) expressed this difference most strikingly: "There are wars in which the nation only takes an interest because of its submission to the Prince; this war is of a different nature; it is the English nation which, by unanimous agreement, has attacked our nation to deprive us of something which belongs to each of us."[60]

In this light, the emphasis Moreau and his fellow authors placed on Jumonville's death takes on added significance. It was not an emissary of the House of Hanover who had cut Jumonville down in the Ohio Valley. Indeed, Britain's King George II barely figured in the war literature at all. No, the villain was an "English barbarian," and, more generally, all "English barbarians." The victim, meanwhile, was no illustrious noble or prince of the blood. He was, wrote Thomas in *Jumonville,* "nothing but a simple

French officer"—but for that very reason the prototype of his nation: "Of the virtuous Frenchman, such is the character."[61]

The difference between the two bodies of propaganda shows just how much had changed in France in the forty years between Louis XIV's death and 1755. The French had grown increasingly accustomed to seeing themselves as a "nation," and more so, a nation which could mobilize itself, instead of simply flocking behind a king. In this respect, the experience of the Seven Years' War contributed to the concept of the nation as a political artifact, something consciously constructed through an act of collective political will. Furthermore, France's ruling elites had become accustomed, in certain important respects, to treating France as a collectivity possessed of its own internal unity and of certain legitimate "rights." In this respect, both the expansion of the public sphere in France and the political earthquake of the early 1750s had an absolutely fundamental importance. By the 1750s the ministry was learning to defend its actions in print, to justify them before the "nation" or "public opinion," through the ever-expanding circuits for the distribution of printed material. It was natural, therefore, to seek to mobilize the nation (in fact, the small percentage of relatively well-off pamphlet readers), presenting the war as one in which every individual citizen had a stake.

National Identity and European Unity

If the war was a war of nations, then it was not only a war of all the French, but a war against all of the English. The publicists needed to demonize not simply an enemy king or his advisors, but an entire enemy nation. This shift from earlier modes of propaganda raised some formidable problems, however, as illustrated particularly by Moreau's contortions on the issue. In October 1755, in the *Observateur hollandois,* he wrote unctuously that he "didn't want to accuse a Friendly Nation"—but he immediately proceeded to ask how one could possibly "separate from the rest of the nation an officer [Washington] whose crime . . . seems to have been the signal for hostilities of all sorts." And he added a few pages later: "Yes, Monsieur, whatever wish you may have to justify the English nation, the facts speak too loudly against it."[62] A month later, he again retreated from this position, in a fascinating disquisition on the English national character.

> I do not attribute to all the English the excesses to which the bulk of the Nation seems pushed today. I do more. I distinguish two Nations, one of

which is presently the small minority, the nation of the wise . . . But there is in England another nation, if you can even give this name to that ill-considered multitude who let themselves be carried away by opinion and subjugated by hatred. A tumultuous assemblage of all sorts of different parties, they are not a Nation who consult, who reflect, who deliberate; they are a people who cry, who agitate, and who demand war.[63]

If elsewhere in his work Moreau (like other authors) drew a deft contrast between true French patriotism and national feeling and the English "fanaticism" that masqueraded under those names, here he drew the boundary line within England itself.[64]

Other writers followed Moreau's example. The *Mémoires de Trévoux* excoriated the "English common people *[petit peuple]*" for "a ferocity which no longer belongs to the mores *[moeurs]* of Europe."[65] A semi-official French publicist, the abbé Le Blanc, denounced "the imbecility of these [English] Fanatics, who take for the voice of the People, the cries of an mindless populace which they themselves have excited."[66] The *Journal encyclopédique* denounced the "wild [English] populace, which, thinking it is embracing the phantom of liberty, can give itself over to horrid insults of other Nations."[67] These passages incidentally illustrate the suppleness of the publicists' vocabulary. While Moreau contrasted a presumably well-constituted and rational "nation" to a disorganized and fickle "people," using the latter in the sense of the (scorned) "common people," Le Blanc distinguished between a divinely wise "People" (as in *vox populi, vox dei*), and a (scorned) "populace."[68]

It was obvious why Moreau and the others distinguished so carefully between the tiny minority of benign English and the crushing majority of malignant ones. As they knew quite well, making collective accusations against the English nation might not have much credibility for the French reading public, because that public had, for more than twenty years, consumed a steady diet of Anglophilic literature, which taught reverence, not hatred, toward the nation across the Channel. From Voltaire's paeans to England in the *Philosophical Lettters*, to Montesquieu's exaltation of the English constitution, to Diderot's prostration before Samuel Richardson ("O Richardson, Richardson . . . I will keep you on the same shelf with Moses, Homer, Euripides and Sophocles"), to the general adulation of Locke and Newton, the major *philosophes* did their part.[69] Anglomania raged in many other domains as well, notably fashion and sport, while the eighteenth-century adoption of words such as "le club" and "le jockey" marked the birth of Franglais.[70] A sizeable literature grew up in the eighteenth century solely to inoculate the French against the disease of Anglomania, and it still could not prevent Mlle. de l'Espinasse from notoriously remarking that "only Voltaire's glory consoles me for not having been born English."[71] The popular novelist and poet Baculard Arnaud acknowledged the problem when he wrote, in a 1762 poem, "Your Lockes and your Newtons / Were not the ones to teach you these barbaric lessons."[72]

Although no other foreign nation elicited anything like the visceral emotional response from the French that England did, this Anglomania itself fit within a broader eighteenth-century phenomenon: French readers' growing awareness of their identity as Europeans. The idea of Europe as a political unit had a long and august pedigree, and the shadow of European empire had not yet vanished from the Continent, but in the eighteenth century, writers began to perceive what we would now call a close European cultural unity as well.[73] Voltaire wrote in his *Le poëme sur la Bataille de Fontenoy* (a war poem, but from the relatively polite War of the Austrian Succession): "The peoples of Europe have common principles of humanity which cannot be found in other parts of the world . . . A Frenchman, an Englishman and a German who meet seem to have been born in the same town."[74] A 1760 review from the *Journal encyclopédique* also put the point in a global context: "There is a perceptible and striking difference between the inhabitants of Asia and those of Europe . . . But it is much harder, and takes much more discernment, to grasp the slight differences that separate the inhabitants of Europe from one another."[75] The young Rousseau, in a plan for universal peace, commented that "Europe [is] not only a collectivity of nations . . . but also a real society, which has its own religion, its own morality, its own way of life, and even its own laws."[76] He returned to the theme more critically in *Emile* and the *Considerations on the Government of Poland*: "Today, whatever one may say, there are no longer any Frenchmen, Germans, Spaniards, or even Englishmen, whatever one may say on the subject there are only Europeans. They all have the same tastes, the same passions, and the same customs, because none of them has acquired a national form through a particular education."[77]

Many factors spurred this new awareness. Among them were improved communications, the burgeoning periodical press, the enormous cultural influence of France itself, and the decline of international religious animosities. The deeply Catholic commitment to a universal human community that pervaded French culture in the eighteenth century could only have reinforced all of these developments. In addition, Europe stood as the embodiment of several of the foundational concepts discussed in Chapter 1: *société, police, civilisation,* and *moeurs.* Nowhere, except perhaps in China, French authors agreed, had progress brought these things to such a high level of development—a verdict that Voltaire celebrated and Rousseau deplored (as we will see in Chapter 5, the status of women was crucial to these arguments, although the issue did not feature prominently in the war literature).[78]

Voltaire's poem and the *Journal encyclopédique* review suggest a final and crucial factor: the vertiginous expansion of interest in and information about non-European cultures during the eighteenth century. Michèle Duchet has remarked that one need read no further than *Candide* and the *Spirit of the Laws* to see how large a place the non-European world occupied in the French Enlightenment's imagination—and Duchet herself, following on several earlier works, has in any case provided ample further evidence.[79] Travel writing, Jesuit *Relations* (accounts of missionary activity), newspapers, atlases, orientalist novels, and synthetic works of philosophy all made the French familiar with a much larger range of human diversity than ever before.[80]

In the context of this new perception of a European identity, the *Mémoires de Trévoux*'s comments that the English common people displayed a "ferocity which no longer belongs to the mores of Europe" takes on particular significance and suggests why the image of the "English barbarian" had such powerful resonance in French propaganda. The casting of the Seven Years' War as a war of nations rather than a war of royal houses conflicted directly with the idea that Europeans were growing steadily closer together, with France and England in particular establishing symbolic bridges across the Channel. How could Moreau, Thomas, and the other publicists make national differences *within* Europe appear unbridgeably vast, when so much of the printed matter consumed by their readership implied the exact reverse?

The power of the image of the "English barbarian" lay precisely in its symbolic removal of the English from Europe—to the shores of Tripoli, or even further, to an outer darkness beyond even the "savagery" of Africans and American Indians. It revealed that the English, or at least most of them, only *appeared* European, but in fact lacked the requisite qualities of politeness, sociability, and respect for the law, and stood at the opposite end of a linear scale of historical developments. The label "barbarian" suggested that the English, unlike the more pliable American "savages," had actually rejected joining the company of advanced nations. In sum, if representations of savage Americans and Africans figured centrally in the invention of the idea of the civilized European, they also provided a radical standard of alien and primitive behavior (of otherness) that could be used, as political necessity dictated, to measure other European peoples against, thereby contributing to the construction of a new, and more specifically national, self-image.

The School of Arts and Humanity

If the image of the English barbarian functioned in this way to de-Europeanize the English, it also helped to place France itself at the symbolic center of Europe. The national self-image it helped to construct had little in common with the one often proposed for England by English publicists in this period: namely, the image of a new Israel of the elect—a chosen people fundamentally set apart from others.[81] The French image was rather that of a new Rome, the open and welcoming center of a universal civilization. And here too the war literature fit in well with the evolution of French nationalism and patriotism over the course of the eighteenth century.

As we have already seen, the way the French defined themselves in the eighteenth century did not rest primarily on a drastic drawing of borders between themselves and foreign "others." They tended to minimize the connotations of exclusivity and fatality that had been associated with the concept of *patrie* from antiquity, and strove to make patriotism compatible with a universal human community in which all nations followed the same linear path of development. This universalism did not, however, imply any modesty about France's own place in the family of nations. Throughout the early modern period, dating back at least to Jean Bodin's *Method for the Easy Comprehension of History*, French writers had generally sought to identify the highest stage of human development not merely with Europe, but with France itself. Most often, they grounded their arguments in theories of climate, arguing that France's temperate weather and fertility made it welcoming soil for spiritual achievement and gave the naturally moderate French—nature's true cosmopolitans—the best qualities of *all* nations.[82] In the eighteenth century, the most subtle contributors to climate theory (particularly Montesquieu and Buffon) eschewed these chauvinistic claims, but many others embraced them. Antoine de Rivarol, for instance, wrote that "nature, in giving [the Frenchman] a gentle climate, could not make him rough: it has made him the man of all the nations."[83] D'Espiard de la Borde similarly argued, in his *The Spirit of Nations*, that "France, among all the nations, can take pride in the fortunate Temperature of its Climate and Minds alike, which produces no bizarre effects, either in Nature or Morals."[84] French mores were perfectly compatible with those of all other nations, and so France, d'Espiard concluded, "is the principal Pole of Europe."[85] The cleric Thomas-Jean Pichon wrote in a work similar to d'Espiard's, *The Physics of History*, that "[French] souls, capable of all modifications, are, in a sense, like their territory, which can produce all sorts of fruits."[86] During the French Revolution the messianic cosmopolitan Anacharsis Cloots asked: "Why, indeed, has nature placed Paris at an equal distance from the pole and the equator, but for it to be a cradle and the metropolis for the general confederation of mankind?"[87]

From these arguments it followed that the French had the duty to act not only as the world's seat of learning (thus fulfilling the venerable promise of a *translatio studii* from Athens to Rome to Paris), but also as the world's schoolmasters.[88] Fellow Europeans might recognize France's superiority and of their own free will copy its fashions and learn its language. Beyond Europe, however, fulfilling the Frenchman's destiny as "the man of all the nations" demanded an early version of what the nineteenth century would call the nation's "civilizing mission."[89] This mission was in fact a tenet of early modern French imperialist theory. The French authorities in Canada, for instance, declared early on that all "savages" who accepted Catholicism would "be considered and reputed native French," while Controller General Colbert even encouraged intermarriage between Indians and French, "in order that, in the course of time, having but one law and one master, they may likewise constitute one people and one race."[90] These ideas permeated travel literature and the missionary *Relations*, which Jesuit *collèges* pressed on their students.[91]

Not surprisingly, the ideas also appeared prominently in the polemical literature of the Seven Years' War—and most strongly in those texts which most insistently deployed the image of the English barbarian. Thomas's *Jumonville*, for instance, describes the American Indians in terms that Colbert himself would certainly have approved:

Les grossiers habitants de ces lointains rivages
Formés par nos leçons, instruits par nos usages,
Dans l'école des Arts et de l'humanité
De leurs sauvages moeurs corrigent l'aprêté . . .
Leur coeur simple et naïf dans sa férocité
Respecte du François la sage authorité.
[The crude inhabitants of those distant shores,
Shaped by our lessons, and instructed by our customs,
Reform the harshness of their savage mores
In the school of Arts and humanity . . .
Their hearts, simple and naïve in their ferocity,
Respect the wise authority of the Frenchman].[92]

In the poem, Jumonville's death itself provides the Indians with a salutary lesson. Until they witnessed it, nothing could overcome their "inflexible roughness," and they remained deaf to pity, taking it for weakness. But on seeing Washington's crime, "Pour la première fois [ils] se sentent ébranler, / De leurs yeux attendris on voit des pleurs couler [For the first time they feel themselves weaken / And one sees tears flow from their eyes].[93] The novelist Lesuire also cast the French as educators—but in this case unsuccessful—of the savage English. As he had one of his few sympathetic English characters remark in a crucial scene: "Our [French] neighbors could, more than any other People, soften our mores, and teach us the bonds of society, which make life precious by making it pleasant; but here we make it a duty to hate them. *As long as we hate the French, we will be barbarians*" (emphasis mine).[94]

It would be wrong to say that these representations of England, France, and the relation between them held unanimous sway in France. The heavy legacy of Anglomania and cosmopolitanism did not dissipate so easily. Besides, these representations were at least in part official ones, elements of a conscious strategy on the part of the ministry to mobilize the population for the war effort. It is impossible to gauge with any degree of accuracy how widely the general population shared them. What can be said, however, is that these representations permanently expanded the field of French political discussion, suggesting ways of seeing nations, foreign and French alike, that would continue to reappear in French political culture (particularly during the Revolution).

What was most original and significant about them, ultimately, was the idea of an essential, unalterable difference between two nations. In the eighteenth century (as we will see in more detail in Chapter 5), the most common criteria for adducing differences in national character were climate, political system, and position on a linear scale of historical evolution, according to which American Indians, for instance, stood roughly equivalent to the early Greeks. For this reason, historians have generally opposed eighteenth-century notions of human difference to nineteenth-century racially based ones, since, according to the earlier criteria, a people's characteristics could easily change (as in Buffon's claim that Africans transplanted to Scandinavia would eventually become white).[95] Certainly the polemical writers of the mid-eighteenth century did not fail to link English faults to all these factors, particularly the turbulence of English politics and weather alike ("a perpetually bloody climate," as Buirette de Belloy concisely put it).[96] But the tactic of stigmatizing the English as barbarians, although rooted in notions of historical evolution, established new criteria of difference. For the writers who deployed it, even "savage" Indians did not ultimately stand beyond the reach of the French civilizing mission. The English did, owing to their perverse refusal of French wisdom. Unlike the Indians, they would never evolve beyond a fundamentally primitive historical state. Lesuire, in *Les sauvages de l'Europe,* again expressed this idea with particular force. At the beginning of his novel, one character observes—in keeping with climate-based theories of difference—that Europe has two true barbaric peoples, both in the north: the Lapps and the English. But then he adds a further difference: "The second are barbarians in their hearts."[97] Similarly, for Lefebvre de Beauvray, the "cruelty of the fierce African" was something the Englishman carried "in [his] breast."[98] In sum, this language served to deepen the concept of a war of nations, to make it seem an inevitable fight to the finish between irreconcilable peoples.

Toward the Revolutionary Wars

When France and Britain signed the Peace of Paris in 1763, official attitudes towards the enemy across the Channel abruptly shifted. Martyrs like Jumonville were no longer in demand, and the specter of the English barbarian rapidly receded. Lefebvre de Beauvray, who only recently had been spitting forth his eternal hatred of the "perjurious race" of Englishmen, suddenly and more than a little hypocritically revealed himself a secret

Anglomaniac, rhapsodizing about "le Français et l'Anglais, par les talents unis, / Emules de tout temps, trop souvent ennemis [The French and English, united by talents / Imitators of each other always, but too often enemies]."[99] As we have seen, even in the two postwar stage plays often cited by historians as prime examples of French Anglophobia (*Le siège de Calais* and C. S. Favart's *L'Anglois à Bordeaux*), a far more nuanced portrait of "English barbarians" emerged. In both, thanks in part to the civilizing influence of French women (particularly important for Favart), the crude and unsociable English protagonists finally proved susceptible to the wisdom of French ways.

Not did "English barbarians" return in force during the War of American Independence. Although again at war with England, the French also found themselves allied with erstwhile English colonists, commanded by the chief barbarian of 1754 (one French volunteer fighting with the Americans simply refused to believe that the imposing general was the same man as Jumonville's murderer).[100] When Lesuire published a revised version of *The Savages of Europe* in 1780, he toned down his portrait substantially and called England "a rival Nation, and one which we should esteem, because it can bear comparison with us from many points of view."[101] French propaganda in this war, including new work by Lefebvre de Beauvray, criticized the English mostly for excessive pride and for trying to establish a universal empire of the seas.[102]

Yet in other ways the pattern set in the 1750s remained influential. For instance, during the War of American Independence the ministry continued to use the press to mobilize domestic opinion behind the war effort. After a major naval defeat, Foreign Minister Vergennes developed what his biographer calls a "veritable press campaign," with the objective, as Vergennes himself put it, of "reestablishing and permanently fixing opinion."[103] The ministry called for patriotic donations to the navy and then assiduously published news of them in supportive newspapers. Vergennes himself admitted that the donations had a greater symbolic than practical value.[104] Once again the ministry popularized the deeds of ordinary French warriors.

The French revolutionaries initially did little to revive the concept of wars of nations. These were the years of the Constituent Assembly's Declaration of Peace to the World and frequent proclamations about the brotherhood of peoples.[105] Such gestures, themselves predicated on the concept of France as the pole of civilization and the world's schoolmaster, expressed the hope that in the brave new world of 1789 there would be no more barbarians, and all peoples would embrace the new gospel emanating from Paris. In 1789–90 Anacharsis Cloots was predicting that one day people would take stagecoaches from Paris to Beijing as they did from Bordeaux to Strasbourg, while Bertrand Barère was asking complacently: "What people would not want to become French?"[106]

But in 1793–94, as the war against the allied powers grew desperate, the ruling Convention changed tack. It enacted a series of repressive measures against foreigners living in France (including a never-realized proposal for them to wear tricolor armbands at all times), and its leading members again began to claim that the English had willfully set themselves outside the universal (and France-centered) human community. Furthermore, the Jacobins most committed to radical theories of popular sovereignty now forthrightly insisted that an irreconcilable and permanent hatred separated the English from the French, even as their moderate opponents continued to distinguish between a supposedly virtuous English people and England's depraved and corrupted government.[107] Robespierre declared famously on January 30, 1794: "I do not like the English, because the very word recalls to me the idea of an insolent people who dare to make war on a generous people who have recovered their liberty . . . Let this people break its government . . . Until then I vow an implacable hatred to it."[108] Saint-Just angrily insisted: "Make your children swear immortal hatred to this other Carthage," and petitions from provincial Jacobin clubs dutifully echoed the message, in one case vowing "eternal hatred to this race of cannibals."[109] Barère hammered the point home most brutally in his report on "England's crimes against the French people": "National hatred must sound forth; for the purposes of commercial and political contacts, there must be an immense ocean between Dover and Calais; young republicans must suck in a hatred of the word Englishman along with their mothers' milk."[110] These leaders clearly believed that to mobilize the French effectively against the nation that seemed, superficially, most to resemble them—indeed, which French leaders in 1789–91 often presented as a political model—the supposed resemblance had once again to be exposed as the vilest sort of deception.[111]

In the service of this cause, the revolutionaries engaged in massive propaganda campaigns against foreign enemies that dwarfed anything seen previously. They also rediscovered, with a vengeance, the image of the English barbarian and the concept of a war of nations. In fact, they literally rediscovered the war propaganda of the 1750s, as shown by the ease with which old poems were simply published under new names and the way Rouget de Lisle, for example, borrowed lines from the earlier literature for the *Marseillaise*. As Sophie Wahnich has demonstrated in a recent book, the radical Jacobins took up the theme of the English barbarian with particular intensity.[112] Provincial clubs and speakers in the Convention railed against "these barbarous islanders, banes of humanity, whom nature has already separated from humanity by the seas"; the "barbarous character and spirit of these inhabitants of an island fertile in infamies"; and "the most ferocious, the most barbarous nation, the most debased of them all."[113] Barère's report fairly bristled with the charges once leveled against Jumonville's killers: "Caesar, in landing on the island [Britain], found only a fierce tribe *[peuplade]*," he declared. "Their subsequent civilization, and their civil wars and maritime wars have all continued to bear the mark of this savage origin." He accused the English of "corrupting the humanity of the savages" in America, and added his truly bone-chilling line: "They are a tribe foreign to Europe, foreign to humanity. They must disappear."[114] The ultimate fate of a people who had refused the revealed truth of superior French wisdom would be the same as Carthage's. An anonymous report, dated 1794, in the archives of the French foreign ministry, made the point with truly chilling concision. The Netherlands were to be "ruined," Spain was to be stripped of its royal house, and Prussia was to be conquered. The English and the Austrians, however, were to be "exterminated."[115] The Jacobins did not apply this logic only to foreign enemies, but even to the counter-revolutionary rebels of the Vendée, whom they similarly labeled "foreigners" and "barbarians" and deemed fit for mass killing, with horrific results. "As long as this impure race exists," said Robespierre of the Vendéens, "the Republic will be unhappy and precarious."[116]

From Wars of Religion to Wars of Nations and Races

In the polemical literature of the Seven Years' War, as throughout eighteenth-century French patriotic writing, religion was both the great absence and the great hidden presence. As previously noted, the authors almost entirely avoided denouncing the English as heretics. And when compared with the anti-Protestant literature of the late sixteenth-century Wars of Religion, or even with Jean de la Chapelle's early eighteenth-century *Letters of a Swiss* (which saluted the Hapsburg candidate for the Spanish throne as "CHARLES III BY GRACE OF THE HERETICS CATHOLIC KING [i.e. *Rey Católico*]"), the difference is stunning.[117] Their very predilection for the image of the English barbarian, with "barbarian" understood as the opposite of a civilized person, underlined their acceptance of the idea that membership in a properly constituted universal community (soon to be called a civilization) did not depend on religion, but on customs (*moeurs*) and cultivation. Religion had become a private matter, an affair of conscience. It should no longer structure international animosities.

Yet the war literature resembled earlier, religiously inspired war propaganda so strongly that it is hard not to see deep connections between the two. To begin with, in order to arouse zeal and sacrifice from the population, French officials explicitly compared the *patrie* to an object of religious devotion. As Foreign Minister Vergennes wrote in 1782: "The Frenchman, proud of the name he glories in, sees the entire nation as his family, and sees his zealous sacrifices as a religious duty towards his brothers. He sees the *patrie* as the object of his worship."[118] Secondly, the most important precedents for using printed matter on a massive scale to mobilize a population for warfare were religious: particularly the efforts of the *politique* party that supported Henri of Navarre against Spain and also against their opponents in the Catholic League.[119] Third, the principal French precedents for the wholesale demonization of an enemy nation, at least since 1500, were religious as well. In the Wars of Religion, even pamphlets aimed at fellow Catholics still managed most often to cast their accusations in religious terms. If Philip II and his subjects were barbarians, as the *politiques* insisted, it was precisely because they were false Catholics: secret atheists, or even Jews, or Muslims. "What!" exclaimed the *politique* Antoine Arnauld in his 1589 pamphlet, *Copy of the Anti-Spaniard.* "Should these Marranos become our Kings and Princes! . . . Should France be added to the titles of this King of Majorca, this half-Moor, half-Jew, half-Saracen? [sic]"[120] The representation of the English as barbaric, false Europeans seems to stand as a secular parallel to these earlier exercises in xenophobia, illustrating the larger parallels between the sixteenth-century process of building a church, and the eighteenth-century one of building a nation, both of which involved not only binding people together, but also purging the body religious or body politic of impure and dangerous elements.

In addition, the "barbarians" and "savages" in the eighteenth century strongly recall earlier, religious modes of characterizing human diversity. Writers who described the American Indians as rude, unfinished people in need of civilizing closely echoed the Jesuit missionaries who had seen the same Indians as lost souls in need of instruction in the true faith. Anthony Pagden has noted that for centuries "barbarian" and "pagan" were virtual synonyms, while Michèle Duchet, in her pioneering study of Enlightenment anthropology, has pointed out that the *philosophes* themselves recognized the connections between the religious and civilizing "missions." It is difficult, she adds, "to conceive of a purely secular model of colonization, not only because history offers no examples of one, but because the very image of savages susceptible to persuasion, relayed by centuries of missiology, is still indissolubly linked to an ideal of evangelization."[121] Meanwhile, the description of the English as barbarians who willfully refused the benefits of French civilization echoed earlier condemnations of groups that had seen, but willfully rejected, the revealed truth of the Gospels: heretics, and especially Jews. Rather eerily, the nefarious qualities attributed to the English in the eighteenth century—overweening pride, irrational hatred of other peoples, a desire to dominate the world, and also an unreasonable love of money and trade (the last a favorite theme for orators in the Convention—Barère called the English "a mercantile horde"), recalled traits that French writers commonly attributed to the Jews.[122] The comparison may seem unlikely, but consider this passage written by Elie Fréron in 1756: "The intolerance of the Jews in religious matters made the entire universe indignant at them. The intolerance of the Tyrians and Carthaginians in commercial matters hastened their destruction. The English should fear the same fate, for all Europe reproaches them for the same principles, the same views and the same vices."[123]

Finally, there is Joseph Coulon de Jumonville himself: an undistinguished man, common, simple and plain but courageous—the very embodiment of French virtue. Previous annals of French military glory held very few precedents for a democratic hero of this sort. Volumes devoted to "great" or "illustrious" Frenchmen before the 1750s drew their military figures almost entirely from the ranks of the high nobility and great warriors (the principal exception, Joan of Arc, was more properly seen as a religious figure). Only from the 1760s would volumes of this sort start to include common soldiers, including Jumonville himself.[124] However, in the thick ranks of Catholic martyrs and saints, men like him had long abounded. In this sense, Jumonville has a strong claim to being the first martyr of modern France (and remember Thomas's pathetic description of his martyrdom: even as his eyes close to the light, his "soul" finds "delight" not in God, but in "the tender memory of France"). He is a direct predecessor of the ostentatiously non-noble heroes of *Le siège de Calais*, and, even more, the Christ-like boy martyrs of the French Revolution, such as the poor Viala, who supposedly choked out his last words: "I die for liberty."[125]

At this point I think it useful to speculate on the implications of this view of Franco-English difference, not only for French nationalism, but also for French ways of understanding human diversity in general, and for the origins of race-based nationalism. It has often been argued that the eighteenth century saw the rise of new, essentialist ideas on the subject of human diversity in France—even the birth of modern racism—above all in order to justify the continuing enslavement of Africans.[126] As intellectual background for the shift, scholars cite the weakening of Christian theology and its insistence on the common descent of the human race from Adam ("monogenesis"), and the increasing influence of the biological sciences with their penchant for classification and ranking. The argument may be convincing as far as peoples of color were concerned, but European racial science in the modern period has sought to prove essential racial differences not only between Europeans and non-Europeans, but within the European family itself. The intellectual framework for investigations into these narrower racial differences was largely the same, but here the "science" developed in the service of nationalism rather than of slavery and imperialism.

I would like to suggest that the essentializing of ethnic and racial differences in fact began at the center as much as it did at the (perceived) periphery.[127] It began as the French struggled to differentiate themselves from the people with whom they often felt the greatest affinity and similarity, yet who had also emerged as the greatest apparent threat to their own honor, prosperity, and understanding of the world: the English. True, even in the Revolution polemicists rarely described the differences between the English and the French in biological terms. The word "race" did occasionally appear, as in the phrase "race of cannibals" or "perjurious race," and its usage in these contexts seems to denote something more than the common eighteenth-century definition of race as "lineage."[128] But most often the fault attributed to the English was a moral one, a failing of the spirit. It infected the English people as a whole, generation after generation, but it did not have its origin in any specific physical difference detectable by biological science.

Yet by making national difference into something as fierce and unforgiving as religious difference had been during the era of the Reformation, the wartime polemicists helped readers to think of human diversity in a way that went beyond the detached, clinical observations of theorists interested in climate, and linear schemes of development. They suggested that national groups, which is to say groups bound together by a common origin rather than by common faith, had characteristics which temperature and humidity could not explain, and which shifts in climate could not alter.

And it is precisely here that the terms "savages" and "barbarians" were so important. They were not scientific terms in the least. But they set forth a problem that biological science could later answer (however mistakenly): the problem of difference. Anthony Pagden has written that when modes of explanation of human difference shifted in the early nineteenth century from the sociological to the physiological, they did so in part because the sociological modes seemed incapable of revealing why some peoples failed to make historical progress.[129] This was precisely the problem highlighted by the figure of the English barbarian (and that would be repeatedly highlighted by emerging nationalist movements over the next century when stigmatizing their enemies—especially the Jews). It suggested that the English, despite their membership in the white race and in a common European civilization, in fact were fundamentally alien, as alien as heretics had been to the mother church. And not only alien but inferior, and deserving of hatred, subjugation, or even extermination. In all the voluminous writings of the French revolutionary period, there is no clearer forerunner of modern expressions of racial hatred than Barère's report on English crimes. "National hatred must sound forth." Without such a rooted sense of profound difference between nations, could nineteenth-century race science have carried any sense of conviction? Would its creators have even pursued their researches in the first place?

Before the middle of the eighteenth century, such a sense of difference was lacking, at least in France. It began to arise only in the period of the Seven Years' War, in response to anxieties about France's changing position in the world, and the demands of a rapidly evolving public sphere, as supporters of the French crown sought to mobilize the nation as a whole against an enemy nation. The image of English barbarians, more alien even than the already frightening American savages, helped teach the French this sense of national difference. It did so, moreover, without challenging the universalism which remained so powerful a force in French culture, and which would express itself so powerfully at the start of the Revolution and again under Napoleon. The English were different precisely because they rejected the universal human civilization that properly revolved around France, as their murder of Jumonville symbolized most vividly. In slaying him, the French publicists were implying, the English had not only taken the life of an unarmed ambassador, but also killed their own membership in the human race.

HATRED OF THEIR
NEIGHBOURS' POINT -
ASSERTS YES -
ESP. ENGLISH
- THOUGH
19th DEVELOPMENTS
AS
IMPORTANT

CHAPTER 4

National Memory and the Canon of Great Frenchmen

To the Great Men, the Grateful Patrie.

—INSCRIPTION ON THE FRONT OF THE
PANTHEON (1791)

*How ridiculous it is for an assembly of slithering, vile and inept men
to set themselves up as judges of immortality.*

—JEAN-PAUL MARAT (1791)

In the last thirty years of the old regime, the French lived amidst a glittering company of ghosts. One could not belong to an academy, walk through the streets of central Paris, attend an artistic *salon* or visit a bookseller without coming across orations, odes, statues, paintings, engravings, and books glorifying the "great men" of France's past. Catinat and Bayard, Duguesclin and Suger, d'Aguesseau and Turenne, and many others passed ceaselessly in review. Their panegyrists placed infinite faith in the ability of images of national greatness to inspire further national greatness. Antoine-Léonard Thomas wrote rhapsodically about an ancient Greece that he saw as a model for modern France: "Everywhere the people saw images of their great men, and . . . surrounded by a crowd of artists, orators and poets, who all painted, sculpted, celebrated and sang of these heroes . . . the free and victorious Greeks saw, felt and breathed nothing but the passion for glory and immortality."[1] Collectively, the attempts to realize this vision in France amounted to nothing less than a conscious reshaping of national memory.

This "cult of great men," as Jean-Claude Bonnet has aptly called it, was, like the political struggles over royal authority and the wars with Great Britain, an arena in which the French found the concepts of the nation and the *patrie* enormously useful.[2] Here, too, the concepts had powerful reso-

107

nance for readers who were coming to understand the human world as something that existed on its own terms rather than being structured from without, and who increasingly saw France as a uniform and homogenous space. Here, too, writers and artists nonetheless found themselves drawing on religious language and symbolism to foster devotion to the secular deity of the *patrie*. Here, too, the concepts were subject to continuous debate and negotiation, involving issues of national character, history, representation, and gender. And here, as well, the debate and negotiation would ultimately promote the idea of the nation as a political construction, an entity that could freely and consciously rebuild itself. This chapter will examine the cult from a new perspective, with particular focus on a fascinating, almost forgotten series of texts: collective biographies of "great Frenchmen" which flowed in profusion from French presses during the eighteenth century.

The Rise of a Cult

As Thomas (the same man who made his reputation as the author of *Jumonville*) freely acknowledged, the idea of a canon of "great men" was hardly a French invention. It reached back to Roman and Greek antiquity, where it had held a central place in political life and had found its defining expression in one of the great classical works of history: Plutarch's *Lives*. In France itself, the canon dated to the Renaissance and initially was a multinational one, as in André Thevet's influential updating of Plutarch, *Les vrais pourtraits et vies des hommes illustres* (*True Portraits and Lives of Illustrious Men*).[3] Plutarch himself, with his parallel listings of Greeks and Romans, exerted an extraordinary influence on the French Renaissance imagination, serving, in the words of one historian, as "the breviary of all cultivated society in the second half of the sixteenth century."[4] His importance extended to the eighteenth century, when Rousseau developed his famous boyhood obsession with the *Lives,* and the moralist Vauvenargues memorably wrote: "I cried with joy when I read those lives. I never spent a night without talking to Alcibiades, Agesilas, and others. I visited the Roman Forum to harangue with the Gracchi, to defend Cato when they threw rocks at him."[5] Of course, French authors also continued to write lives of classical heroes and great men of other nations (notably, in the eighteenth century, Russia's Peter the Great).

The first works to celebrate France alone predictably featured canons of kings, as in Ronsard's Renaissance epic the *Franciade* (the poet joked of having "the weight of 63 kings on my shoulders").[6] Yet a broader, non-royal canon celebrating notable French lives did not take long to emerge in this period, which saw a great flourishing of the biographical genre in general. In 1600, Gabriel Michel de la Rochemaillet's *Portraits of the Illustrious Men Who Flourished in France from 1500 to the Present* presented 144 clerics, military leaders, statesmen, poets, and scholars. Two years later, Scaevole de Sainte-Marthe's Latin *Eulogy of Illustrious Learned Frenchmen* recounted the lives of 137 recent French writers. Both works held up great Frenchmen to demonstrate France's worth as successor to Greece and Rome, not to mention its superiority to Italy.[7]

What distinguished the late eighteenth-century celebration of great Frenchmen from these Renaissance predecessors was less its novelty than its scale, its relentless emphasis on patriotic pedagogy, and its definition of "greatness." To begin with, virtually every artistic and literary medium embraced the subject. Louis XVI's effective minister for the arts, the Marquis d'Angiviller, put the enormous patronage power of the crown firmly behind the celebration of great Frenchmen, commissioning his series of history paintings and sculptures which duly took pride of place in the artistic Salons of the late 1770s and 1780s. There visitors could contemplate the brave Constable Duguesclin receiving his final honors after a heroic death in the Hundred Years' War, the "fearless knight" Bayard saving the honor of a female prisoner, and many other statesmen and soldiers, as well as Descartes and Fénelon (see Table 1).[8] On the stage, Buirette de Belloy's *The Siege of Calais* fit into the pattern, and inspired numerous, even more forgettable imitations.[9] Several authors, in an obvious foreshadowing of the revolutionary Pantheon, developed plans for galleries, sculpture gardens, or cemeteries of great men, again focusing primarily on statesmen and military figures. Most often, they proposed that their statues surround a statue of the king, and more than one envisioned the ensemble at the entrance to a new national museum in the Louvre. King Louis XV himself approved one such plan in 1768, although nothing came of the idea until the Revolution.[10]

The genre that the eighteenth century made peculiarly its own was the academic eulogy, which functioned as something of a successor to the older oratorical art of the funeral oration.[11] The eulogy owed its promi-

Figure 6. One of the paintings commissioned by the Marquis d'Angiviller to stimulate patriotic sentiment in France, it depicts the selfless conduct of the Renaissance hero Pierre Bayard in sparing the honor of a female prisoner. Louis-Jacques Durameau, *La continence de Bayard* (Bayard's Continence), 1777.

Table 1. D'Angiviller's Sculpture Commissions for the Salons

1777	Michel de l'Hôpital (chancellor); Fénelon (bishop and philosopher); Sully (statesman and minister); Descartes
1779	D'Aguesseau (chancellor); Corneille; Montesquieu; Bossuet (religious)
1781	Catinat (military); Tourville (military); Montausier (royal tutor); Pascal
1783	Vauban (military, minister); Molière; La Fontaine; Turenne (military)
1785	Racine; Molé (magistrate); Duquesne (military); Condé (prince, military)
1787	Bayard (military); Rollin (scholar); Luxembourg (military); Vincent de Paul (religious)
1789	Duguesclin (military); Poussin; Cassini (astronomer); Lamoignon (magistrate)

Source: Bonnet, *Naissance du Panthéon.* 395–6.

nence above all to the Académie Française, which decided in 1758 (as it was falling into the hands of the *philosophes*) to change the form of its periodic eloquence competition. Henceforth, orators would deliver eulogies of the "great men of the nation" instead of discourses on devotional religious topics, as they had done for more than a century. Over the next thirty years the Académie selected sixteen great men as subjects, including two kings, ten military figures and statesmen, and four men of letters (see Table 2). France's many provincial academies took up the eulogy as well, and it therefore came to occupy a central position in French cultural life.[12] Such was the genre's importance during the last thirty years of the regime that few *philosophes* and future revolutionaries failed to try their hand at it. Even Marat composed a eulogy of Montesquieu. D'Alembert (who became recording secretary of the Académie) wrote more than sixty.[13] But the Enlightenment's master eulogist was Thomas, who, after making his reputation with *Jumonville*, won the first five of the Académie's new competitions, published an enormously long, well-received *Essay on Eulogies* in 1773, and helped inspire d'Angiviller's artistic program. Thanks to these achievements, he stood for some time in the front ranks of the *philosophes*, although his reputation has since fallen drastically.[14]

Finally, there was a genre which has fallen into even greater historical oblivion than Thomas's work: the collective biography. Indeed, these fascinating works have never received systematic historical study. In recent years, one eminent historian has called Antoine-François Sergent's 1786 *Portraits of Great Men and Illustrious Women* "an important event in the

Table 2. Subjects of the Académie Française's Eloquence Competitions

1759	Maurice de Saxe (military)
1760	D'Aguesseau (chancellor)
1761	Duguay-Trouin (military)
1763	Sully (minister, statesman)
1765	Descartes
1767	Charles V
1769	Molière
1771	Fénelon (bishop, philosopher)
1773	Colbert (minister, statesman)
1775	Catinat (military)
1777	Michel de l'Hospital (chancellor)
1779	Suger (cleric, regent)
1781	Montausier (tutor to the royal family)
1783–4	Fontenelle (author)
1785	Louis XII (postponed until 1788)
1787	Vauban (military, minister—postponed until 1790)

Source: Bonnet, *Naissance du Panthéon,* 391–2.

creation of a new, exclusively French pantheon of heroes," apparently unaware that the book had more than a dozen very similar precedents, stretching back across more than a century (see Table 3).[15]

These volumes bore some resemblance to the collections of Thevet and Michel de la Rochemaillet, but they traced their origins most directly to a different Renaissance source: portrait galleries. In 1600, the astronomer royal Antoine de Laval, reacting against the use of profane myth and allegory as decoration in royal palaces, had advocated the establishment of portrait galleries modeled after the palace of Emperor Augustus, who had displayed statues of meritorious citizens, accompanied by inscriptions recounting their deeds, in order to inspire emulation. Laval himself designed a gallery of 68 kings for the Louvre, providing a visual equivalent to the *Franciade,* not to mention a didactic history lesson that assimilated the story of France to the story of its monarchs. Cardinal Richelieu then took the idea in a new direction with the portrait gallery he placed in his grand Parisian palace (today's Palais-Royal), for which he commissioned Simon Vouët and Philippe de Champaigne to depict twenty-five French kings, ministers, prelates, and warriors. The captions and other ancillary decorations left no doubt that Richelieu meant each portrait to express a trait he

Table 3. Seventeenth- and Eighteenth-Century Collective Biographies

B. Griguette, *Eloges des hommes illustres peints en la gallerie du Palais Royal* (Dijon, 1646). *Eloges des illustres François* (Caen, 1652).

Marc Vulson de la Colombière et al., *Les portraits des hommes illustres françois, Qui sont peints dans la galerie du Palais Cardinal de Richelieu, avec leurs principales Actions, Armes & Deuises* (Paris, 1655, 1668 [twice] & 1673).

Charles Perrault, *Les hommes illustres qui ont paru en France pendant ce siècle*, 2 vols. (Paris, 1697).

[Jean-Baptiste Morvan de Bellegarde], *Les vies de plusieurs hommes illustres et grands capitaines de France, Depuis le commencement de la Monarchie jusqu'à présent*, 2 vols. (Paris, 1726).

Mémoires contenant les principales actions de la vie des hommes illustres du règne de Louis XIV, 2 vols. (Avignon, 1734).

Jean Du Castre d'Auvigny, Gabriel Pérau, and François-Henri Turpin, *Les vies des hommes illustres de la France, depuis le commencement de la monarchie jusqu'à present*, 26 vols. (Amsterdam, 1739–1768). See also Jean Du Castre d'Auvigny, *Avis pour l'histoire des hommes illustres de la France* (Paris, 1741).

Le nécrologe des hommes célèbres de France, 17 vols. (Paris, 1764–82).

Jean-Zorobabel Aublet de Maubuy, *Les vies des femmes illustres de la France*, 6 vols. (Paris, 1762).

Jacques Gautier Dagoty, *Galerie françoise, ou Portraits des hommes et des femmes célèbres qui ont paru en France* (Paris, 1770), continued by Jean-Bernard Restout, *Galerie françoise*, 2 vols. (Paris, 1771).

Tablettes historiques et chronologiques où l'on voit d'un coup-d'oeil le lieu, l'époque de la naissance & de la mort de tous les Hommes célèbres en tous genres que la France a produits (Amsterdam, 1779).

François-Henri Turpin, *La France illustre, ou le Plutarque français*, 5 vols. (Paris, 1777–90).

François-Henri Turpin, *Annales pittoresques de la vertu française, ou Recueil d'estampes destinées à représenter les belles actions qui honorent notre nation et notre âge* (Paris, 1783; separate abridged edition of same, 1782)

[Antoine-François Sergent], *Portraits des grands hommes, femmes illustres, et sujets memorables de France, gravés et imprimés en couleurs* (Paris, 1786).

Faits et actions héroïques et historiques des Grands Hommes (Paris, 1786).

Louis-Pierre Manuel, *L'année françoise, ou Vies des Hommes qui ont honoré la France, ou par leurs talens, ou par leurs services, & surtout par leurs vertus*, 4 vols. (Paris, 1789).

François-Henri Turpin, *Histoire des illustres françois sortis du ci-devant tiers-état*, 2 vols. (Paris, 1792).

associated with himself, such as loyalty, piety, or military valor, and to highlight aspects of his own career. Yet in creating the gallery, he helped establish a new French canon, centered less on the monarchy than on the institutions and servants of the state.[16]

Unlike Horace's poetry, Richelieu's monument was *less* durable than bronze, for the gallery perished in an eighteenth-century fire. But for a century it featured prominently in descriptions of Paris and was memorialized in verse.[17] And in 1655, the engravers Heince and Bignon published a volume of reproductions of the paintings and enlisted a courtier, Marc Vulson de la Colombière, to write accompanying biographical essays. The book went through four editions in eighteen years, shrinking in the process from an in-folio to an in-quarto, and then finally an in-octavo.[18] With this shift from painting to print, a new genre had been born.

Between 1697 and 1792, at least fourteen more collective biographies appeared, many in multivolume sets. The first came from an author illustrious in his own right, Charles Perrault, who intended his paean to a hundred illustrious men of the *grand siècle* primarily as a salvo in the ongoing quarrel of the Ancients and Moderns. Like Richelieu, Perrault limited his canon to France and insisted in the preface that he had "nothing but the honor of France in mind."[19] Later contributions tended to take both Perrault and the engravings in Richelieu's gallery as their models—indeed, they not infrequently plagiarized these sources and each other. While a few remained essentially collections of engravings, overall the tendency, starting with the abbé Morvan de Bellegarde in 1726, was toward smaller or no illustrations, and ever more voluminous essays. In some cases, individual biographies expanded to hundreds of pages each and merited volumes to themselves, as in the successful series started by Jean Du Castre d'Auvigny. The selection of great men in this genre differed substantially from those found in others, and the canon changed markedly over the course of the century.

With the exception of Perrault's work, these biographies are less interesting, aesthetically and intellectually, than the paintings, statues, and eulogies. They seem to be hastily written and their style is unremarkable, which is not surprising, as their authors mainly belonged to the profit-obsessed "Grub Street" of French publishing immortalized by Robert Darnton.[20] Louis-Pierre Manuel, for instance, was a former Bastille prisoner and future Jacobin who had failed at numerous literary endeavors. Police files described Jean-Zorobabel Aublet de Maubuy as an unemployed attorney's

PETRVS BAYARD EQVES

Figure 7. Renaissance hero Bayard; the engraving is copy of a painting in Cardinal Richelieu's portrait gallery in the Palais Royal. From Marc Vulson de la Colombière, et al., *Les hommes illustres* (The Illustrious Men), Paris, 1658

clerk who would lend his poison pen to whatever cause would pay him.[21] Nonetheless, the books have a capital importance. In the first place, they served as a principal source of information for the other genres. The painters who filled d'Angiviller's commissions, for instance, drew on material from François-Henri Turpin's many works on great men.[22] The authors of eulogies clearly relied on the information that the collective biographies provided.[23] Secondly, the works reached far more members of the public than the paintings and sculptures and all but the most successful eulogies and stage plays. As with most eighteenth-century works, measuring their diffusion is difficult. It is worth observing, however, that publishers would probably not have committed themselves to works that often extended to a score of volumes and that faced considerable competition (particularly between 1770 and 1789, when eight came out), unless the genre had commercial potential. Furthermore, several of the works sold by subscription—readers received new installments at regular intervals, in a sort of "great-man-of-the-month club"—and would hardly have continued, in Du Castre d'Auvigny's case for thirty years, without the subscribers' support.[24]

In all these media, the cult of great men had a tirelessly pedagogical, patriotic character. Expose the French to an endless parade of meritorious examples, so the assumption went, and imitation would naturally take place. "Great men," wrote the author of one collective biography, "are, so to speak, mirrors in which one contemplates oneself, so as to better oneself."[25] D'Angiviller told the Royal Academy of Painting and Sculpture in 1775 that his purpose was to "revive virtue and patriotic sentiments," while the dramatic authors who copied Buirette de Belloy generally hoped to elicit the sort of swooning responses elicited by the *Siege of Calais*. Recall the words of his admirer Manson: "People will say: 'Why can I not do what this person has done? He was French; I am as well.'"[26] The advocates of public galleries or cemeteries of great men tended to justify the project in the terms stated by Maille Dusaussoy, in a 1767 proposal for rebuilding the Louvre: "The revered statues . . . placed in the Palace of our Kings, will produce more Great Men who will equal and perhaps surpass them."[27]

At the same time, eighteenth-century works tended increasingly to distinguish between the "illustrious," whose reputation rested on heroic—even accidentally heroic—deeds, and the "great," whose notable qualities supposedly suffused every aspect of their lives. As Bonnet has shown, this distinction owed its wide acceptance in the eighteenth century to the philosopher-bishop Fénelon, and especially to that irenic philosopher of European peace, the abbé Saint-Pierre, who emphasized that greatness arose from "inner qualities of the mind and heart alone, and from the great benefits that one brings to society."[28] Following this lead, the *philosophes* frequently belittled military heroes as little more than successful brigands, and reserved their admiration for true benefactors of humanity. The eulogists thus dwelt endlessly on their subjects' diligent cultivation of native talents, their selfless dedication to others and to the state, their humble rejection of material rewards, their wise simplicity, their steadfast courage in moments of despair and disgrace, and their magnanimity in moments of triumph. They delighted in images of Montesquieu chatting with his Gascon peasants, d'Aguesseau lost in contemplation of ancient philosophers, the medieval abbé Suger tirelessly working to reconcile warring barons.

In the last decades of the old regime, some authors had taken the distinction even further, finding a person's true greatness less in public acts than in private, intimate behavior. As Manuel remarked concisely in the preface to his *French Year* (1789), "private life is the surest testimony of public life."[29] Plutarch himself, as his eighteenth-century French translator emphasized, had focused on the "inner," as opposed to the "public" man alone.[30] But just as French lawyers of the 1770s and 1780s treated private, familial disputes as windows into public politics, so the biographers now frankly privileged the private over the public, preferring to capture the great man in the bosom of his family instead of on the battlefield, in the courtroom, or on any other public arena. "It is in domestic obscurity," Manuel continued, "that I have observed my great men."[31]

Still, celebrations of illustrious figures and heroic actions continued, and the line between "illustrious" and "great" remained less rigid than has sometimes been suggested.[32] François-Henri Turpin's *Illustrious France* freely mixed discussions of "heroes" and "virtuous" men, while collections of engravings continued to glorify the military triumphs that Voltaire, among others, usually sneered at.[33] Antoine-François Sergent's elaborate series of *Portraits* (1786–1792) borrowed freely from Thomas's *Eloge de d'Aguesseau* in praise of the late Lord Chancellor's selfless actions on behalf of the starving population in 1709, but the author went back to Heince, Bignon, and Vulson to hail the victories of Duguesclin and Joan of Arc. Indeed, he copied several of his engravings directly from theirs.[34]

The national cult of great men had its provincial equivalents in count-

Figure 8. Louis Joseph de Montcalm, the commander of French forces in North America during the Seven Years' War, was killed at the Battle of the Plains of Abraham outside Québec in 1759. In this engraving, Indians drawn to resemble Europens serve to witness the general's heroic death. "La Mort de Montcalm" (The Death of Montcalm), engraving from Antoine-François Sergent, *Portraits des grands hommes, femmes illustres et sujets mémorables de France* (Portraits of the Great Men, Illustrious Women and Memorable Subjects of France), Paris, 1786.

less eulogies delivered at provincial academies, in sculptures and engravings, and in collective biographies dedicated to the *grands hommes* of Burgundy, Provence, Brittany and so forth. This material still awaits its historian. Still, even a brief glance indicates that it in no way constituted an expression of minority nationalism, and did not (unlike some of the pre-revolutionary material discussed in Chapter 2) present any sort of challenge to French national unity. Rather, it seems to constitute a predecessor to the sort of nineteenth-century local patriotism recently studied by Anne-Marie Thiesse: a patriotism which taught that allegiance to the national whole began with allegiance to, and an appreciation of, what was nearby and familiar. In this sense, the provincial cults of great men only strengthened the larger, national one.[35]

The Great Men and the Domain of the Sacred

The cult of great men illustrates much the same religious dynamic that I have discussed in the context of politics and warfare: on the one hand, an effort to imagine and reorder the world without reference to divine Providence; on the other, a recourse to the forms and practices of Counter-Reformation Catholicism. In this case, the echoes of Catholicism are entirely obvious. The celebrations of the great men clearly marked them out as sacred. It reserved special spaces for them, free from all possible profanity and pollution, as in the plans for a Pantheon; and it emphasized their transcendence through sacrifice, as in the Calais burghers' acceptance of imminent martyrdom in Belloy's play, or in the actual martyrdom of Jumonville or Montcalm. Furthermore, the exemplary conduct that great men reportedly displayed at every moment of their lives, and the way they served as models for others, with their images placed relentlessly before the population, recalled nothing so much as the saints of the Roman Catholic Church. Some authors came close to making the comparison explicit. Manuel's *French Year,* for instance, proposed a great Frenchman for every day of the year: contemporaries could hardly have missed the parallel to the church's calendar of saints. A few canonical great men—for instance, Charlemagne—were lauded as Christlike figures who had saved France from its sins.[36] A future Jacobin named Baumier wrote a poem about a well-celebrated hero—the Chevalier d'Assas of Seven Years' War fame—in which he suggested that "reading the lives of Great Men" could start a "holy fire" burning in susceptible breasts. He continued:

> Ta tombe, en s'écroulant, se transforme en Autel.
> O mânes d'un Héros à qui le sang me lie,
> Sur cet Autel sacré qui s'élève à mes yeux,
> J'incline avec respect un front religieux,

> Et dépose en ce jour L'HOMMAGE A LA PATRIE!
> [Your tomb, falling down, becomes an Altar.
> O shades of a Hero linked to me by blood,
> On this holy Altar which is rising before my eyes,
> I bend a religious brow with respect
> And lay down today HOMAGE TO THE PATRIE!][37]

Such words recall Carl Becker's famous contention about the eighteenth century, that "there is more of Christian philosophy in the writings of the *Philosophes* than has yet been dreamt of in our histories."[38]

The idea that the cult simply amounted to a substitute religion, however, is misleading. Its development does confirm just how much eighteenth-century attempts to forge a new French nation owed to earlier, Catholic attempts to forge a new church. But it is not as if some eternal, "furious need to believe" (to quote Bonnet) turned the French towards the cult of great men when an emotionally impoverished Catholicism had ceased to slake their spiritual thirst.[39] In the 1790s, the Revolution's cult of great men did indeed sometimes veer into a sort of substitute Christianity—as when the Cordeliers carried Marat's heart through the streets of Paris chanting "heart of Jesus, heart of Marat," or when a Jacobin preacher talked of a revolutionary martyr rising up to heaven on tricolor wings.[40] The old regime cult, however, was different. The admirable qualities of its great men derived from, and their admirable lives were lived in, a purely human, terrestrial sphere. Neither owed anything to any supernatural force. Thomas's eulogies, for instance, virtually never mentioned God or the supernatural, while they implicitly celebrated humanity's ability to create value and meaning from within itself.[41] Even the most obviously "miraculous" great figure in French history, Joan of Arc, underwent a rigorous disenchantment in the few eighteenth-century collections which still acknowledged a public role for women in French history (as we will see, few did). In 1655, Vulson's text for the engraving of Joan's portrait in Richelieu's gallery presented her as a pure instrument of God's will.[42] But Aublet de Maubuy, in his 1762 *Lives of Illustrious Women of France,* resolutely minimized the role of divine inspiration, arguing that Joan's visions, while not frauds, were delusions which grew out of her excessively "ecstatic devotion."[43] In this sense, the cult fits into the pattern of the interiorization of religious life described in Chapter 1.

Furthermore, what made the great men great was precisely their devotion *to* their fellow humans. If they deserved respect and commemoration, it was not for their great love of God, or for Homeric, superhuman feats, but, as Saint-Pierre wrote and the eulogists repeated, for the benefits they brought to human society or the "patrie." Thus to the prize-winning eulogist de la Harpe, an eminent seventeenth-century soldier like Catinat was remarkable less for his military acumen than for the humanity he showed in sparing Savoy the ravages of his armies. Thomas similarly praised the seventeenth-century sailor Duguay-Trouin for preferring the merchant marine and commerce to the navy and war.[44] Great men "need only have devoted their talents to France to have the right to our gratitude," wrote the painter Jean-Bernard Restout in his 1771 *French Gallery*.[45] And Manuel commented in the preface to his *French Year*: "I have above all looked for useful citizens. He who discovers a new form of subsistence or a new branch of commerce for his country, deserves to stand in the same rank with him who enlightens or defends it."[46] The cult of great men may have attempted to bathe its subjects in an aura of sacrality, but the men themselves were models, not icons.

To be sure, Renaissance readers had already found in Plutarch the spectacle of exemplary lives in which Christian inspiration had no part.[47] What the eighteenth-century cult added was the idea that great men rendered their services first and foremost to the *national* community, and that they helped consciously to build that community by their efforts and examples. Saint-Pierre, in the early years of the century, might still have spoken in general terms of society, echoing Fénelon's embrace of a universal human community.[48] But the Académie in 1758 limited itself to the "great men of the nation," and the eulogists and biographers of the 1770s and 1780s wrote almost exclusively of the nation, the *patrie*, and France. The eighteenth-century cult also added the idea that the nation itself should take charge of putting images of the great before the population. It thereby transformed the experience of reflecting on great men from an individual, voluntary act of edification into a public project of nation-forming.

The Great Men, the Monarchy, and Royal Patriotism

Like the war propaganda of the Seven Years' War, the cult of great men helped establish the nation itself as the most important reference point in French political culture. For this reason, it is tempting to think of it as subversive, perhaps even deliberately subversive, of the monarchy which had previously occupied this position. Jean-Claude Bonnet has recently made an argument much along these lines. The eulogy in particular, he writes, "far from being a dusty rhapsody concerned exclusively with the past, revealed itself to be a little machine of power which affected the immediate present, and the future of the polity."[49] Despite the monarchy's best attempts to control the cult, Bonnet claims, a "fatal rivalry began" between the king and the great men, which ultimately left him symbolically evacuated from the national space which the cult defined.[50]

This argument, while compelling in some respects, disregards important features of the context in which the cult developed. To begin with, it downplays the extent to which celebrations of great Frenchmen, insofar as they had an explicit polemical purpose, were directed principally against France's supposed subjection to Greek and Roman antiquity. The architects of the cult rarely compared the great men to French monarchs, but they routinely and explicitly argued that the French needed great men of their own rather than distant and alien classical ones. "The Greeks dealt with national subjects," the *Journal des Savants* claimed in a scathingly witty 1781 article on the theater, "and we have concluded from this that we should deal with Greek subjects. Horace praised Roman authors who had dealt with national subjects, and we have concluded simply that we can deal with Roman subjects too."[51] Buirette de Belloy wrote similarly, in his dedication to the *Siege of Calais,* "Let it not be said by those who come out of our theater: 'The great men I have just seen played were Romans; I was not born in a country where I can emulate them.' Let it be said, sometimes at least: 'I have just seen a French hero; I can be such a one too.'"[52] Or consider the argument endorsed by Lefebvre de Beauvray in his 1770 *Social and Patriotic Dictionary:* "The great actions of the Greeks and Romans touch only our minds, and prompt only our admiration; those of our own Nation would impress on our souls a livelier sentiment: emulation."[53] One of the most prolific authors of collective biographies, François-Henri Turpin, emphasized the competition with the ancients by giving one of his works the title *The French Plutarch,* incidentally joining the company of British and Russian Plutarchs that also appeared in the eighteenth century.[54]

In this sense, the cult traces its lineage back less to Fénelon and Saint-Pierre than to the Quarrel of the Ancients and the Moderns of the late seventeenth century. And beyond the Quarrel, it threads its way further back, to the long struggle of French authors to see their own language and literature recognized as the equal of Latin and Greek. In the Renaissance,

Du Bellay had already sounded a clear call to arms: Were the French, he asked, inferior to the Greeks and Romans, to make so little of their own language?[55] In the seventeenth century, François Charpentier similarly wrote that if the Greeks had used Greeks in their public Inscriptions, and the Romans had used Latin, then the French should use French.[56] By the eighteenth century, the debate had shifted to primary education and the desire to banish Latin from that domain as well. As the educational reformer La Chalotais quipped in the 1760s, "a foreigner to whom one explained the details of our education would imagine that France's principal goal was to populate Latin seminaries, cloisters, and colonies."[57]

From this perspective, the celebration of great Frenchmen, like the celebration and use of the French language, hardly dimmed the luster of the king; to the contrary. The glory of French writers and great men redounded on him, increasing his stature and historical reputation, indeed putting him on a level with the Roman emperors. Perrault, a collaborator of Colbert's, made the point explicitly in his *Hommes illustres,* when he stressed that extraordinary figures tended to be born at a time when "the heavens have decided to give to the earth some great prince," and that great men served "either as the instruments of the prince's great actions, the builders of his magnificence, or the trumpets of his glory."[58] It is hardly a coincidence that most of the eighteenth-century plans for sculpture gardens of great Frenchmen envisioned the men surrounding the king like so many jewels in his crown.

It is precisely because France's kings hoped to gain luster from the glory of France's great men that much of the cult amounted to a quasi-official enterprise, sanctioned and sponsored by the monarchy itself. The most direct cases involved d'Angiviller's commissions for paintings and sculptures. But as we have seen, the presentation of great Frenchmen on the stage, particularly in Belloy's *Siege of Calais,* enjoyed, at the very least, enthusiastic royal support. As for the eulogies, it is hardly a coincidence that the Académie Française decided to change the form of its eloquence competition in 1758, the year in which the Seven Years' War started to turn desperate for France, and the anti-English propaganda campaign described in the last chapter reached its height. (This is when the master eulogist Thomas wrote the rabidly anti-English *Jumonville* and served as secretary to Foreign Minister Choiseul.) And the subject of the first competition, which Thomas won, was none other than the Maréchal de Saxe, who had won the old regime's last great military victory at Fontenoy, in 1745. As for

the subject of the third competition, Duguay-Trouin, his military reputation paled before that of a Vauban or Duguesclin (to put it charitably), and
his selection only made sense in the context of the ongoing royal campaign
to elicit voluntary donations for ship building. (Thomas, again the winner
of the competition, wrote his entry while working at Versailles.) In fact,
eleven of the sixteen figures chosen by the Académie between 1758 and
1790 were faithful servants of the monarchy, and the winning eulogists
rarely failed to praise them for their love of the king (see Table 2). "What
perhaps contributed no less to developing his talents than so much com-
bat, study and reflection," wrote Thomas of Duguay-Trouin, "was his love
for Louis XIV, and Louis XIV's esteem for him."[59] Another prize winner,
who had served as one of Lord Chancellor Maupeou's chief defenders after
the 1771 coup, used his eulogy to praise the king and lambaste the *parlements*.[60] In the last years of the old regime, Sergent's collection of 96 colored engravings included 46 military heroes and 30 kings and queens.[61]

Indirectly, the cult did express a profound displeasure with the social hierarchy and the world of the royal court. As early as 1697, Perrault drew
criticism for not organizing his *grands hommes* of the *grand siècle* by social
rank, and for including men of low birth.[62] Thomas, in the same prize-
winning eulogy of Duguay-Trouin, praised the sailor for "being born without ancestors" and contrasted his simple and upright figure to the "idle
and disdainful courtiers" of Versailles. "True nobility comes from serving
the state," he commented. "It is very difficult for those who have titles to
forgive those who have virtues."[63] Such comments ran through the eulogies
and the collective biographies, which almost always found the origins of
their subjects' greatness not in blood, title, or position, but in inner qualities and merit, in keeping with the general theme that great men exemplified the potential of the human spirit.

This egalitarianism, however, was not incompatible with a powerful attachment to the French monarchy. The authors in question simply distinguished between the monarchy, which they adored, and the court, which
they despised. In this sense, they followed Voltaire, who notoriously combined a loathing for court society and the aristocracy which had spurned
him with support for virtually unrestrained royal authority (he even wrote
pamphlets in support of Chancellor Maupeou's coup). Thomas, not coincidentally, admired Voltaire more than any other contemporary figure.[64]
Although the French revolutionaries would later turn the cult of great men
to their own democratic purposes, under the old regime the sort of senti-

ments Thomas expressed accorded well with the enlightened absolutism advocated by Voltaire and figures like the Marquis d'Argenson, who were explicitly hostile to the *parlements*. It fit in directly with the project of royal patriotism discussed in the last two chapters: the attempt to ground the king's authority not in divine right, social contract, or constitutional tradition, but in the direct, affective bond between the king and individual citizens. Thomas's celebration of the Maréchal de Saxe, d'Aguesseau, Duguay-Trouin, and Sully during the last four years of the Seven Years' War thus served much the same political purpose as his concomitant celebration of Jumonville.

The cult of great men, like the project of royal patriotism, did raise a potential danger for the monarchy, for the citizens' love of the king depended on his remaining a worthy object of affection. "He loved Louis XIV, not as a Master, but as a great man," wrote Thomas of Duguay-Trouin.[65] Similarly, Manuel remarked of Renaissance France's Louis XII: "Under this citizen king, the people barely realized they had a master: serving a king whom one loves is not obedience."[66] The authors poured scorn on what Manuel called "these do-nothing kings" who had vanished into obscurity.[67] But until the Revolution, the greatness of the *reigning* king was taken, publicly at least, as axiomatic. Illicit pamphlets might mock and revile Louis XV and Louis XVI, but not until the Revolution did freely circulating works openly discuss the current monarch's failure to live up to the standard of greatness, still less argue that this failure justified his removal.

Masculine Republicanism

Although the cult of great men did serve the project of royal patriotism, its significance for the political culture of the late old regime did not stop there. In other ways, like royal patriotism itself, it contributed deeply to the cultural shifts which made French revolutionary radicalism thinkable.

Most important, the cult not only helped popularize classical republican ideas (from the Roman tradition revived and modified in Renaissance Italy and then in England and America), but suggested that these ideas had a direct relevance to modern France. As a good deal of recent historical work has shown, republican ideas held a fascination for French elites in the last decades before the Revolution. From the writings of Rousseau and Mably, to the neoclassical paintings of David, to the court speeches and printed briefs of barristers denouncing corruption and injustice, reverent images of the ancient republics proliferated at the end of the old regime, along with praise for political systems in which free, independent, and equal citizens, effortlessly resistant to the blandishments of luxury and *amour propre*, joined together in governing and in defense of the commonwealth.[68] In strictly political terms, however, this republicanism remained for the most part an abstraction with no direct relation to the realities of French government. As Rousseau and Montesquieu themselves had stressed, republics simply could not serve as the proper form of government in large Christian monarchies located in the temperate climate of Western Europe. The very notion of a true French republic remained largely unthinkable.

The cult of great men, however, presented a canon of recognizably French, Christian figures who possessed, in the new retelling of their stories, the essential attributes of exemplary republican citizens. The shift from equating distinction with heroic actions and accomplishments to equating it with inner, domestic qualities, had particular importance here. Great feats of military valor or great artistic achievements, such as those the seventeenth-century panegyrists celebrated, had nothing intrinsically republican about them. To the extent they brought classical models to mind, the names in question were Caesar, Alexander, or Achilles, not Marius or Brutus. But the qualities commonly attributed to great men in the eighteenth-century eulogies—independence, steadfastness, virtue defined as a solemn dedication to the common good, immunity to the seductions of luxury, lucre, and sensual pleasure—were precisely those that the republican tradition identified as the hallmarks of proper citizenship, and indeed those that Montesquieu had recently identified with republics (by contrast, illustrious feats and heroic actions belonged more to the realm of honor, which Montesquieu identified with monarchies).[69] However high their birth, however well placed in the social hierarchy, however exposed to wealth and temptation, truly great men, so the eulogies and collective biographies insisted, behaved like Roman citizens in the heyday of the Republic. The concern on the part of the cult's architects to demonstrate France's parity with or even superiority to Greece and Rome only highlighted these republican attributes further, by setting up inescapable parallels between the French figures and their classical predecessors. And given the cult's relentless presentation of great men as models to be emulated, its gallery of supposedly familiar French historical figures in fact constituted nothing less than a school of republican politics.

The cult's intrinsic republicanism shows through particularly in the way its participants attempted to establish stark and unforgiving gender divisions. As many scholars have argued, French republicanism of the revolutionary era derived its polemical energy in large part from the contrast it set up between properly organized polities, where male citizens dominated the public arena and women remained in the private realm of the home, and corrupt polities, where gender boundaries became hopelessly blurred. In this perspective Versailles, a place of feminine influence and intrigue, could only be seen as the *nec plus ultra* of corruption and political degeneration. Rousseau, the key figure in French republicanism of this era, first articulated the contrast, but it remained in force through the period of the radical Revolution.[70]

These ideas permeated the cult of great men of the eighteenth century. The oratorical competitions of the Académie Française proposed no women as subjects for eulogies, and following them, d'Angiviller chose none as the subjects of portraits or sculptures. Women often received the appellation *célèbre* (famous) or *illustre* (illustrious), but French authors made no attempt to find a female equivalent for the phrase "*grand(s) homme(s)*" (*grande femme* means a large woman, rather than a great one).[71] In other words, while women could perform glorious and heroic actions, as Joan of Arc and innumerable saints had done, they did not, according to the architects of the cult, have the qualities requisite for republican citizenship.

The collective biographies seem at first to offer an exception to this rule. Richelieu's portrait gallery included three women: an improbably elegant Joan of Arc (treated as the vessel of God's will), Marie de Médicis (mother of the reigning Louis XIII), and Anne of Austria (Louis XIII's queen). At the end of the old regime, Sergent's *Portraits* included 12 women, along with 84 men. Aublet de Maubuy devoted an entire book to French women, in which he dismissed notions of natural male superiority as "prejudice," attacked a certain Monsieur R., obviously Rousseau, for trying to lower women to the status of domestic animals, and added, in reference to women's literary skills: "Give them an education like that given to men, excite their emulation, cultivate their talents, and soon we will see them our rivals."[72] His work fit into an established tradition of proto-feminist portraits of famous women.[73] Yet in Sergent's book, which spanned French history from the Gauls to Louis XVI, while half the 84 "great men" came from the seventeenth and eighteenth centuries, the most recent of the 12 women had died in 1550 (and four before 1000 A.D.).[74] It is as if the author only felt comfortable dealing with women in the public sphere if they had lived so long before as to make them into virtual legends. Even Aublet suggested that women deserved a serious education in large part so that they could serve as properly stimulating and sympathetic companions to men. He explicitly warned against taking the mostly royal and aristocratic members of his female canon as role models, and lovingly recounted their crimes and follies alongside their achievements.[75] The very consignment of women to a volume of their own testified to a literal separation of the sexes in French history.

The cult's republicanism implicitly criticized the belief that a nation's treatment of women was a measure of its civilization. But then, the cult of great men implicitly criticized the concept of civilization itself, holding up instead the classical concept of the *patria* as the proper foundation of human existence. To the extent that it reshaped France's national memory, therefore, it replaced the story of a nation struggling to rise out of barbarism towards civilization by the story of a nation struggling to restore itself to a pristine condition of republican health, from which it had fallen into dangerous degeneration, in large part because of the reckless freedoms it allowed women.

The Market and the Public

Thus far I have been able to generalize about the cult of great men and to fit it into the story of pre-revolutionary French nationalism and patriotism laid out in the previous chapters. The cult, I have argued, helped the French to see the nation and the *patrie* as the fundamental background against which human activity took place; its architects consciously treated it as a means of establishing just order in a disenchanted world, although they often adopted the language and practices of the Catholic Church to achieve their ends. Their implicitly republican vision of the nation stood in stark contrast to portraits of France as a hierarchical society of orders. Yet to the extent the cult had an explicit political role, it was the monarchy which sought most insistently to develop and manipulate it. In these respects, the story of the cult complements the stories of political conflicts and war propaganda.

In another area, however, the cult of great men resists such generalization: the attitudes it embodied towards French history and memory. Here,

PVELLA AVRELIACA,

Figure 9. This engraving of Joan of Arc, copied from a painting in Cardinal Richelieu's gallery in the Palais Royal, appeared in Marc Vulson de la Colombière, et al., *Les hommes illustres* (The Illustrious Men), Paris, 1658.

the collective biographies followed a unique path of their own, and they more fully anticipated the nationalism and patriotism of the Revolution than did the quasi-official eulogies, plays, paintings, and statues. Indeed, in the years before the Revolution, the biographies leaned less toward reshaping France's collective memory for patriotic purposes than toward the beginning of a desire to wipe it clean altogether.

The biographies parted company with the quasi-official genres most obviously in the size of the canon of great men they celebrated. Over a period of thirty years, the Académie Française proposed only sixteen men as subjects of its oratorical competition. D'Angiviller, in the twelve years before the Revolution, commissioned twenty-eight statues of great men and twelve history paintings highlighting their actions.[76] By contrast, the canon presented in the printed biographies expanded vertiginously during the eighteenth century. Heince, Bignon, and Vulson, following Richelieu in his gallery, had presented only 25 great men. But Perrault, in 1700, chose an even hundred. His immediate successors fell back from this mark, limiting themselves to 30 or 40 each. But the series begun by Jean Du Castre d'Auvigny in 1739 reached 50, and the first solo venture by his successor François-Henri Turpin, in the 1770s, reached 65. The 1770 collection *Historical Tablets* went up to 296, Turpin's 1782 *French Plutarch* to 112, Sergent's 1786 *Portraits* to 96, and the same year's *Heroic and Historical Deeds and Actions of Great Men* (*Faits et actions héroïques et historiques des Grands Hommes*) to 82. And of course Manuel's *French Year* included no fewer than 365 great men of the nation, one for each day of the year.[77]

These differences resulted from strikingly different dynamics at work in the two cases. The Académie was the prisoner of its biennial schedule, and d'Angiviller faced constraints of time, money, and available talent; in any case, he wanted to focus the attention of viewers in the Salons on a relatively small number of artworks.[78] Nor was there any pressure to find new great men to honor. Nine of the Académie's sixteen also appeared in d'Angiviller's selections, and virtually all of d'Angiviller and the Académie's choices had previously appeared in one or another collective biography. The point was rather to call renewed attention to what were, after all, canonical figures; to find new and striking ways of presenting familiar stories, in the same way that artists returned incessantly to the story of Jesus.

The authors of the collective biographies, on the other hand, felt a constant pressure to innovate and to discover new great men to honor. They did not work on commission and could not easily slip into the role of semi-official pedagogues instructing the semi-captive audience of the academy and the Salons. They were authors competing in a commercial marketplace, who had to convince their readers that they had something novel to offer, something not found in previous collections. Consider the abbé Morvan de Bellegarde. Morvan clearly based his 1726 *Les vies de plusieurs hommes illustres* on Heince, Bignon, and Vulson—to put it more plainly, he shamelessly pirated them. He included 19 of their 25 subjects, leaving out only Joan of Arc, kings, and members of the royal family, and he freely plagiarized Vulson's text. Nonetheless, he strove to make his book *look* as different as possible from its predecessor. He expanded the essays, tacking onto Vulson's rather bare lists of heroic accomplishments some new details and many homiletic asides. He updated the canon, adding eleven statesmen and soldiers who had achieved fame after the construction of Richelieu's gallery. Most important, whereas Richelieu had designed his gallery as a celebration of the French state, Morvan's publisher, Le Gras, cast the new work as a celebration of the nobility (which explains the removal of Joan and the kings), and suggested, in a sycophantic dedicatory epistle, that France's present-day nobles would find the book a source of pride and inspiration.[79] Le Gras and Morvan may indeed have had a sincere admiration for the nobility, but they were also shrewd marketers, who hoped to find new buyers for their work among the wealthiest order of the kingdom.

Similarly, when Jean Du Castre d'Auvigny launched his own hugely successful series thirteen years later (it would remain a going concern for three decades, and expand to 26 volumes), he soon felt the need to issue a prospectus explicitly distinguishing the work from those of Vulson, Perrault, and Morvan:

> [There are] those who have reproached me for stealing the materials which make up the first part of my Book, and who have called it, without having read it, a compilation and collection of Histories; but the Public has certainly compared the Lives I have given it with what can be read elsewhere on the subject, with the works of *Perrault*, of [Morvan de] *Bellegarde*, with the *Gallery of the Palais Royal* [Heince, Bignon, and Vulson], or individual Histories . . . These Works are, for the most part,

nothing more than very short, badly written eulogies, long Genealogies, or cold Panegyrics, or tissues of lies, dictated by private interest, fear or baseness.[80]

Du Castre d'Auvigny added many more great men, as did his successors at the helm of the project, abbé Gabriel Pérau, and Turpin. By 1782, when Turpin was launching yet another collection of his own, novelty had become the principal selling point: "nothing has yet been written on most of the Great Men whom I have given to history. I have cleared new and uncultivated land."[81] As for Manuel, he implicitly made the same claim when he dipped deep into the well of obscurity to find not merely a few good men, but 365 great ones. Had many of his readers ever heard of such figures as Baron d'Espagnac, Etienne Geoffroi, or Pierre Carlet?

The collective biographies clearly belonged, then, to the dynamic commercial publishing sector of the French economy.[82] The expansion of this sector, I have already argued, helped teach French elites to see their nation as a single, homogeneous territory, while at the same time revising the very definition of the nation, as publishers competed to sell readers an ever larger array of novel pieces of information about their new favorite subject: the French nation, a.k.a. themselves. Even more directly than the histories and pamphlets discussed in the previous two chapters, these books represented, in the visions of France they put before the public, a response to commercial and political stimuli alike.

If commercial pressures helped expand the canon, however, they did not, in and of themselves, dictate where to look for new examples of greatness. Here again, the biographers parted company with d'Angiviller and the Académie. Both these quasi-official authorities, following Perrault's example, had included artists and writers in their canons of great men but kept them in a distinct minority (a third and a quarter, respectively) among the dominant statesmen, soldiers, and prelates. Their great men also came predominantly from the relatively recent past (more than half from the sixteenth and seventeenth centuries), and fewer than a fifth had died within half a century of their selection. In short, these canons remained centered firmly on the absolutist state in its heyday.[83]

Among the biographical works, two—Sergent's *Portraits* and the anonymous *Deeds and Heroic Actions*—moved back from this focus towards an imagined Age of Chivalry. They chose overwhelmingly from the ranks of kings, queens, and noble military men (roughly two-thirds in Sergent,

BATHILDE, REINE DE FRANCE,

FEMME DE CLOVIS II;

Née vers l'an 636, morte le 30 Janvier 680.

Figure 10. Bathilde, queen to France's seventh-century King Clovis II, was one of several medieval queens depicted in this expensive collection of colored engravings from Antoine-François Sergent, *Portraits des grands hommes, femmes illustres et sujets memorables de France,* Paris, 1786.

nearly all in *Deeds and Heroic Actions*), and in each, more than half the figures had died before, or within in a few years of, 1600. Both works, in fact, clearly belonged to the late eighteenth-century's rediscovery of the Middle Ages and medieval chivalry.[84] Both celebrated their subjects for great actions rather than great inner qualities. The *philosophes* would have labeled these men and women illustrious, not great.

The rest of the late eighteenth-century collective biographies, those which did adopt the Enlightenment definition of "greatness," took almost precisely the opposite tack. Restout's 1771 *French Gallery* (started the year earlier by Jacques Gautier Dagoty) included just 12 princes, statesmen, and military leaders (and two of the latter had risen from the ranks of common soldiers). The other 26 came primarily from the world of learning, literature, and the professions, and included not only painters and playwrights, but doctors, jurists, novelists, architects, and astronomers.[85] Furthermore, all the figures except King Louis XIII had lived in the late seventeenth or eighteenth centuries. Turpin's 1782 *French Plutarch* similarly chose its 118 men overwhelmingly from these modest social groups, and again, primarily from the eighteenth century. In his dedication (to Catherine the Great's Lord Chamberlain), Turpin wrote: "No, Prince, nature has not been exhausted by the productions of the centuries which have preceded us . . . What do we have to envy the centuries of Augustus, of Leo X, of Louis XIV, when our own has produced Voltaire, Buffon and Montesquieu?"[86]

The hundreds of great men profiled in the 1779 *Tablets* and Manuel's 1789 *French Year* omnivorously included nearly all the figures selected by d'Angiviller, the Académie, *and* the previous collective biographies. Even so, in each case more than two-thirds of the total came from outside the ranks of kings, statesmen, and soldiers, and more than two-thirds had died within the past century. Manuel included architects, bankers, merchants, and even a few artisans. "I have missed no occasion," he wrote, "to honor the hands that till the earth and weave our clothes, the farmers and artisans, those to whom we owe our surpluses while lacking their own necessities."[87] He had a particular fondness for poor scholars like Jean-Baptiste Ludot, whom he praised for jumping into the Seine in winter to see how long the human body could stand exposure to freezing water, and philanthropic doctors like Augustin Roux, who devoted himself entirely to the rural poor. As we have seen, he also devoted several pages to that emblematic martyr of the modern French nation, Jumonville.[88]

Manuel heightened the effect of raising these men, many of whom had

Figure 11. The inclusion of the famous eighteenth-century Doctor Jean Astruc among the portraits in this collection illustrates the broadening of the canon of "great Frenchmen" in the decades before the French Revolution. Engraving from Restout, *Galerie Françoise, ou Portraits des hommes et des femmes célèbres qui ont paru en France* (French Gallery, or Portraits of Famous Men and Women Who Have Lived in France), two vols., Paris, 1771.

enjoyed little or no social recognition during their lives, to the ranks of the great by making the order of his *French Year* entirely random. The reader paging through late January, for instance, would come across the following sequence of men, appearing on an entirely equal footing: the geographer Guillaume de Lisle, the soldier François de Chevert, the doctor Jean-Baptiste-Michel Bucquet, the clerical author Pierre Huet, the war minister Belle-Isle, and then, almost contemptuously, Charlemagne, greatest of French monarchs.[89] Given the loud criticism earlier authors had received for not organizing great men by social rank, the reader would have had to be singularly obtuse not to grasp Manuel's ideological point. Clearly, the book of this journalistic hack *par excellence,* while not illegal, like many that came out of his milieu, nonetheless amounted to a weapon in a cultural battle aimed at a radical restructuring of France's historical canon.[90]

Therefore, despite sharing much of the rhetoric of the Academy's *éloges*—even blatantly plagiarizing them on occasion—Manuel's project in fact subverted them, as did most of the collective biographies of the last twenty years of the old regime. Whereas the Academy and d'Angiviller, acting in a quasi-official capacity, presented historically distant, socially eminent subjects mostly linked to the service of the absolute monarchy, Manuel and his colleagues, acting in their own capacity and competing in a commercial marketplace, presented contemporary, ordinary civilians very much like the image the reading public of the late old regime was forming of itself: virtuous and meritorious heads of households who could offer just as great service to their *patrie* as any grandee. Furthermore, whereas the Academy and d'Angiviller presented a relatively stable canon, casting a shadow from the century of Louis XIV over the centuries to come, Manuel, Turpin, and the other biographers, with their claim that "nature has not been exhausted," implied, none too subtly, that true French greatness was still very much in the making. In short, whereas the cult of great men as a whole amounted to a public project of nation-forming within the symbolic space vacated by the retreat of organized religion, it nonetheless took two very different forms. For the orators of the Academy and for d'Angiviller, the nation was a project to be undertaken by the monarchical state under the banner of royal patriotism. For the biographers, it was a project that implicitly arose from within the public as a whole—not the entire population, to be sure, but the learned, largely middle-class public represented in their pages. In a sense, their work amounted less to a cult of great men, than to a cult of the public itself.

To the extent that the celebration of great men as a whole pointed forward to the Revolution, the quasi-official genres and the collective biographies again did so in strikingly different ways. In this realm of national memory, as with the politics of sovereignty and with war propaganda, the Revolution marked an intensification and transfiguration of trends that had begun under the old regime. The successive authorities held up great lives as examples to the citizenry, from boy martyrs cut down in battle against counter-revolutionaries to assassinated leaders like Marat and Le Pelletier de Saint-Fargeau.[92] In September 1793, the National Convention

Figure 12. The Pantheon, Paris. The former Church of Sainte-Geneviève was transformed during the French Revolution into a monument to (and final resting place for) "the great men of the *Patrie*."

decided to establish, as its principal vehicle of civic and patriotic education for the masses, an official periodical entitled *Collection of Heroic and Civic Actions of French Republicans,* to be distributed to the armies and popular societies and used as mandatory texts in primary schools. The government sent out thousands of circulars requesting that incidents of patriotic heroism be reported to the periodical's editor, and hundreds of responses filtered back in. Five issues of the paper appeared before the fall of Robespierre in 1794, with print runs ranging from 80,000 to a spectacular 150,000.[93] In an equally important move, the Revolution took the newly built, gloomy neoclassical Church of Sainte-Geneviève, which lowered over much of the Left Bank of Paris, and expensively transformed it into a National Pantheon on the Roman model. Several reconsecrations and deconsecrations later, it again has this function today, complete with the eighteenth-century motto over its entrance: "Aux Grands Hommes la Patrie Reconnaissante" (To the Great Men, the Grateful *Patrie*).

This revolutionary cult of great men exhibited an intense concern for history, in the sense that the revolutionaries saw themselves as the founders of a new history and strove anxiously to influence posterity's judgment of their achievements.[94] At the same time, they rejected the actual history of pre-1789 France almost entirely, and with few exceptions celebrated only titans and martyrs of the Revolution itself. Even the Pantheon welcomed only Voltaire and Rousseau among pre-revolutionary "great men." The entire panoply of Frenchmen so rhapsodized over by old regime panegyrists, from Clovis and Charlemagne to Chevert and Jumonville, suffered a total eclipse, although the nineteenth century would again recover them for France's national memory. The doughty François-Henri Turpin, author of more biographies than any other writer, made one last attempt in 1792 (at age 81) to publish a *History of Illustrious Frenchmen from the Former Third Estate,* which drew together eleven of his more humbly born historical subjects. But the book vanished without a trace.[95]

As Mona Ozouf has cogently argued, the various revolutionary attempts to institute an official canon of great men, and particularly the Pantheon itself, for the most part proved crashing, embarrassing failures. The factions in the successive assemblies could rarely agree on which figures deserved admittance, and even when they did, a great man interred in the crypt with great pomp one year often faced eviction the next, following some political shift that revealed him a traitor and criminal. This was the case with Mirabeau and also Marat.[96] Furthermore, from the very beginning of the Revolution, the radical left—led, ironically enough, by Marat himself—inveighed bitterly against the very idea of a national canon of greatness, as in the passage quoted at the start of this chapter.[97] The rather mournful, and carefully choreographed ceremonies of interment at the former Sainte-Geneviève contrasted sharply with the wild, spontaneous outpourings on behalf of Marat after his death at the hands of Charlotte Corday. The Club des Cordeliers invented rituals for Marat involving his heart, and (somewhat grotesquely) featuring the bathtub in which he had met his death as a sort of substitute crucifix, in the most emotional and bizarre public expression of religious passion in the city since the cult of the convulsionaries, sixty years earlier.[98]

In the old regime cult of great men, it was the collective biographies which pointed most directly towards this revolutionary future. In their emphasis on men from the recent past, in their claim that "nature is not exhausted," and in their effective devaluation not only of kings, but of the entire quasi-official canon celebrated by the academy and d'Angiviller, they anticipated the revolutionary rejection of the French past, and the ambition of the revolutionaries to cast themselves as the protagonists of a new, more perfect history, in a nation that was consciously rebuilding itself. In their freewheeling celebration of whatever figures the authors thought might sell, they anticipated somewhat the spontaneity of radical revolutionary commemorations and the radicals' rejection of any official canon whatsoever. In their virtual canonization of men like Ludot and Jumonville, common men who sacrificed themselves for the *patrie,* they anticipated the revolutionary cult of martyrs and the transformation of men like Marat into virtual saints of the *patrie.* In sum, most of the cult of great men under the old regime, despite its distinct republican accents, remained constrained within a tradition which saw the nation embodied in the king, those who served him, and those whom he designated. The collective biographies, however, looked ahead to a revolutionary vision in which the nation was embodied, potentially, in every citizen; in which every citizen partook, potentially, of its sacred qualities.

SELECTIVE USE
OF HISTORY

CHAPTER 5

National Character and the Republican Imagination

If there were in the world a nation which had a sociable humor, an openness of heart, a joy in life, a taste, an ease in communicating its thoughts; which was lively, pleasant, playful, sometimes imprudent, often indiscreet; and which had with all that, courage, generosity, frankness, and a certain point of honor, one should avoid disturbing its manners by laws, in order not to disturb its virtues. If the character is generally good, what difference do a few faults make?

—MONTESQUIEU, *THE SPIRIT OF THE LAWS*

Here there arises an obstacle to be overcome, and that we cannot overcome without rigorous resolution and a vehement, continuous push forwards. This obstacle is habit . . . whose dominion in the long term shapes a national character distinctive from that of other peoples and other men . . . To dissolve all the ties that bind a degenerate nation to ancient usages, to ingrained passions, to vicious inclinations, it seems that one must, so to speak, strike oneself down, sacrificing the interests of the moment.

—JACQUES-NICOLAS BILLAUD-VARENNE, *PRINCIPES RÉGÉNÉRATEURS DU SYSTÈME SOCIAL* (1793)

In 1769, the novelist Jean-Louis Castilhon paid the aging magistrate François-Ignace d'Espiard de la Borde the most sincere of compliments: he plagiarized d'Espiard's 1752 *The Spirit of the Nations,* republishing it under his own name and a new title.[1] The compliment was limited, however, for this ambitious literary pirate systematically altered d'Espiard's work. To begin with, he trimmed and smoothed out d'Espiard's repetitive and ungainly prose—a fact that became his principal line of defense after d'Espiard caught him in the theft and started a minor if entertaining literary controversy over the book's paternity.[2] More seriously, he modified d'Espiard's conclusions, especially on the subject of the French national character. D'Espiard had remarked that in France "women . . . soften the pride that is natural to Reason, and oblige us, if we wish to be pleasing, to disguise Philosophy and Science."[3] Castilhon changed the passage to: "The women who, in France, exert a despotic sway over the tastes and pleasures of society, oblige the French to disguise philosophy and its science as much as is needed to please them."[4] D'Espiard had also stated that "the French character is established on a foundation of reasonable Obedience, which is never unreserved, except for the sovereign."[5] Castilhon rewrote as follows: "the French are distinguished from other Europeans by their subordination, by a voluntary, enlightened, and never blind obedience, by a submission which is only unlimited in the case of beloved sovereigns."[6]

Finally, d'Espiard had linked the French character to a particular social class. "The lordly manner [*l'air Seigneur*] is the manner of the Frenchman," he wrote; by contrast, "bourgeois customs [*moeurs*] are the customs of the Citizen . . . But all this has been sacrificed and ridiculed by the spirit of French society." He added that "bourgeois customs . . . are the true customs of Republics."[7] Castilhon, in his version, came close to turning this idea on its head:

> It is in the depths of bourgeois customs that we must search for the true national character—a happy, solid and truly estimable character, despite the scorn expressed for it by those French who do not belong, or blush to belong, to the most numerous class in the state . . . but all these virtues have been cruelly ridiculed by the ingeniously wicked spirit of brilliant French society [the aristocracy]. The great ambition of the Frenchman in all classes other than the one I have just mentioned is to behave in a noble, easy-going way . . ., in a lordly manner.[8]

Do the differences between the two versions of the book simply reflect the contrasting personalities of a sober, tradition-minded noble magistrate and a risk-taking middle-class hack? Castilhon's specific alterations—the horror of female influence in public life, the tepid and conditional support for the monarchy, the strong condemnation of aristocratic manners—suggest that something more was at work, for they all fit in with the rise of a republican sensibility. D'Espiard himself had a certain sympathy for the ancient republics, but it was more in the traditional manner of the judicial nobility as exemplified by d'Aguesseau. That is to say, it was based on a strict compartmentalization of attitudes, with admiration for the ancients kept separate from acceptance of Christian monarchy in France. Recall the fearful note in d'Espiard's original 1743 work, insisting on his utter lack of "republican sentiments."⁹ Castilhon made no such disclaimers. He doubtless did not imagine an end to the monarchy, but he hoped for the triumph of republican *moeurs*, with social distinctions reduced, female influence eliminated, and the king's power kept in check. His identification of French national character with implicitly republican "bourgeois customs" certainly suggests as much.

In addition to confirming the growth of republican sensibilities in France, Castilhon's revisions reveal that the people who held such sentiments believed that the greatest obstacle to their ambitions was the French "national character" itself. To an extent that has not been recognized, in the decades after 1750 French writers devoted enormous time and energy to analyzing the general phenomenon of "national character" or "national spirit." Works by the major *philosophes* form only the most visible part of a huge mass of writing on the subject, including books specifically devoted to it, articles in periodicals, and long discussions in history and travel literature.¹⁰ The results of these inquiries generally suggested that the French were incapable of becoming good republican citizens. Even Castilhon, who had more confidence than most in a French population he chose to see as essentially "bourgeois," recognized that the seductions of "brilliant society" posed a perhaps insuperable obstacle to the advance of good republican *moeurs*. The republicanism that emerged during the last decades of the old regime and triumphed during the Revolution therefore saw no more fundamental task than *changing* the national character.

These issues lay at the very heart of the discussion of nation-*building* that began in France at the end of the old regime. As we have seen, nation-building was proposed as a response to two separate problems, both of which seemed to call the very existence of the nation into question: France's regional diversity, and its supposedly corrupt moral condition. The first problem was initially posed as one of juridical diversity—the particular legal rights and privileges of France's historic provinces—and then, after the Revolution eliminated these rights and privileges, primarily as one of linguistic diversity. Here, the issue of national character did not arise directly. But it did in discussions of the second problem, for if France was "the most immoral nation" in Europe, where did the fault lie if not in the collective national character? The republicans' diagnosis of France's moral ills and the program for curing them that the Jacobin regime developed in 1792–1794 were predicated on the study of national character as it had evolved during the Enlightenment. It has often been remarked that the idea of the "new man" was, in Mona Ozouf's phrase, the "central dream of the French Revolution."[11] Yet the revolutionaries spoke just as often of a "new people," a collective entity, and they had very specific views, grounded in decades of investigations and polemics, as to the nature of the "old" people they hoped to toss on the scrapheap of history.[12]

This chapter will first explore eighteenth-century French understandings of national character, proceed to the republican critique of it, and finally consider Jacobin republican efforts to reshape it. These efforts were, in theory, wholly secular, representing the logical culmination of attempts to reshape the terrestrial order without reference to the dictates of God or a divinely-ordained king. But the means which republican reformers adopted again reveals how deeply indebted they remained, in their project of building a nation, to the older, Catholic project of rebuilding the Church. Not only did they seize upon the originally theological concept of "regeneration" to express their hopes and ambitions; when they found themselves in a position actually to realize these ambitions, they proceeded in a manner that derived directly from clerical examples and that amounted to a literal campaign of conversion.

National Character Investigated

It hardly needs saying that national stereotypes, usually based on the attribution of exaggerated individual characteristics to an entire people, long predate the eighteenth century and remain ubiquitous in our own day. They may or may not have a basis in fact, but they have certainly provided a simple and comforting way for people to come to terms with the array of human diversity.[13] Medieval literature overflowed with them. "The peoples of Spain are very light-hearted," one typical thirteenth-century poem began. "The French seem valiant knights . . . The English are handsome and false-hearted / The Lombards greedy and the Germans perfidious."[14] As far back as Aristotle, natural philosophers sought what we would now call scientific explanations for differences in national character. In the late sixteenth century Jean Bodin renewed and popularized this tradition in France, and it continued through such writers as François La Mothe le Vayer, Charles Saint-Evremond, Jean-Baptiste Dubos, and d'Espiard.[15] La Mothe notably composed a "Discourse on the Opposition of Humors between Certain Nations," which attributed to the French and Spanish "as perfect an antipathy as there is in nature."[16]

In the eighteenth century, the literature on national differences and national character grew to massive and unprecedented dimensions, ranging from learned treatises to the crude propaganda of the Seven Years' War. The authors wrote for different purposes and in wildly varying styles. Nonetheless, they generally saw national character determined by three broad factors: climate, political action, and historical evolution. *Moeurs*, manners, and religion, all of which they also frequently invoked, generally depended in their schemes on politics or evolution, while the phrase "moral causes," which appears frequently in their works, usually amounted to a conflation of the two.[17]

French authors generally did not ascribe "national character" to the entire population of a nation. Until 1789, as we have seen, few authors even acknowledged the enormous demographic, social, and cultural diversity of France's 28 million inhabitants. But in any case, most authors elided the problem altogether by straightforwardly associating the *true* national character with a particular slice of the population. Thus Voltaire wrote that "the spirit of a nation always resides with the small number who put the large number to work, are fed by it, and govern it." Charles Pinot-Duclos put things even more simply: "It is in Paris that you have to consider the Frenchman, because there he is more French than elsewhere." Rousseau, by contrast, in a vision pregnant with implications for later, Romantic nationalism, found the "genius" and *moeurs* of a nation in the "most distant provinces." "It is the countryside that makes the country [*pays*], and the people of the countryside who make the nation."[18]

Of climate, political action, and historical evolution, it was the first which perhaps most completely seduced the French of the eighteenth century. "Climate is, for a Nation, the fundamental cause . . . the principal cause presiding over the genius of peoples" wrote d'Espiard, the most uncompromising advocate of this point of view.[19] Temperature, humidity, wind, the quality of the soil: all of these shaped a person's body and behavior, with the result that national characters varied from one climate to the next. His work almost certainly influenced Montesquieu, who would soon make the importance of climate to national character a piece of utterly conventional wisdom.[20] In some of the most famous chapters of *The Spirit of the Laws*, he pursued the idea with rigor, describing how, for instance, thanks to the influence of cold weather on "surface fibers" and "tufts of nerves" (something he claimed to have verified by freezing a sheep's tongue), northern peoples were stronger, less sensitive to pain and love, and ultimately more suitable to liberty than southern ones.[21] Eighteenth-century wits quipped that where Malebranche had seen everything in God, Montesquieu saw everything in climate.[22] Voltaire, Diderot, Buffon, and Helvétius all embraced theories of climate enthusiastically as well.[23]

None of these authors, however, truly saw climate as all-determining. "Many things govern men," Montesquieu wrote: "climate, religion, laws, the maxims of the government, examples of past things, *moeurs*, and manners; a general spirit [of the nation] is formed as a result."[24] Other than climate, laws and maxims were the most important. And on this subject, if he did not exactly create a piece of conventional wisdom, he certainly helped to popularize it. Throughout the rest of the eighteenth century, French authors routinely expressed their confidence in the ability of political action to affect national character. To quote just a few examples: "republican government produces a particular character, and monarchical government produces another"; "it is princes who form the national character"; "the character [of the French] is a soft and flexible clay, out of which the Men in place can make vessels of glory or vessels of ignominy."[25] Above all, the idea ran like a bright thread through the political works of Rousseau, who claimed in his *Confessions* to have seen early on that "everything fundamentally depended on politics . . . and that no people would ever be anything other than what its Government made of it."[26] Only "national institutions," Rousseau admonished his readers, could shape the character, tastes, and mores of a people, distinguishing it from others and stimulating the ardent patriotism conducive to proper social relations.[27]

Yet even Rousseau, along with the classical republicans he resembled in so many ways, acknowledged another crucial factor in the shaping of national character. For his ideal legislators fought against a powerful enemy: time itself, which slowly and insidiously leeched virtue away and infected the healthiest body politic with the bacillus of self-interest. To Rousseau, time was a purely negative factor, which reduced well-defined, particular national characters to a common human sludge. Other authors, however, treated time far more favorably. They discerned in the history of the world a slow, irregular, but nonetheless visible evolution from savagery to civilization. For them, the character of a nation therefore depended in large part on how far it had scaled this chronological ladder.

French authors applied this historical theory most insistently to their own past, emphasizing France's evolution away from cruder standards of behavior. "Nearly all of us started out as sorts of savages, shut away in forests under a gloomy sky," wrote Antoine-Léonard Thomas in his history of eloquence, while the playwright P. J. B. Chaussard even put the idea in verse: "Ces généreux Français n'étaient à leur berceau / Qu'une horde stupide: un servile troupeau" [In the cradle these generous French were nothing / But a stupid horde, a servile flock].[28] More systematically, the Marquis de Mirabeau likened the process to the course of nature itself and warned in *L'ami des hommes,* in the accents of biblical lyricism, that it could not continue indefinitely: "There is a circle prescribed to all nature, moral as well as physical, of birth, growth, fullness, decline and death. Thus are the days from morning to night, the years in their solar revolution, the life of man from cradle to tomb, and that of states from their foundation to their fall."[29] Voltaire, in the *Essai sur les moeurs,* provided the fullest exposition of the theory, attempting to trace the progress of nearly every nation on earth. While bemoaning the capacity of stupidity, greed, intolerance, and sheer accident to block or even reverse progress, he nonetheless concluded that European nations, at least, had overall moved in the proper direction.[30]

To the extent that French authors believed that political action and historical evolution determined national character, they also generally saw these two factors working through a particular intermediary: women. For if national character was heavily shaped by that elusive product of politics and history called *moeurs, moeurs* themselves were the province of women, both because of their general influence on social interactions and their specific role in educating the young. "Women," d'Espiard wrote, "are the essential part of *moeurs.*" The military reformer Guibert agreed with him. "Men make laws," but "women make *moeurs,* there lies their true empire."[31] Montesquieu, in his warning against altering a good national character (see the epigraph to this chapter), could envision only one way of actually doing so: "One could constrain [the] women, make laws to correct their *moeurs,* and limit their luxury."[32] Not coincidentally, these very measures, which Montesquieu himself hesitated to apply, formed the heart of Rousseau's misogynistic prescription for preserving the *moeurs* of Geneva in his famous *Letter to d'Alembert.*[33] Women, in short, constituted at once a measure of a nation's civilization and the key to the preservation of its character.

A Bearable Lightness of Being

Armed with these conceptual tools, eighteenth-century French authors went eagerly about investigating national characters, and particularly the one they saw reflected in the mirror. They were not always consistent, to say the least. At different times Voltaire described the French as "the most sociable and polite people on earth" (the preface to a stage play in the 1730s), "a people of heroes . . . a gentle and terrible people" (a war poem from the 1740s), and "monkeys and tigers" (his bitter exile in the 1760s).[34] Still, outside of wartime literature, which predictably saw a Bayard or Jumonville in every French male, the French national character was still, most generally, associated with a relatively well-defined and consistent constellation of closely related traits.[35] To be French was to be particularly social, particularly refined and polite, and particularly cheerful or flighty (*léger*, implying a mix of vivaciousness, inconstancy, and perhaps also superficiality). Sometimes these traits were invoked all at once, as in d'Holbach's umbrella comment that "the general character of the French nation is gaiety, activity, politeness, *sociabilité*."[36] Yet if the traits themselves provoked few disagreements, their desirability provoked many: the same term that served as a warm commendation in one context could become a stinging criticism in another, even from the same author. Certain authors were consistently critical, and it was they who shaped the emerging republican critique of French national character.

Of the traits, "social" or "sociable" attracted attention from nearly all the major *philosophes*, eager as always to encompass a given subject in a single, overarching abstraction.[37] Thus Montesquieu had a character remark, with characteristic bite, in *Persian Letters:* "It is said that man is a sociable being. On this score it seems to me that a Frenchman is more human than anyone else." Diderot similarly wrote that "there is no nation that is more like a single family. A Frenchman swarms about in his town more than ten Englishmen, fifty Dutchmen, or a hundred Moslems do in theirs."[38] Beyond the ranks of the *philosophes,* many other writers adopted the same motif— notably patriotic authors who wished to contrast the cheerful, sociable French to the gloomy, unsociable English.[39] As Bernardin de Saint-Pierre commented, "*most* of our writers brag about our nation's spirit of *société*"[40] (emphasis mine).

Légèreté and related terms had equal popularity. To quote the *Encyclopédie:* "It is a sort of proverb to say, *léger* like a Frenchman . . ."[41] D'Espiard repeatedly stresssed this aspect of the French character, as did the elder Mirabeau, who called the French the most fickle, vivacious, and *léger* of nations, and the radical journalist Louis-Sébastien Mercier, who cited their "extreme penchant" for *légèreté*.[42] The term often carried a critical bite and easily elided into frivolity, luxury, and superficiality. Republican-minded critics routinely used it as a term of abuse, and probably for this reason many adopted "gay" (*gai*) as a substitute (they contrasted *léger* and gay to "heavy," "gloomy" and "pedantic"—again, characteristics often associated with the English). The Jesuit Joseph-Antoine Cerutti wrote a twenty-page essay on "French gaiety," which he attributed in turn to the nation's sociability. Laughter, he wrote, is the distinctive quality of the French nation.[43] Yet *légèreté* did have its defenders. Jean-François Sobry, in his survey of French characteristics and institutions, said that "if [the Frenchman] has *légèreté*, it is not at all of the sort which is fickle and superficial, but rather that *légèreté* which recoils from heaviness and monotony. The Athenians were also *léger,* and they were the foremost people in the world." The novelist Jacques-Antoine Perrin likewise commented: "Our neighbors may well call us *léger,* frivolous, inconsequential. But this lightness, this frivolity is the source of our amusements and our pleasures; it is to delicacy and even gallantry that we owe our happiness, they are virtues for us."[44]

Politeness and refinement, meanwhile, went almost without saying. It was a commonplace to remark, as Voltaire did, that the French were not simply polite, but the *most* polite, as well as the most sociable of nations.[45] D'Holbach, Servan, Thomas, d'Espiard, Sobry, and Turgot all echoed the claim.[46] Eighteenth-century French understandings of politeness were complex, but in the discussions of national character the complexities faded somewhat, and such disparate concepts as urbanity, *honnêteté,* delicacy, and civility blended together to signify simply an elaborate attention to form and style in personal interactions.[47]

The sociability, *légèreté,* and politeness of the French were all easily explained by reference to climate, political action, and history. France, possessed as it was of a perfectly temperate climate, had succeeded, so it was claimed, in avoiding the solitude, seriousness, and moroseness of northern peoples, and the weakness, indolence, and debauchery of southern ones.[48] An innate moderation allowed the French to seek out pleasure and to delight in polite human interaction without necessarily corrupting and enslaving each other (although also without seeking true freedom). In addition to climate, the French character reflected the country's monarchical government and aristocratic social system, in which *les grands* set the tone and everyone else scrambled to imitate them. Thus the same traits that foreigners associated with the French in general, the French themselves associated particularly with the royal court and the high aristocracy. As d'Espiard had said, the Frenchman's manner was the lordly manner.

Above all, if the French were said to maintain a degree of polite social interaction unknown elsewhere and to devote themselves to endless
rounds of pleasure, it was because they stood at the end point of that long
historical evolution which had taken them away from their "savage" or
"barbarian" origins and rendered them steadily more "polite," "policed," or
"civilized." Sociability, *légèreté*, and politeness were all closely linked to the
concept of "civilization," which took shape in the mid-eighteenth century
and depended on a vision of historical progress and cosmopolitan exchange between civilized people. As we saw in Chapter 1, "civilization," one
of the key foundational concepts in eighteenth-century culture, stood in
stark opposition to "patrie" and "republic." Thus to the extent that eighteenth-century authors saw the French national character in terms of sociability, *légèreté*, and politeness, and approved of it, they were defining
France less as a classical *patrie* and more as the center and apogee of a universal civilization.

For most French authors, the civilized traits of sociability, *légèreté*, and
politeness reflected the extraordinary influence of women. D'Espiard and
Montesquieu agreed that women, to whom vivaciousness and love of society came naturally, ruled French *moeurs*, obliging men to strive to please
them.[49] Sébastien-Marie-Mathurin Gazon-Dourxigné, author of a historical essay on the "principal absurdities of different nations," attributed the
politeness and sociability of the French particularly to the "company of
women."[50] Many observers considered the position of women the main
difference between France and nations which restricted women to what
Rivarol called "the domestic tribunal."[51] D'Espiard stressed that "society
cannot exist without women," and nations like the Chinese "have destroyed Society by this eternal imprisonment of women, which is the least
philosophical and most unjust thing in the world."[52] An anonymous author similarly suggested that if the English stopped banishing women from
the table after dinner, the nation would grow less misanthropic. "The
Frenchman," he remarked, "owes the amiable qualities which distinguish
him from other peoples to interchange with women."[53]

The Degenerate, Effeminate French

Yet it was precisely over the position of women that French students of national character also revealed their greatest anxieties. D'Espiard, for all his
solicitude where Chinese women were concerned, had also commented
that "foreigners say that in France, men are not men enough, and women

are not women enough."[54] Gazon-Dourxigné added a similarly caution-
ary note to his celebratory history of the French character: "Some women
were reproached for taking on the character of men, and many men for
too closely resembling women."[55] Rivarol noted severely that "it is from
women's vices and ours, the politeness of men and the coquetry of women,
that was born this gallantry of the two sexes which corrupts both in
turn."[56] These remarks recall Rousseau's remark in the *Letter to d'Alembert*
that the two sexes should "live separated ordinarily," and that "no longer
wishing to tolerate separation, unable to make themselves into men, the
women make us into women."[57]

These men nonetheless had ambiguous attitudes towards the reform of
the French character, because they thought that thanks to a favorable climate, beneficial historical evolution, and a political system they would not
dream of challenging, this character was generally acceptable. They agreed
with Montesquieu that trying to alter it might prove dangerous. But in the
final decades of the old regime, in the context of political collapse and military challenges, moderate assumptions of this sort increasingly came into
question. More observers adopted a caustic, Rousseauian view of history,
held up the ideal of the *patrie* over that of civilization, and started to think
of impaired national virility as an urgent problem in need of a solution. In
1762, for instance, a *Discours sur le patriotisme*, read in the Academy of
Lyon, warned that the French had developed a tendency to become "syba-
rites, plunged into a voluptuous stupor, breathing and thinking only for
pleasure, deaf to the voice of the *patrie*." The speaker added sternly that "if
fashion, modes and frivolity take the place of *moeurs* and reason . . . then a
nation is done for."[58] Castilhon similarly called for the authentic bourgeois
character of the French to reassert itself in the face of corrupting female
aristocratic influences. In 1787, an entrant in the Academy of Châlons-sur-
Marne's essay competition on patriotism called the French "too *léger* and
too dissipated" and warned they might perish unless they grew more civic-
minded.[59] Even the ardent patriot Antoine-Léonard Thomas could turn
scathing on the subject of the French character. France, he wrote in his history of eloquence, was a "*léger* and impetuous nation, ardent for pleasures,
concerned always with the present, soon forgetting the past, talking of
everything and caring about nothing."[60]

Almost without exception, as Antoine de Baecque has stressed, these critiques associated supposedly typical French traits with the corporeal failings of lethargy, sickness, physical corruption, and old age.[61] "The French

nation has changed . . . We are no longer as robust, as strong, as the ancient Gauls from whom we descend."[62] The French nation had become "indolent, apathetic, carefree," in a modern period described as "a long lethargy" or "a coating of rust." The French were "an immense people grown old in despotism," "a degraded, debased people," "a society grown old in slavery and sensual pleasure and corrupted by the habit of vice."[63] In the diagnosis of a flawed national character, political writers were questioning the future existence of the nation and calling, in the accents of classical republicanism, for immediate reform.

But would such a reform necessarily entail wiping the slate clean and imprinting an entirely new character on the population? Until the first years of the Revolution, republican-minded observers rarely went this far. Instead, they generally suggested that modern French traits reflected the perversion and corruption of a older, authentic Frenchness, which needed somehow to be restored. As Rabaut de Saint-Etienne remarked, following Rousseau, in modern times the true national character had simply been "erased."[64] Blame for this corruption was attributed to historical evolution in general, which had leeched away the original, pristine virtues of the French, and on the form of government—namely, absolute monarchy and "feudalism." Abbé Charles Chaisneau wrote in 1792 that although France's temperate climate had endowed its inhabitants with an innate love of virtue, "despotism ruined everything with its impure breath; this monster infected the truest feelings at the source." Many echoed him.[65] France's regional diversity, which came to be perceived as an urgent problem at the time of the Revolution, was similarly interpreted, in the manner of the Physiocrats, not as a natural state of affairs, but as a historical aberration caused by the nefarious effects of the feudal system.[66] Overcoming divisions of privilege and region, and bringing the French back to a state of original, authentic homogeneity, therefore demanded not simply a reversal of the historical clock—the typically republican promise of a return to the pristine past—but an end to despotism and a check on the powers of the king.

Republican-minded critics of the national character were hardly original in their call for a return to an idealized past. From a different angle, noble and *parlementaire* opponents of the crown under the old regime did very little other than assert the claims of the distant past upon the present. Occasionally, they invoked the subject of national character to support their point, as when Boulainvilliers wrote grandiloquently of "the French,

born free and independent . . . who fell prey to the conquest, not of a foreign nation, but of a single family."[67] But national character mattered far
less to them than specific constitutional arrangements and the specific historic rights they claimed for their own institutions and groups. In contrast,
the later republican texts increasingly eschewed any consideration of an
ancient French constitution which, no matter how favorably presented,
still could not match up to the Roman republican one. They preferred
more historically vague, although often lushly evocative, invocations of the
earlier, unspoiled national personality.

How far one had to go into the past to find the golden age of Frenchness
was a question open to discussion. Republican critics of the national character in the 1770s and 1780s most often located it either in the Middle Ages
or the Renaissance. The earlier era had experienced something of a vogue
in the late eighteenth century, spurred in particular by the meticulous
historical researches of La Curne de Sainte-Palaye, which fed a colorful,
proto-Romantic celebration of chivalry and the Troubadours. "O happy
times! O forever lamented days!" wrote the poet Pierre-Laurent Bérenger
in one typical effusion. "Brilliant and fortunate nation! . . . Egoism, that
poison which destroys all sensitivity, had not yet attacked the *patrie*, society, nature itself . . . In those days the Nation had a character that was simple, and, if I dare say so, poetic and full of grandeur."[68] Historical works
such as Claude de Sacy's twelve-volume study of *L'honneur françois* chroni-
cled the history of chivalry in detail, while, as we have seen, in the 1780s
devotees of the cult of great Frenchmen put new emphasis on medieval
heroes.[69] As for the Renaissance, it was not only the age of great Frenchmen
like Bayard, but also of the paradigmatic good king, Henri IV. When Louis
XVI inherited the throne in 1774, hopeful Parisian graffiti artists painted
the word "Resurrexit" ("he has arisen") on the statue of Henri IV on Paris's
Pont Neuf, and Renaissance-style clothing enjoyed a brief vogue at Versailles.[70] A 1789 pamphlet referred to Henri's famous culinary pledge to the
poor in predicting that with the Revolution, the French, "regaining the
gaiety and vigor of our fathers, . . . will dance, sing, and rejoice in the shade
of those ancient oaks under which they used to gather to eat chicken in
the pot."[71]

During the Revolution, the association of chivalry with the nobility and
of even Henri IV with royal "despotism" made these particular allusions
politically incorrect, and so the search for a usable pristine past proceeded
further back in time, to the era of the Franks or even the Gauls. Pithou's *Le*

triomphe des parisiens, published after the fall of the Bastille, proclaimed: "Frenchmen, you have reconquered your liberty, that liberty of which the first Franks, your ancestors, were jealous; you will again become like them, strong and healthy; like them you will let your beards grow, and you will wear the long hair that they favored."[72] Other pamphlets identified the conquerors of the Bastille with the "sturdy Gauls," while Barère, in August of 1793, asked his listeners in the Convention to emulate the Gauls who had once conquered Rome.[73] A particularly curious revolutionary pamphlet demanded that the country reject the name of France and call itself Gaul once again.[74] Even the National Convention's choice of a giant Hercules as the emblem of the Republic, in 1793, conformed to this revived Celtophilia. For in French iconography the mighty Hercules had a particular association with the Gauls, whom he had brought out of barbarism. The emblem therefore managed simultaneously to invoke the classical mythology so beloved of the revolutionaries, and also a more specifically national past.[75]

Even when invocations of national character did not refer to any particular era in the French past, the authors almost reflexively used the language of recovery, awakening, rebirth, and regeneration. "Century eighteen! Return to France all its energy, return to it all its virtues," the future Girondin Pétion wrote in a 1789 pamphlet. "People, awaken! Break your chains! Rise once again to your initial grandeur," chimed in an anonymous poet. At the end of 1789, Mercier hailed "the year which has brought equality, liberty and justice back to Gaul . . . which ended the abasement of the people; which ennobled it, in revealing to it titles which had been lost."[76] Such opinions were ubiquitous.

Yet how could a fatally sick and corrupt nation possibly accomplish such an act of revival? By 1789 it had become commonplace to take images of indolence and corruption to an extreme, with France described as a nation on its deathbed. Many authors therefore implied that it could only rise up again through a sort of miracle, similar to cures brought about by saints, or even the resurrection of Jesus. The popular concept of regeneration perfectly expressed this belief. Certain authors went even further, however, and couched images of national recovery in language taken blatantly from the Gospels. Pamphlets appeared with titles such as *La Dies Irae, ou les trois ordres au jugement dernier* ("The Day of Wrath, or the Three Orders at the Last Judgment"), and *La Passion, la mort, et la resurrection du peuple* ("The Passion, Death and Resurrection of the People"), which recounted that the

French body politic had lain on its deathbed until the God of Mercy had finally stepped in save it. Priests favorable to the Revolution, not surprisingly, used such language with particular fervor and frequency.[77] Such writing usually came in the form of parables; few went so far as to claim that God literally stood on the side of the Revolution. But the religious language nonetheless suggests that when it came to addressing the problem of how a nation and its national character might actually be transformed, French republicans still instinctively reached for religious models.

Man and Citizen

While the idea of recovering an earlier, more authentic, and more natural national character may have prevailed under the old regime and the start of the Revolution, it was not the only form that the republican critique took. Particularly during the Terror, another, more radical approach to the subject of national character also took shape: instead of a return to nature and an original French national character, the call went out for a complete and utter break with both.

This approach rested above all on an opposition between the abstract categories of "man" and "citizen," that is, between the human being as found in nature, complete with natural instincts and feelings, and the human being as found in the *patrie*, conditioned to heed the call of civic duty. Under the old regime, Christian writers generally tried to deny the opposition, lest it lead to the Machiavellian conclusion that a good Christian could not be a good citizen of the *patrie*. Thus the Jansenist orator Soanen, in his 1683 sermon on patriotism, affirmed that "it is impossible to be truly a man without being a good citizen, and it is similarly impossible to be a good Christian without cherishing one's country."[78] The notion that people might turn away from their natural feelings in favor of their patriotic duty was often actively condemned and associated with countries other than France. "The *Patrie*," wrote a pamphleteer of the Seven Years War, "is the idol to which the English sacrifice all the feelings which the voice of nature tells them to have for their fellow men. Their love for it has dried them up entirely."[79] The Jesuit and future revolutionary, Joseph-Antoine-Joachim Cerutti, sought more neutrally to associate such behavior with the ancient republics: "In Man, the Romans and Athenians sought only to fashion the Citizen."[80]

It was Rousseau who sketched out the opposition in the strongest terms.

Indeed, it underlies much of his work. His *Discourse on the Origins of Inequality* famously portrayed man in the state of nature and in the intermediary stage of contented savagery, before concluding that in modern times the insidious enticements of *amour propre* had led humans fatally astray, with the only salvation lying in the adoption of a new, wholly civic nature. The *Social Contract* then continued the story, suggesting how this new nature might be created through politics. "The passing from the state of nature to the civil society," Rousseau emphasized, "produces a very remarkable change in man; it puts justice as a rule of conduct in the place of instinct, and gives his actions the moral quality they had previously lacked."[81] In *Emile*, Rousseau proposed a different possible course, that of sheltering men from the nefarious effects of corrupt social institutions so as to preserve their natural instincts. He admitted, however, that a man sheltered in this manner would not grow up into a dutiful patriotic citizen. "Forced to fight nature or social institutions," he wrote, "we must choose between making a man or making a citizen; we cannot do both."[82] Diderot likewise lamented that mankind had never managed to unify the three categories of "man, citizen and religious person."[83]

Like Soanen, the French revolutionaries for the most part initially attempted to deny the need for Rousseau's choice. How else could they have named the single most important document of 1789 *The Declaration of the Rights of Man and of the Citizen?* Clerical revolutionaries seeking to put the Church under the tricolor and the Revolution under the cross, such as Adrien Lamourette, Henri Grégoire, and Hyancinthe Sermet, argued zealously that the Revolution might yet achieve a precious union between the demands of citizenship and human nature.[84]

But even as these men fought to reconcile (Christian) man and (revolutionary) citizen, other, more radical voices were restating Rousseau's formulation and insistently severing the two categories again. As early as 1788, an anonymous pamphlet entitled *Discours sur le patriotisme* responded to the Academy of Châlons-sur-Marne's essay question about whether patriotism could exist under monarchies with this explanation of the word's meaning:

What is Patriotism? Patriotism is the continual practice of all the political virtues. . . . It is the sacrifice of one's goods, one's relatives, one's family: it is contempt for life itself, when the safety of the City is at stake. What is Patriotism? *Patriotism is the forgetting of the man, to be nothing other than a citizen* [my emphasis]. In the heart of the true Patriot, personal interest constantly cedes to the general interest. He generously sacrifices all his passions to the passion for the *Patrie*. So what, finally, is Patriotism? Patriotism is the total abnegation of all feelings which are not directed towards the happiness of the City.[85]

The passage reads like pure classical republicanism, yet in his conclusion to the pamphlet the author retreated somewhat. Adapting (without attribution) the passage from Montesquieu with which this chapter opens, he asked a number of similar questions, beginning with: "[What] if there were a people who possessed to the highest point the social virtues; who were gentle, human, generous, charitable; whose general character was gaiety, vanity, inconsistency. . .?"[86] He concluded that if such a people existed, it could not be patriotic. Again in echo of Montesquieu, he insisted that "if ever Patriotism took root in the heart of this people, it would no longer be the same, its constitution would have changed."[87] Unlike Montesquieu, however, he did not suggest that this change would be a bad thing.

Within a few years, the pamphleteer's suggestion had become, for others, a manifesto. If the Revolution began, in 1789, with the rejection of specifically French constitutional precedents, it quickly proceeded to a rejection of French history altogether. "It is France's salvation you must consult, not its archives," Cerutti instructed the deputies to the Estates General, while Rabaut de Saint-Etienne made his famous comment about France being fit not to follow examples, but only to give them.[88] Barère grandiloquently asserted that "all must be new in France; we wish to date only from today," while Boissy d'Anglas borrowed from the Bible to swoop even higher in his rhetoric: "To set the destinies of the world, you have but to will it. You are the creators of a new world. Say let there be light, and light will be."[89] Robespierre made the same point more darkly: "Considering the depths to which the human race has been degraded by the vices of our former social system, I am convinced of the need to effect a complete regeneration, and, if I may so express it, to create a new people."[90] From this point, it was only a short step to a rejection of nature itself in favor of the demands of the *patrie*. Thus Danton could famously tell the Convention that children belong to the Republic before belonging to their parents, and the legislator Lepeletier de Saint-Fargeau could propose (in a plan endorsed by Robespierre) to remove all French children from their families and send them to state-run boarding schools for periods of six years or longer.[91] Thus Saint-Just could proclaim to the Convention that "there is something terrible in the sacred love of the *patrie*. It is so exclusive that it sacrifices everything without pity, without fear, without human respect, to the public interest."[92]

The call to reject nature came with particular persistence in the arts. Already in 1789, Jacques-Louis David's neoclassical masterpiece, *Lictors Bringing Brutus the Bodies of His Sons*, celebrated the Roman hero who ordered his own sons killed as a punishment for treason. The painting brilliantly contrasted the still, unfeeling Brutus, staring straight ahead without visible emotion on one side of the tableau, to his wife and daughters weeping hysterically on the other. Under the Terror, revolutionary theater repeatedly returned to such themes, with a series of plays celebrating the same sort of chillingly stern and unforgiving heroes, drawn mostly from the history of republican Rome. In Joseph Lavallée's 1794 *Manlius Torquatus, ou la discipline romaine,* for instance, a Roman father, in the manner of Brutus, kills his son for disobedience. The son pleads repeatedly with his father, but the stern Roman responds only with the words "la patrie!" Finally, he adds this explanation:

> To save unhappy morals from chains,
> Let us break, burst the chains of paternal affection;
> And whether they finally call me just or barbaric,
> Let me be the father of the people, and not the father of a man.[93]

Similarly, in Antoine-Vincent Arnault's *Quintus Cincinnatus,* also from 1794, a Roman learns that his father-in-law has committed treason, whereupon his wife warns him not to let family sentiment soften his reaction:

> Stifle the murmur of protesting blood,
> Conquer yourself; enslave nature to the *patrie,*
> Feeling to laws, and the man to the citizen;
> This is the effort worthy of your heart and mine.[94]

From Soanen's reconciling of "man" and "citizen," to Rousseau's injunction to choose between them, to the 1789 pamphleteer's suggestion to forget the first in favor of the second, the French had finally arrived at the ultimate stage of the republican critique: demanding the enslavement of man, and nature itself, to the *patrie.*

From this perspective, of course, any national character shaped by climate, historical evolution, and monarchy was nothing other than an ob-

Figure 13. Jacques-Louis David, *Les licteurs rapportent à Brutus les corps de ses fils* (Lictors Bringing to Brutus the Bodies of His Sons), 1789. David's stern, neoclassical masterpiece depicts a famous incident from the Roman Republic, in which Junius Brutus ordered the execution of his own sons for treason.

stacle to be overcome, which is precisely how the Jacobin and Terrorist Jacques-Nicolas Billaud-Varenne described it in his 1793 work, *Principes régénérateurs du système social,* in the passage quoted at the start of this chapter. In *Manlius Torquatus,* Lavallée drew a contrast between the Roman and Latin peoples whose conflict lay at the heart of his story, stressing that even though they were neighbors sharing a common history, climate, and language, the thirst for liberty had changed the Roman character unalterably. Robespierre expressed the same sentiment when he strikingly asserted, in a report to the Convention on religious ideas and national festivals, that the Revolution had put the French two thousand years ahead of the rest of the human race, so that "one is tempted to see them . . .] as a different species."[95] If France *was* to have a national character, it should have an entirely new one, reflecting its newly republican constitution. As we have seen, the playwright Chénier told the National Convention that the state should take as its purpose "to make Frenchmen, to give the nation a physiognomy of its own."[96]

The single most sustained exposition of this point of view came a few years after the Terror, in a remarkable short book called *De l'influence de la Révolution française sur le caractère national* ("On the Influence of the French Revolution on the National Character") by Jacobin magistrate Gilles Boucher-Laricharderie. Composed at a time when the achievements of the republican revolution seemed ever more precarious, Boucher hoped to encourage the left by sounding a tone of revolutionary optimism and confidence, declaring that the national character *had* changed, positively, completely, and irreversibly, since 1789. Before that date, he argued in a familiar manner, despotism had caused the French to lose whatever national character they might once have possessed. Therefore, to consolidate itself, the Revolution needed to entirely recast that character. "This is what it began to do," he continued, "with a success that even the most penetrating minds could not have predicted."[97] In keeping with earlier diagnoses of national character, Boucher devoted the heart of the book to the role of women. Quoting Rousseau, he argued that before 1789 French women had taken advantage of the deference shown them by men to make themselves the true sources of power "in all conditions and ranks," right up to the royal court. But, he continued sententiously: "This strange domination expired on July 14, 1789." Since then, women's dominion had been restricted to the "interior of their families" and "the exercise of domestic virtues," with beneficial results for France in general.[98] Boucher did admit that the French possessed a natural gaiety which had suffered under the Terror. But he also insisted that the "frivolity" and *légèreté* which had accompanied this gaiety had disappeared, replaced by "decency, gravity, . . . simplicity."[99] The French had acquired a "new character," a martial, conquering disposition that allowed their armies to march through Europe in triumph. And Boucher concluded, in echo of a thousand revolutionary speeches: "Thus the love of liberty has made of the French an entirely new people."[100] Although issued in the twilight of the First Republic, it was the perfect republican vision of a France transformed.

The Means of Conversion

It was one thing to pontificate about the weaknesses of the French national character. It was quite another to do something about it. And over the course of the Revolution, the task came to seem steadily more daunting, as the bounds of the political nation expanded. In the spring of 1789, with the French still divided into their three traditional estates and with voting rights strictly circumscribed by property requirements, it was still possible—just—to follow Voltaire or Duclos and restrict the problem of the national character to a small, influential, easily describable minority. But by the fall of 1792, when the National Convention had extended the suffrage, in theory, to nearly all adult males, the problems of the larger nation could no longer be overlooked, and the biblical and classical examples of nation-building cited by Rousseau in the *Considerations on the Government of Poland* came to seem less and less relevant. For eighteenth-century France was not a small desert tribe knit together by painfully tight bonds of kinship and obedience, nor was it a walled classical city-state in which slaves supported the leisure of free citizens. Shaping the character of a population that numbered in the millions, most of whom had little formal education, many of whom could not read or understand any but rudimentary French, and who varied enormously in everything from language and folklore to village organization and forms of agriculture, was a project without any real secular precedent.

How was the task to be accomplished? Mona Ozouf has suggested that the revolutionaries had two, almost diametrically opposed ways of talking about what she calls the problem of the "new man": the miraculous and the laborious.[101] In the first, the change would simply happen, in a single instant, through a simple, immense, and fundamentally miraculous act of political will. In a period of such rapid and extraordinary change that one month's "unimaginable" regularly became the next month's "insufficient," the notion was not quite so naive as it appears with hindsight. Yet given the disappointment that followed upon nearly all the supposedly transformative moments during the Revolution, it is not surprising that, just as often, the revolutionaries saw change in the national character as a long, painstaking project involving the massive use of state resources and personnel. As one member of the Convention wrote in a report on the new revolutionary calendar: "A revolution that involves a total change in political opinions can lead, in very little time, to a similar change in government and the laws . . . but when it comes to destroying religious opinions and the customs of private life, which habit has turned into a sort of necessity, then it takes centuries."[102]

It was this notion of slow, laborious change driven by the central state which animated the enormously ambitious cultural policies of 1792–94 in education, religion, the arts, and daily life. These policies, although directed at everything from language to the calendar to book publishing, derived their fundamental unity precisely from their goal of transforming the

French people as a whole and giving them new unity and uniformity. The legislators in question cared remarkably little about giving the French the intellectual tools to act as free, independent citizens. They wanted, rather, to purge the population of old attitudes, habits, and knowledge and to reshape it according to a particular, predetermined idea of what a good republican state required.

In undertaking this vastly ambitious project, the Jacobins had only one clear model before them. From the middle of the sixteenth until well into the eighteenth century, the Catholic Church throughout Europe had engaged in a massive campaign to instruct the common people in orthodox Catholic doctrine and to purge them of "superstitious" "pagan" beliefs and practices. In Brittany, one of the best-studied cases, a typical mission might involve a score of priests spending a month in small villages, dispensing more than 7,000 hours of Christian education. The Jesuit Julien Maunoir probably oversaw the instruction of hundreds of thousands of Bretons during his career. The missionaries brought with them, along with new catechisms, new songs, new parables and stories, new almanacs, and new instructions for the parish priest, whose activities became subject to regular, stringent inspections by the ecclesiastical authorities. In a word, the campaign aimed at nothing less than a wholesale transformation of popular culture. It cannot be said to have fully succeeded. It varied in intensity over time and from place to place, and everywhere the common people appropriated the missionaries' message in their own way and for their own purposes.[103] Nonetheless, under the old regime it represented the only concerted cultural project of its sort. After 1789, the revolutionaries had every reason to reject a comparison between it and their own project, given the fundamental difference of kind which they believed separated them from the priesthood. Yet many of them could not resist the model. As Rabaut Saint-Etienne had stressed in his 1792 speech to the Convention: "Why should we not do in the name of truth and freedom what [the priests] so often did in the name of error and slavery?" The Jacobin club of Paris, in February, 1792, similarly urged its affiliates in the provinces to emulate the spread of Christianity by sending apostles of liberty and equality into France's villages. The Girondin Armand Kersaint wrote in 1791: "What the imposters did in the name of God and the King, so as to enslave minds and captivate men, you must do in the name of liberty and the *patrie*."[104]

This is certainly not the place for an exhaustive survey of the Jacobin cultural program, a subject which would require a book of its own. Here I will simply offer a brief survey of the policies that explicitly aimed at the reform of France's national character, and point out the ways in which they took inspiration from the earlier, clerical project.[105] The next chapter will examine in more depth one particular aspect of the program: the attempt to make French a truly national language.

The most important means that the revolutionaries envisaged for transforming the French national character was primary education. Between 1789 and 1794, the successive assemblies devoted enormous amounts of time to proposals for reforming the educational system.[106] Marat, with his usual savage wit, scornfully compared the proposals to "planting trees so that they may bear fruit for the future nourishment of soldiers who are already dying of starvation."[107] In the midst of war, civil war, economic desperation, and political turmoil, most of them indeed ended up as dead letters. Nonetheless, they illuminate radical revolutionary attitudes exceptionally well.

Particularly between 1792 and 1794, the would-be fathers of republican education devoted far more attention to the inculcation of correct moral and political attitudes than to the imparting of basic knowledge.[108] In this respect, their authors followed a distinction first made by Rabaut in his 1792 speech between "public instruction" and "national education." While the first "enlightens and exercises the mind" through schools, books, and instruments, the second "shapes the heart" through festivals, circuses, public games, and "the spectacle of the fields and nature."[109] Indeed, for Rabaut and most of his successors, "national education" had relatively little to do with schooling. "All the doctrine consists of taking hold of man from the cradle, indeed even before birth, for the unborn child already belongs to the *patrie*. It takes hold of the man and never leaves him, so that national education is not an institution for childhood, but for all of life."[110]

Rabaut's speech inspired most of the subsequent republican educational proposals, and particularly Lepeletier de Saint-Fargeau's draconian plan for placing all children in boarding schools, which Robespierre strenuously advocated after Lepeletier's assassination in early 1793.[111] "At age five," Lepeletier wrote, "the *patrie* receives the child from the hands of nature; at twelve, it returns him to society . . . the totality of the child's existence belongs to us . . . it never leaves the mold."[112] Lepeletier called for a "surveillance of every day, every moment," with children eating the same food, wearing the same clothing, and cut off from most contact with the outside world: "Thus there will take shape a renewed, strong, hard-working, well-regulated, disciplined race, which an impenetrable barrier will have separated from impure contact with the prejudices of our aged species."[113] In its foreshadowing of modern totalitarian practices, the project had no equals.

But even if they pointed towards the twentieth century, the radical educational proposals also followed older models. Most obviously, they recalled ancient Sparta, with its severe regimentation of male youth. But as was so often the case during the Revolution, the invocation of the ancients hid the equal, indeed perhaps greater, importance of the clerical example, which the French of the eighteenth century knew far more intimately. It is an obvious but too-often-ignored point that nearly all of the French revolutionary generation's personal experience of education had come at the hands of the Catholic Church, which had maintained a virtual monopoly on education under the old regime. Furthermore, the rigid separation of the young from outside society and the twenty-four-hour-a-day surveillance proposed by Lepeletier had a more recent and more exact precedent than Sparta (where a rigid quarantine of youth was not practiced): namely, the monasteries.[114]

While the educational projects confronted the problem of France's rural masses, other types of cultural reform focused on a far narrower, predominantly urban population. For instance, the theater, arguably the central cultural institution of the old regime, attracted more than its share of Jacobin reforming energy. In March of 1793, the Paris Commune voted to establish a free theater for "the instruction of the people." That summer, the Convention ordered Parisian theaters to present only certifiably republican plays and provided a list of works, dealing mostly with Roman history, to be performed three times a week over the next month. In March 1794, the government voted to rename the Comédie Française the Theater of the People, and it instructed every French municipality possessing a stage to put on free "patriotic" productions every ten days.[115] These reforms were aimed at the servants and artisans of the *parterre* as well as the grandees and bourgeois of the box seats, but not the rural population.

The use of the theater for civic education had been widely discussed during much of the century. This discussion itself reflected the progress of what Marcel Gauchet calls "disenchantment," for as early as in the decades around 1700, quarrels over the theater started focusing less on Christian morality and more on the institution's possible contributions to civic harmony.[116] In the 1760s, the crown touted patriotic plays such as *Le siège de Calais*. Meanwhile Mercier, who sympathized with the patriotic opposition to Lord Chancellor Maupeou, argued that the theater, which he compared to the pulpit, had a unique ability to shape *moeurs* and to bind the French together into one nation.[117] Mercier and other critics of the Comédie Française's rigid monopoly on theatrical performance in Paris suggested that one benefit of ending the monopoly would be to encourage the performance of plays with more patriotic content. The notorious journalist Restif de la Bretonne made particularly vast claims for patriotic theater: "The strength of national or patriotic tragedy is that it is the only one capable of reviving . . . ancient virtues, and giving descendants of great men the possibility of representing on the stage the model that the descendant must then copy in life."[118] By 1790 the Paris Commune was being pressured to dictate which plays should be performed, and from there it was not too far a step to the rigid politicization of the theater under the Terror, when only didactic republican plays like *Manlius Torquatus* were allowed on the French stage.[119]

It was this strict control of the theaters, as much as the content of the plays, which most strongly marked off revolutionary drama from its predecessors (crudely pedagogical and patriotic plays were hardly an eighteenth-century invention, after all). Even at the height of the campaign of royal patriotism, works like the *Le siège de Calais* shared the boards with apolitical comedies and tragedies. Only with the Revolution did the notion take shape that the political authorities should pass on all the plays that appeared and use them to pursue a particular didactic agenda—as opposed simply to censoring plays they deemed offensive. Yet if these practices had no real secular precedent, they did have something of a religious one, in the dramas performed until the 1760s in French *collèges* (high schools), particularly under the aegis of the Jesuit order. According to L. W. B. Brockliss, *collège* instructors did not just choose the plays; they generally wrote the scripts. "Through a careful control of plot and theme," he emphasizes, "they intentionally imparted moral and political lessons." Moreover, "the themes explored by these plays . . . scarcely deserved the name of tragedy. They examined neither the problems of inner conflict nor the effect of an obsessive passion, but through the portrayal of stereotyped saints and sinners indoctrinated the audience in the need to be obedient to the commands of their father, prince and God."[120] Few of the texts have survived, but the titles and programs indicate that the plays most frequently celebrated the monarchy and the great men of French history.[121]

In their campaign for national regeneration the radical republicans also made heavy use of the periodical press, using its columns to report news, make political arguments, and also to enlighten their readers and to impart proper political attitudes. One newspaper in particular, the inexpensive weekly *La Feuille villageoise,* aimed explicitly at educating the peasantry about politics and the events of the Revolution and achieved a fair degree of popularity (although admittedly, peasants accounted for well under half of the 15,000 subscribers).[122] At first glance, this particular means of conversion seems to differ from the other two in lacking important religious precedents. Certainly, newspaper publishing was not a practice of the Counter-Reformation clergy. Yet revolutionary journalists, too, borrowed from the priesthood in surprising ways. The principal editors of the *Feuille villageoise* were clerics: none other than the former Jesuit Cerutti, and Rabaut Saint-Etienne. The newspaper often covered the efforts of priests to educate the peasants, and more than half the letters to the editor printed in the *Feuille* allegedly came from priests and pastors.[123] More generally, Jeremy Popkin has noted that radical revolutionary journalists made large-scale use of "language and imagery drawn from religious sources," which would make their message "easily comprehensible for a wide audience." None did so more insistently than Marat: "Addressing the ordinary people of France in language they had previously heard on the most solemn occasions, he conveyed to his audience the sense that they were called upon to play a leading part in a great drama of redemption."[124]

One final arena for the project of reshaping the French national character, and the one with the most obvious religious precedents, was the festival. Between 1789 and 1799, in cities and hamlets alike, revolutionaries organized hundreds of large, carefully choreographed festivals to celebrate their accomplishments, render homage to their heroes and themselves, and to instruct and transform the common people through images, words, music, and pageantry. On June 8th, 1794 (the date of the traditional holiday of Pentecost), the Jacobin government organized in Paris the most remarkable such affair, the Festival of the Supreme Being. In the morning, 2,400 Parisians dressed in white robes sang hymns. In the afternoon a parade took to the streets, featuring a triumphal chariot drawn by eight oxen, their horns painted gold, and bearing a printing press and a plow, symbols of labor. Ahead, in a cart, a group of blind children sang a Hymn to Divinity; they were followed by columns of mothers bearing roses, and fathers leading sons carrying swords. In the center of the field was an enormous plaster-and-cardboard mountain, on top of which stood a huge tree beside

Figure 14. The great Festival of the Supreme Being, staged in Paris during the Terror under the direction of Maximilien Robespierre and Jacques-Louis David. Naudet, *La fête de l'être suprême*, 1794.

a fifty-foot column bearing a statue of Hercules. After more hymns had been sung, a man dressed in a sky-blue coat descended from the mountain in the manner of Moses, bearing a torch, applauded by ranks of patriots dressed in red, white, and blue and singing the *Marseillaise*. It was Maximilien Robespierre. If Condorcet had earlier warned against treating revolutionary doctrine as "tablets brought down from heaven, to be worshipped and believed in," Robespierre here gave his unambiguous response.[125]

Such episodes reveal just how profoundly the republicans of 1792–94 obeyed, if often unconsciously, Rabaut Saint-Etienne's words about following the example of the priests "with their catechisms, their processions . . . their ceremonies, sermons, hymns, missions, pilgrimages, patron saints, paintings, and all that nature placed at their disposal."[126] Mona Ozouf, in her analysis of the festivals, has exhaustively catalogued the "vertigo of imitation" of Christian practices evident in them: hymns, processions, sermons, altars, the Declaration of Rights taking the place of the Bible, the obsessive use of words such as "holy," "temple," "catechism," and "gospel."[127] From this perspective, the festival seems to have amounted to little more than a laughable pastiche of Christianity, centered upon a kitschy cardboard Sinai.

Yet Ozouf cautions that the festivals were *not* a simple imitation of Christianity, for through them the revolutionaries also hoped to purge the world of superstition, of the metaphysical, of ideas of sin and redemption. The formal content of the festivals overwhelmingly referred not to Christianity, but to pagan antiquity—although an antiquity curiously shorn of nearly all specific references to Rome or Greece. Ozouf concludes that the festivals amounted to an attempt to "transfer sacrality" to the human world, to the Revolution itself, and to the *patrie*.[128]

In this sense, the festivals perfectly illustrate the relationship between nationalism and religion. The architects of the festivals, who were also the principal architects of nationalism in France, were not acting on behalf of any God, not even a God dressed up in the clothes of the Nation—a supernatural idol in secular guise. They were following the example of the priests so as to establish harmony and order in a wholly human world that existed on its own terms, according to its own laws. In particular, they sought to do this within a particular, limited space, which they called the nation. And they sought to do it by transforming the very character of the people who lived within this space by giving them new attitudes, opinions, and habits—and also, crucially, the *same* attitudes, opinions, and habits, to ensure that they acted as a single body. Education, the theater, the press, and the festivals were all mobilized to this end.

But as France's revolutionary assemblies recognized on many different occasions between 1789 and 1794, even a successful transformation of the French national character might not suffice to arrive at the desired state of harmony. For within France there existed, so they believed, another deadly source of division, misunderstanding, and conflict, a deeper one that destroyed any chance of achieving true republican homogeneity and might lead even the best of republican citizens inadvertently to threaten the safety of the republic. Overcoming it would require an effort as arduous as any proposed by the radical educational reformers, perhaps more so. This source of division was language itself.

CHAPTER 6

National Language and the
Revolutionary Crucible

*The poor of this country should be able to say, like the poor of other
nations such as the French, Spanish, Italian, &c.: "we dare to speak
in our own language of the grandeurs of God and of the articles of
our Faith."... What flaw might the language of Toulouse have, not
to be worthy of expressing the word of God, just like all others? What
could the poor people of this country have done, not to deserve the
consolation and honor of hearing of a matter as great as eternal salvation in their own language? To speak truly, experience... teaches
us that there is no tongue which reaches further into the heart, and
that touches more to the quick, than the maternal.*

—*LA DOUCTRINO CRESTIANO MESO EN RIMOS*
[CHRISTIAN DOCTRINE SET TO RHYMES]
(TOULOUSE, 1641)

*Federalism and superstition speak Breton, emigration and hatred of
the Republic speak German; counter-revolution speaks Italian and
fanaticism speaks Basque. Let us break these instruments of injury
and error.*

—BERTRAND BARÈRE (1794)

On July 14, 1790, the first anniversary of the fall of the Bastille, the French
staged one of the most impressive displays of national unity ever seen in
Europe, in the first of the great revolutionary festivals. At noon, in Paris, on
the Champ de Mars (future site of the Eiffel Tower), delegations of National Guardsmen from across France swore oaths of loyalty and pledged
to join in a great national Federation. Under the ecstatic gaze of the guard
commander, Lafayette, and the cooler eye of the presiding bishop, Talleyrand, guardsmen paraded past specially built pavilions, dignitaries delivered speeches, and masses of spectators applauded and broke into patriotic
song (including "Ça ira," as yet without its famous refrain about hang-

ing aristocrats from lampposts). Everywhere—on flags, banners, uniforms, and cockades—floated the new symbol of the nation, the tricolor. At as close to the same moment as the technology of the age permitted, cities and villages across France marked the occasion with their own parades, songs, oaths, and speeches. In short, the idea of the nation as a political construction built by the conscious action of patriotic citizens—an idea unimaginable to the French just a few decades before—here enjoyed its apotheosis.[1]

In one of the localities celebrating the Federation, the hamlet of Saint-Ginest on the outskirts of the southern city of Toulouse, the assembled guardsmen heard a sermon from a distinguished speaker. Hyacinthe Sermet was an ambitious and progressive-minded clergyman who had preached before the king at Versailles and contributed sprightly notices, in the manner of the day, to learned publications. Already firmly identified with the cause of Revolution, he was widely considered the leading candidate for bishop of Toulouse under the new Civil Constitution of the Clergy.[2] For his text on July 14, Sermet adroitly chose Galatians 4:31–5:1, in which Paul warns his readers against falling back into the grip of the old Mosaic law: "So then, brethren, we are not children of the bondwoman, but of the free. Stand fast therefore in the liberty wherewith Christ hath made us free, and be not entangled again with the yoke of bondage." In the sermon itself, Sermet compared Christ's abrogation of the Mosaic law to the Revolution's abrogation of the old regime, and suggested that Paul himself, in heaven, was smiling on the achievements of the Constituent Assembly.[3]

Yet even as he participated in this great ceremony of nation-building, the actual words Sermet used testified to what, from our modern perspective, stands as one of the most important signs of French disunity at the time. This is how he started:

Jamay nou debignayots, mous efans, & brabés Camarados, à qui l'Apoustoul Sent-Pol, le plus grand des Predicairés qu'ajo parescut sur la terro, desempey la naissenço del Christianismé, adressabo aquel lengatgé. Aco ero, afin qu'au sapiats, à nostrés illustrés Aujols, as mainatgés d'aquelis Gauloisés, que quitteguen y a enbiron tres milo ans aquesté Pays, al nombré de may de cent cinquanto milo, per ana al dela de las mars, al bout del moundé counescut alabets, al fin found de l'Asio founda la superbo Bilo d'Anciro, & poupla la Proubinço que prenguec lour noum & s'apelec Galatio.[4]

The sermon was not in French, but rather in the Romance language now called Occitan, which then served as the vernacular for most of southern France and was just one of the many non-French languages then spoken on French territory. From the perspective of the twentieth century, which saw so much bloodshed in the name of self-determination for minority language groups, one would think that France in 1789 stood poised on the brink of dissolution into half a dozen smaller states—or at the very least, that any program of French nation-building had very far to go indeed.

The Politicization of Language

In fact, it was only in the Revolution itself that French multilingualism acquired real political significance and became the principal sign of the nation's regional diversity (before that, as I argued in Chapter 2, provincial rights and privileges served this purpose). Although France's kings had promoted French as a learned language and tried to associate its glory with their own, they had given very little attention to the speech of their humbler subjects. François I's 1539 Edict of Villers-Cotterêts, which ordered that all judicial and administrative documents be written "in maternal French language," originally had more to do with reducing the role of Latin in public life than with propagating Parisian French in the provinces.[5] Occitan verse stayed in print to the end of the old regime, while Alsace sheltered a vibrant German publishing trade until the Revolution.[6] In fact, the idea that language could be altered by legislative fiat remained largely unimaginable before 1789. "There is no Power capable of reforming manners of speech consecrated by usage," wrote d'Espiard de la Borde in a typical statement.[7] Other authors made much the same point by recounting an anecdote about a Roman emperor who failed in his bid to legislate new words into Latin.[8] A few isolated works did call for the elimination of local dialects, but they had little resonance.[9] Most authors agreed with the view of sixteenth-century Lord Chancellor Michel de l'Hôpital: "The division of languages does not cause the separation of kingdoms."[10]

True, it did not take legislation to render the position of the local languages increasingly marginal in secular society. As early as 1567, the Gascon poet Pey de Garros had tellingly mourned "the damned cause of our despised language, [which] everyone is leaving and abandoning, and calling barbaric."[11] Local elites in the seventeenth and eighteenth centuries oriented themselves increasingly to the court and the capital, and therefore to the French language, and the process was abetted by the expansion of the royal administration and the periodical press. By 1789, French reigned unchallenged in nearly all print media, in courtrooms and administrations, in the drawing rooms of educated bourgeois and nobles, and throughout most French cities.[12] Men and women who might previously have read and taken pride in local literary productions now bought handbooks with titles like *Gasconisms Corrected,* which promised to eliminate all embarrassing traces of dialect from their speech.[13]

The use of the local languages in print, except in religious contexts, now served principally to mark a piece of writing as carnivalesque, capable of expressing meanings not permitted by the conventions of polite usage, without necessarily crossing into the territory of the obscene and forbidden.[14] Grammarians tended to define correct speech by the usage of the royal court. They and many others dismissed regional languages and French dialects as "patois," a derogatory term derived from *patte* (an animal's paw), signifying an earthy, unsophisticated, variable speech part way between animal grunts and true human speech.[15] Although some scholars were starting to devote serious attention to the local languages, glimpsing in them stable remnants of Europe's older, more primitive tongues, most educated people simply ignored them altogether, or treated them as corrupt versions of French itself.[16] In a 1790 speech, Mirabeau casually described France as "a nation of twenty-four million people speaking the same language."[17]

Even at the start of the Revolution, concern about linguistic diversity remained almost nil among France's secular elites. The grievance petitions drawn up for the Estates General in 1788 and 1789 barely mentioned the subject.[18] When a prominent article in the *Mercure national* in 1790 demanded a wholesale reform of language, the recommendations boiled down to nothing more than the removal of forms of aristocratic politeness from the language.[19] Consider also an early revolutionary pamphlet which called on the government to abolish all differences of language and accent among the citizenry. "What good will it have done to eliminate the divisions of the provinces," the author asked, "as long as one can say, from someone's first phrase, *this person is Provençal and that one is Picard?*"[20] The proposal sounds radical—but the pamphlet was actually a satire on the advanced revolutionaries' calls for social equality. It also proposed, *inter alia,* to nourish all children exclusively with a special "patriotic bouillon" so as to render them physically identical.

Starting in 1790, however, the way the French perceived and represented

their linguistic situation became a point of angry political contention.
Sermet's July 14 sermon itself had political importance, not simply because
he delivered it in patois—already an unusual step for a man of his stature—but because it then appeared in print in no fewer than four cities.[21]
The very typography, precisely the same used in French-language publications, gave graphic visual evidence that the language of Toulouse could express the same range of meanings and opinions as French itself, and so
perhaps deserved something closer to equal status. Sermet's confident, elegant Occitan prose, nourished by a deep familiarity with Toulouse's native
literary traditions, implicitly made the same point.[22]

The sermon in fact signaled the beginning of a remarkable efflorescence
of France's regional languages in 1790–92. The Department of Finistère
organized the translation and printing of numerous laws in Breton.[23]
A well-known antiquarian translated the Constitution of 1791 into
Provençal and had it published by the Imprimerie Nationale.[24] Jacobin
clubs in non-French speaking areas, while generally deliberating in French,
commonly organized public sessions at which members orally translated
new laws and newspapers into the local language.[25] In the south, they also
sponsored original speeches and subsidized publications in patois, to
which counter-revolutionary authors responded in kind.[26] Over two hundred printed Occitan songs, poems, and pamphlets appeared between 1788
and 1800.[27] In Alsace, a strong tradition of German-language publishing
continued, with thousands of items published, including a weekly newspaper aimed at "artisans and peasants."[28] In 1790, after complaints that some
citizens could not follow its debates, the National Assembly even voted to
translate all new laws and decrees into the various regional tongues. Following this moment of enthusiasm, however, it passed on to other business, and despite the zeal of volunteers hoping for lucrative translating as-
signments, the policy functioned only fitfully, and few printed translations
appeared.[29]

Even as these hundred flowers were blooming, however, other revolutionaries were beginning to see linguistic diversity—which they identified
above all with the peasantry—as a curse.[30] The key figure was abbé Henri
Grégoire, a Lorraine priest who first made a national reputation as champion of civil rights for Jews. As early as 1790 he blamed rural resistance to
the Revolution on ignorance of French, claiming that disruptive south-
western peasants were confusing the *décrets* (decrees) of the revolutionary
National Assembly with the old regime's *décrets de prise de corps* (arrest or-

DISCOURS

PROUNOUNÇAT le 14 Juillet 1790 , à l'houro de mietjon , en preſenço de la Municipalitat & de la Legiou de SANT-GINEST , à l'ouccaſiou de la Federatiou generalo ,

Pel R. P. HYACINTHO SERMET ,

Exproubinciai des Carmés Deſcauſſés , Predicairé ourdinari del Rey , de l'Academio Rouyalo de las Scienços , Inſcriptious & Belos-Lettroſ de Toulouſo, d'aquelo de Mourtalba , & Aumounié de la Legiou de Sant Gineſt , dins le Cantou de Bruyeros & le Diſtriĉt de Toulouſo.

Fratres , non ſumus filii ancillæ , ſed liberæ , quâ libertate Chriſtus nos liberavit. State & nolite iterum ſervitutis jugo contineri. Gal. c. 4 , v. 31 , & c. 5 , v. 1.

Frairés , nou ſen pas les mainatgés de l'eſclabo , mes de la fenno libro , & acos Jeſus Chriſt que nous a proucurat aquelo libertat : damourats dounc fermés , & bous tournets pas may bouta de noubel jouts le joug de l'eſclabatgé.

JAMAY nou debignayots , mous eſans , & brabés Camarados , à qui l'Apouſtoul Sent-Pol , le plus grand des Predicairés

A

Figure 15. Antoine-Hyacinthe Sermet, a noted cleric from Toulouse, delivered his speech celebrating the Festival of the Federation in Occitan, and had it printed in the same language. The typeface and layout are exactly the same as in French-language publications of the period. Title page from his *Discours prounounçat le 14 juillet, 1790* (Toulouse, 1790).

ders). The same year he sent out to a wide audience a questionnaire "concerning *patois* and the customs of the people of the countryside." As his revolutionary career flourished, he made regular calls for the nation's linguistic unification and found considerable support for his ideas. Legislative reports, pamphlets, and newspaper articles alike denounced linguistic diversity as a barrier to social equality, contrasted the success of French abroad to its failure at home, and labeled the translation of laws cumbersome and unreliable.[31]

By 1794, the Jacobins had begun an official campaign to eradicate patois entirely and make the French language uniform throughout the Republic (although they recognized the continuing short-term need for translators).[32] Bertrand Barère put the matter starkly in a legislative report that demanded the establishment of French-language schools in four peripheral areas of the Republic: Brittany, Alsace, the Basque Country, and Corsica. Directing his ire at their "foreign" idioms, he let loose his usual overboiled rhetoric, notably in the passage quoted at the start of this chapter.[33] Four months later, Grégoire submitted a much more detailed report that targeted not merely peripheral languages, but Occitan and northern French dialects as well.[34] In its pages, what had been material for satire, now became grist for policy. "We no longer have provinces, but we have thirty *patois* which recall their names," Grégoire proclaimed. He also repeated the old anecdote about the Roman emperor who tried to legislate on language but, with aplomb, turned it on its head: "A tyrant of Rome once wished to introduce a new word; he failed, because the legislation of languages was always democratic."[35] The Convention instituted French-language requirements for promotion to officer grades in the armies, and a ban on all non-French languages in judicial documents.[36] In Alsace and in Catalan-speaking Roussillon, something of a limited "linguistic terror" took place, with non-French publications and commercial signs suppressed, non-French-speaking personnel dismissed, and plans drawn up for forcible transfers of population.[37] A visiting *conventionnel* in Strasbourg proposed a horrific solution for gallicizing Alsace: to guillotine a quarter of the population and expel all others who had not actively participated in the Revolution.[38]

Grégoire and a few others held out as an ultimate goal not merely the diffusion of French through France, but the transformation of French itself into a perfectly pure, clear, and rational tongue, purged of aristocratic corruptions and of all grammatical and lexical irregularities and confusions.

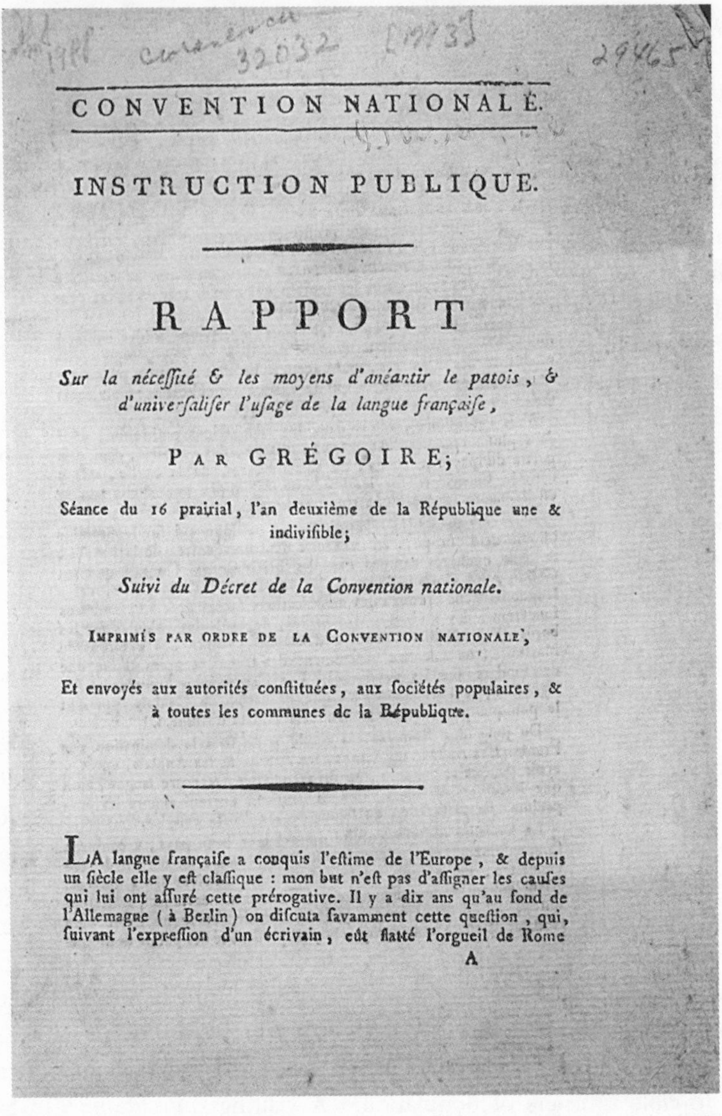

CONVENTION NATIONALE.

INSTRUCTION PUBLIQUE.

RAPPORT

Sur la néceſſité & les moyens d'anéantir le patois, & d'univerſaliſer l'uſage de la langue françaiſe,

PAR GRÉGOIRE;

Séance du 16 prairial, l'an deuxième de la République une & indiviſible;

Suivi du Décret de la Convention nationale.

IMPRIMÉS PAR ORDRE DE LA CONVENTION NATIONALE,

Et envoyés aux autorités conſtituées, aux ſociétés populaires, & à toutes les communes de la République.

LA langue françaiſe a conquis l'eſtime de l'Europe, & depuis un ſiècle elle y eſt claſſique : mon but n'eſt pas d'aſſigner les cauſes qui lui ont aſſuré cette prérogative. Il y a dix ans qu'au fond de l'Allemagne (à Berlin) on diſcuta ſavamment cette queſtion, qui, ſuivant l'expreſſion d'un écrivain, eût flatté l'orgueil de Rome

A

Figure 16. The title page from Henri Grégoire, *Rapport sur la nécessité et les moyens d'anéantir le patois* (Report on the Necessity and Means for Annihilating Patois), Paris, 1794: his proposal for eradicating local languages and making French the sole and uniform language of France.

This perfect language could then spread, they suggested, to all the world. They hoped that its development would eliminate misunderstandings and "abuses of words," which they presented as the root causes of all conflict and disharmony in the terrestrial sphere. It was a dream which recalled the ancient religious desire to overcome the legacy of the Tower of Babel; it also testified to the process of "disenchantment" discussed in Chapter 1. For now the perfect language would come from nature, not God, and would belong to the natural world alone.[39]

The idea was dazzling. In practice, though, even the radicals devoted most of their effort to the problem of spreading the French language—the one spoken and written by Parisian elites—to the rest of the Republic. Barère, the hardheaded and opportunistic Terrorist, even claimed that most language abuses had *already* disappeared, along with their aristocratic authors.[40] Grégoire himself spent most of his report justifying the destruction of patois, and only in the last few pages turned to the "vast project . . . of revolutionizing language."[41] His program was nationalist first, universalist second.

In any case, even the relatively limited nationalist program of uniformization never had a real chance for success. Long before a single language teacher had arrived in Brittany or Alsace, the Ninth of Thermidor had come, and with it the end of this and many other radical dreams. While subsequent regimes remained cognizant of language differences, until the late nineteenth century they mostly gave up on any attempt to eliminate the problem. It would take the Third Republic, endowed with far greater material resources and a far greater degree of political stability than the First, to start putting Grégoire's program into action. And even the Third Republic remained tolerant of patois insofar as it constituted part of a region's folklore and did not threaten national unity.[42]

The Ear of the Listener

To modern readers, this politicization of language during the French Revolution has generally seemed an obvious and inevitable phenomenon, one that arose naturally when the revolutionaries tried to bring democracy to a multilingual country.[43] But was the problem so obvious to contemporaries? Consider the enormous differences of opinion on the very *extent* of the problem. In 1792, the deputy Dentzel estimated that three million people, out of a population of 28 million, could not speak French. Grégoire himself variously put the figure at eight million and six million, and claimed that scarcely three million spoke French itself properly.[44] His report to the Convention enumerated thirty separate patois ripe for eradication. Moreover, he treated French dialects and the non-Indo-European Basque as equal barriers to the progress of the Revolution.[45] In contrast, Barère echoed the common old regime view that northern and southern patois amounted simply to variations on French, and saw a problem only in four relatively small peripheral regions.[46] Other prominent revolutionaries, such as Mirabeau, remained oblivious to the language problem altogether. Seeming to relegate the matter to the past, Saint-Just speculated in the spring of 1794 that if old regime feudalism had continued for longer, "soon the French would no longer have spoken the same language."[47]

Consider also Grégoire's earliest revolutionary remarks on the subject, when he told the Constituent Assembly, in reference to the southwestern riots, that "the municipal authorities in the areas where these troubles are taking place think that they are caused first of all by ignorance of the [French] language."[48] In fact the municipal authorities thought nothing of the sort. Nor did the other deputies charged with investigating the riots, who tended to blame counter-revolutionary agitators, or peasant brigands, rather than any confusion over the meaning of *décret*. Nor have subsequent historians, who have rather highlighted such factors as long-standing peasant hostility to seigneurialism and the hopes raised when the Assembly proclaimed the end of the feudal regime on August 4, 1789. At best, linguistic confusion has merited a footnote in their works.[49]

Two recent studies support the views of those who failed to see major language barriers in France. One shows that French emigrants to Québec—who came primarily from a wide swathe of dialect-speaking western France—adapted to the standard French of the colony quickly and without difficulty.[50] The other concludes that litigants and defendants in old regime Languedoc do not seem to have been seriously inconvenienced by linguistic differences.[51] In fact, very few eighteenth-century sources from outside the peripheral regions of Brittany, Flanders, Alsace, Savoy, Corsica, the Basque Country, and Roussillon mention linguistic difference at all, or suggest that speakers of French or Occitan dialects had trouble understanding the decrees and *monitoires* read out to them in church. Differences of language may have been obvious, but the extent to which they posed problems of mutual comprehension is much less so. It is no coincidence that Grégoire's revolutionary writings are the most often-cited evidence for the existence of linguistic barriers in France in the eighteenth century, outside of the periphery. He was one of the very few observers who paid more than passing attention to them.[52]

On one level, this confusion as to the very existence of difficulties caused by multilingualism seems somewhat absurd—surely the French knew if they understood each other. Yet as sociolinguists have long recognized, when it comes to the extent that closely related languages (like French and Occitan) differ from one another, perceptions not only vary enormously, but easily get tangled up with politics. The extent to which people succeed in communicating with each other always depends on the subject discussed, and on a host of contingent social and psychological factors. One person's slang or patois is another's oppressed minority language, as in the case of Ebonics, or Black English, whose very existence has been the subject of heated political debate in the United States.[53] The ability to understand a limited range of orders (as in the army) or to complete a transaction in the marketplace is not the same as the ability to engage in a lengthy conversation about religion or politics. So it should not be surprising that while Grégoire's old regime predecessors—and even his revolutionary colleague Barère—perceived only relatively minor differences at the periphery of the country, he himself could see massive and paralyzing heterogeneity. Language differences are real, but their extent, and the extent to which they matter, lie at least partly in the ear of the listener.

In this connection, it is worth remarking that the representation of early modern France as a nation of vast and overpowering linguistic diversity has been widely promoted, largely because it has nicely served two very different ideological agendas. Republicans and educational reformers have promoted it because it suggests that French national unity is fragile, necessitating a vigorous program of republican centralization. Modern regional militants have promoted it as well, because it helps them to equate centralization with imperialism and to distinguish their own culture as sharply as possible from that of Paris.[54] Particularly in the French and Occitan dialect areas, therefore, it is simply not correct to say that the French revolutionaries confronted an obvious, inevitable "language problem." Rather, a relatively small number of them simultaneously invented this problem and kindled a desire to solve it. Furthermore, they proposed solving it in radically different ways. While Sermet and many others advocated translating revolutionary ideas into the languages of the people, Grégoire and his allies insisted on teaching the people a new language: standard French.

The question remains, however, *why* the revolutionaries invented this problem—why they seized on language as the ultimate sign of national disunity when this issue had previously received such scant political attention. It is an important question, not only for understanding this particular historical moment, but also for making sense of the powerful republican vision of the French nation that was born out of the Revolution. Certainly up until World War I, most of those who subscribed to the republican vision of the nation interpreted the language question much in the way Grégoire had done: as a sign of excessive heterogeneity and backwardness requiring civilizing and standardizing instruction from republican schoolmasters and officials. The vision lay behind much of the educational policy of the Third Republic, which explicitly attempted to universalize the use of French and to confine regional languages to the domain of folklore. It has even colored some of the best scholarship on French nation-building—notably Eugen Weber's *Peasants into Frenchmen,* which opens with a stark tableau of the isolation, backwardness, and diversity of the French countryside before 1870 (Weber entitled his first chapter, with insufficient irony, "A Country of Savages").[55] Recent scholarship has done much to uncover the ideological roots of this vision, but it has done much less to explore where the vision came from in the first place.[56]

Previous interpretations of the revolutionary initiatives with regard to the language, to the extent they have gone beyond the notion that the Revolution simply tried to solve an obvious problem, have generally highlighted either the heritage of the Enlightenment or the experience of the radical revolution itself. For instance, it has been argued that Grégoire and his correspondents were representatives of a cosmopolitan, urban, and ultimately imperial Enlightenment who sought in essence to colonize and domesticate a peasantry they perceived as alien, primitive, and incapable of abstract reasoning.[57] It has also been suggested that these revolutionaries were driven principally by their theoretical concerns about misunderstanding and "abuse of words," and the utopian idea of creating a perfect language.[58]

This complex Enlightenment background certainly has great importance for understanding the language initiatives, but any interpretation of the revolutionary initiatives that refers solely to the Enlightenment runs up against one, simple, frustrating question. Why, if the Enlightenment taught the French to see patois as primitive and unable to handle complex political discussions, did the years 1790–92 see such important efforts to translate documents into patois and to use the local languages to educate the people in revolutionary politics? Hyacinthe Sermet was no less a product of the provincial Enlightenment than Grégoire, yet he saw no trouble with expressing complex political arguments in the Toulouse dialect. The Jacobin clubs to which Grégoire sent his questionnaire were much the same institutions which promoted the flowering of regional tongues during the early Revolution. Indeed, while few of Grégoire's correspondents questioned the ultimate desirablity of linguistic uniformity, many, as they reported back to him, instinctively used patois in their efforts to persuade peasants to support the Revolution. Some contributors to the revolutionary debate on language even suggested standardizing the regional languages so as to make them more effective tools of political instruction.[59]

Interpretations which highlight the experience of the radical revolution, meanwhile, fail to explain *either* this patois-friendly phase of revolutionary language politics *or* the wide disagreements among proponents of linguistic uniformity.[60] To be sure, the demand for linguistic uniformity fit in well with the general Jacobin struggle against social and cultural heterogeneity, as well as the radical republican efforts to have all male citizens participate in government.[61] Grégoire, by far the most important figure in the story, described mastery of French as a key element of full republican citizenship and presented linguistic unification as a weapon against the malign forces of feudalism and federalism (the latter a reference to revolts against the Jacobin government).[62] Yet whatever additional impetus the radical revolution provided, there is also the inconvenient fact that Grégoire himself, at least, had already come to his views on language *before* the Revolution, in a prize-winning *Essay on the Physical, Moral and Political Regeneration of the Jews*, which called forthrightly for the "annihilation of patois."[63] Talleyrand similarly advocated linguistic uniformity as early as 1790, well before the Jacobins had dreamed of a new calendar, new forms of dress, or a Cult of the Supreme Being.[64] However well it *fit in* with the agenda of the radical revolution, the politicization of language did not derive *from* the radical revolution.

The revolutionary language initiatives might also be put in the context of long-term social and economic developments of the sort discussed by Gellner and Anderson in their influential theories of nationalism.[65] However, even leaving aside the fact that the late-eighteenth-century French countryside had not yet experienced widespread industrialism (a key part of Gellner's theory), and that most patois-speaking peasants were poor and illiterate (Anderson's theory puts great emphasis on the expanding market for books), such long-term explanations offer little help in understanding why the issue erupted into politics so abruptly in 1789–90, and what precipitated the subsequent variety of attitudes towards multilingualism. In short, to understand the problem fully, we need to move into a very different historical territory.

"L'Empire des Prêtres"

Some time in late 1790 or early 1791, the Society of the Friends of the Constitution of Albi, in Languedoc, published a twenty-seven-page speech in the local dialect delivered by a wool merchant named Salivas to the "good people of the countryside."[66] The title gave little clue to the content, and indeed the first few lines amounted to standard early revolutionary boilerplate. Soon, however, Salivas's principal purpose became clear. Not only did the Revolution pose no threat to the Catholic religion, he argued; it represented the fulfillment of Catholic prayers. Indeed, it meant something close to the literal coming of the Millennium. As he made this hyperbolic point, his literary style, which had begun as a fairly literal rendering into Occitan of the rhetoric of the National Assembly, quickly strayed into a different, older mode:

> It is now that the reign of God will flourish in this Kingdom . . . now, in this age of miracles . . . France will be the first [country] to spread and propagate the law of our Lord . . . and thus the desire for our Redemption will be fulfilled; the name of the Lord, of God Almighty, will spread and be hallowed first throughout Europe, and from here will reach to all parts of the universe . . . God has heard our oath, it is written in the book of life, it is pleasing to Heaven and has brought joy to all the martyrs crushed by the former despotism, the former tyranny.[67]

Salivas also contrasted the "purity of the Gospel" to the corruption of the Catholic clergy in France. He insisted that among all the tasks faced by the Revolution, none ranked higher than putting an end to the church's myriad "abuses." Soon, however, the light of reason would prevail, and then "France will not be better compared than to that Zion triumphant, that heavenly Zion of which the Scripture speaks."[68]

In publishing this unlikely attempt to drape the mantle of Hebrew prophets over the shoulders of revolutionary Liberty, the club of Albi did not wish to indulge the religious fantasies of an addled merchant, but rather to address a pressing political problem. In 1790, the National Assembly had unveiled a plan for the greatest reform ever undertaken in the history of French Catholicism, the Civil Constitution of the Clergy. From now on, it decreed, the people (including non-Catholics) would elect priests and bishops; clerics would become, in effect, civil servants under the control of the state. This action stirred more resistance than any previously taken by the revolutionary authorities, and in response, the Assembly insisted that priests take an oath of loyalty to the new regime (including the Civil Constitution) or face dismissal. The breach widened, and both sides in the dispute resorted massively to the newspaper and pamphlet press to win adherents.[69]

In the overall corpus of revolutionary publications, the dispute over the Civil Constitution amounts to only one large body of texts. In the more limited corpus of publications in the local languages, however—both revolutionary and counter-revolutionary—it represents by far the single largest issue under discussion.[70] A concern for the religious future of France suffused these texts. They alternately spoke of the Revolution as the coming of Christ or the Antichrist. They alternately praised the priests as faithful shepherds of their flocks or damned them as iniquitous monsters (in the words of one Montpellier pamphleteer, the clergy was a "great beast with a red head, purple claws, all the rest a black body, and motley fur.")[71] Furthermore, they did not hesitate to confront the ultimate fear raised by the dispute in the minds of uneasy believers: its consequences for their personal salvation.[72] While most opinions came from the Occitan-speaking areas of France, the pattern seems to have held for the other non-French-speaking areas. The most substantial of the rare Flemish texts published in revolutionary France is a pastoral letter sent by a "constitutional" bishop to assure his parishioners of the "complete conformity between Catholic belief and the Civil Constitution."[73] A similar letter from the bishop of Finistère makes up one of the two longer pieces of revolutionary rhetoric translated into Breton, and the two known Breton addresses drawn up by Jacobin clubs focused on the issue as well.[74] In Alsace, a German-language newspaper came out that dealt exclusively with the religious issue.[75]

Did the non-French texts dwell so heavily on the Civil Constitution simply because it dominated political discussion at the time the Revolution was extending toleration to the regional languages?[76] The chronological and geographical patterns of revolutionary publishing in Occitan suggest a much more fundamental importance for religious issues in the revolutionary engagement with linguistic diversity. To begin with, of the 140-odd Occitan works published between 1789 and 1794, over half appeared in 1790–91. The majority of these texts dealt principally with the Civil Constitution (including Sermet's July 14 sermon), and nearly all mentioned it in some way.[77] In 1789, by contrast, there had been only 19 publications, mostly "burlesque" verses and addresses typical of the pre-revolutionary role set aside for patois. In 1792 the figure fell to 20, in 1793 to 13, and in 1794 to just 10.[78] For the period of the Terror, the anti-patois policies of Barère and Grégoire can plausibly take the blame for the decline, but throughout 1792, the successive governments in Paris remained committed to a policy of translation. In 1792, however, other conflicts eclipsed the disputes over the Civil Constitution. As for the geography of publication, two French cities in 1789 still had strong traditions of Occitan publishing: Toulouse and Marseilles.[79] In the Revolution, it was Toulouse—where only a minority of priests accepted the Civil Constitution, and a bitter conflict ensued—which by itself produced forty percent of all Occitan texts, including the only (unsuccessful) attempt to launch a newspaper in the language. Marseilles, where most priests acceded to the new clerical regime, produced less than half that number.[80]

Even after 1790–91, religion remained the most important single theme in the diminishing number of non-French-language publications. The most substantive of the Occitan texts from 1794 were devoted to the Cult of Reason, including one speech published at the behest of a Jacobin club.[81] The second substantial piece of revolutionary rhetoric translated into Breton was Robespierre's report of 18 Floréal on the Cult of the Supreme Being and national festivals. In Finistère, the departmental authorities ordered the revolutionary Tribunal to publish its sentences in Breton, but in only one case does the court actually seem to have done so: the death sentence of a "refractory" priest.[82] In sum, patois was a language of choice for addressing the peasantry on religious issues—even when the purpose was to attack or supplant religion itself.

The regional-language texts that dealt with religion followed its literary models as well. On the laws and decrees translated into Breton during the Revolution, one specialist has commented: "The translation is not, as I was going to say, into kitchen Breton—that would be as false as it is unfair, for unfortunately kitchen Breton is better—but rather into Church Breton. It seems to me on the level of the more successful [Breton] catechisms."[83] The most thorough expert in Provençal writings from the period also points to the prevalence of "the form of the sermon, but secularized."[84] Among the titles of the Occitan texts, words like *Epistle, Hymn, Homily, Exaudiat, Credo,* and *Profession of Faith* were considerably more prevalent than in the French-language equivalents.[85] Blatant biblical language found its way into many texts unconcerned with religious conflict, such as a set of plaintive 1790 verses which urged the Virgin Mary and the Holy Ghost to aid the representatives of the nation, and a "Christmas Carol of the Sans-Culottes" sung in Marseilles in 1792.[86]

Religion thus permeated publications in the local languages. But what of the other ways in which the Revolution engaged with linguistic issues? Consider the background and concerns of those revolutionaries most active in this area, starting with the most important one, Henri Grégoire. Not only was Grégoire a priest; unlike many other revolutionary priests, he never wore the cassock lightly and never abjured his calling. He had been known before 1789 as the very model of the enlightened *curé,* and during the Terror he insisted on attending the Convention in clerical garb, at real risk to his life.[87] Moreover, Grégoire consistently defended his linguistic initiatives in religious as well as political terms. His first systematic discussion of patois, in his 1789 essay on the Jews, mentioned a "purified knowledge of religion" as one reason to impose linguistic uniformity.[88] The questionnaire on patois that he sent out in 1790 actually gave precedence to religion over politics in its crucial leading question ("What would be the religious and political importance of entirely destroying this patois?")[89] This document itself, with its attention not only to the language but to the morals of the peasantry, had an obvious clerical model: the questionnaires used in the so-called pastoral visits carried out by Tridentine bishops to monitor the health of the church in their dioceses.[90]

Most of Grégoire's colleagues in the legislature who helped formulate language policies admittedly lacked this sort of clerical pedigree (although Talleyrand, the least pious of priests, did write one important report). But the same is not true of the more numerous revolutionaries engaged with the issue in the provinces. Here the model is Sermet, who throughout the Revolution defended a liberal, enlightened Catholicism and, like Grégoire, never abjured his calling (indeed the two men became fast friends).[91] Sermet pioneered the idea of preaching in patois to propagate the gospel of Revolution, and many other priests followed his example. In the Breton village of Plouénour-Trez, the local *curé* preached in Breton and translated the Constitution of 1791 into this language.[92] In Flanders, priests took the lead in translating the Declaration of the Rights of Man and also published a short-lived Flemish-language newspaper.[93] In Perpignan in 1791, the bishop prevented the revolutionary abbé Cambon from preaching, so Cambon instead founded a "patriotic school" and spent every evening and holiday lecturing in Catalan on the decrees of the Assembly, and more broadly on "the double duty of Christian and citizen."[94] Other priests enthusiastic about the Revolution set themselves up as their parishioners' instructors in French. The idea of priests as language instructors runs through the writings of Grégoire's correspondents, and fully a third of them came from the clergy.[95]

Yet despite all the efforts of these patriotic clerics, in the canons of revolutionary demonology the figure of the patois-speaking priest most often signified something very different: hideous reaction. Despite the widespread use of patois by Jacobin clubs and priests favorable to the Revolution, the fear that counter-revolutionaries might somehow make occult use of patois to turn ignorant peasants against the Revolution gnawed powerfully at revolutionary officials. A certain Brassard, for example, offering his services to the Justice Ministry as a translator in 1792, warned that while the local priests had done much to translate the decrees of the Assembly, they had done so for the worst of reasons: "They had mutilated or envenomed the terms, and had thus managed to make our Constitution seem odious not only to the people in our countryside, but also to our neighbors, the Belgians and Flemings."[96] Many of Grégoire's correspondents similarly raised the specter of patois-speaking priests misleading their flocks.[97] The ex-Capuchin (and future Terrorist) François Chabot, who himself tried to conduct patois classes for the peasantry, warned that "the members of the parish tremble at the sight of a pastor, who appears in their eyes like the Sultan of Constantinople."[98]

It was Barère who managed best (as in his speeches on England) to distill a general fear of conspiracy into an elixir of concentrated hyperbole. In his report to the Convention on language, the deputy from the Pyrenees excoriated German and Italian dialects because these were the languages of the foreign enemy. He cast Breton and Basque beyond the pale, however, largely because of the use priests made of them. "It is with this barbaric instrument of their superstitious thoughts [Breton] that the priests and the intriguers hold [the people] under their sway, direct their consciences and prevent citizens from knowing the laws and loving the Republic."[99] Only with the teaching of French, he insisted, would the "empire des prêtres" (dominion of the priests) come to an end.[100]

The Clerical Precedents

To get an inkling as to *why* the "dominion of the priests" weighed so heavily in the Revolution's linguistic initiatives, one can do no better than to read a response to Grégoire's questionnaire sent by the Jacobin club of Auch, in Gascony. The anonymous author reported that nearly everyone in the area *spoke* Gascon in preference to French. However, he continued, "no one writes in patois, unless it is some *curé* or some missionary monk." He mentioned that the peasants did not know of the seventeenth-century Gascon poet Jean-Géraud d'Astros, nor, curiously, could the literate ones even manage to decipher his verses. They could, however, make out the Gascon hymns with which Capuchin missionaries had "flooded" the countryside. "Our peasants," he concluded, "have less trouble reading in their patois everything which maintains their rusticity and their false ideas on religion."[101]

Behind these brief and dismissive remarks lie two centuries of history which explain a great deal about the linguistic policies of the French Revolution. It is true that patois stirred relatively little concern in *secular* circles in France before the Revolution. The same was not true, however, of religious circles. In this period, as part of the great enterprise of evangelization undertaken under the auspices of the Catholic Reformation, French priests devoted enormous time and energy to learning the many languages of France, speaking them, cataloguing them, and above all using them to spread the word of God. Far more than the still-hesitant efforts of a handful of late eighteenth-century *savants*, it was this long-standing clerical engagement with the languages of the common people which, for the first time in France, seriously raised the questions of whether linguistic uniformity could be achieved in a modern state, what it would take to achieve it, and whether or not this achievement was desirable.

The involvement of the clergy stemmed from an obvious dilemma, took inspiration from a prominent model, and followed well-established examples. The dilemma lay in the fact that whereas approximate, rough-and-ready translations between French and the local languages might suffice for many ordinary transactions (including most forms of interaction with the state), they were woefully inadequate when it came to convincing peo-

ple of sacred truths and of the need to reform their most intimate behavior.[102] The model was that of the Apostles, in Acts, chapter II: "And they
were all filled with the Holy Ghost, and began to speak with other tongues,
as the Spirit gave them utterance . . . When this was noised abroad, the
multitude came together, and were confounded, because that every man
heard them speak in his own language." As for the examples, at least since
late antiquity, the demands of Christian evangelization had provided the
most important spur for the study and systematization of non-written
tongues.[103] From the age of European exploration to the present day, Christian missionaries have done the most to study and systematize such languages in the Americas, Africa, and Asia, and to compose their first written
texts: translations of the Scriptures.[104] The same Jesuit Order which took
the lead in studying supposedly primitive dialects in France was, at the
same time, doing much the same work in relation to the Amerindian languages of New France.[105]

In France itself, the work began in earnest in the late sixteenth century,
with Jesuits like Julien Maunoir in Brittany. He and his colleagues had little
or no interest in language for its own sake: they wanted to save souls. Unlike their contemporaries at court, however, they could not afford to ignore
linguistic differences. Maunoir himself spoke Breton fluently and insisted
on the same skills from his missionaries.[106] Similar attitudes prevailed in
the south. A bishop of Grasse wrote of his crusading predecessor, Antoine
Godeau, that "if God had given him the choice of the gift of miracles or the
Provençal language, he would have chosen to speak this language well, so
as to instruct his people more faithfully."[107] In the Vivarais, another bishop
asked his clergy, "If you don't know patois, what have you come here for,
fools that you are?"[108]

The missionaries and crusading bishops not only spoke the local languages, they also influenced them in important ways. To begin with, they
wrote in them and worked to replace many traditional peasant composi-
tions with their own. Maunoir composed scores of hymns in Breton, which
he urged the peasantry to sing in place of their old profane songs, and the
southern clergy did likewise.[109] Passion plays, largely composed by Jesuits,
also proliferated in several dialects, as did religious poetry and funeral orations.[110] Most important, a profusion of dialectal catechisms appeared in
the seventeenth century.[111] The efforts of the reforming clergy in this domain did, however, have one important limit: the local priests rather than
the peasants themselves were to read these works and then, as spiritual in-

tercessors and cultural intermediaries, transmit the words orally to their flocks.[112]

Nonetheless, thanks to these efforts, most written texts in the local languages between 1600 and 1789, both manuscript and printed, were religious in nature.[113] Indeed, if religious observance began to decline in French culture as a whole in the eighteenth century, the same cannot be said of the remnants of those local cultures tied to non-French languages.[114] If anything, these non-French cultures grew *more* exclusively religious in character as the educated classes abandoned the local tongues, leaving great Occitan baroque poets such as Pèire Godolin and Guillaume Ader without audiences or secular successors. When Grégoire asked his correspondents in 1790 to list the principal uses of patois and any examples they knew of patois publications, again and again the same responses came back to him: carols and hymns, books of devotions, reports on preaching and catechizing, and references to the clerical compilers of dictionaries and grammars.[115]

The reforming clergy also influenced the development of the local dialects in another way. Even priests from humble backgrounds undertook their formal education in French and Latin and lost almost all contact with local dialects once they entered clerical milieus.[116] Maunoir tellingly lamented that even his native-Breton missionaries had "forgotten part of the vocabulary of the Breton idiom, with the result that in their Catechisms and sermons they use many French words with Breton endings, and most of their listeners do not understand."[117] Priests who came from French-speaking areas often had not the slightest inkling of their parishioners' tongues. To carry out the program of evangelization, they needed instruction in the local languages based on a formal knowledge of their grammar and vocabulary. The seventeenth and eighteenth centuries thus saw the large-scale publication, for the first time, of French-Languedocien, French-Provençal, and French-Breton dictionaries and grammars, ranging from small, loosely bound affairs of a hundred pages to imposing, multivolume folio sets.[118] Given the great variation in dialects, the project entailed effectively devising *standard* versions of the local languages, the first ever attempted. Not surprisingly, later generations have looked back to these works as early examples of regionalism, but it was the demands of the clergy that usually generated them. Fully six of the seven Breton works were written explicitly for the use of the clergy, including one by Maunoir, a native French-speaker sometimes called the father of modern Breton.[119]

Did these various clerical projects have any effect on actual speech patterns? Certainly the priests had no ambition to impose a new "standard" Breton or Gascon on their flocks. Yet to the extent that the local languages developed a new lexicon in the seventeenth and eighteenth centuries, it was not the lexicon of Enlightenment or of secular politics, but rather of Tridentine Catholicism. The French-Breton and French-Occitan dictionaries proposed translations for such terms as *grace* and *hérésie* (rendered in Breton as *Huguenaudage,* that is, Huguenotism), even *Jansénisme* (most often listed as a synonym for *hérésie*), and then gave detailed definitions to help parish priests explain the new words.[120] Evidence about actual speech patterns is sparse, but Yves Castan has tantalizingly suggested that litigants in Languedoc tended to use Occitan religious vocabulary to translate French legal terms. As already noted, Breton and Occitan specialists have demonstrated the persistence of religious terminology in revolutionary publications.[121]

In short, even as the secular status of the local languages was falling precipitously, the clergy, for its own evangelical reasons, was preserving for them a measure of dignity. The words of the Toulouse priest quoted at the start of this chapter make the point movingly.[122] The efforts of teaching, catechizing, and preaching that the priest referred to, and the linguistic knowledge that went into producing the catechism itself, show clearly that the non-French-speaking areas of France had not been lingering in some linguistic state of nature from which the revolutionaries would work to remove them after 1789. The Catholic Church had already made strong attempts to influence linguistic practices.

Catholics and Protestants

Overall, this story offers insight into at least part of the revolutionary engagement with the local languages. In 1789–90, adherents of the Revolution in the French provinces found themselves confronted with an awesome and difficult task: helping the peasant masses become good citizens of a democratic polity. The only previous enterprise that had much relevance was the Catholic Reformation's attempt to turn the ancestors of those same peasants into good Catholics. In both cases, the same thing was at stake: the conversion of hearts and minds. So it is hardly surprising that the revolutionaries, and particularly those trained as clergymen themselves, took the Church's earlier efforts as a sort of template for their own.

In the provinces, revolutionary leaders eagerly launched their own campaigns of catechizing, sermonizing, hectoring, and instructing, particularly in their weekly "popular sessions" held mostly on Sundays and often led by priests, but also on special occasions such as that of July 14, when Sermet delivered his sermon.[123] From their clerical predecessors they took the notion that "no tongue reaches further into the heart" than the maternal, and so they carried out the campaigns in patois, not in French.

The story also suggests one reason why, among all the prominent revolutionaries, the one who cared most about language, and saw the unfortunate effects of language difference everywhere at work, was Henri Grégoire. For not only did he grow up in rural Lorraine speaking a distinct dialect of French; as a vicar and parish priest in Lorraine villages from 1776 to 1789, he himself ministered to peasants who spoke the dialect exclusively. Furthermore, Grégoire saw himself as a paradigmatic "bon curé," bringing what he later called "enlightened piety" to his flocks. Among other things, he established a library for their use. He therefore directly confronted the problem of how to communicate complex ideas to peasants.[124]

Yet Grégoire, unlike Sermet and many others, did not believe the local languages were suited for this sort of communication. He wished to make the peasants speak standard French, and it was his view which became the official policy of the First Republic and subsequent regimes. Why? Part of the answer lies in a quirk of the priest's biography—but it is a quirk that illuminates the overall course of the revolutionary policies in a surprising manner.

Grégoire lived in Lorraine, in eastern France, and in the 1780s this region had two intellectual poles: Paris, and also, perhaps even more important, Strasbourg, the capital of neighboring Alsace. A vibrant, bilingual city, still retaining something of the glow generated by its glorious role in the German Renaissance and Reformation, Strasbourg had an active circle of bilingual men of letters, drawn particularly from the venerable university and the clergy. They gathered in such settings as the informal "table society" of Johann Daniel Saltzmann (where Goethe first met Herder), the more ambitious French-language Société des Philanthropes, and the German-speaking Gesellschaft zur Ausbildung der Deutschen Sprache (Society for the Promotion of the German Language), which helped nurture early German Romanticism.[125] The Société des Philanthropes played what one biographer calls "an essential role in Grégoire's intellectual development."[126] The young priest also developed a close friendship with two sons of a professor at Strasbourg's German Gymnasium: Jeremias-Jakob and Johann-Friedrich Oberlin. Jeremias-Jakob, a polymathic philosopher, philologist, and classicist, was one of the first scholars to give serious study to regional languages, notably in a 1775 study entitled *Essai sur le patois lorrain.*[127] Grégoire wrote Jeremias in 1798 of his own inquiry into patois: "It was you who once gave me the idea by your writings."[128]

Just as important was Grégoire's relation with Johann-Friedrich, the famous "enlightened pastor" for whom Oberlin College is named. In his rural Lorraine parish of Waldersbach, this Oberlin worked with maniacal energy to advance education, improve roads, modernize farming techniques, and develop commerce. Significantly, he also struggled to eradicate the local patois, which he barely understood. According to one historian, he "succeeded, if not in eradicating it, at least in relegating it to the interior of the family and substituting French as the public and official language."[129] Grégoire, ten years Oberlin's junior, fell entirely under the charismatic pastor's spell and called his conduct "a lesson and a reproach to many Catholic priests." In 1794, he would persuade the Convention to commend Oberlin for his "contributions to the universalization of the French language."[130] In sum, Grégoire's attitude towards patois, so different from that of most Catholic clergy, derived in large part from these two men.[131]

The Oberlins' attitude towards common speech, in turn, stemmed above all from their Protestant heritage. During the Reformation, Protestant clerics, like their Catholic counterparts, had embarked on ambitious programs of evangelizing the peasantry. Yet they quickly took a different approach to language differences, because of their insistence that the faithful read the Scriptures for themselves. While Catholic priests could render the message of the Gospel orally into the hundreds of distinct dialects that existed at the time, producing printed texts in each dialect was clearly impossible, in the first place because of the limitations of the technology, and also because faulty translations could conceivably produce theological error. The Protestants therefore strove for amalgamation and uniformization: the production of a single, standard translation that could appeal to as broad a population as possible, followed by education to bring groups initially incapable of comprehending it into the charmed circle. Protestants also preferred to standardize only the speech of the princes who stood at the head of the new churches. For instance, the High German of Luther's Saxony became the basis for the standard form of the language.[132] When practical difficulties proved too great, however, they could also opt for producing printed, standardized versions of widely spoken minority languages such as Welsh. Significantly, the two known revolutionary-era proposals for raising at least some regional languages to the level of standard languages, equal to French, came from Protestants: Jeremias-Jakob Oberlin, and the Montauban agriculturist Antoine Gautier-Sauzin.[133]

The case of Protestant Great Britain, with its large non-English-speaking populations in Wales, Ireland, and Highland Scotland, provides a particularly useful comparison with France. Draconian legislation on language in these areas dates from long before the late eighteenth century—from the early years of the Reformation, when Henry VIII's ministers feared that the Celtic lands would provide a refuge for Catholicism.[134] Thus the 1536 Act of Union between England and Wales commanded Welsh justices and sheriffs to use only English in their proceedings. A year later, a law for Ireland stated in its preamble that "There is nothing which doth more conteyne and keep many of [the King's] Subjects of the said Land in a certain savage and wilde kind and manner of living, than the diversitie that is betwixt them in Tongue, Language, Order and Habit."[135] The first Welsh religious primer appeared in 1547, but in Ireland and Scotland it was only after attempts to impose English had failed miserably that efforts were made to establish standard versions of Irish and Scots Gaelic, with their own approved translations of the Scriptures.[136]

Had Protestantism succeeded in France, it is virtually certain that the French language would have spread far more rapidly than it did. The Protestant churches that mushroomed in the mid-sixteenth century used the French of the court and the high nobility almost exclusively, even in the south of the country.[137] The Calvinist preachers who swarmed through the Occitan-speaking regions in those years came bearing small, cheap printed books which taught literacy, the French language, and the new faith all at once.[138] The only exception occurred in the tiny remnant of the Kingdom of Navarre north of the Pyrenees, the only place where an Occitan dialect remained the official language.[139]

In short, when Grégoire proposed to abolish patois and universalize the use of French in France, he was effectively introducing a Protestant solution to the problem of linguistic diversity. It was not the only possible Protestant solution. Conceivably, Grégoire might have heeded Jeremias-Jakob Oberlin's advice and called for raising at least some local speech to the level of standard, official languages. Instead, he ended up following Johann-Friedrich and historical precedent and opted for a single standard:

the language of power. Interestingly, in later years Grégoire's ideas on language earned him abuse as a crypto-Protestant, for after the Terror one of his principal causes was the translation of the Catholic liturgy itself into French.[140]

'LANGUAGE A DIALECT WITH AN ARMY BEHIND IT'?

The Jacobins and the Law

The question remains, of course, why Grégoire's "Protestant" solution should have had such great appeal in an overwhelmingly Catholic nation. Most obviously, one answer is the French Revolution's violent turn against Catholicism, which began in the debates over the Civil Constitution and reached a climax in the violent campaign of de-Christianization launched by the Jacobins in 1793, and later Robespierre's Cult of the Supreme Being. Barère's report on language, infused as it was by violent anticlericalism, certainly reflected this rejection of the Christian God.

Another reason may have to do with the attitude taken towards language by those Catholic cousins of Calvin, the Jansenists, who had had enormous influence in eighteenth-century French political culture, and nowhere more than in the religious debates that led up to the Civil Constitution.[141] From the mid-seventeenth century, these advocates of rigorous Augustinianism helped produce a new French translation of the Bible and defended the legitimacy both of translation and of Bible study for all, just as Luther and Calvin had done.[142] Intriguingly, Jansenism had particular purchase in Lorraine, and after the Revolution Henri Grégoire became an ardent defender of the Jansenist legacy. The extent to which he followed this religious current himself as a young man remains a matter of debate, however, and there is no direct evidence to tie Jansenism to the revolutionary language projects.[143]

Perhaps of greater importance to the drive for imposing French as the national language was a fundamental shift in the status of the written word in French culture during the revolutionary period. Marie-Hélène Huet and Sarah Maza have suggested that during the Revolution, "the traditional symbolism of power, which centered on the visible, theatricalized body of the father-king, was displaced by a competing semiotic system, which vested social authority in such linguistic abstractions as 'public opinion' or 'the Law.'"[144] Carla Hesse has similarly pointed to a growing conviction on the part of revolutionary criminal authorities that written words, particularly in the form of private correspondence, provided the most authentic portrait of defendants' most intimate feelings.[145] In a society where such a shift was taking place, it follows that the full exercise of citizenship demanded a full understanding, not simply of the principles of the Revolution in general, but of the specific written laws that incarnated most authentically the convictions and decisions taken by the sovereign people.

Indeed, it was precisely the problem of how to teach the common people the new written law that centrally preoccupied the radicals who argued for the elimination of patois. The problems that linguistic diversity might have posed for the peasants' active participation in politics—for acting as electors or elected officials, for instance—received far less attention. "The people must understand the laws to sanction and obey them," Grégoire wrote in his report to the Convention.[146] His correspondents echoed this idea, and again and again voiced the fear that translating the written law would expose it to the danger of *mis*translation, whether innocent or malevolent. Chabot cautioned that "an insidiously translated word can totally change the meaning of a law." Fonvielhe, a *curé* of Bergerac, wrote: "However well the law is explained to the people, they will interpret it badly, they will suspect the fidelity of the translation . . . they will stick to their own ideas, interpret it themselves according to their own personal interests."[147] At Aix, in 1790, certain members of the Jacobin club opposed the public explanation of laws in Provençal on the grounds that "only the legislator has the right to interpret the law . . . it can happen that the instructor without meaning to can make a mistake, or even that a well-explained decree will be poorly understood by an almost entirely illiterate audience."[148]

These warnings suggest that the radical revolutionaries found themselves in much the same situation vis-à-vis linguistic difference as Protestant reformers who insisted that individual believers read holy Scripture for themselves. If what mattered was access to a text endowed with quasi-sacred qualities, then all citizens needed to know the language in which the text was written. (The revolutionaries assumed that a perfectly clear, rational legislation would need no particular legal expertise to be understood.) This need would have seemed particularly great at the height of the Terror. When deception and treason seemed to lurk almost behind every visage, representatives of the people like Grégoire and Chabot could no more imagine entrusting the political salvation of the citizenry to potentially deceitful translators than pious Protestants could imagine entrusting the care of their souls to Catholic priests. In these circumstances, regardless of the practical difficulties facing Grégoire's plan to eliminate patois, the

Convention could hardly refuse its support or refrain from acting to discourage translation wherever possible.

To conclude, then, although the French revolutionary engagement with the language issue did not derive from religious precedents alone, in a real sense these precedents structured the debates and lurked behind them at every stage. The initial efforts to use patois to spread the revolutionary message followed from the evangelizing enterprises of the Counter-Reformation clergy (and indeed were partly carried out by a portion of that same clergy, who tried for a time to mix the old and new gospels). Later attempts to impose linguistic uniformity arose in part from suspicion that ill-intentioned priests were using patois as a sort of occult, mysterious tool to control a superstitious and ignorant peasantry. These efforts also stemmed, however, from much the same concerns about the relationship of the common people to the law as those that were first articulated by Protestants, concerns which did not lose their relevance when linguistic diversity became a secular, rather than religious issue. The revolutionaries were seeking to seize the linguistic power of the priest for themselves, and this meant either destroying or seizing control of his occult language: patois. In the Year II, they opted decisively for the former, just as Luther had done before them.

If the religious precedents dominated in this manner, they did so above all because, during the Revolution, the question of linguistic diversity was essentially a rural question, and the world of the peasant was still the world of the priest. For revolutionaries seeking to reach into the hearts and minds of the peasant masses and to effect what amounted to a mass conversion, the priests offered the only available model. At the same time, the priest himself remained the dominant cultural influence in the countryside, and had to be overcome if the Revolution were to triumph. Peasants might not have had salons and *cabinets de lecture* and academies structuring their cultural lives, the way educated city dwellers did, but, as Grégoire's correspondents themselves readily attested, they had a curate who relayed news, told them what (if anything) to read, and possibly even made notes on their grammar and vocabulary. In a real sense, he *was* their salon and *cabinet de lecture* and "Académie de Patois." He gave a structure to their cultural lives, and the linguistic reformers knew they could not pursue their own program without either winning him over or in some way replacing him.

Until 1789, the priests carrying out their projects of evangelization in local languages operated in virtually a separate sphere from elite discussions of the nation and the *patrie,* but the coming of the Revolution marked the eventual doom of their work on behalf of France's many "maternal languages." Thereafter, a state newly committed to molding the diverse populations of France into a single nation ran unavoidably, and at full speed, into the previous efforts of the Catholic clergy to mold them all into a single church. It was at this moment that the French state came to share the clergy's perception of France as radically multilingual, and also to interpret multilingualism as a potent barrier to the construction of a properly revolutionary nation. And it was at this moment, therefore, that the idea of French as a uniform *national* language, rather than just the language of an educated elite, acquired the powerful ideological charge which it has retained ever since. As a result, the regional languages have now become virtually extinct (with—again—the exception of Alsace, which spent much of the Third Republic under German rule). Recent reforms by the Fifth Republic allowing them to be taught in public schools only underline how small a threat they now pose. Indeed, if Hyacinthe Sermet were to return today to Toulouse and deliver once again his July 14 sermon, he would find virtually no one capable of understanding him.

CONCLUSION

Toward the Present Day
and the End of Nationalism

*We do not have to renounce the nation. France cannot live without
its own identity. The French people cannot live as a people whose
destiny is to melt away among others.*
— LIONEL JOSPIN, INTERVIEWED IN *LE MONDE*,
JANUARY 7, 1999

"We have made Italy. Now we have to make Italians." Historians of nationalism delight in quoting this famous saying of the *Risorgimento* leader Massimo d'Azeglio, but usually only to echo his own point, namely that the formal creation of the Italian nation had little meaning to most of its new citizens.[1] Whatever their formal nationality, they remained first and foremost, in language, customs, historical traditions, and political allegiances, inhabitants of their villages and regions: Sicilians, Piedmontese, Tuscans, Calabrians, Romans, Umbrians, Venetians; not "Italians."

Yet the saying is important for another reason. It perfectly and concisely expresses what I have argued in this book lies at the heart of modern nationalism: the idea of the nation as a political artifact whose construction takes precedence over all other political tasks. This idea is today utterly familiar. In the catalogue of the Library of Congress, the phrase "nation-building" itself appears in the titles of no fewer 334 books, going back as far as 1902 and dealing with subjects ranging from Estonian architecture to the Singapore police.[2] Yet this familiarity has bred a forgetfulness of origins. The idea of taking a population, *en masse,* and transforming everything about it—from political allegiances to dress, manners, and daily language—so as to "build a nation" is not an eternal feature of human history, but a specifically modern phenomenon. Before 1750 or so, the idea of imposing the same language and "the same, uniform ideas" (Rabaut's phrase) on Basque shepherds and Breton fishermen, Picard farm laborers and

198

Lyonnais servants, Parisian lawyers and Marseilles merchants, to say nothing of Versailles courtiers, would have struck observers as self-evidently absurd. It was only in the later eighteenth century that it became thinkable, as Marie-Joseph Chénier put it, "to form Frenchmen, to endow the nation with its own, unique physiognomy." It was this shift which made nationalism itself possible: the shift from treating nations as organic bodies that grow and wither according to biological rhythms, to treating them as man-made entities that humans freely create through the exercise of political will.

I have argued that nationalism took shape in France in the eighteenth century in response to a dynamic that was primarily, although by no means exclusively, religious. Building on the work of several philosophers and social theorists, I suggested that in the decades around the year 1700, a series of religious, philosophical, political and material changes combined to produce a fundamental shift in the way educated French men and women saw the world around them. They came to perceive God as absent from the sphere of human affairs. They felt the need to exclude potentially homicidal religious passions from all but carefully delineated areas of human activity. And they experienced material and political changes which made it possible for them to think of France as a uniform and homogeneous space. These far-reaching cultural shifts allowed them to imagine forms of harmonious human coexistence whose ordering principles did not derive from any entity or authority external to the human community itself. An important part of this change was the birth or transformation of foundational concepts that allowed the French to represent these forms of coexistence, including the concepts of *société, civilisation, public,* and also *nation* and *patrie.*

Over the course of the eighteenth century, these concepts were developed and contested in a variety of contexts. *Nation* and *patrie* were at the heart of powerful disputes over the nature of the French constitution. They were systematically deployed by the monarchy to mobilize resources for the war effort against Britain during the Seven Years' War. And they were at the heart of the "cult of great men" which had so prominent a place in French culture at the end of the old regime. As a result, by the time the French monarchy shuffled toward collapse in the 1780s, *nation* and *patrie* had emerged as the key organizing principles in French political debate, put forward loudly and insistently as justification and legitimation for nearly all political claims. Yet precisely as the regime *did* collapse, opening up the awesome question of how to replace it, doubts arose concerning the French nation's very existence. The word nation was coming to signify not merely a particular group of people living on a particular territory, but an intense political and spiritual union of like-minded citizens—a union that manifestly remained to be built, and whose construction stood logically prior to all other political tasks. The Revolution itself therefore came to embody the odd paradox at the heart of modern nationalism: claiming as justification and legitimation a nation which, as even its adherents admit, is not yet there.

What would it take to "make Frenchmen"? In 1789, the more republican-minded of the revolutionaries still thought of the problem in largely classical terms, essentially treating France as an ancient city-state writ large, and prescribing measures that a Pericles or Cicero would have found appropriate for stimulating patriotic, civic devotion: spectacles, in the form of festivals and theater; speeches, statuary, and inscriptions celebrating the great men of the past; some form of civic religion. Rousseau, of course, had advocated precisely these measures in his political works. As I have argued, all these measures also had important Catholic precedents, although they went largely unacknowledged as such.

But the radicalization of the Revolution forever altered the terms of the debate, and, ironically, forced France's would-be nation-builders to embrace far more directly and intensely the example of the institution they most despised: the Roman Catholic Church. For during the Revolution it became clear that building the nation was not, and could never be, the same thing as building a classical republican city-state. It was something that required not only a transformation of the character of some twenty-eight million human beings spread over a large territory, but even more important, the homogenization of those twenty-eight million human beings, the reduction of their tremendous diversity to a single, national essence, and the overcoming of supposed mass ignorance. Making Frenchmen did not just entail turning a small population of sociable, elegant, pleasure-loving fops into grave, sober republican citizens. It required giving a civic education to millions of people still believed to be in thrall to the worst superstitions, uneducated—indeed heavily illiterate—and a great many speaking little or no French. Faced with this monumental task, the revolutionaries adopted the methods of the Reformation-era priesthood, proposing to send their own well-drilled republican versions of the Jesuits out into the countryside to teach, persuade, and indoctrinate by every possible means, and to provide the diverse population with a common education, a common set of allegiances, and a common language.

The radical revolutionaries did not come close to succeeding in this goal. In the midst of war against external and internal enemies alike and in the throes of economic collapse, they did not have the resources to build chains of boarding schools or to send armies of French-language teachers into the provinces. Indeed, by far the most successful instrument of national integration created by the radical revolutionaries was one that was never thought of primarily in these terms, and in which patriotic education, while provided, took a back seat to more immediate and prosaic tasks: the army. Here, men drafted from the various provinces of France, kept away from home for months or years, speaking French, singing republican songs, and receiving the occasional patriotic lesson or group reading of Jacobin newspapers, found a unity and forged a common identity that civilian institutions were as yet incapable of imparting to the general population.[3]

Yet despite its failure to achieve integration, the revolutionary program remains a milestone in the history of nationalism, for it not only engendered the idea of building a homogeneous, unified nation in a modern, diverse, European polity, but provided a practical plan for doing so, modeled heavily on the practical, and at least partially successful efforts of the Reformation-era clergy to reshape the peasantry into a new community of believers. The ideas first developed in the crucible of revolutionary conflict would resound throughout the history of France, and beyond France, down to the present day. D'Azeglio's saying about making Italians, unconsciously echoing Chénier's about making Frenchmen, is itself a good piece of evidence for this diffusion.[4]

During the two centuries since the Revolution, French nationalism has hardly remained static or uncontested. In the early nineteenth century, virtually all its forms took a strongly historical turn. Whereas the radical revolutionaries had briefly envisaged the construction of the nation as an entirely new process, set upon foundations swept clean of the corrupt historical detritus of despotism and feudalism, nineteenth-century nationalists for the most part preferred the language of "regeneration" and "recovery." Like many of their eighteenth-century predecessors, they envisaged a new structure, but one lovingly put together out of hallowed, ancient material. In keeping with their counterparts across Europe, they engaged in a massive effort of recuperating, preserving, and displaying what now came to be called the nation's heritage or patrimony, including folklore, artworks, music, monuments, costumes, and historical personalities such as Joan of Arc. The construction of the nation through the rediscovery of its past animated new cultural forms ranging from the museum to the souvenir shop to the postage stamp. Of course, much of this supposed rediscovery amounted to pure invention.[5]

This historical turn also helped open the door for a new, if limited, toleration of regional diversity even among committed republicans. As Grégoire himself had believed (following Oberlin and other local *savants*), insofar as patois reflected the unchanging mental world of the peasant, it offered a glimpse into the remote past and thus deserved study and preservation.[6] Radical republicans of the late nineteenth century saw no contradiction in advocating the universal teaching of French and also supporting the folkloric Occitan revival movement known as the Félibrige, which treated the southern dialects not as potential languages of state, business, or education, but as living, oral museum exhibits (its leader, Frédéric Mistral, won the Nobel Prize in literature for his pastoral writings in Provençal). When coupled with the Romantic movement's celebration of countryside and wilderness, this new attitude towards the regions fostered a widespread perception and celebration of France as a large *patrie* consisting of a mosaic of distinct, but organically linked "little *patries*."[7]

Within this broad framework, a new variety of French nationalism emerged which defined itself in direct opposition to the republican, revolutionary version. This monarchical, ultra-Catholic nationalism, expressed most forcefully in the late nineteenth- and early twentieth-century writings of Charles Maurras, Maurice Barrès, and the political platforms of the far-right Action Française, saw the national past not merely as a heritage, but as a literal destination.[8] For them, France's regional diversity in no sense constituted an obstacle to be overcome. Regional cultures were to be powerfully and consciously strengthened, not merely to be celebrated as folklore. The Third Republic's efforts to reduce France's natural variety represented, from this point of view, the true alien presence in French life. Going further, Barrès, in his novel *Les déracinés* ("The Uprooted"), associated these efforts not with the French Enlightenment or Revolution so much as with *German,* above all Kantian philosophy.[9] Significantly, until recent gestures in favor of the now-moribund regional languages by the Fifth Republic, the only regime in modern French history to attempt to reintroduce regional speech into the school system as anything more than an aid to the teaching of French was precisely the one regime most animated by this right-wing nationalism: Vichy. In 1941, it permitted an hour and a half per week of instruction in the local dialects.[10] Needless to say, in this vision of the French nation, "Frenchness" was not something *made*, but something inherited, something in the blood, even if political action was still necessary to purge France of impure alien influences.

If this right-wing French nationalism was so at odds with the republican, revolutionary version, the reason was as much religious as political, for its advocates consciously and explicitly rejected the transformations in the religious sphere that had occurred in France since 1700—indeed, in important respects, since the end of the *sixteenth* century. In their writings France remained a Christian, Catholic nation, part of a great and unbroken chain that extended from the people through the king and the pope to God and the kingdom of heaven. In their attempts to recreate an idealized medieval world of hierarchy and deference, modern right-wing French nationalists asserted a role for the (ultramontane) church in French affairs that a Richelieu or Louis XIV, to say nothing of a Mirabeau or Robespierre, would have found intolerable. It was perhaps precisely because these nationalists considered the nation so directly and completely subject to external determinations, and so firmly a part of a larger universal scheme, that they could depict the national community itself in such limited and exclusive (indeed, racial) terms. Significantly, important aspects of this modern right-wing nationalism recall sixteenth-century French writings on the nation. In this early period, too, writers tended to put a strong emphasis on blood and descent, presented radical regional and linguistic diversity as a natural tapestry, and of course stressed the place of France in a larger, divinely inspired hierarchy.[11] For modern right-wing nationalists, the ultimate symbol of France—still the key symbol for the extreme-right National Front—was Joan of Arc, the woman who saved France in the name of God and in direct response to his command. In short, this is a nationalism which, while ultimately owing as much as any other variety to the "disenchantment of the world," nonetheless set itself explicitly against this disenchantment and denied it.

This right-wing nationalism has had great importance at certain moments in modern French history (for instance, the time of the Dreyfus Affair). In the final analysis, however, it has belonged consistently to a minority. The only regime that systematically attempted to act upon it and to remake the nation according to its tenets was Vichy, which owed its existence to a foreign power. Even the Restoration of 1815–30 mostly attempted a futile compromise between the old regime and the French Revolution. The July Monarchy and the two empires, not to mention the republics that have now existed for over 130 years, have all remained essentially loyal to the national idea as it was formulated under the First Republic. Of course, the republican idea itself has hardly remained static since 1794, and the republican left fully shared in the nineteenth century's historical turn. One has only to consider the importance of Joan of Arc to a convinced republican like Jules Michelet to recognize this point (although Michelet would not have granted his female contemporaries the same freedom of expression he praised in Joan—it was one thing to be a saint, another to be a citizen).

Thus I would argue that, in its fundamental elements, there has been a basic continuity in French republican nationalism over the past two centuries. The republicans, unlike their opponents on the right, distinguished between the past as heritage and the past as blueprint, and they remained true to the conviction that constructing the nation amounted to more than simply purging an idealized medieval structure of ethnic and ideological contaminants. As Michelet wrote, the era when religion still permeated French life had definitively ended, and "extinguished Christianity" had passed its torch to the republican *patrie*.[12] In the last pages of this book, I will speculate briefly on this continuity and on its implications for what is often called the "crisis of French national identity"—what I would in fact define as the end of nationalism in France.

The most basic element of continuity involved the conception of the nation as a product of political will. French republican nationalists have always expressed the idea of the nation as a political construction in the most pure sense, because they have insisted that the nation can remake itself, if not wholly as it pleases, then at least with great liberty. From this perspective, what ultimately defines the nation is less history, or race, or language, or a particular territory, although these remain important, but the common desire to join together *as* a nation, accepting common laws, values, institutions, and perhaps a common culture and language as well. Likewise, from this perspective the particular frontiers of France are not sacrosanct, and the status of citizen versus foreigner is defined less by birth or mother tongue than by political stance and cultural sympathies. The revolutionaries pushed these arguments to an extreme. "The only foreign-

UNFRENCH = FOREIGN

ers in France are the bad citizens," Tallien famously declared in 1795, while
counter-revolutionaries were frequently dismissed as "foreigners," and
"barbarian" ones at that—like the English, they had willfully and per-
versely written themselves out of the universal human community centered on France.[13] By contrast, foreign sympathizers of the Revolution
flocked to Paris, and, for a time, many easily gained French citizenship.[14]
Republican nationalism was, as it is now said, assimilationist, or "integrationist."[15]

The region which has offered the most important illustration of this
conception of the nation is Alsace. Largely German in language and Lu-
theran in religion, under the old regime it still possessed important ves-
tiges of German imperial law and noble privileges. Indeed, such was the
fluid and porous nature of early modern frontiers that many areas of the
province still fell under the feudal jurisdiction of, and paid feudal dues to,
lords living beyond the Rhine. The city of Strasbourg had a glorious German past as a center of German humanism and the German Reformation.
Even in the 1760s, as we have seen, its influential Society for the Promotion
of the German Language helped give birth to German Romanticism.[16] But
none of this mattered to the deputy Merlin de Douai, who declared in
1790: "What do people of Alsace, or the French people, care about those
treaties which, in the time of despotism, joined the first to the second? The
Alsatian people joined the French people because it wished to; it is therefore its will alone, and not the Peace of Westphalia, which has legitimized
the union."[17] And none of these qualities mattered eighty years later, when
the newly united German empire defeated France and annexed Alsace,
claiming as justification its German language, history, and race. It was precisely in response to these German claims that Ernest Renan delivered his
famous lecture, "Qu'est-ce qu'une Nation?" ("What is a Nation?") which
summarizes better than any other single text the republican nationalist
creed: "A nation is therefore a large-scale solidarity, constituted by the feeling of the sacrifices that one has made in the past and of those that one is
prepared to make in the future . . . A nation's existence is, if you will par-
don the metaphor, a daily plebiscite."[18] Renan continues to be cited copiously in France in discussions and defense of the republican ideal of the
nation, including in speeches by President Chirac.[19]

Yet despite this ideal, French republican nationalism over the past two
centuries has also been distinguished by something else, something that
comes close to contradicting it. For despite the frequent declarations that

membership in the French nation depends on the will of individual citizens freely to embrace the elements of a common nationality, in practice French republicans have never quite trusted individuals to come to the correct decision on their own. As we have seen, in the Revolution they sought to ensure the proper result through a concerted program of what can only be called indoctrination, following on the model of the priesthood. Recall Rabaut Saint-Etienne's words on how the French could in fact be transformed into a "new people": what was needed was "an infallible means of transmitting, constantly and immediately, to all the French at once, the same, uniform, ideas."[20] This is not quite the same thing as a "daily plebiscite," any more than adherence to correct Catholic doctrine was a matter of choice for the peasants under the old regime.

We should be careful before using this reason to label French republican nationalism, as an influential recent study has done, "collectivist-authoritarian," in contrast to a supposedly "libertarian-individualist" Anglo-American alternative.[21] Still less should we assume that this coerciveness implies any necessary relationship between French republican nationalism and the Terror. It is too often forgotten that if French republicans brought about the Terror, French republicans also ended it, and after less than two years (the Thermidorians were admittedly the least savory of deliverers, an evaluation that has significantly colored later interpretations). A total military defeat was not required to end it, nor was it necessary to wait decades for an institutionalized Terror to grow slack and corrupt and ultimately to collapse under its own weight, as was the case with the twentieth-century dictatorships sometimes described as the spiritual heirs of the French Revolution. In fact, since the late nineteenth and early twentieth centuries, French republican nationalism has coexisted with a succession of generally democratic and tolerant regimes, and its record as far as minorities within the nation are concerned, though far from ideal, certainly stands comparison with the United States or Britain. Today, critics often condemn France's Third Republic for suppressing the language and culture of Celtic Brittany, but who would trade the history of Brittany, or even that of the Vendée, hideous as it is, for that of Ulster?

Let us remember that most modern nationalist movements, regardless of whether we choose to label them "civic," "cultural," or other, have insisted on some form of compulsory patriotic education to instill common values, loyalty to the nation, and perhaps also a common culture and language. French republican nationalism is no different from others in this respect, and we should give due consideration to the centrifugal forces that nationalists have struggled against before condemning them for it. What has made French republican nationalism different has been the astonishing missionary zeal with which the goal has been pursued—with which the apostles of the nation have set out to "make Frenchmen," the way the Jesuits set out to "make Christians" in China or the Americas.

I would go so far as to argue that French republican nationalism owed its peculiar character and extraordinary vigor, from the late eighteenth century to the mid-twentieth, precisely to the extraordinary sense of mission and purpose that animated its principal agents: administrators, soldiers, and above all educators. In this sense, France's experience has differed greatly from that of its neighbors.[22] Generations of teachers formed in the *écoles normales* were trained to see themselves not merely as instructors, but as the "black hussars of the Republic" sent out to convert the young and to form them into good republican French citizens. Furthermore, French republican nationalism was genuinely universalistic, for what gave it its purpose was, in addition to building the nation, expanding it indefinitely so as to embrace as large a portion of humanity as possible.

The first large effort to fulfill this mission, under the First Republic and then under the Napoleonic Empire (which inherited some, though hardly all, of the Republic's ideas and principles), was a brief blazing triumph that quickly collapsed into an abject failure. This effort was, of course, a military one, which expanded the frontiers of France across Europe, in the process integrating areas without a shred of French tradition seamlessly into the system of French *départements*. By 1812, in theory, Schleswig-Holstein and the Adriatic coast of Croatia belonged to France every bit as much as the Ardèche or the Morbihan. The effort was a failure in part because the French soldiers and administrators proceeded with brazen hypocrisy, declaring their new subjects the equals of French citizens while ruthlessly exploiting them for the war effort. The hypocrisy was not all-pervasive; in the last years of the Empire, more than a third of Napoleon's (admittedly powerless) Senate came from territories well outside France's 1789 boundaries.[23] Nonetheless, the French attitudes spurred widespread resentment and rebellion, which in turn led to the birth of new nationalist movements throughout Europe, all of which tended to define themselves against France and the French.

Yet after the defeat of the Empire, and particularly from 1870 to 1940, efforts to fulfill the early republican national mission met with considerably more success, despite France's reduced military capacities and international prestige. These efforts aimed at three separate and very different population groups: French peasants, inhabitants of France's colonial territories, and foreign immigrants. In each case, the republican state set itself a "civilizing mission" whereby assimilation into civilization meant—as had often been the case in the eighteenth century—assimilation into the *patrie*.

Peasants, of course, were the original targets of the First Republic's efforts at national integration, from its grandiose plans for public education and the deployment of newspapers like *La Feuille villageoise*, to the "public sessions" of the Jacobin clubs and the language policies discussed in the last chapter. These peasants were the French citizens routinely described by their educated, urban compatriots in the nineteenth century as belonging to an alien, animalistic world. Adolphe Blanqui in 1851 could speak of "two different peoples living on the same land a life so different that they seem foreign to each other."[24] True, after the Terror, and particularly after Napoleon's rise to power, the campaign to make Frenchmen out of these country-dwellers fell into abeyance. Universal primary education, the most important means of conversion for the Jacobins, remained a distant dream until well into the nineteenth century.[25] After 1830, however, the July Monarchy began to set up a nationwide system of public schools. The Second Republic of 1848 revived the ideals of the First, and in the 1860s Louis-Napoleon's Ministry of Education began to formulate the problem of peasant integration in a systematic manner, notably carrying out the first truly large-scale survey of the spoken languages of France. In 1867, the reforming minister Victor Duruy again put forward an ambitious plan for universal elementary schooling.[26]

The Third Republic, which arose out of the disasters of the Franco-Prussian War and the Commune, built on these foundations with such energy and zeal that its black-clad schoolmasters became its most famous and visible servants. The high temple of French education, the Ecole Normale Supérieure, in theory a school for training *lycée* teachers, served as the nursery for France's leading politicians and intellectuals and had no equivalent in most other European countries. Eminent educators proclaimed that apprentice teachers "must above be told that their first duty is to make [their charges] love and understand the *patrie*"; the school is "an instrument of unity" and an "answer to dangerous centrifugal tendencies."[27] School texts like Ernest Lavisse's enormously successful French history primer, and Bruno's *Tour de France par deux enfants* took up the task once shouldered by *La Feuille villageoise,* educating the rural population not only in the language, history, and constitution of France, but in patriotic duty.[28] While usually not committed to the eradication of local languages, teachers in patois-speaking regions nonetheless saw the teaching of standard French as their main mission. Patois had, at best, a minor, auxiliary role in the classroom.[29]

Even as republican efforts to civilize the peasantry reached their peak towards the end of the nineteenth century, the Third Republic reached out to embrace a far larger field in which to sow its language, ideals, symbols, and ultimately, perhaps, its nationality: the colonial empire, which by 1900 included vast areas of north and west Africa.[30] Just as seventeenth- and eighteenth-century Catholic missionaries had employed much the same methods of conversion in France as in the Americas or Asia—and indeed had drawn explicit parallels between the different fields of operation—so the republicans of the age of imperialism easily translated their approach towards the peasants into an approach towards their colonial subjects.[31] In the service of an explicit civilizing mission, not only did they expose these subjects to the usual panoply of "integrationist" policies, above all schooling and linguistic instruction; they went further than any other European colonial power in breaking down the distinction between the colonies and the metropole. Certain areas of the empire became legally part of France, theoretically indistinguishable in this regard from Paris or Marseilles. Furthermore, legislation opened the door for at least an elite of colonial subjects to become full French citizens. School texts like Louis Sonolet's *Moussa et Gi-gla: Histoire de deux petits noirs,* modeled on Bruno's *Tour de France,* taught that French and blacks belonged to the same *patrie.*[32]

The extent to which the empire offered its colonial subjects true equal membership in the French nation was, of course, strictly limited. The enterprise proceeded with a predictably large share of racism, hypocrisy, hesitation, and doubt—particularly after World War I, and particularly where Muslims were concerned.[33] Yet the "civilizing mission" was not simply a mask for exploitation. And regardless of the realities on the ground, it mattered deeply to republican nationalists in France that the nation was expanding in this way, and that it might someday welcome millions of fully civilized Africans and Asians into the great circle of the *patrie.*

The final, and most contested field of expansion and integration was immigration. Unlike the missions to civilize the peasantry and the colonies, the assimilation of immigrants was not an enterprise that the republic gloried in. France has repeatedly opened its doors to large numbers of immigrants: Belgians and Italians in the nineteenth century, Poles in the early twentieth, and more recently Spanish, Portuguese, North Africans, black Africans, and Southeast Asians. But it has almost always done so initially as a temporary measure, to provide badly needed labor. Citizenship came later, after the communities had already established themselves. Nor was immigration ever anything less than controversial. The Belgians and Italians met as much hostility and prejudice in their time as Algerians and black Africans have done in contemporary France, and sometimes more. In part as a result, the French government and the French academy for many years practically ignored the long history of immigration into France. No less a prestigious scholar than Pierre Nora could write, as recently as 1986, that immigration was "a novelty of the country's present-day situation."[34]

Unremarked as it may have been, the immigration did take place. Indeed, after the United States drastically curtailed immigration in the wake of World War I, France became the leading immigrant nation in the Western world, with policies far more welcoming than those of any other European country.[35] It is a powerful but relatively little-known fact that today nearly a quarter of all French citizens have at least one grandparent born elsewhere.[36] Furthermore, in large part thanks to the same republican institutions that strove to civilize the peasants and the colonies—above all, the schools—the immigrants did indeed assimilate, and to a greater extent than their American counterparts. As has sometimes been remarked, there is no such thing as a "hyphenated French person," in contrast to the millions of hyphenated Americans taking pride in an (often mostly invented) ethnic identity, and expressing a residual if largely nostalgic loyalty to an ancestral homeland. The phrase "Italian-American" suggests an individual; the phrase "Italian-French," a treaty. Few French people know that one of their most celebrated film stars of the twentieth century, Yves Montand, was born Ivo Livi, or that the nineteenth-century novelist Emile Zola also came from an Italian background. When President François Mitterrand named a son of Ukrainian immigrants, Pierre Bérégovoy, as his prime minister, his background generated far less interest and comment than it would have done in the United States.

In all these ways, then, the French republican nationalism born in the eighteenth century remained powerful and active through the middle of the twentieth, shaping the policies of the French state both at home and abroad and providing to its elites, educated in large proportion at the Ecole

Normale Supérieure, a unique sense of mission. In this somber building on the rue d'Ulm in Paris, within sight of the Pantheon, so reminiscent of a monastery in its architecture, with its cloister and cells and high, echoing corridors, the Republic trained its own secular Jesuits to go forth and forge, not the church, but the nation.

Today, the Ecole Normale still stands on the rue d'Ulm, and some of the smartest and best-prepared of France's university-age students still pass through its doors each year, under an inscription beginning "By Decree of the Convention, 9 Brumaire, Year III." But it is diminished. The most ambitious and successful students have largely abandoned it for the Ecole Nationale d'Administration, which trains high civil servants and virtually the whole top layer of what the French call the "political class" (including the present president, prime minister, and a majority of the Cabinet). While some of its pupils still take the republican mission seriously and teach in the countryside (or, more often, the suburban slums), most are simply academics using it as a stepping stone to eventual professorships. The scientists who make up half the student body compete strenuously for postdoctoral fellowships abroad, above all in the United States. And they publish almost exclusively in English.

As such the Ecole Normale can stand as a symbol, among many such symbols, for what is often today called a "crisis of French national identity." This crisis has been endlessly discussed, both in France and abroad, over the past twenty years.[37] It is significant that perhaps the single most important work of scholarship published in the Mitterrand years, the massive collection *Les lieux de mémoire*, edited by Pierre Nora (himself a descendant of North African Jews), began with the assumption that long-standing French forms of self-identification were disappearing, and that the republican tradition in particular was unraveling. Indeed, despite Nora's presentation of the work as a dispassionate analysis of the workings of national memory, much of it adopted a frankly elegiac, rueful tone, particularly when discussing the great institutions of the French state and French culture.[38] Meanwhile, the great *livre de scandale* of 1993 was a book gloomily entitled *Voyage au centre du malaise français* ("Voyage to the Center of the French Malaise"), which discerned a virtual disintegration of French national identity, thanks to multiculturalism and the flood of revelations about French conduct towards the Jews under Vichy (the author found them pathological, whence the scandal).[39]

The usual suspect in these discussions of the crisis is France's diminished position in an increasingly interconnected, Americanized world. The fingers point to France's decline as a military and diplomatic power, the increasing integration of the European Union (as of this writing, the French currency has recently given way to the euro and the dictates of the European central bank, and plans are afoot for a pan-European military force), and of course the invasion of France by everything from McDonald's and Pizza Hut to American pop music, movies, The Gap, Starbucks, and the Internet (the long-suffering French language must now accommodate phrases like "le netsurfing des sites cools du web"). In the spring of 2000, a farmer who vandalized a new McDonald's in the Languedoc town of Millau, José Bové, became something of a French folk hero. Prime Minister Jospin's recent statement on French identity, quoted at the start of this chapter, was made above all in reference to Europeanization and the euro. Commentators were not slow to notice its defensive tone. Immigration also comes up frequently, of course, and is generally discussed in blissful ignorance of the subject's long and complex history.

All these factors indeed have enormous relevance for the way the French now view their nation. What is much less well understood is why these factors, common to all nations, seem to have had such a particularly strong negative effect in France. There has been less talk of crises of Dutch, Irish, or Italian national identity, although the developments that go by the name of globalization have arguably had a stronger impact in any of these countries than in France. Of course, as Michelet liked to quip, the world thinks; France speaks. But I would argue that the sharpness with which the French have experienced these global changes should in fact be attributed to particular changes that the nation underwent *before* most of the trends associated with globalization made much of an impact on France. It was in the period of strong economic growth between World War II and the early 1970s, often called the "Glorious Thirty [years]," that the sense of mission attached for so long to French republican nationalism, along with the drive to assimilate new populations and to put France at the center of a universal civilization, virtually evaporated. The areas in which these changes took place are, again, the peasantry, the empire, and immigration. The changes were reinforced by significant transformations in the French educational system and in the sphere of religion.

Few French schoolmasters today can take on the role of republican missionaries sent out into the depths of the countryside to civilize the peasantry, and for a simple reason: there is no more peasantry. As recently as

World War II, with France lagging behind many other industrialized Western states, fully 45 percent of the population lived in rural districts, and a quarter of the labor force worked directly on the land. The peasantry remained, in the words of the sociologist Henri Mendras, "the central social class."[40] But then came the thirty years of rapid economic growth and transformation. Today, only five percent of the labor force is employed in agriculture, and in villages across France homes stand empty and decaying. In the 1960s, 100,000 workers a year left the land.[41] They have flocked to cities and suburbs where patois is a distant memory, and send their children to *lycées* and universities. They have indeed been "melted into the national mass," and are melting into the global mass as well. I still remember vividly my own first encounter with a French farming family, in Brittany, in 1978. Invited by their suburb-dwelling cousins, my summer hosts, for an afternoon, I was expecting rural tradition and quaintness, and found it in the lovely old stone farmhouse, the farm animals, the weather-beaten face of the farmer, and the *galettes* and cider on the table. But the effect was rather spoiled by the fact that we spent dinner watching "Happy Days" on television.

Just as France retains only tiny remnants of its once vast peasantry, so it has only kept shreds of its once vast empire: Guadeloupe, Saint-Pierre and Miquelon, Martinique, New Caledonia and so forth—a small, thin, and widely scattered archipelago where one can still use French currency, speak the French language, and walk into post offices identical to the ones on Parisian street corners. The rest disappeared in the great wave of decolonization in the 1950s and 1960s. Beyond this tiny formal empire, there is also a much larger informal one, for France still maintains legions of civil servants, businessmen, and aid workers in its former African colonies, not to mention soldiers. But if French influence remains strong in these nations, its civilizing mission has almost entirely vanished. Far from granting French citizenship to "meritorious" Africans, the French state devotes considerable efforts to keeping them out of France, lest they swell an already large immigrant population.

The issue of immigration itself is, as it has always been, fraught and complex. Nearly every party to the ongoing debate in France over immigrants has an interest in presenting the problems of the current wave of immigrants (especially the millions of Arabs and Berbers who have made Islam France's second largest religion, after Catholicism) as more serious than any similar problems in the past. The National Front and other rightists do so to garner support for an absolute halt to immigration and intensified efforts of repatriation. Opposing political forces do so in order to justify large-scale public efforts to relieve the misery in which many immigrants live. Even though, in a recent poll, no less than 38 percent of the French population confessed to some racist feelings about immigrants, and even though the National Front routinely has won up to 15 percent of the vote, the prejudice and even violence dealt to *previous* waves of immigrants ironically offer some hope that eventually the North Africans, too, may find themselves integrated more fully into French society and culture.[42] Southeast Asians, and to a lesser extent black African immigrants, are becoming so already. On the other hand, at least two phenomena do suggest a need for caution. One is the growing popularity of anti-Western fundamentalism in some sectors of France's Muslim communities, leading to a radical rejection of assimilation. The other is the ghettoization of immigrant communities, characterized by high levels of unemployment and crime, and physical isolation in the miserable suburban confines of vast, sterile housing projects.

Even if the North African Muslims do eventually follow the example of their Belgian, Italian, Polish, and Iberian predecessors, a different fact is now becoming clear: they will most likely have no successors. In the present French political climate, and thanks above all to the National Front, even the Socialist Party has strongly committed itself to ending immigration, cracking down on clandestine immigration, and shipping illegal immigrants back to their countries of origin. Meanwhile, the president of the Republic has openly remarked that he sympathizes with his compatriots who must put up with the "noise" and the "smells" generated by an "overdose" of immigrants.[43] In the 1980s and 1990s the United States has again become the leading immigrant nation in the West, and is being transformed by immigration to an extent not seen for a century. By contrast, the French are making it clear that once they have digested the current immigrant populations, they have no appetite for more. In this sense, the field of immigration, too, is closed to republican nationalism.

Supposing that France did still have peasants, an empire, and ongoing waves of immigration, would there still be a vigorous republican national impulse to instill republican values in these outsiders and to integrate them seamlessly into the national community? The answer is far from obvious. As Pierre Nora and others have noted, French republicanism in many ways reached its peak a century ago, thanks above all to its conflict with a frankly anti-republican Catholic right. This opponent remained a serious threat throughout the interwar years, and of course took power in 1940 thanks to the Nazi conquerors. But the experience of Vichy wholly discredited it, and it has never regained its electoral base. The National Front is itself a largely republican party; it flies the republican tricolor even as its supporters celebrate Joan of Arc. After the war, not only did French republicanism find itself without a powerful opponent to justify its continued vigilance and activity; it was also sapped by the competing forces of Gaullism and Marxism. They have declined in their turn in the past twenty years, but it has not been to either the ideological or electoral advantage of Third Republic-style republicanism and the political parties that embodied it.[44] Whether or not the French Revolution is finally over, as François Furet famously claimed, it has ceased to matter in mainstream French politics, where middle-of-the-road parties with often identical policies compete to dominate a Republic of the Center largely similar to other Western European democracies.[45]

Just as important, republicanism has in a sense lost its principal instrument of spreading the creed, the public education system. Obviously, French public education itself is larger than ever (French civil servants once liked to boast that "l'éducation nationale" was the single largest organization in Europe, after the Red Army—now, presumably, it is the largest). But since the war it has undergone some fundamental transformations. First, its center of gravity has shifted upwards. Whereas once the *lycées* were elite institutions and the universities and *grandes écoles* were reserved for a tiny minority, now virtually all French children receive secondary education. François Mitterrand set a goal of bringing 80 percent of the population at least through the *baccalaureat,* and the intolerable crowding in many universities testifies to the system's progress towards this goal. As the system increasingly came to center on adolescents rather than young children, it would inevitably have moved away from the sort of heavy-handed patriotic indoctrination characteristic of the Third Republic. But that indoctrination has in any case faded away for very different reasons, and *instituteurs* now rarely treat patriotic and moral education as more important tasks than the imparting of basic skills.[46]

In this context, one cannot overestimate the importance of the events of May 1968. Whatever else this extraordinary episode accomplished, it came close to destroying the magisterial authority previously enjoyed by French educators, and their overweening confidence in their ability to shape their charges to fit a pattern of their own devising. While students had helped lead previous French rebellions, they had not done so directly against their own teachers and educational institutions. In the wake of 1968, teachers could no longer occupy the same moral position they had held before—especially after the students of 1968 became teachers in their turn.[47]

Beyond all these social, political, and cultural reasons why the republican vision of the nation has dissolved, leaving a perceived crisis in its wake, there is another, perhaps more fundamental reason. Nationalism, while developing in large part *against* religion, also developed *out* of it, and did so at a time of general, profound religious faith. Above all, the order and harmony that nationalists hoped to establish in this world, while seen as *part* of this world and not a reflection or extension of celestial order, was nonetheless envisioned as a terrestrial *counterpart* to the order and harmony discerned by Christians in heaven. Hence it is doubtful that nationalism

can remain the same in an era characterized not merely by the interiorization of religion, but by the thorough evaporation of religious faith, to the extent that the original, religious conception of order and harmony no longer resonates in most people's minds with anything like the strength it did in the eighteenth century. What are the successors of Rabaut Saint-Etienne to do when they no longer need to fight against the priests—when, moreover, what the priests themselves were trying to accomplish no longer has any meaning to most of the population?

In our own profoundly disenchanted world, it is perhaps not surprising that in fact, most of the foundational concepts discussed in Chapter 1 are losing their centrality, in France and beyond. The word "civilization" is spoken with irony more often than not. The same is true for "patrie"—indeed, this word seems to be fast disappearing from the French lexicon, to the extent that if the abbé Coyer returned to France today, he would undoubtedly see the need to reprint his little dissertation lamenting the word's absence. "Society," as is often remarked, is steadily giving way to "culture" in everything from the most abstruse academic discourse to the most popular media. We may not be at the "end of history," but we do seem to be at the end of a period in which reshaping human society into some sort of ideally harmonious order was seen as the central task for human beings to accomplish. Assuring a reasonable degree of comfort and security is now often seen as all that is possible. As in the decades around 1700, inhabitants of the West are again living in a time of "anti-enthusiasm," though now they are reacting against ideological, as opposed to religious enthusiasms.

And what of the nation? In this not-so-brave new world, which admittedly extends over only the small portion of the globe that can take a reasonable degree of comfort and security for granted, will it simply become irrelevant? Will France steadily dissolve into Europe, cyberspace, and the global marketplace, whatever stubborn words the prime minister may summon against this fate? I do not think so. But if the nation does remain a central organizing principle of human life, it will do so in a very different manner from the past two centuries. It will do so not as a field of homogeneity, but as a site of exchange, where different cultures meet and mix, in constant movement. National identity and national character will survive, but they will refer as much to the particular style of the meeting and mixing as to the things that are meeting and mixing.

Parts of France itself have already become this sort of kaleidoscope nation, as a stroll through central Paris, with its overwhelming selection of foods, music, and clothing from around the world, easily demonstrates. Many prominent French commentators and politicians, attached by a blend of conviction, nostalgia, and self-interest to the old national creed and the institutions that embodied it, may decry the change, but they have so far proved incapable of doing anything to reverse it (legislation on protecting the French language, for instance, has been an often ludicrous failure). They are unlikely to become more effective in the near future. Today, with France more prosperous, peaceful, and secure than at any time in its history, the nationalism that flourished between the late eighteenth century and the mid-twentieth is distant from the experiences and concerns of most of the French. This change may be partly regrettable, for French republican nationalism, if party to much that was terrible, particularly at its origins, had something noble and grand to it as well. Nonetheless, the French will be fortunate if they are able, in the years to come, to look back on their nationalist past with sympathy and admiration, but also with a degree of puzzled incomprehension.

Notes

Introduction: Constructing the Nation

1. Maximilien Robespierre, *Discours et rapports à la Convention,* ed. Marc Bouloiseau (Paris, 1965), 79.
2. On Rabaut, see André Dupont, *Rabaut Saint-Etienne, 1743–1793: Un protestant défenseur de la liberté religieuse* (Strasbourg, 1946, repr. Geneva, 1989).
3. *Réimpression de l'ancien Moniteur,* 32 vols. (Paris, 1840), Dec. 22, 1792, 803. The speech was reprinted as Jean-Paul Rabaut, *Projet d'éducation nationale* (Paris, 1792).
4. Cited in Mona Ozouf, "La Révolution française et la formation de l'homme nouveau," in *L'homme régénéré: Essais sur la Révolution française* (Paris, 1989), 116–157, at 125.
5. *Moniteur,* 802–3.
6. Ibid., 802–3.
7. Ibid., 803.
8. Ibid.
9. Ibid., 804.
10. Rabaut de Saint-Etienne, *Projet.*
11. It has principally been noticed for its influence on the subsequent educational projects. See Jean-Louis Labarrière, "De la vertu du citoyen éclairé," in Josiane Boulad-Ayoub, ed., *Former un nouveau peuple? Pouvoir, éducation, révolution* (Quebec, 1996), 57–69, esp. 66–67; Robert J. Vignery, *The French Revolution and the Schools: Educational Policies of the Mountain 1792–1794* (Madison, 1965), 45, 77; Dominique Julia, *Les trois couleurs du tableau noir: La Révolution* (Paris, 1981), 46, 89–96; and Bronislaw Baczko, *Une éducation pour la démocratie: Textes et projets de l'époque révolutionnaire* (Paris, 1982), which reproduces the later, printed version of the speech on 295–301.
12. On this subject, see notably Colette Beaune, *Naissance de la nation France* (Paris, 1985), and Myriam Yardeni, *La conscience nationale en France pendant les guerres de religion (1559–1598)* (Louvain, 1971).

13. Here I am taking issue with influential scholars who see the rise of nations and the rise of nationalism as the same essential phenomenon. See for instance Ernest Gellner, *Nations and Nationalism* (Oxford, 1983); Benedict Anderson, *Imagined Communities: Reflections on the Origin and Spread of Nationalism* (London, 1983); John Breuilly, *Nationalism and the State* (New York, 1982); Eric Hobsbawm, *Nations and Nationalism since 1780: Programme, Myth, Reality* (Cambridge, 1989). These scholars all take a "modernist" approach, locating the origins of nations and nationalism alike around 1800, but the same conflation is also typical of scholars who project the phenomenon further back in time, for instance Adrian Hastings, *The Construction of Nationhood: Ethnicity, Religion and Nationalism* (Cambridge, 1998), or Anthony D. Smith, *National Identity* (Reno, 1991).

14. For an excellent synthesis of this aspect of nationalism, see Anne-Marie Thiesse, *La création des identités nationales: Europe XVIIIe–XXe siècle* (Paris, 1999). For a discussion of the language of restoration and reconstruction, even in the most radical moments of the French Revolution, see Chapter 5 below.

15. This point is valid for the "civic" (as opposed to "ethnic") form of nationalism, to borrow the distinction formulated most notably by John Plamenatz in "Two Types of Nationalism," in Eugene Kamenka, ed., *Nationalism: The Nature and Evolution of an Idea* (New York, 1976). The distinction has recently been challenged, notably by Anne-Marie Thiesse.

16. Geoff Eley, "State Formation, Nationalism, and Political Culture: Some Thoughts on the Unification of Germany," in *From Unification to Nazism: Reinterpreting the German Past* (London, 1986), 66. See also Celia Applegate, *A Nation of Provincials: The German Idea of Heimat* (Berkeley, 1990), and Thiesse, passim.

17. In making an argument about how new ways of looking at the world become "thinkable," I am drawing on numerous works in cultural theory, political theory, and cultural anthropology. Among the most important are Quentin Skinner, "Meaning and Understanding in the History of Ideas," *History and Theory* VIII/1 (1969), 3–53; J. G. A. Pocock, "Political Languages and Their Implications," in Pocock, *Politics, Language and Time: Essays on Political Thought and History* (New York, 1971), 3–41; Clifford Geertz, "Ideology as a Cultural System," in Geertz, *The Interpretation of Cultures* (New York, 1973), 193–233; Michel Foucault, *The Archaeology of Knowledge,* trans. A. M. Sheridan (New York, 1973). I am also indebted to the example of Keith Michael Baker in *Inventing the French Revolution: Essays on French Political Culture in the Eighteenth Century* (Cambridge, 1990).

18. The argument that for centuries "nation" meant primarily communities of foreign university students, developed particularly by Guido Zernatto in "Na-

tion: The History of a Word," *Review of Politics,* 6 (1944), 351–66, has been too easily accepted by many scholars. See the persuasive evidence presented by Hastings, *The Construction of Nationhood,* 14–17 (although the author proceeds to draw unwarranted conclusions about the antiquity of nationalism itself); Jean-Yves Guiomar, *La nation entre l'histoire et la raison* (Paris, 1990), 13; and Claude-Gilbert Dubois, ed., *L'imaginaire de la nation 1792–1992* (Bordeaux, 1992), 20.

19. Cited in Hastings, *The Construction of Nationhood,* 17; *Dictionnaire de l'Académie Françoise* (Paris, 1694), s.v. "nation."

20. For Richelieu's project, which never came to fruition, see Nicolas Legras, *Académie royale de Richelieu* (n.p., 1642). For Mazarin's, which quickly lost its "integrative" purpose and became simply a prestigious Parisian *collège,* see Alfred Franklin, *Recherches historiques sur le collège des quatre nations* (Paris, 1862).

21. I here take issue with recent attempts to push the origins of nationalism further back in time, such as Anthony D. Smith's *National Identity* and *The Ethnic Origins of Nations* (Oxford, 1986), and Liah Greenfeld, *Nationalism: Five Roads to Modernity* (Cambridge, Mass., 1992). A compelling recent synthesis making the same case, and arguing for the centrality of the early modern Netherlands and England, is Philip S. Gorski, "The Mosaic Moment: An Early Modernist Critique of Modernist Theories of Nationalism," *American Journal of Sociology,* CV/5 (2000), 1428–68. Even Gorski, however, still tends to conflate nationalism and national identity (e.g. p. 1430, where he takes the antiquity of the word "nation" as evidence for "nationalism qua ideology" antedating the modern era).

22. On the origins of the word, see Beatrice Hyslop, *French Nationalism in 1789 According to the General Cahiers* (New York, 1934), 22; Jacques Godechot, "Nation, patrie, nationalisme et patriotisme en France au XVIIIe siècle," in *Annales de l'histoire de la Révolution française,* 206 (1971), 481–501.

23. This formulation is based on a reading of Anderson, *Imagined Communities,* esp. 17–23.

24. The limits of Louis XIV's ambitions comes through quite clearly in the recent revisionist work of scholars such as William Beik, *Absolutism and Society in Seventeenth-Century France: State Power and Provincial Aristocracy in Languedoc* (Cambridge, 1985), and Roger Mettam, *Power and Faction in Louis XIV's France* (Oxford, 1988). The perils of reading modern "language politics" back into the early modern period have been amply demonstrated by Henri Peyre, *La royauté et les langues provinciales* (Paris, 1933), 58–91; Danielle Trudeau, "L'ordonnance de Villers-Cotterêts et la langue française: Histoire ou interprétation," *Bibliothèque d'humanisme et Renaissance,* XLV (1983), 461–472; and Paul Cohen, "Courtly French, Learned Latin, and Peas-

ant Patois: The Making of a National Language in Early Modern France," 2 vols., Ph.D. diss., Princeton University, 2000.

25. A good starting point in the immense literature on this subject is still John Bossy, "The Counter-Reformation and the People of Catholic Europe," *Past and Present*, 47 (1970), 51–70. More recently, see Louis Chatellier, *The Europe of the Devout: The Catholic Reformation and the Formation of a New Society*, trans. Jean Birrell (Cambridge, 1989), and R. Po-Chia Hsia, *The World of Catholic Renewal, 1540–1770* (Cambridge, 1998). On the case of Brittany, see the superb study by Alain Croix, *La Bretagne aux 16e et 17e siècles: La vie, la mort, la foi*, 2 vols. (Paris, 1981). On the Catholic clergy see also Timothy Tackett, *Priest and Parish in Eighteenth-Century France: A Social and Political Study of the Curés in the Diocese of Dauphiné, 1750–1791* (Princeton, 1977), and Philip T. Hoffman, *Church and Community in the Diocese of Lyon, 1500–1789* (New Haven, 1984). Keith P. Luria provides an interesting revisionist view on the Catholic Reformation in *Territories of Grace: Cultural Change in the Seventeenth-Century Diocese of Grenoble* (Berkeley, 1991).

26. On Britain, see Linda Colley, *Britons: Forging the Nation 1707–1837* (New Haven, 1992). For the "peripheral" states, see especially Franco Venturi, *Settecento Riformatore*, III and IV (Turin, 1979 and 1984). Colley (p. 86) has recently noted that "it remains unclear why this resurgence of interest in matters patriotic occurred in so many different countries at the same time."

27. See, for instance, the copious publications of Robert Lafont on "Occitania." Maryon McDonald, *"We Are Not French!": Language, Culture and Identity in Brittany* (London, 1989), offers a valuable corrective to this point of view. On the supposed crisis of French identity, see David A. Bell, "Paris Blues," *The New Republic*, Sept. 1, 1997, and the Conclusion, below.

28. Colley, *Britons;* Eugen Weber, *Peasants into Frenchmen: The Modernization of Rural France* (Stanford, 1976), are the most prominent general works on their subjects. On Britain, see also Gerald Newman, *The Rise of English Nationalism: A Cultural History* (London, 1987); Steven Pincus, *Protestantism and Patriotism: Ideologies and the Making of English Foreign Policy, 1650–1688* (Cambridge, 1996); Richard Helgerson, *Forms of Nationhood: The Elizabethan Writing of England* (Chicago, 1992); Brendan Bradshaw and Peter Roberts, eds., *British Consciousness and British Identity: The Making of Britain, 1533–1707* (Cambridge, 1998); Colin Kidd, *British Identities before Nationalism: Ethnicity and Nationhood in the Atlantic World, 1600–1800* (Cambridge, 1999). On nineteenth-century France, see also Caroline Ford, *Creating the Nation in Provincial France: Religion and Political Identity in Brittany* (Princeton, 1993), and James Lehning, *Peasant and French: Cultural Contact in Rural France during the Nineteenth Century* (Cambridge, 1995). Nearly all the general works on nationalism listed in the bibliography (available at www.davidbell.net) accord considerable attention to French history.

29. See particularly Gellner, *Nations and Nationalism;* Hobsbawm, *Nations and Nationalism;* Weber, *Peasants into Frenchmen.*

30. Cited in Ferdinand Brunot et al., *Histoire de la langue française, des origines à 1900,* 13 vols. (Paris, 1905–53), IX, pt. I, 4.

31. See notably Anderson, *Imagined Communities;* Greenfeld, *Nationalism;* Smith, *The Ethnic Origins of Nations* and *National Identity;* Josep R. Llobera, *The God of Modernity: The Development of Nationalism in Western Europe* (Oxford, 1994); John Armstrong, *Nations before Nationalism* (Chapel Hill, 1982); Carla Hesse and Thomas Laqueur, "Introduction: National Cultures before Nationalism," *Representations* 47 (1994), 1–12; Hagen Schulze, *Staat und Nation in der europäischen Geschichte* (Munich, 1994).

32. The fundamental introductory works on the political culture of the old regime are: Baker, *Inventing the French Revolution;* Roger Chartier, *The Cultural Origins of the French Revolution,* trans. Lydia G. Cochrane (Durham, 1991); Keith Michael Baker, ed., *The Political Culture of the Old Regime* (Oxford, 1987). See also Jeffrey Merrick, *The Desacralization of the French Monarchy in the Eighteenth Century* (Baton Rouge, 1990) and Dale Van Kley, *The Damiens Affair and the Unraveling of the Old Regime, 1750–1770* (Princeton, 1984).

33. See especially Pierre Nora, ed., *Les lieux de mémoire,* 7 vols. (Paris, 1984–93); Peter Sahlins, *Boundaries: The Making of France and Spain in the Pyrenees* (Berkeley, 1989); Sahlins, "Fictions of a Catholic France: The Naturalization of Foreigners, 1685–1787," *Representations,* 47 (1994), 85–110; Sahlins, with Jean-François Dubost, *Et si on faisait payer les étrangers? Louis XIV, les immigrés et quelques autres* (Paris, 1999). Also important are two stimulating, if more narrowly focused new works on patriotism: Edmond Dziembowski, *Un nouveau patriotisme français, 1750–1770: La France face à la puissance anglaise à l'époque de la guerre de Sept Ans* (Oxford, 1998), and Hélène Dupuy, "Genèse de la Patrie Moderne: La naissance de l'idée moderne de patrie en France avant et pendant la Révolution," Ph.D. diss., Université de Paris-I (1995). Other recent works on early modern French national sentiment include Greenfeld, 89–188; Sophie Wahnich, *L'impossible citoyen: L'étranger dans le discours de la Révolution française* (Paris, 1997); and the books discussed in David A. Bell, "French National Identity in the Early Modern Period," *Journal of Modern History,* LXVIII/1 (1996), 84–113. Steven Englund is currently writing an ambitious history of modern French nationalism. Michael Rapport's *Nationality and Citizenship in Revolutionary France: The Treatment of Foreigners, 1789–99* (Oxford, 2000) appeared too late to be consulted for this book.

34. See on this point especially Yardeni, *La conscience nationale,* and Alphonse Dupront, "Du sentiment national," in M. François, ed., *La France et les français* (Paris, 1972), 1423–74.

35. For a sharp criticism of Pierre Nora, Colette Beaune, and Miriam Yardeni on this point, see Steven Englund, "The Ghost of Nation Past," *Journal of Modern History,* LXIV (1992), 299–320.

36. Jean Soanen, "Sur l'amour de la patrie" (1683), in J. P. Migne, ed., *Les orateurs sacrés,* 99 vols. (Paris, 1844–66), XL, 1280–95.

37. [François-Ignace d'Espiard de la Borde], *Essais sur le génie et le caractère des nations, divisé en six livres,* 3 vols. (Brussels, 1743).

38. It sold well enough to have three subsequent editions and an English translation: [François-Ignace d'Espiard de la Borde], *L'Esprit des nations,* 2 vols. (The Hague, 1752 and 1753; Geneva, 1753); d'Espiard, *The Spirit of the Nations* (London, 1753). D'Espiard's continuing obscurity was such that in 1769 Jean-Louis Castilhon plagiarized large portions of the book for his own *Considérations sur les causes physiques et morales de la diversité du génie des moeurs, et du gouvernement des nations,* 2 vols. (Bouillon, 1769). In addition, Oliver Goldsmith plagiarized several long sections of the English translation in writing his "The Effects Which Climates Have upon Men, and Other Animals." See Michael Griffin, "Oliver Goldsmith and François-Ignace Espiard de la Borde: An Instance of Plagiarism," *Review of English Studies,* L (1999), 59–64.

39. As Robert Shackleton noted in *Montesquieu: A Critical Biography* (Oxford, 1961), 308–9, Montesquieu almost certainly derived part of his theory of climate from d'Espiard. If anything, Shackleton probably underestimates the importance of d'Espiard's work for Montesquieu.

40. D'Espiard, *Essais,* II, bk. IV, 41.

41. Montesquieu, *The Spirit of the Laws,* Anne M. Cohler, Basia Carolyn Miller, and Harold Samuel Stone, trans. and ed. (Cambridge, 1989), e.g. 310 (section entitled "How careful one must be not to change the general spirit of a nation"); Voltaire, *Essai sur l'histoire générale et sur les moeurs et l'esprit des nations* (Paris, 1756).

42. Jean-Jacques Rousseau, *Considérations sur le gouvernement de Pologne et sur sa réformation projetée* (1772), in *Oeuvres complètes,* 4 vols. (Paris, 1964), III, 960–1.

43. See Martin Papenheim, *Erinnerung und Unsterblichkeit: Semantische Studien zum Todenkult in Frankreich (1715–1794)* (Stuttgart, 1992), 156–200; Jean-Claude Bonnet, *Naissance du Panthéon: Essai sur le culte des grands hommes* (Paris, 1998).

44. Voltaire to Charles Bordes, March 23, 1765, in *Les oeuvres complètes de Voltaire,* Theodore Besterman, ed., 134 vols. (Oxford, 1970–76), CXII, 477. On the plays, see most recently Anne Boës, *La lanterne magique de l'histoire: Essai sur le théâtre historique en France de 1750 à 1789* (Oxford, 1982). It is also worth noting that the Academy of Inscriptions and Belles-Lettres, following

its reorganization in 1701, concerned itself almost entirely with French history and literature, and helped lead a rebirth of scholarly interest in these subjects.

45. See Roger Bickart, *Les parlements et la notion de souveraineté nationale au XVIIIe siècle* (Paris, 1932), and Chapter 2, below.

46. René Louis de Voyer de Paulmy d'Argenson, *Journal et mémoires,* Rathéry, ed., 8 vols. (Paris, 1859), VIII, 315 (June 26, 1754); history work cited in Elisabeth Fehrenbach, "Nation," in Rolf Reichardt and Eberhard Schmitt, eds., *Handbuch politisch-sozialer Grundbegriffe in Frankreich, 1680–1820,* vol. VII (Munich, 1986), 75–107, at 98.

47. Jacques Godard to Cortot, Nov. 7, 1788, in Archives Départementales de la Côte d'Or, E 642.

48. See Jean Locquin, *La peinture d'histoire en France de 1747 à 1785* (Paris, 1912); Jacques Silvestre de Sacy, *Le comte d'Angiviller, dernier directeur général des batiments du roi* (Paris, 1953); Francis H. Dowley, "D'Angiviller's *Grands Hommes* and the Significant Moment," *The Art Bulletin,* XXXIX (1957), 259–77; Andrew McClellan, "D'Angiviller's 'Great Men' of France and the Politics of the Parlements." *Art History,* 13/2 (1990), 177–92; and Chapter 4, below. Sergent's engraving was almost certainly inspired by West's famous rendition of the death of Montcalm's opponent, General Wolfe, in the same 1759 battle.

49. See Dziembowski, *Un nouveau patriotisme,* and Chapter 3, below.

50. [Manson], *Examen impartial du Siége de Calais* (Calais, 1765), pp. 8–9.

51. Bedos, *Le négotiant patriote* (Amsterdam and Paris, 1784); Maupin, *Projet patriotique sur la vigne, les vins rouges, les vins blancs et les cidres* (Paris, 1787); Philippe-Nicolas Pia, *Avis patriotique concernant les personnes suffoquées par la vapeur de charbon qui paroissent mortes et qui ne l'étant pas peuvent recevoir des secours pour être rappellées à la vie* (Paris, 1776).

52. De Forges, *Des véritables intérêts de la patrie* (Rotterdam, 1764), 20.

53. French National Library Catalogue, available at catalogue.bnf.fr. The following list, drawn from the ARTFL database (humanities.uchicago.edu/ARTFL), gives the frequency, per 100,000 words:

Date	Nation	Patrie
1690–1709	4.7	4.8
1710–1729	10.0	18.5
1730–1749	20.8	12.0
1750–1769	22.2	13.2
1770–1789	22.5	18.8

In addition, the use of the neologism "national" went from 0 in 1710–29, to 1.0 per 100,000 in 1730–49, to 1.3 in 1750–69, and 3.8 in 1770–89. The neologisms "patriote" and "patriotique," often used interchangeably, went from 0 in 1730–49 to 0.4 in 1750–69, and 1.5 in 1770–89.

54. *Declaration of the Rights of Man*, art. III; cited in Albert Mathiez, *L'origine des cultes révolutionnaires, 1789–92* (Paris, 1904), 31.

55. Cited in Josephine Grieder, *Anglomania in France, 1740–1789: Fact, Fiction and Political Discourse* (Geneva, 1985), 140.

56. *Discours sur le patriotisme* (n.p., 1788), 82.

57. Cited in C. Berlet, *Les tendances unitaires et provincialistes en France à la fin du XVIIIe siècle* (Nancy, 1913), 151; Emmanuel-Joseph Sieyès, *Instructions envoyées par M. le duc d'Orléans pour les personnes étrangères de sa procuration aux assemblées de bailliages relatives aux Etats-généraux* (Paris, 1789), 44.

58. Cited in Fehrenbach, "Nation," 98.

59. *Réimpression de l'ancien Moniteur*, XVIII, 351.

60. See J. H. Elliott, "A Europe of Composite Monarchies," *Past and Present*, 137 (1992), 48–71.

61. Henri Grégoire, *Essai sur la régénération physique, morale et politique des Juifs*, ed. Rita-Hermon-Belot (Paris, 1989, orig. 1788), 141; Grégoire, *Rapport sur la nécessité et les moyens d'anéantir le patois et d'universaliser l'usage de la langue française* (Paris, Year II [1794]), 10. On the language question, see Chapter 6, below.

62. See Labarrière, Julia, and Baczko.

63. See notably Weber, 8–12, 67–114. On the influence of French policies beyond France, see Hobsbawm, 44; Federico Chabod, *L'idea di nazione* (Bari, 1961), 55–58; Lorenzo Renzi, *La politica linguistica della rivoluzione francese* (Naples, 1981), 171.

64. It would require reading against the grain in archival sources largely compiled by state officials, to glean remarks indicative of sentiments towards the nation and the *patrie*. A pioneering work of this sort is Arlette Farge, *Dire et mal dire: L'opinion publique au dix-huitième siècle* (Paris, 1992). A very different attempt to gauge widespread attitudes through an analysis of a particular text, the *Cahiers de doléances* of 1789, may be found in Gilbert Shapiro and John Markoff, *Revolutionary Demands: A Content Analysis of the Cahiers de doléances of 1789* (Stanford, 1998).

65. Eighteenth-century Gallicanism remains a subject in search of a historian. On the doctrine itself, see most recently Jotham Parsons, "Church and Magistrate in Early Modern France: Politics, Ideology and the Gallician Liberties, 1550–1615," Ph.D. diss., Johns Hopkins University (1998). On the eighteenth-century theological controversies see Catherine Maire, *De la cause de Dieu à la cause de la Nation: Le jansénisme au XVIIIè siècle* (Paris, 1998), and esp. Dale Van Kley, *The Religious Origins of the French Revolution: From Calvin to the Civil Constitution, 1560–1791* (New Haven, 1996).

66. Nora, in *Les lieux de mémoire*, pt. III, I, 29. Another influential work in this tradition is Beaune, *Naissance*. For criticism of Nora on this point see Bell, "Paris Blues," and Englund, "The Ghost of Nation Past."

67. See notably Greenfeld, *Nationalism*, 89–188, Guiomar, *La nation*, and Englund, "The Ghost of Nation Past."

68. Liah Greenfeld comes close to treating it in this matter (esp. see 1–26). See the counterarguments made by Maurizio Viroli, *For Love of Country: An Essay on Patriotism and Nationalism* (Oxford, 1995).

69. On "national sovereignty," see esp. J. K. Wright, "National sovereignty and the National Will: The Political Program of the Declaration of Rights," in Dale Van Kley, ed., *The French Idea of Freedom: The Declaration of the Rights of Man* (Stanford, 1994), 199–233. Here, I am departing from the linguistic approach of Keith Baker in *Inventing the French Revolution*, itself grounded in the work of Quentin Skinner and J. G. A. Pocock, and also of Michel Foucault. Briefly, I would contend that it is possible and necessary to elucidate a broader social and cultural context to which the changing meanings of words ultimately relate, even if they do not reflect it in any simple, causal sense.

70. Foreign Minister Vergennes, cited in J.-F. Labourdette, *Vergennes: Ministre principal de Louis XVI* (Paris, 1990), 207; *Lettre d'un jeune homme à son ami, sur les Français et les Anglais, relativement à la frivolité reprochée aux uns, & la philosophie attribuée aux autres, ou Essai d'un paralelle [sic] à faire entre ces deux nations* (Amsterdam, 1779), 50; Adrien Lamourette, cited in Dupuy, *Genèse*, 131; Club of Auch to Grégoire, in Augustin Gazier, ed., *Lettres à Grégoire sur les patois de France* (Paris, 1880), 94; Commentary on decree of Dec. 22, 1789, cited in Brunot, *Histoire*, IX, pt. 2, 667.

71. Lynn Hunt, *The Family Romance of the French Revolution* (Berkeley, 1992).

72. See notably Joan Landes, *Women and the Public Sphere in the Age of the French Revolution* (Ithaca, 1988); Hunt, *Family Romance;* Sarah Maza, "Response to Daniel Gordon and David Bell," *French Historical Studies*, XVII/3 (1992), 935–53.

73. W. V. Quine, *Quiddities* (Cambridge, Mass., 1987), 90.

74. My thinking here is much indebted to discussions with Dr. Dror Wahrman and his work-in-progress, tentatively titled *A Cultural History of the Modern Self.* See also the works cited in n.17 above.

75. Kathleen Wilson, "The Island Race: Captain Cook, Protestant Evangelicalism and the Construction of English National Identity, 1760–1800," in Tony Claydon and Ian McBride, *Protestantism and National Identity: Britain and Ireland, c. 1650–c. 1850* (Cambridge, 1999), 265–90, at 268. For some interesting criticisms of Colley, see the other essays in this book. For criticism of Weber, see Ford, *Creating the Nation*, and Lehning, *Peasant and French*.

76. I have not paid commensurate attention to the name France itself, a name so

widely used, in so many differing contexts and with so many different meanings, that I have found tracing patterns of usage not to be a useful exercise. Still for an interesting attempt, see Dupront, "Du sentiment national."

77. On the origins of "patriotism" and "nationalism," see Hyslop, *French Nationalism in 1789*, 22, and Pierre Nora, "Nation," in François Furet and Mona Ozouf, eds., *Dictionnaire critique de la Révolution française* (Paris, 1988), 801–4.

78. In my understanding of patriotism and nationalism I rely above all on Gellner, *Nations and Nationalism;* Anderson, *Imagined Communities;* and Viroli, *For Love of Country.* For reasons that will become clear in Chapter 1, I am less convinced by the description of nationalism as an ideology by Elie Kedourie, in *Nationalism* (New York, 1960), or Greenfeld, in *Nationalism.*

79. E.g. those self-styled "national republicans," MM. Pasqua and Chevènement, who have recently and preposterously suggested that additional protection for the moribund Breton and Occitan languages will mean the Balkanization of France. Quoted in *The Economist,* July 3, 1999, 40.

80. See notably Suzanne Citron, *Le mythe nationale: L'histoire de France en question* (Paris, 1987), and the works of Robert Lafont on Occitania, and, for the neoliberal perspective (following on the work of François Furet), Greenfeld, 3–26 and 89–188.

81. Mona Ozouf, *La fête révolutionnaire, 1789–1799* (Paris, 1976), 469.

82. Two recent, important works which have raised a cheer and a half, respectively, for nationalism and Jacobinism, are David Miller, *On Nationality* (Oxford, 1995), and Patrice Higonnet, *Goodness beyond Virtue: Jacobins during the French Revolution* (Cambridge, Mass., 1998).

1. The National and the Sacred

1. "How sweet and fitting it is to die for one's country." Horace, *Odes,* III, ii, 13.

2. See esp. Carlton Hayes, "Nationalism as a Religion," in *Essays on Nationalism* (New York, 1928), 93–125; Hayes, *Nationalism: A Religion* (New York, 1960); Llobera, *The God of Modernity* (for publishing data, see Intro., n.31); Hans Kohn, *The Idea of Nationalism* (New York, 1944); George L. Mosse, *The Nationalization of the Masses: Political Symbolism and Mass Movements in Germany from the Napoleonic Wars through the Third Reich* (New York, 1975); Conor Cruise O'Brien, "Nationalism and the French Revolution," in Geoffrey Best, ed., *The Permanent Revolution: The French Revolution and Its Legacy, 1789–1989* (Chicago and London, 1988), 17–48; O'Brien, *God Land: Reflections on Religion and Nationalism* (Cambridge, Mass., 1993); Anderson, *Imagined Communities* (see Intro., n.13); Gorski, "The Mosaic Moment" (see Intro., n.21); Adam Zamoyski, *Holy Madness: Romantics, Patriots, and Revo-*

lutionaries, 1776–1871 (New York, 1999); Mary Anne Perkins, *Word and Nation, 1770–1850: Religious and Metaphysical Language in European National Consciousness* (London, 1999), esp. 262–76 ("The New Religion of Nationalism").

3. Liah Greenfeld, "The Modern Religion?" *Critical Review,* X/2 (1996), 169–91, quote from 169.

4. Jules Michelet, *Journal,* Paul Viallaneix, ed., 4 vols. (Paris, 1959), I, 83 (August 7, 1831). Quoted in O'Brien's thoughtful "Nationalism," 17.

5. Anderson, *Imagined Communities,* 19.

6. Ibid. Anderson quickly adds that nationalism did not simply "supersede" religion.

7. Again, see Greenfeld, *Nationalism* (see Intro., n.21), 89–188; Guiomar, *La nation* (see Intro., n.18); Englund, "The Ghost of Nation Past" (see Intro., n.35); Bickart, *Les parlements* (see Intro., n.45).

8. Henri de Boulainvilliers, *Essais sur la noblesse de France* (Amsterdam, 1732).

9. See again Greenfeld, *Nationalism,* 89–188; Guiomar, *La nation;* Englund, "The Ghost of Nation Past."

10. See William Farr Church, *Constitutional Thought in Sixteenth-Century France* (Cambridge, Mass., 1941); François Hotman, *Francogallia,* ed. Ralph Giesey (Cambridge, 1972).

11. Boulainvilliers did use the phrase "natural rights." See the cogent discussion in Robert Morrissey, *L'empereur à la barbe fleurie: Charlemagne dans la mythologie et l'histoire de France* (Paris, 1997), 270–80.

12. I have developed this point in reference to Louis-Adrien Le Paige in David A. Bell, *Lawyers and Citizens: The Making of a Political Elite in Old Regime France* (New York, 1994), 117–19. For a recent survey of the ongoing debate over these matters, see Michael Sonenscher, "Enlightenment and Revolution," *The Journal of Modern History,* LXX/2 (1998), 371–83.

13. On semantic changes in general in France, see Rolf Reichardt et al.'s indispensable *Handbuch politisch-sozialer Grundbegriffe* (see Intro., n.46), which is in turn indebted to Otto Brunner, Werner Conze, and Reinhart Koselleck, eds., *Geschichtliche Grundbegriffe: Historisches Lexikon zur politisch-sozialen Sprache in Deutschland* (Stuttgart, 1972). In his general introduction (I, 39–148), Reichardt suggests (p. 40) that there was a general shift of "leading representational and behavior-directing fundamental concepts" ("vorstellungs- und handlungssteuernden Grundbegriffe") between 1680 and 1820. But he does not attempt to analyze any particular group of concepts. His explanatory framework (70–78) draws on Habermas in a manner similar to my section below, "The Realm of Material Organization."

14. Lucien Febvre, "*Civilisation:* Evolution of a Word and a Group of Ideas," in *A New Kind of History: From the Writings of Febvre,* Peter Burke, ed., K. Folca,

trans. (New York, 1973), 219–57; also Joachim Moras, *Ursprung und Ent-wicklung des Begriffs der Zivilisation in Frankreich (1756–1830), Hamburger Studien zu Volkstum und Kultur der Romanen,* VI (Hamburg, 1930); Pierre Michel, "Barbarie, civilisation, vandalisme," in Reichardt and Schmitt, *Handbuch,* VIII (1988), 1–43; Anthony Pagden, "The 'Defence of Civilisation' in Eighteenth-Century Social Theory," *History of the Human Sciences,* I/1 (1988), 33–45.

15. Keith Michael Baker, "Enlightenment and the Institution of Society: Notes for a Conceptual History," in Willem Melching and Wyger Velema, eds., *Main Trends in Cultural History* (Amsterdam, 1992), 95–120, quote from 119; Daniel Gordon, *Citizens without Sovereignty: Equality and Sociability in French Thought, 1670–1789* (Princeton, 1994), esp. 43–85.

16. The most useful starting points remain Mona Ozouf, "L'opinion publique," in Baker, ed., *The Political Culture of the Old Regime,* 419–34 (see Intro., n.32), and Baker, *Inventing the French Revolution* (see Intro., n.17), 167–99.

17. On *moeurs,* see Roberto Romani, "All Montesquieu's Sons: The Place of *esprit général, caractère national,* and *moeurs* in French Political Philosophy, 1748–1789," in *Studies on Voltaire and the Eighteenth Century,* 362 (1998):189–235; Arthur M. Wilson, "The Concept of *moeurs* in Diderot's Social and Political Thought," in W. H. Barber et al., eds., *The Age of the Enlightenment: Studies Presented to Theodore Besterman* (Edinburgh, 1967), 188–99. On *peuple,* see Gérard Fritz, *L'idée de peuple en France du XVIIè au XIXè siècle* (Strasbourg, 1988); Henri Coulet, ed., *Images du peuple au XVIIIè siècle* (Paris, 1973). On *police,* see Gordon, 9–24. All in all, eighteenth-century French writers showed such a talent for such neologisms, redefinitions, and quarrels over words that industrious German disciples of Reinhart Koselleck have seen fit to create, in the *Handbuch politisch-sozialer Grundbegriffe,* a virtual encyclopedia on the subject.

18. On commerce, see Albert O. Hirschman, *The Passions and the Interests: Political Arguments for Capitalism before Its Triumph* (Princeton, 1976); J. G. A. Pocock, *Virtue, Commerce and History* (Cambridge, 1985). On politeness, see especially Roger Chartier, "From Texts to Manners, A Concept and Its Books: *Civilité* between Aristocratic Distinction and Popular Appropriation," in *The Cultural Uses of Print in Early Modern France* (Princeton, 1987), 71–109. On citizenship, see Peter Sahlins, "Fictions of a Catholic France" (see Intro., n.33); and Sahlins, "The Eighteenth-Century Revolution of Citizenship," unpublished paper presented to the conference "Migration Controls in Nineteenth Century Europe and the United States," Université de Paris (June 1999), which summarizes some theses of his forthcoming book on the subject.

19. On this point, I am endebted to Craig Calhoun, "Nationalism and Difference: The Politics of Identity Writ Large," in his *Critical Social Theory: Culture, History and the Challenge of Difference* (Oxford, 1995), 231–82, esp. 233.

20. Thus Baker and Gordon identify "society" as fundamental (e.g. Gordon, *Citizens without Sovereignty*, 7), while Greenfeld, by contrast, calls the idea of the nation the "constitutive element of modernity" (Greenfeld, *Nationalism*, 18). Gordon argues that "nation" has a more specifically political, statist resonance than "society." Without attempting to go into this point in detail, I would suggest that such resonances are historically variable and that in some historical situations "nation" may well seem a more inclusive, neutral term than "society," which itself can carry resonances of hierarchy and exclusion. See on this last point Linda Colley, "Whose Nation? Class and National Consciousness in Britain, 1750–1830," *Past and Present*, 113 (1986), 96–117, and Sarah Maza, "Luxury, Morality and Social Change: Why There Was No Middle-Class Consciousness in Prerevolutionary France," *Journal of Modern History*, LXIX/2 (1997), 199–229. It is precisely to avoid assigning priority to any particular term that I resort here to terms such as "community," "human coexistence," and "human relations."

21. Particularly Marcel Gauchet, *The Disenchantment of the World: A Political History of Religion*, trans. Oscar Burge (Princeton, 1998), Reinhart Koselleck, *Kritik und Krise: Eine Studie zur Pathogenese der bürgerlichen Welt* (Frankfurt, 1959, repr. 1979); and Jürgen Habermas, *The Structural Transformation of the Public Sphere: An Inquiry into a Category of Bourgeois Society*, Thomas Burger and Frederick Lawrence, trans. (Cambridge, Mass., 1989). I have also benefited greatly from J. G. A. Pocock's article "Conservative Enlightenment and Democratic Revolution: The American and French Cases in British Perspective," *Government and Opposition*, XXIV (1989), 81–106.

22. This idea of distinct if connected realms is indebted to Daniel Bell's discussion of the "disjunction of realms" in *The Cultural Contradictions of Capitalism* (New York, 1976), 3–30.

23. Paul Hazard, *La crise de la conscience européenne, 1680–1715* (Paris, 1961). See especially the preface, vii–xi, in which Hazard gives full rein to his fondness for martial metaphors.

24. Gauchet, *Disenchantment*. While Gauchet obviously borrows the term "disenchantment" from Weber, he uses it to refer not to the progress of reason, but to the liberation of mankind from divine "determination."

25. Ibid., 162.

26. Ibid., 23–24.

27. "Rationality, individual freedom, and appropriation of the natural world . . . All three are incipient in the new articulation of the visible and the invisible presupposed by the Christian deity." Ibid., 62.

28. Ibid., 57.

29. He mentions Jansenism only in passing (61), but then again, in attempting to write a universal history of religion in just 200 pages, he abandons specificity more or less entirely.

30. On Jansenism, most recently, see Monique Cottret, *Jansénismes et lumières: Pour un autre XVIIIè siècle* (Paris, 1998); Maire, *De la cause de Dieu* (see Intro., n.65); Van Kley, *The Religious Origins* (see Intro., n.65).

31. An important recent work on this period of French history that supports the idea of placing "orthodox" religious and skeptical philosophical works side by side is Alan Charles Kors, *Atheism in France, 1650–1729,* vol. I (Princeton, 1990).

32. Soanen, "Sur l'amour de la patrie" (see Intro., n.36), 1281.

33. Ibid., 1281–82.

34. Baker, "Enlightenment and the Institution of Society," esp. 119–20.

35. Marcel Gauchet, "Les *Lettres sur l'histoire de France* d'Augustin Thierry," in Nora, ed., *Les lieux de mémoire* (see Intro., n.33), Part 2, I, 247–316. See esp 286: "the Nation is the consequence [*résultante*] and expression of the passage from a society structured by subjection to an external principle of order to a society structurally subject to itself . . . The root of the transformation is religious; it rests on the exploitation of a fundamental virtuality of Christianity, namely the unlinking of the celestial order and the terrestrial order."

36. Pocock, "Conservative Enlightenment," 84. Pocock has recently put this idea at the heart of his magisterial work on Edward Gibbon, *Barbarism and Religion,* 2 vols. to date (Cambridge, 2000).

37. "O ruined France! O bloody land, / Not land, but ash." Agrippa d'Aubigné, *Les tragiques,* Jean-Raymond Fanlo, ed., 2 vols. (Paris, 1995, orig. 1616), I, 61–62.

38. Voltaire, *La Henriade: Poème en dix chants* (Paris, 1869), esp. *chant II* (42–52). Voltaire also dwelt at length on the period in his *Essai sur les moeurs,* in much of his poetry, and indirectly in his fiction, including *Candide.* On the cult of Henri IV, and in general on the persistence of the memory of the wars, see Marcel Reinhard, *La légende de Henri IV* (Saint-Brieuc, 1935).

39. Diderot, *Essai sur le mérite,* quoted in Gordon, *Citizens without Sovereignty,* 82.

40. On the theater, see Clarence D. Brenner, "Henri IV on the French Stage in the Eighteenth Century," *P.M.L.A.,* XLVI/2 (1931), 540–53; Jean-Alexis Rivoire, *Le patriotisme dans le théâtre sérieux de la Révolution* (Paris, 1950), esp. 44–45.

41. *La voix du vrai patriote catholique, opposée à celle des faux patriotes tolérans* (n.p., 1756), 229.

42. Quoted in Koselleck, *Kritik und Krise,* 118.

43. Quoted in Bonnet, *Naissance du Panthéon* (see Intro., n.43), 260.

44. "It is religion whose inhuman zeal / Puts weapons in every Frenchman's hands." Voltaire, *La Henriade,* 42.

45. See Yardeni, *La conscience nationale* (see Intro., n.12), 81; Peter Campbell, *Power and Politics in Old Regime France, 1720–1745* (London, 1996); Isabelle

Storez, *Le chancelier Henri François d'Aguesseau (1688–1751): Monarchiste et libéral* (Paris, 1996), esp. 360–61.

46. See Yardeni, *La conscience nationale*, 77–98; Beaune, *Naissance* (see Intro., n.12), 4–5. "This threat to the very survival of the *patrie* called forth one of the most massive outbursts of patriotic writing in the early-modern period": William Farr Church, "France," in Orest Ranum, ed., *National Consciousness, History and Political Culture in Early Modern Europe* (Baltimore, 1975), 43–66, at 46.

47. Koselleck, *Kritik und Krise*, 11–39.

48. Koselleck argues that the theorists of absolute monarchy demanded, in the name of civic order, that individuals sever the connection between their exterior actions and their interior convictions, effectively splitting human beings into public and private halves. But in the eighteenth century, the new private conscience ironically emerged as the basis for a powerful moral critique of absolutism. Despite the way it underestimates the religious underpinnings of absolute monarchy, Koselleck's argument remains enormously valuable.

49. "O Charles! It is time to expiate the crime / Impious corpse, leave your royal tomb!" Ponce-Denis Ecouchard ("Lebrun"), "Fragment sur Charles IX," in *Poésies nationales de la Révolution française* (Paris, 1836), 9. See also Marie-Joseph Chénier, *Charles IX, ou l'école des rois* (Paris, 1790); Louis-Sébastien Mercier, *La destruction de la Ligue, ou la réduction de Paris* (Amsterdam, 1782).

50. The classic theoretical expositions of this perspective are Karl Deutsch, *Nationalism and Social Communication* (Cambridge, Mass., 1966), and Gellner, *Nations and Nationalism*.

51. Two works exemplifying the cultural historical approach to nationalism are Ford, *Creating the Nation*, and Lehning, *Peasant and French* (see Intro., n.28). More generally, see J. G. A. Pocock, *Politics, Language and Time* (Cambridge, 1985), 1–34; Gareth Stedman Jones, *Languages of Class: Studies in English Working Class History, 1832–1982* (Cambridge, 1983); Dror Wahrman, *Imagining the Middle Class: The Political Representation of Class in Britain, c. 1780–1840* (Cambridge, 1995). On the French state as nation-builder, see Englund, "The Ghost of Nation Past," and Bell, "Paris Blues" (see Intro., n.27).

52. See Chapter 6, below.

53. See James B. Collins, *The State in Early Modern France* (Cambridge, 1995).

54. See Theodore K. Rabb, *The Struggle for Stability in Early Modern Europe* (Oxford, 1975), 116–45.

55. Michael Kwass, "A Kingdom of Taxpayers: State Formation, Privilege, and Political Culture in Eighteenth-Century France," *Journal of Modern History*, LII/2 (1998), 295–339, quote from 301–2.

56. Quoted in Lionel Rothkrug, *Opposition to Louis XIV: The Political and Social*

Origins of the French Enlightenment (Princeton, 1965), 284–85. See also Daniel Nordman and Jacques Revel, "La connaissance du territoire," in Jacques Revel and André Burguière, eds., *Histoire de la France: L'espace français* (Paris, 1989), 71–115, esp. 83–87 ("La naissance de la statistique") and 108–15. See also "Instruction pour les Maîtres des Requêtes, commissaires départis dans les provinces," Sept. 1663, in *Lettres, instructions et mémoires de Colbert,* ed. Pierre Clément (Paris, 1877), IV, 27–43. My thanks to Orest Ranum for pointing out this text to me.

57. See Rothkrug, 356–60.
58. On the Dutch papers, see Jeremy D. Popkin, *News and Politics in the Age of Revolution: Jean de Luzac's Gazette de Leyde* (Ithaca, 1989). Good surveys of the press are found in Jack Censer, *The French Press in the Age of Enlightenment* (London, 1994); Jeremy D. Popkin, "The Prerevoluionary Origins of Political Journalism," in Baker, ed., *Political Culture,* 203–224.
59. Habermas, *Structural Transformation,* 14ff.
60. Margaret C. Jacob, *Living the Enlightenment: Freemasonry and Politics in Eighteenth-Century Europe* (New York, 1991), 27; Dena Goodman, *The Republic of Letters: A Cultural History of the French Enlightenment* (Ithaca, 1994), 74–77.
61. See Chartier, *Cultural Origins* (see Intro., n.32), 20–35. Chartier notes the shift from seventeenth- to eighteenth-century ideas of the public.
62. Robert A. Schneider, *Public Life in Toulouse, 1463–1789: From Municipal Republic to Cosmopolitan City* (Ithaca, 1989), esp. 255–61, quote from 255. For a view of somewhat similar processes occurring in Britain, see Dror Wahrman, "National Society, Communal Culture: An Argument about the Recent Historiography of Eighteenth-Century Britain," *Social History,* XVII/1 (1992), 43–62.
63. Jean-François Sobry, *Le mode françois, ou discours sur les principaux usages de la nation françoise* (Paris, 1786), 10. On the book, see Barbier's *Dictionnaire des anonymes.* The book was suppressed by the Breteuil ministry because of its attack on state finances.
64. Quoted in Moras, *Ursprung,* 6.
65. John Brewer has made much this argument about politeness in the first chapter of his *The Pleasures of the Imagination* (London, 1997). See also Hirschman, *The Passions and the Interests;* Pocock, *Virtue, Commerce and History,* and Chartier, "From Texts to Manners."
66. See Sahlins, "The Eighteenth-Century Revolution of Citizenship."
67. See Chartier, *Cultural Origins,* 92–110.
68. Bernard Groethuysen, *The Bourgeois: Catholicism versus Capitalism in Eighteenth-Century France,* trans. Mary Ilford (New York, 1968, orig. 1927), 39, 40. See on this subject Daniel Gordon, "Bernard Groethuysen and the Human Conversation," *History and Theory,* 36/2 (1997), 289–311.

69. On this point, see esp. Koselleck, 18–32.

70. Rousseau, *Oeuvres,* III, 464–5. Maurice Cranston's admittedly too free trans-lation (*The Social Contract,* London, 1968), renders "the religion of man" as "the religion of the private person" (182).

71. On this point see Gordon, *Citizens without Sovereignty,* 76–85.

72. *Encyclopédie,* XII (1765), 510. Cited in Gordon, 83.

73. Ernst H. Kantorowicz, *The King's Two Bodies: A Study in Mediaeval Political Theology* (Princeton, 1957), 232–72, quote from 267. On the original reli-gious connotations of *patria,* see also Viroli, *For Love of Country* (see Intro., n.68), 18–19.

74. Quoted in Church, "France," 49, and Yardeni, *La conscience nationale,* 107.

75. Chateaubrun, *Philoctète* (Paris, 1756), 5; Métal, *Description et explication de la Philopatrie, personnage iconologique* . . . (Paris, 1782), 27; Chevalier de Jaucourt, "Patrie," in *Encyclopédie* (1765), XII, 178–80, quote from 178; Fran-çois Ferlus, *Le patriotisme chrétien* (Montpellier, 1787), 12; [Claude-Rigobert Lefèbvre de Beauvray], *Adresse à la nation Angloise, poème patriotique* (Am-sterdam, 1757), 6; Foix, *Le patriotisme, ou la France sauvée* (n.p., 1789), 3.

76. Quoted in Perkins, *Nation and Word,* 270.

77. Rousseau, *Oeuvres,* III, 347–470, and esp. 381–84 on the Lawgiver and 460–69 on Civil Religion.

78. Ibid., III, 956.

79. Ibid., III, 957–58. Rousseau put Numa and Moses alongside the Spartan Lycurgus.

80. On *patrie,* see Nathalie Elie-Lefebvre, "Le débat sur l'idée de patrie et sur le patriotisme, 1742–1789," unpublished Mémoire de Maîtrise, Université de Paris I, 1974; Dupuy, "Genèse de la Patrie Moderne"; Dziembowski, *Un nou-veau patriotisme français* (see Intro., n.33), 321–68.

81. Voltaire, in *Philosophical Dictionary,* http://www.voltaire-integral.com/20/ patrie.htm; quoted in Alphonse Aulard, *Le patriotisme français de la Renais-sance à la Révolution* (Paris, 1921), 58, and Goodman, *The Republic of Letters,* 50.

82. Montesquieu, *The Spirit of the Laws,* 25–27 (III, chs. 5–7). The point is con-vincingly demonstrated by Viroli, in *For Love of Country,* esp. 63–94. The di-vergence of meaning in France, however, does call into question Viroli's as-sertion that patriotism was a coherent "language," as opposed to a loose set of associations.

83. On notions of time in republican thought, see J. G. A. Pocock, *The Machia-vellian Moment: Florentine Political Thought and the Atlantic Republican Tra-dition* (Princeton, 1975), esp 3–80.

84. The word *civilisation* did exist before the eighteenth century, but meant the transformation of a criminal trial into a civil one. The verb "to civilize" dated back to the seventeenth century. See Michel, "Barbarie . . . ," 10.

85. Marie-Jean-Antoine-Nicolas de Condorcet, *Esquisse d'un tableau historique du progrès de l'esprit humain* (Paris, 1966), 203. On the general question of the value of human progress, see also the helpful work of Jean-Marie Goulemot, *Discours, histoire et révolutions* (Paris, 1975). On "civilization," see Febvre, "Civilization"; Moras, *Ursprung;* Michel, "Barbarie"; Pagden, "The 'Defence of Civilization.'"

86. As in this 1767 poem: "Toute Société languit, se décompose, / Dès qu'on desserre ce lien. / La chute des Etats n'a jamais d'autre cause / Que le relâchement de l'esprit Citoyen" ("Every Society languishes and decomposes, once this bond slackens. The fall of States never has any cause other than the loosening of the Citizen spirit"). *Le patriotisme, poème qui a été présenté a l'Académie françoise pour le prix de 1766 et dont on n'a fait aucune mention* (Paris, 1767), 6.

87. This point is made by Sahlins, "Fictions of a Catholic France."

88. See Godechot, "Nation, patrie, nationalisme et patriotisme" (see Intro., n.22), 486; Guiomar, *L'idéologie nationale: Nation, représentation, propriété* (Paris, 1974), 31; Boës, *La lanterne magique* (see Intro., n.44), 5; quote from Fehrenbach, "Nation" (see Intro., n.46), 76.

89. See the discussion of these points by Pierre Nora, "Nation" (see Intro., n.77), esp. 802.

90. Victor de Riquetti de Mirabeau, *L'ami des hommes, ou traité de la population,* ed. Rouxel (Paris, 1883). On the enormous popularity of the book in the 1760s, see vi. Mirabeau, often identified with the physiocrats, was the father of the revolutionary orator.

91. On his use of "civilization," see Moras, *Ursprung*, 5; on his use of "regeneration," see Morrissey, *L'empereur à la barbe fleurie*, 268. D'Alembert had used the originally theological concept of "regeneration" in the preliminary discourse to the *Encyclopédie,* but far more sparingly. See Alyssa R. Sepinwall, "Regenerating France, Regenerating the World: The Abbé Grégoire and the French Revolution, 1750–1831," Ph.D. diss., Stanford University (1998), 83–87.

92. Mirabeau, *L'ami des hommes,* 247–68.

93. See esp. ibid., 316–29, on the question of whether France itself had yet reached the point of decrepitude.

94. Robert-Martin Lesuire, *Les sauvages de l'Europe* (Berlin, 1760), quote from 41. The novel had sufficient success to be reprinted during France and England's next war (Paris, 1780); it was even translated into English (*The Savages of Europe,* London, 1764).

95. Ibid., 22, 35–9, 126, 42.

96. C.-S. Favart, *L'anglois à Bordeaux* (Paris, 1763, repr. 1771), 5; Jean-Bernard Leblanc and La Coste, quoted in Grieder, *Anglomania* (see Intro., n.55), 42; *Lettre d'un jeune homme* (see Intro., n.70), 44; Louis-Charles Fougeret de

Montbron, *Préservatif contre l'Anglomanie* ("Minorca," 1757), 51; Edmond-Jean-François Barbier, *Chronique de la régence et du règne de Louis XV*, 7 vols. (Paris, 1885), III, 273. In general, see Grieder, Dziembowski, *Un nouveau patriotisme;* and Frances Acomb, *Anglophobia in France: An Essay in the History of Constitutionalism and Nationalism* (Durham, 1950).

97. Acomb's *Anglophobia*, which focuses on attitudes toward the English constitution, concludes that "Anglophile liberalism" declined towards the end of the old regime. Grieder, whose *Anglomania* takes in a broader spectrum of cultural influences, argues for the persistence of a dialectic between Anglophobia and Anglomania, as does Dziembowski in *Un nouveau patriotisme français.*

98. See also Edmond Dziembowski, "Les débuts d'un publiciste au service de la monarchie: L'activité littéraire de Jacob-Nicolas Moreau pendant la guerre de sept ans," *Revue d'histoire diplomatique*, 4 (1995), 305–22; J. Labourdette, *Vergennes*, 205–8 (see Intro., n.70).

99. For an overview of this literature, see Thomas J. Schlereth, *The Cosmopolitan Ideal in Enlightenment Thought: Its Form and Function in the Ideas of Franklin, Hume, and Voltaire, 1694–1790* (South Bend, 1977); Gerd van den Heuvel, "Cosmopolite, cosmopolitisme," in Reichart and Schmitt, eds., *Handbuch politisch-sozialer Grundbegriffe*, VI (Munich, 1986), 41–55.

100. Ferlus, *Le patriotisme*, 29; abbé Baudeau, quoted in Elie-Lefebvre, 170; *Journal encyclopédique, par une société de gens de lettres*, I (Jan. 15, 1756), 31; ibid., 30; *Apologie du caractère des anglois et des françois* (n.p., 1726), 65.

101. Elie-Lefebvre, 169–81; Montesquieu, *Cahiers, 1716–1755*, Bernard Grasset, ed. (Paris, 1941), 9–10.

102. Sobry, *Le mode françois*, 12, 431.

103. *Discours sur le patriotisme* (see Intro., n.56), 10; A. J. de Baptestein de Mouliers Rupe, *Mémoire sur un moyen facile et infallible de faire renaître le patriotisme en France, dans toutes les classes des citoyens, comme dans les deux sexes* (Amsterdam, 1789), 1; *Le patriotisme, poëme*, 6; Claude-Rigobert Lefèbvre de Beauvray, *Dictionnaire social et patriotique* (Amsterdam, 1770), unpaginated preface; Jean-Baptiste-Jacques Elie de Beaumont, *Discours sur le patriotisme dans la monarchie* (Bordeaux, 1777), 9.

104. Pierre-Laurent Buirette de Belloy, *Le siège de Calais* (Leyden, 1765), 48–49. See Acomb, *Anglophobia*, 55–59, for a representative interpretation of the play.

105. See, for instance, Acomb, *Anglophobia*, 55.

106. Favart, *L'anglois à Bordeaux;* Lesuire, esp 61.

107. The evidence for this assertion will be discussed in Chapter 3.

108. See Bernard Cottret, ed., *Bolingbroke's Political Writings: The Conservative Enlightenment* (New York, 1997).

109. See on this subject Newman, *The Rise of English Nationalism*, esp. 1–47.

110. Colley, *Britons* (see Intro., n.26), 36; Newman, *The Rise of English Nationalism* (see Intro., n.28); Kathleen Wilson, *The Sense of the People: Politics, Culture, and Imperialism in England, 1715–1785* (Cambridge, 1995). Jeremy Black, however, argues against taking the conclusion too far in "Confessional State or Elect Nation? Religion and Identity in Eighteenth-Century England," in Claydon and McBride, *Protestantism and National Identity*, 53–74. T. H. Breen, "Ideology and Nationalism on the Eve of the American Revolution: Revisions Once More in Need of Revising," *Journal of American History*, LXXXIV/1 (1997), 13–39, emphasizes that Britain's exclusionary nationalism could even be directed at its own colonists in North America.

111. Johann Georg Zimmermann, *Vom Nationalstolze* (Zurich, 1768), 177. The book was published in at least four editions and translated into both English and French.

112. See Colley, esp. 1–54; Newman, esp. 49–120; Wilson, *The Sense of the People*, 140–65.

113. James Axtell, *The Invasion Within: The Contest of Cultures in Colonial North America* (New York, 1981).

114. Colley, 11–54.

115. Newman, *The Rise of English Nationalism*, 109–18, quotes from 115, 112.

116. See Lionel Gossman, *Medievalism and the Ideologies of the Enlightenment: The World and Work of La Curne de Sainte-Palaye* (Baltimore, 1968). See also below, Chapter 5.

117. Again belying Maurizio Viroli's claim that the "language of patriotism" had a single, essential meaning. See Viroli, *For Love of Country*, 1–2.

118. The English language, of course, has no real equivalent of *patrie;* "fatherland" and "motherland" are almost always used in reference to foreign countries. Nonetheless, the phrase "love of country" does convey much the same sense as "amour de la patrie."

119. Colley, *Britons*, 29–33. On the Netherlands, see G. Groenhuis, *De Predikanten: De sociale positie van de gereformeerde predikanten in de Republiek der Verenigde Nederlanden voor 1700* (Groningen, 1977), 77–86; Gorski, "The Mosaic Moment," 1434–52. In general on this theme, see William R. Hutchison and Hartmut Lehmann, eds., *Many Are Chosen: Divine Election and Western Nationalism* (Minneapolis, 1994).

120. See Tony Claydon and Ian McBride, "The Trials of the Chosen Peoples," in Claydon and McBride, *Protestantism*, 13–15.

121. On English patriotism in the sixteenth and seventeenth centuries, see Helgerson, *Forms of Nationhood* (see Intro., n.28); Greenfeld, *Nationalism*, 27–87; Philip Corrigan and Derek Sayer, *The Great Arch: English State Formation as Cultural Revolution* (Oxford, 1985), 55–71, and William Hunt, "Civic Chivalry and the English Civil War," in Anthony Grafton and Ann Blair, eds.,

The Transmission of Culture in Early Modern Europe (Philadelphia, 1990), 204–37.

122. Montesquieu, *Spirit of the Laws*, 463 (bk. XXIV, ch. 5).

2. The Politics of Patriotism

1. Henri-François d'Aguesseau, "De l'amour de la patrie" (1715), in *Oeuvres*, 13 vols. (Paris, 1759), I, 205–13, quote from 208.

2. Aulard, *Le patriotisme français* (see Ch. 1, n.81), 27. Similar, if more muted opinions are expressed by Church, "France," 63–4 (see Ch. 1, n.46), and Philippe Contamine, "Mourir pour la Patrie: Xe-XXe siècle," in Nora, ed., *Les lieux de mémoire* (see Intro., n.33), pt. II, III, 31.

3. Understandably enough, perhaps, since Aulard initially made the pronounce- ment in a public lecture during World War I, when the historical continuity of patriotism was a matter of more than academic interest.

4. To take just one example, in November of 1730, when a group of obstreper- ous barristers claimed that the king was bound to his subjects by contract, d'Aguesseau himself insisted on drafting the royal declaration that con- demned their offending document to the flame, and threatened the signato- ries with dire penalties unless they formally retracted. See Bell, *Lawyers and Citizens* (see Ch. 1, n.12), 92–3. D'Aguesseau's *arrêt de conseil* can be found in Bibliothèque Nationale, Cabinet des Manuscrits, Fonds Joly de Fleury 97, fols. 281–82. On d'Aguesseau in general, see most recently Storez, *Le chancelier Henri-François d'Aguesseau* (see Ch. 1, n.45).

5. D'Aguesseau never mentioned the king by name and insisted that whatever Louis's failings, his subjects suffered from them as well.

6. The only real predecessor I can find for d'Aguesseau in this respect is Soanen, in "Sur l'amour de la patrie" (see Intro., n.36).

7. D'Aguesseau, 207–8.

8. Ibid., 211.

9. See Viroli, *For Love of Country* (see Intro., n.68), 18–62.

10. Emmanuel Le Roy Ladurie, *L'ancien régime, De Louis XIII à Louis XV,* 2 vols. (Paris, 1991), II, 7.

11. The chancellor never engaged in open theological debate and never made any public profession of faith, but as Storez shows (535–48), his sympathy for and acceptance of Jansenist ideas was obvious.

12. See Storez, 197–236.

13. Bibliothèque de Port-Royal, Collection Le Paige, 449.

14. D'Aguesseau, 211–12.

15. Among these studies are Aulard, *Le patriotisme;* Church, "France"; Clive Emsley, "Nationalist Rhetoric and Nationalist Sentiment in Revolutionary

France," in Otto Dann and John Dinwiddy, eds., *Nationalism in the Age of the French Revolution* (London, 1988), 39–52; Fehrenbach, "Nation" (see Intro., n.46); Godechot, "Nation, patrie" (see Intro., n.22); Greenfeld, *Nationalism* (see Intro., n.21); Jean-Yves Guiomar, *L'idéologie nationale* (see Ch. 1, n.88); Guiomar, *La nation entre l'histoire et la raison* (see Intro., n.18); Norman Hampson, "La patrie," in Colin Lucas, ed., *The Political Culture of the French Revolution* (Oxford, 1988), 125–37; Hyslop, *French Nationalism in 1789* (see Intro., n.22); Hans Kohn, *Prelude to Nation States: The French and German Experience, 1789–1815* (New York, 1967); W. Krauss, "'Patriote,' 'patriotique,' 'patriotisme' à la fin de l'Ancien Régime," in W. H. Barber, ed., *The Age of the Enlightenment* (London, 1967), 387–94; Jean Lestocquoy, *Histoire du patriotisme en France des origines à nos jours* (Paris, 1968); Nora, "Nation" (see Intro., n.77); O'Brien, "Nationalism" (see Ch.1, n.2); Robert Palmer, "The National Idea in France before the Revolution," *Journal of the History of Ideas*, I (1940), 95–111; Boyd Shafer, "Bourgeois Nationalism in the Pamphlets on the Eve of the French Revolution," *Journal of Modern History*, X (1938), 31–50; Michel Vovelle, "Entre cosmopolitisme et xénophobie: Patrie, nation, république universelle dans les idéologies de la Révolution française," in Michael O'Dea and Kevin Whelan, eds., *Nations and Nationalisms: France, Britain and Ireland and the Eighteenth-Century Context* (Oxford, 1995), 11–26. See also the following dissertations: Dupuy, "Genèse de la patrie moderne" (see Intro., n.33); Elie-Lefebvre, "Le débat" (see Ch. 1, n.80); Clarke Garrett, "French Nationalism on the Eve of the French Revolution," Ph.D. diss., University of Wisconsin (1961).

16. Dziembowski, *Un nouveau patriotisme français* (see Intro., n.33), esp. 1–15, 491–96. The reason may be that Dziembowski focuses on the *patrie;* the concept of the *nation,* by contrast, owed more of its importance to internal politics.

17. Jean Egret's *Louis XV et l'opposition parlementaire* (Paris, 1970) is now badly out of date, but remains the most general survey of the *parlements* in the eighteenth century. Among more recent works, see particularly Campbell, *Power and Politics* (see Ch. 1, n.45); Van Kley, *The Damiens Affair* (see Intro., n.32); Julian Swann, *Politics and the Parlement of Paris under Louis XV, 1754–1774* (Cambridge, 1995); Durand Echeverria, *The Maupeou Revolution: A Study in the History of Libertarianism, France, 1770–1774* (Baton Rouge, 1985); and Bailey Stone, *The French Parlements and the Crisis of the Old Regime* (Chapel Hill, 1986).

18. See most recently Bell, *Lawyers and Citizens,* and Sarah Maza, *Private Lives and Public Affairs: The Causes Célèbres of Prerevolutionary France* (Berkeley, 1993).

19. See Chartier, *Cultural Origins* (see Intro., n.32), 38–66.

20. Works emphasizing tradition and continuity in *parlementaire* history are Swann, *Politics*, and John Rogister, *Louis XV and the Parlement of Paris, 1737–55* (Cambridge, 1995). See also David A. Bell, "How (and How Not) to Write *Histoire événementielle*: Recent Work on Eighteenth-Century French Politics," *French Historical Studies*, XIX/4 (1996), 1169–89.

21. See Robert Darnton, *The Literary Underground of the Old Regime* (Cambridge, Mass., 1982), 167–208.

22. [Jacob-Nicolas Moreau], *Le Moniteur françois*, 2 vols. (Avignon, 1760), I, 14. See also Jacob-Nicolas Moreau, *Mes souvenirs*, Camille Hermelin, ed., 2 vols. (Paris, 1898), esp. I, 57–62; Baker, *Inventing* (see Intro., n.17), 61–5; Dieter Gembicki, *Histoire et politique à la fin de l'ancien régime: Jacob-Nicolas Moreau (1717–1803)* (Geneva, 1976); Dziembowski, *Un nouveau patriotisme*, esp. 60–7.

23. Thus Keith Baker identifies the early 1750s as the moment when French politics broke out of the "absolutist mold." Baker, *Inventing*, 170. See also, in general, Van Kley, *The Damiens Affair*.

24. See in general on this literature, Shanti Marie Singham, "'A Conspiracy of Twenty Million Frenchmen': Public Opinion, Patriotism, and the Assault on Absolutism during the Maupeou Years, 1770–1775," Ph.D. diss., Princeton University (1991), and Echeverria, *The Maupeou Revolution*, esp. 37–122.

25. On the vicissitudes of the concept of public opinion, which has received enormous attention in the last decade, see above all Ozouf, "L'opinion publique" (see Ch. 1, n.16), and Baker, *Inventing*, 167–99.

26. Henri de Boulainvilliers, *Etat de la France*, 2 vols. (London, 1727), I, 15–49.

27. See Renée Simon, *Henry de Boulainviller [sic]: Historien, politique, philosophe, astrologue: 1658–1722* (Paris, 1941); Paul Vernière, *Spinoza et la pensée française avant la Révolution*, 2 vols. (Paris, 1954), I, 306–22. The most recent biography, and the most sophisticated in its study of Boulainvilliers' political writings (even if it does not do enough to integrate his religious and political thought) is Harold A. Ellis, *Boulainvilliers and the French Monarchy: Aristocratic Politics in Early Eighteenth-Century France* (Ithaca, 1988).

28. Ellis, 78, and more generally, 57–91.

29. For an excellent overview of these arguments see Wright, "National Sovereignty and the General Will" (see Intro., n.69). The works had a wide readership as shown by the new research on eighteenth-century French political culture cited above in Intro., n.32. See particularly Chartier, *Cultural Origins*, and Van Kley, *The Damiens Affair*.

30. For the fullest discussion of this material, see Bickart, *Les parlements* (see Intro., n.45), and Daniel Carroll Joynes, "Jansenists and Ideologues: Opposition Theory in the Parlement of Paris (1750–1775)," Ph.D. diss., University of Chicago (1981).

31. The quotes are from the controversial legal brief that prompted d'Aguesseau's comments on public opinion, [François de Maraimberg], *Mémoire pour les Sieurs Samson Curé d'Olivet, Couët curé de Darvoi, Gaucher chanoine de Jargeau, Diocèse d'Orléans* (Paris, 1730), 3. At least 3,000 copies of the brief were circulated. On this text and the controversy surrounding it, see Bell, *Lawyers and Citizens,* 91–104.

32. *Parlements* of Rouen, Paris (twice) and Besançon, quoted in Bickart, *Les parlements,* 54. In general on the phenomenon, see Bickart, 71–142, and more recently, Joynes, "Jansenists and Ideologues"; and Van Kley, *The Damiens Affair,* 166–225. The same strategists promoted the theory of the "union des classes," according to which the individual provincial *parlements* each formed a part of a larger national *parlement.* On the newspapers, which were the principal independent sources of news in France before the 1760s, see Popkin, *News and Politics,* and his "The Pre-Revolutionary Origins of Revolutionary Journalism" (see Ch. 1, n.58).

33. [Louis-Adrien Le Paige], *Lettres historiques sur les fonctions essentielles du Parlement, sur les droits de Pairs, et sur les lois fondamentales du Royaume,* 2 vols. (Amsterdam, 1753–54); and his, *Lettre sur les lits de justice* (n.p., 1756).

34. Jacques-Bénigne Bossuet, *Politics Drawn from the Very Words of Holy Scripture,* trans. and ed. Patrick Riley (Cambridge, 1990), 16.

35. Jean-Baptiste Dubos, *Histoire critique de l'établissement de la Monarchie française dans les Gaules* (Amsterdam, 1735).

36. Jules Flammermont, ed., *Remontrances du Parlement de Paris au XVIIIe siècle,* 3 vols. (Paris, 1888), II, 186.

37. "The Session of the Scourging," in Keith Michael Baker, ed., *The Old Regime and the French Revolution* (Chicago, 1987), 47–50, quote from 49.

38. See Bickart, 68–70.

39. Paul A. Friedland, "Representation and Revolution: The Theatricality of Politics and the Politics of Theater in France, 1789–1794," Ph.D. diss., University of California, Berkeley (1995); Baker, *Inventing,* 224–51. Friedland likens the process at one point to Catholic notions of transsubstantiation (105).

40. Montesquieu, *The Spirit of the Laws* (see Intro., n.41), 544.

41. For example, see the following works: Michel Desjardins, *Le patriotisme* (n.p., 1759); François-Charles Vallier, *Le citoyen, poème* (Nancy, 1759); Claude-François-Xavier Millot, *Discours sur le patriotisme françois* (Lyon, 1762); Louis Basset de la Marelle, *La différence du patriotisme national chez les françois et chez les anglois* (Paris, 1766); Joseph-Antoine-Joachim Cerutti, *Discours qui a remporté le prix de l'éloquence à l'Académie de Toulouse, le 3 mai 1760* (Lyon, 1760); Antoine-Jacques Roustan, *Offrande aux autels et à la patrie, contenant Défense du Christianisme ou réfutation du chapitre VIII du [livre IV du] Contrat Social; Examen historique des quatre beaux siècles de Mr.*

de Voltaire; Quels sont les moyens de tirer un peuple de sa corruption (Amsterdam, 1764).

42. Chevalier de Jaucourt, "Patrie" (see Ch. 1, n.75), 178.

43. Elie-Lefebvre, in "Le débat," 100–108, agrees that very few texts put the *patrie*'s autonomy from the king at the heart of political arguments.

44. See, for instance, Théodore Lombard, *Discours . . . sur ses paroles: L'amour de la patrie* (Toulouse, 1742); Jean-Baptiste Geoffroy, *De amore patriae oratorio* (Paris, 1744).

45. *Plaidoyer* of Louis Chevalier, May 9, 1716, in *Plaidoyers de Mr. Joly, en faveur des trois chanoines, & des trois Curez de Reims, pour être déchargés de la sentence d'excommunication prononcée contr'eux, le 17. juin 1715, au sujet de la Constitution Unigenitus* (Paris, 1716), in Bibliothèque Nationale, main collection. Ld-4 802, p. 24. On the context for the remarks, see Bell, *Lawyers and Citizens*, 75–9.

46. For instance, *De la nature de la Grâce . . . dédié à Messieurs les Avocats du Parlement de Paris* (n.p., 1739), 6.

47. [abbé Coyer], *Dissertations pour être lues: La première, sur le vieux mot de patrie; la seconde, sur la nature du peuple* (The Hague, 1755), 9, 31. The first part of this work has recently been republished: Edmond Dziembowski, ed., *Ecrits sur le patriotisme, l'esprit public & la propagande au milieu du XVIIIe siècle* (La Rochelle, 1997), 41–53.

48. Jaucourt, "Patrie"; Jean-Jacques Rousseau, *Emile, ou de l'éducation* (Paris, 1966), 40. See also his article "Political Economy" for the *Encyclopédie*, in which he claimed that love of the *patrie* is treated with derision.

49. Basset de la Marelle, *La différence*, 3; Rossel, *Histoire du patriotisme françois*, 8 vols. (Paris, 1769), I, vi; Geoffroy, *De amore patriae*, 3. Norman Hampson, in "La patrie," 127, argues that during the pre-revolution of 1787–1789, "conservatives" tended to use the word "patrie," while opponents of the monarchy used "patriote." His observation is quite correct, but he does not examine the reason for this dichotomy, namely that the "patriotes" did not believe the *patrie* actually existed and had to be created, while their opponents believed that it did exist and indeed was inseparable from the monarchy.

50. Quoted in Contamine, "Mourir pour la patrie," 31. On later French expressions of the idea, see Viroli, 73–6. Chantreau, quoted in Dupuy, "Genèse," 68.

51. Baptestein, *Mémoire* (see Ch. 1, n.103), 2.

52. Coyer, 42.

53. Quoted in Bickart, *Les parlements*, 30.

54. [Edme-François Darigrand], *Antifinancier* (n.p., 1763), 7.

55. I reject the argument of Steven Englund in "The Ghost of Nation Past" (see Intro., n.35), 315: "Who is using *patrie* and its derivations, *patriotisme, patriote*? Is it kings and ministers vis-à-vis popes or ultramontanes? Or is it

more often municipalities, parlements, and aristocracies in opposition to centralizing monarchs?" In fact, the evidence shows that it was precisely the centralizing monarchs who used the word *patrie* most often.

56. Millot, *Discours sur le patriotisme françois* (Lyon, 1762), 3, 15.

57. Philippe-Auguste de Sainte-Foix, chevalier d'Arcq, *La noblesse militaire* (1756), iii; Beausobre, quoted in Elie-Lefebvre, "Le débat," 102.

58. Rossel, *Histoire du patriotisme françois.* The manuscript essays submitted to the contest do not appear to have survived in the archives. Entries that were printed include Baptestein, *Mémoire;* Clément-Alexandre de Brie-Serrant, *Ecrit adressé à l'Académie de Châlons-sur-Marne, sur une question proposée par voie de concours, concernant le patriotisme* (n.p., 1787); Johan Meerman, *Discours présenté à l'Académie de Châlons-sur-Marne en 1787* (Leiden, 1787); E. Mignonneau, *Réflexions politiques sur la question proposée par l'Académie de Châlons* (Paris, 1787); and the winner, Charles-Joseph Mathon de la Cour, *Discours sur les meilleurs moyens de faire naître et d'encourager le patriotisme dans une monarchie; qui a remporté le prix dans l'Académie de Châlons-sur-Marne, le 25 août, 1787* (Paris, 1787). All of these works stressed the compatibility of monarchy and patriotism, although the anonymously published *Discours sur le patriotisme* of 1788 (see Intro., n.56), which appears to have been provoked by the contest but not submitted for the prize, argued the opposite case.

59. *Mémorial pittoresque de la France, ou recueil de toutes les belles actions, traits de courage, de bienfaisance, de patriotisme et d'humanité, arrivés depuis le règne de Henri IV jusqu'à nos jours* (Paris, 1786). On depictions of the great men, see Chapter 4, and Bonnet, *Naissance du Panthéon* (see Intro., n.48), 131–32.

60. Pierre Buirette de Belloy, *Oeuvres complettes de M. de Belloy, de l'Académie Française* (Paris, 1779), 32. This text probably first appeared in 1775. See Simon Schama, *Citizens: A Chronicle of the French Revolution* (New York, 1989), 37.

61. The exact degree of royal sponsorship of the play has been the subject of considerable discussion. See especially Clarence D. Brenner, *L'histoire nationale dans la tragédie française du dix-huitième siècle* (Berkeley, 1929), 253–65; Margaret M. Moffat, "'Le siège de Calais' et l'opinion publique en 1765," *Revue d'histoire littéraire de la France,* 39 (1932), 339–54; Lennard Breitholz, *Le théâtre historique en France jusqu'à la Révolution* (Uppsala, 1952), 191–202; Carmen Biondi, "Le siège de Calais di Dormont de Belloy [sic]: Ragioni di un successo," in *Intorno a Montesquieu* (Pisa, 1970), 5–20; Boës, *La lanterne magique* (see Intro., n.44), 98–103.

62. Belloy, *Le siège de Calais* (see Ch. 1, n.104), 48. The eulogist, in Belloy, *Oeuvres,* 33, makes clear the line was directed against the *philosophes.*

63. Louis-Sébastien Mercier, *L'an 2440* (London, 1772), 267.

64. [Louis Petit de Bachaumont, et al.], *Mémoires secrets pour servir à l'histoire de la république des lettres en France*, 36 vols. (London, 1777–1789), VI, 39; Baron Grimm similarly reported that those who dared criticize the play and its obsequious royalism "are regarded as bad citizens." Quoted in Boës, *La lanterne magique*, 70.

65. The point has been exhaustively demonstrated by Dziembowski in *Un nouveau patriotisme français*.

66. "Six months ago you caused one revolution in the opinions of this country; now you must cause another one." Moreau, *Mes souvenirs*, I, 59.

67. In the newspaper he identified his enemies as "so-called *philosophes*," and people "who have tried to restrict the exercise of authority," and explicitly linked the former to the English enemy: "A contagious epidemic malady has come to us from England: it is called the philosophical spirit." Moreau, *Le Moniteur*, I, 77, 19. On Moreau's enterprise, see Dziembowski, "Les débuts d'un publiciste" (see Ch. 1, n.98). Two introductory essays from the *Moniteur* have been published in Dziembowski, ed., *Ecrits*, 57–74 and 75–83.

68. On this literature, see Darrin McMahon, *Enemies of Enlightenment* (New York, 2001).

69. *Le patriotisme, poème* (see Ch. 1, n.86), 4, 11.

70. See Beaune, *Naissance* (see Intro., n.12), esp. 417–53.

71. Moreau, *Moniteur françois*, I, 27.

72. *Recueil des pièces d'éloquence et de poësie qui ont remporté les Prix de l'Académie Françoise, depuis 1747 jusqu'en 1753* (Paris, 1753). See also Denis-Ponce Ecouchard Lebrun, "Ode: L'amour des Français pour leurs Rois, consacré par les monuments publics," in Denis-Ponce Ecouchard Lebrun, *Oeuvres*, P. L. Ginguené, ed., 4 vols. (Paris, 1811), 16–22. Nathalie Elie-Lefebvre writes that "in sum, one can say that the idea of *patrie* is practically inseparable from love for the king" (108).

73. Basset de la Marelle, 24. See also, for instance, Sobry, *Le mode françois* (see Ch. 1, n.63), 11; *Annonces, affiches et avis divers ou Journal général de France*, 156 (1782), 1317–18; Ferlus, *Le patriotisme chrétien* (see Ch. 1, n.75), 5; Fourot, *Code patriotique de rivalité et d'émulation nationale, pacifique et guerriere* (London, 1788), 25; Fauchet, *De la religion nationale* (Paris, 1789), 2.

74. Thomas Kaiser, "*Louis le Bien-Aimé* and the Rhetoric of the Royal Body," in Sara E. Melzer and Kathryn Norberg, eds., *From the Royal to the Republican Body: Incorporating the Political in Seventeenth- and Eighteenth-Century France* (Berkeley, 1998), 131–61.

75. The reference is to Jacques-Bénigne Bossuet, *Politics*, which was first published posthumously in 1709. See Merrick's authoritative *The Desacralization of the French Monarchy* (see Intro., n.32).

76. Bibliothèque de Port-Royal, Collection Le Paige, 17, 794.

77. In general on this shift, see Singham, "A Conspiracy," Echeverria, *The Maupeou Revolution*, and Van Kley, *The Religious Origins* (see Intro., n.66), 249–302. Even so, the "patriote" pamphlets still used the words "patriote" and "patriotique" less frequently than "nation."

78. *Lettre à M. le Comte de xxx sur l'obéissance que les militaires doivent aux commandements du Prince* (n.p., [1771]), 12.

79. See, for instance [Darigrand], *Antifinancier*, 7; Pierre-Etienne Regnaud, *Histoire des evenemens arrivés en France depuis le mois de septembre MDCCLXX concernans les Parlements & les changements dans l'Administration de la justice & dans les loix du Royaume* (Paris, 1772), in Bibliothèque Nationale, Cabinet des Manuscrits, Manuscrits Français 13733–35, I, 1; [Bachaumont, et al.], *Mémoires secrets*, V, 223 (March 7, 1772).

80. See, for a summary of this literature, Singham, "A Conspiracy," 77–161. Among the most notable examples of the literature are *L'avocat national, ou lettre d'un patriote au Sieur Bouquet, dans laquelle on défend la vérité, les loix et la patrie contre le système qu'il a publié dans un ouvrage intitulé* Lettres provinciales (Paris, 1774).

81. In the ARTFL database there are 14 words beginning with "patriot-" out of a total of 1,387,549 for the period 1765–1769, or a frequency of 1.00 per 100,000. For the period 1770–1774 there are 88 out of 2,286,660, or a frequency of 3.85 per 100,000.

82. On "revolution," see Baker, *Inventing*, 203–23.

83. Louis Brancas, Comte de Lauragais: *Extrait du droit public de la France* (n.p., [1771]), 45.

84. Quoted in Singham, "A Conspiracy," 137. See also notably Mathieu-François Pidansat de Mairobert, *Journal historique de la Révolution opérée dans la constitution de la monarchie française par M. de Maupeou*, 5 vols. (London, 1775); Guy-Jean-Baptiste Target, *Lettres d'un homme à un autre homme sur les affaires du temps* (n.p., 1771).

85. Bibliothèque de la Société de Port-Royal, Collection Le Paige 571, no. 26 (Le Paige to Murard, 20 May 1772). See also Van Kley, *The Damiens Affair*, 193.

86. *Maximes du droit public françois* (Amsterdam, 1772). On the influence of this work, see Dale Van Kley, "The Jansenist Constitutional Legacy in the French Pre-Revolution," in Baker, *The Political Culture of the Old Regime* (see Intro., n.32), 169–201.

87. [Jacques-Claude Martin de Mariveaux], *L'ami des loix, ou les vrais principes de la législation françoise* ([n.p.], 1775), 6, 25.

88. [Guillaume-Joseph Saige], *Le catéchisme du citoyen*, quoted in Baker, *Inventing*, 143.

89. As several recent studies have concluded, the changes in French political cul-

ture unleashed by Maupeou's coup were irreversible. See for instance, Maza, *Private Lives*, esp. 313–24; Bell, *Lawyers and Citizens*, 148–81

90. See Ozouf, "L'opinion publique," 431–32. Measuring the popularity of terms is a difficult call, and the assertion here is based above all on my general sense from having read widely in the primary literature. However, the ARTFL database again provides a suggestive comparison. The use of "nation," as shown below, jumped dramatically both during lead-up to the Maupeou crisis and the crisis itself (1771–74), and then again during the pre-revolution (1785–1789). "Public opinion," on the other hand, registered a decline during the Maupeou crisis, and even in the pre-revolutionary conflict it did not jump dramatically.

	"Nation"	*"Public Opinion"*	*(use per 100,000 words)*
1760–64	0.77	1.67	
1765–69	3.39	1.20	
1770–74	3.79	0.63	
1775–79	1.24	1.38	
1780–84	1.20	0.88	
1785–89	3.31	1.36	

91. According to the on-line catalogue of the Bibliothèque Nationale de France: http://catalogue.bnf.fr.

92. [Jurieu], *Les voeux d'un patriote* (Amsterdam, 1788).

93. As recently demonstrated by Dale Van Kley in "From the Lessons of French History to Truths for All Times and All People: The Historical Origins of an Anti-Historical Declaration," in Van Kley, ed., *French Idea*, 72–113, and esp, 80–91.

94. [Pierre-Jean Agier], *Le jurisconsulte national, ou principes sur la nécessité du consentement de la nation pour établir et proroger les impôts* (n.p., 1788).

95. Quoted in Van Kley, "From the Lessons of French History," 81–82.

96. This assertion, based on my reading in the pre-revolutionary pamphlet literature, is also supported by Fehrenbach, "Nation"; Godechot, "Nation, patrie, nationalisme et patriotisme"; Hampson, "La patrie"; and Garrett, "French Nationalism."

97. Godard to Cortot, May 29, 1788, Archives Départementales de la Côte d'Or, E 642. On the "national party" see also, for instance, *Le roi et ses ministres, dialogues* (n.p., [1788]), 3–4.

98. Emmanuel Sieyès, *Qu'est-ce que le Tiers Etat?* (Paris, 1789). On Sieyès and his influence, see most recently William H. Sewell, Jr., *A Rhetoric of Bourgeois Revolution: The Abbé Sieyès and 'What Is the Third Estate?'* (Durham, 1994).

99. "Manifeste aux Normands," and "Manifeste aux Bretons," reprinted in

Maupeouana, ou Recueil complet des écrits patriotiques publiés pendant le regne du Chancelier Maupeou, 7 vols. (Paris, 1775), VI, 1–21, 84–97, quote from 1.

100. Quoted in Berlet, *Les tendances unitaires* (see Intro., n.57), 10, 59; Aulard, *Le patriotisme,* 103; and Jules Keller, *Le théosophe Frédéric-Rodolphe Saltzmann et les milieux spirituels de son temps,* 2 vols. (The Hague, 1985), I, 194; Provençal material quoted by Rafe Blaufarb in unpublished conference paper, Society for French Historical Studies, Washington D.C., 1999.

101. See on this subject David A. Bell, "Nation-Building and Cultural Particularism in Eighteenth-Century France: The Case of Alsace," *Eighteenth-Century Studies,* XXI/4 (1988), 472–90. On the absence of secessionist movements during the redrawing of France's internal boundaries, see Marie-Vic Ozouf-Marignier, *La Formation des départements: La représentation du territoire français à la fin du 18è siècle* (Paris, 1989); Ted Margadant, *Urban Rivalries in the French Revolution* (Princeton, 1992).

102. See particularly on this subject Antoine de Baecque, *The Body Politic: Corporeal Metaphor in Revolutionary France, 1770–1800,* trans. Charlotte Mandel (Stanford, 1997), 132–38.

103. Quoted in ibid., 138.

104. J. Villier, *Nouveau plan d'éducation et d'instruction publique dédié à l'Assemblée nationale dans lequel on substitue aux universités, seminaires et collèges des établissements plus raisonnables, plus utiles, plus dignes d'une grande nation* (Angers, 1789), vi–viii. For further discussion of this discourse of "degeneration" see Chapter 5 below.

105. In this analysis I take issue somewhat with Jacques Revel's important article, "La région," in Nora, ed., *Les lieux de mémoire,* 851–83, pt. III, I, in which, drawing on the work of Mona Ozouf and Catherine Bertho, he argues that the "regional problem" was invented in the early years of the Revolution itself.

106. Toussaint Guiraudet, *Qu'est-ce que la nation et qu'est-ce que la France* (n.p., 1789).

107. See Van Kley, "From the Lessons of French History," and esp. Joseph John Zizek, "The Politics and Poetics of History in the French Revolution, 1787–1794," Ph.D. diss., University of California, Berkeley (1995).

108. For this section I am relying on the rich literature already available on the concept of "regeneration" in the era of the French Revolution. See particularly Mona Ozouf, "Régénération," in Furet and Ozouf, eds., *Dictionnaire* (see Intro., n.77), 821–31; de Baecque, *The Body Politic,* 131–56; and most recently, Sepinwall, "Regenerating France" (see Ch. 1, n.91), esp. 83–7.

109. On this shift to a social, statistical description of the nation, and the influence of the physiocrats (which was particularly strong on Sieyès), see esp. Baker, *Inventing,* 238–50.

110. Pierre-Louis de Lacretelle, *De la convocation de la prochaine tenue des états-*

généraux (Paris, 1789), quoted in Shafer, "Bourgeois Nationalism," 35; Guiraudet, *Qu'est-ce que la nation*, 63, Sieyès, passim.

111. Here I am following Baker, *Inventing*, 238–51; Friedland, "Representation," esp. 1–60.

112. Sepinwall, 85–6.

113. Jean Starobinski, "Eloquence et liberté," *Revue suisse de l'histoire*, XXVI (1976), 549–63, quote from 562.

114. Cited in Fehrenbach, "Nation," 58.

115. Quoted in Vovelle, "Entre cosmopolitisme et xénophobie," 15.

116. For two examples from 1789, see Fauchet, *La religion nationale*, 2; Foix, *Le patriotisme* (see Ch. 1, n.75), 3–4.

3. English Barbarians, French Martyrs

1. For the most recent, complete, and impartial accounts of the incident, see Francis Jennings, *Empire of Fortune: Crowns, Colonies and Tribes in the Seven Years War in America* (New York, 1988), 67–70, and Richard White, *The Middle Ground: Indians, Empires and Republics in the Great Lakes Region, 1650–1815* (Cambridge, 1991), 240–41. Jennings concludes that Jumonville was most likely killed by Tanaghrisson. See also Gilbert F. Leduc, *Washington and the "Murder of Jumonville"* (Boston, 1943). For an account critical of Washington, see abbé Georges Robitaille, *Washington et Jumonville* (Montreal, 1933).

2. The French literature invariably identified the enemy as "England" rather than "Britain." When discussing the literature, I will follow this usage.

3. Among works that discussed Jumonville's death, see Antoine-Léonard Thomas, *Jumonville* (Paris, 1759); [Jacob-Nicolas Moreau], *Mémoire contenant le précis des faits avec leurs pièces justificatives* (Paris, 1756); Moreau, *L'Observateur hollandois, ou seconde lettre de M. Van ** à M. H** de la Haye* (The Hague, 1755), esp. 20–35; *L'Observateur hollandois, troisième lettre . . .* and *cinquième lettre . . .* (The Hague, 1755); [Edme-Jacques Genet], *Petit catechisme politique des Anglois, traduit de leur langue* (n.p., n.d. [1757]), 4; [Lefebvre de Beauvray], *Adresse* (see Ch. 1, n.75), 7; Audibert, "Poëme," in *Recueil général des pièces, chansons et fêtes données à l'occasion de la prise du Port-Mahon* ("France," 1757), 48; Denis-Ponce Ecouchard ("Lebrun"), *Ode nationale contre l'Angleterre* (Paris, 1758), 2–3; Séran de la Tour, *Parallèle de la conduite des carthaginois à l'égard des romains, dans la seconde guerre punique, avec la conduite de l'Angleterre, à l'égard de la France, dans la guerre déclarée par ces deux puissances, en 1756* (n.p., 1757), 185–91.

4. Thomas, *Jumonville*, 22. I am assuming "souleva" is a misprint for "soulève."

5. Zimmermann, *Vom Nationalstolze* (see Ch. 1, n.111), 177.

6. *Mémoires de Trévoux (Mémoires pour servir à l'histoire des sciences et des arts)*, 1756, II, 1756–57.

7. See Claude de Sacy, *L'honneur françois, ou Histoire des vertus et des exploits de notre nation, depuis l'Etablissement de la Monarchie jusqu'à nos jours*, 12 vols. (Paris, 1769–84), XI, 284–86; and Louis-Pierre Manuel, *L'année françoise, ou Vies des Hommes qui ont honoré la France, ou par leurs talens, ou par leurs services, & surtout par leurs vertus*, 4 vols. (Paris, 1789), III, 12–15.

8. [Lefebvre de Beauvray], *Adresse*, 11; Lebrun, *Ode aux françois* (Angers, 1762), 1. Lebrun's poem also contains the *Marseillaise*-like line "L'entendez-vous gémir cette auguste Patrie?" See David A. Bell, "Aux origines de la 'Marseillaise': L'*Adresse à la nation angloise* de Claude-Rigobert Lefebvre de Beauvray," *Annales historiques de la Révolution française*, 299 (1995), 75–77. Lefebvre himself may well have borrowed from N. de Coulange, *Ode sur les anglois au sujet de la Guerre présente* (Paris, 1756), 7: "Puissiez-vous aborder sur leurs propres rivages / Et de leur sang parjure arrosant les sillons." Dziembowski, in *Un nouveau patriotisme* (see Intro., n.33), has also noticed these borrowings (82) and found further precedents in the 1656 verses by Boileau: "Et leurs corps pourris dans nos plaines / N'ont fait qu'engraisser nos sillons."

9. Dziembowski, in *Un nouveau patriotisme*, has provided the first scholarly survey of this literature. He states that the French propagandists treated Jumonville's death as England's "original sin" (76) but does not explore the representations of this event in a systematic way.

10. The exception is Audibert, "Poëme," 47: "Réunis autrefois dans le sein de l'Eglise / L'Hérésie aujourd'hui les guide & les divise." On British anti-Catholicism in the period, see Colley, *Britons* (see Intro., n.26), 11–54. The fascinating evidence of a possible plot involving French Protestants has been unearthed by John D. Woodbridge in *Revolt in Prerevolutionary France: The Prince de Conti's Conspiracy against Louis XV, 1755–1757* (Baltimore, 1995).

11. Jacobin clubs quoted in Wahnich, *L'impossible citoyen* (see Intro., n.33), 322–3; Bertrand Barère, *Rapport sur les crimes de l'Angleterre envers le Peuple français, et sur ses attentats contre la liberté des Nations* (Paris, 1794), 18. On the treatment of Pitt, and on the "take no prisoners" decree, see Norman Hampson, *The Perfidy of Albion: French Perceptions of England during the French Revolution* (Houndmills, Basingstoke, 1998), 103–19, 142–43.

12. See John Brewer, *The Sinews of Power: War, Money and the English State, 1688–1783* (New York, 1989); James C. Riley, *The Seven Years' War and the Old Regime in France: The Economic and Financial Toll* (Princeton, 1986).

13. For examples from the Hundred Years' War, see, for instance, the material collected in Marie-Madeleine Martin, *The Making of France: The Origins and Development of the Idea of National Unity*, Barbara and Robert North, trans.

(London, 1951), 108–20. An amusing catalogue of national invective in the Renaissance can be found in John Hale, *The Civilization of the Renaissance in Europe* (New York, 1994), 51–66. More recently, many seventeenth-century French authors copiously indulged in the delights of Hispanophobia. See for instance François de La Mothe le Vayer, *Discours de la contrariété d'humeurs qui se trouve entre certains nations, et singulièrement entre la française et l'espagnole* (Paris, 1636).

14. On the use of print in the wars of the Reformation, see especially Denis Pallier, *Recherches sur l'imprimerie à Paris pendant la Ligue, 1585–1594* (Geneva 1975); R. W. Scribner, *For the Sake of Simple Folk: Popular Propaganda for the German Reformation* (Cambridge, 1981). See also David A. Bell, "Unmasking a King: The Political Uses of Popular Literature under the French Catholic League, 1588–89," *Sixteenth-Century Journal*, 20 (1989), 371–86.

15. This assertion is based on holdings of the French Bibliothèque Nationale, in my own survey of the number of publications that qualify as wartime propaganda—including plays and poems as well as pamphlets—and on material cited in Dziembowski, *Un nouveau patriotisme*. On wartime propaganda in the War of the Spanish Succession, see Joseph Klaits, *Printed Propaganda under Louis XIV: Absolute Monarchy and Public Opinion* (Princeton, 1976). On the Seven Years War, in addition to the fundamental work of Dziembowski, see also Nicholas Rowe, "Romans and Carthaginians in the Eighteenth Century: Imperial Ideology and National Identity in Britain and France during the Seven Years' War," Ph.D. diss., Boston College (1997); Charles Gevaert Salas, "Punic Wars in France and Britain," Ph.D. diss., Claremont Graduate School (1996); and Brenner, *L'histoire nationale* (see Ch. 2, n.61), esp. 243–66.

16. *Journal encyclopédique par une société de gens de lettres,* 1756, VI, Sept. 15, 78.

17. According to Moreau, *Mes souvenirs* (see Ch. 2, n.22), I, 59–63.

18. As an indication of the diffusion of the works, see the lengthy and favorable reviews of Moreau's *Mémoire* in *Mémoires de Trévoux*, 1756, II, 1734–90, and of his *Observateur hollandois, ou deuxième lettre* in *Journal encyclopédique*, 1756, V, July 1, 12–22. The British replied to the second in the pamphlet *L'Observateur observé* (n.p., [1756]), which the *Journal encyclopédique* mentioned as well (12). Lengthy and favorable reviews of Thomas's *Jumonville* included *Mémoires de Trévoux*, 1759, II, 1116–33, and *Journal encyclopédique* 1759, IV, pt. III, 123–40; *Journal des Savants*, June 1759, 429–31.

19. See the *Recueil général des pièces, chansons et fêtes,* and the discussion in Rowe, "Romans and Carthaginians," 10–63.

20. For instance, Voltaire's *Le Poème sur la bataille de Fontenoy* (Amsterdam, 1748). The only text I have found of a violence remotely close to those of the Seven Years' War is Pezé d'Anglincourt's *Ode à la France* (Paris, 1744), which

calls on Louis XV to "cut off the ferocious heads of a Cohort of Brigands," but then almost immedieately checks itself: "What am I saying? Where is my mind wandering? LOUIS, magnanimous victor, don't grant this barbarous desire" (6–7).

21. Lefebvre de Beauvray, *Adresse*, 9; Coulange, *Ode*, 3; *Considérations sur les différends des couronnes de la Grande-Bretagne et de France, touchant l'Acadie et autres parties de l'Amérique septentrionale* (Frankfurt, 1756), 23.

22. On this comparison, see above all Rowe, "Romans and Carthaginians," 64–97, and Salas, "Punic Wars," 287–314. One play, entitled *Asdrubal,* took the other tack, comparing France to a virtuous Carthage and England to an expansionary, grasping Rome. See Dziembowski, *Un nouveau patriotisme,* 411.

23. Moreau, *L'Observateur hollandois, ou deuxième lettre,* 37, and *cinquième lettre,* 4.

24. Moreau, *Cinquième lettre,* 40.

25. "Quod genus hoc hominum? Quaeve hunc tam barbara morem / Permittit patria?" *Aeneid* I, 539–40.

26. *Mémoires de Trévoux,* 1759, II, 1118. It also noted, in the poem, "un contraste frappant de la simplicité & de la droiture des Sauvages avec la perfidie des Anglois" (1132).

27. Lebrun, *Ode Nationale,* in *Oeuvres,* 403.

28. Séran de la Tour, 187–91, 250. The book attracted sufficient attention to warrant a nine-page review in the *Journal encyclopédique,* 1757, III, pt. II, 81–89.

29. For instance, Lefebvre de Beauvray, *Adresse,* 12: "De l'affreuse Discorde agitant le flambeau, / Fais de ton Isle entière un immense Tombeau."

30. Audibert, in *Recueil,* 49.

31. *L'Albionide, ou l'Anglais démasqué: Poëme héroï-comique* (Aix, 1759), 80.

32. Lefebvre de Beauvray, 8.

33. Lesuire, *Les sauvages de l'Europe* (see Ch. 1, n.94). As noted above, the book was reprinted in Paris in 1780 under the title *Les amants françois à Londres,* and translated as *The Savages of Europe* (London, 1764). Despite the English translation, there is no indication that Lesuire did not intend his criticisms seriously. As Grieder demonstrates in *Anglomania* (see Intro., n.55), 33–63, the novel obeyed the conventions of contemporary satirical Anglophobia. Furthermore, Lesuire himself felt obliged to tone down his criticisms in the 1780 version.

34. Lesuire, 18–19.

35. On this terminology, see Anthony Pagden, *The Fall of Natural Man: The American Indian and the Origins of Comparative Ethnology* (Cambridge, 1982), 15–26; Pagden, *Lords of All the World: Ideologies of Empire in Spain, Britain and France, c. 1500–c. 1800* (New Haven, 1995); Olive Patricia Dickason, *The Myth of the Savage and the Beginnings of French Colonialism in*

the Americas (Calgary, 1984), esp. 61–94; Michèle Duchet, *Anthropologie et histoire au siècle des lumières* (Paris, 1973, repr. 1995), 217.

36. My thanks to Stéphane Pujol for this observation.

37. See notably the *politique* pamphlets, *La fleur de lys, qui est un discours d'un François retenu dans Paris* (n.p., 1590), and *Exhortation d'aucuns Parisiens, n'agueres eslargis de la Bastille de Paris, au peuple François* (n.p., 1592).

38. Barthélémy-François-Joseph Mouffle d'Angerville, *Vie privée de Louis XV, ou principaux événements, particularités et anecdotes de son règne* (London, 1785), III, 84–85, quoted in Dziembowski, *Un nouveau patriotisme*, 106–7.

39. Dziembowski, *Un nouveau patriotisme*, while paying close attention to the ministry's efforts, occasionally errs somewhat in this direction (e.g. 491–96).

40. On Moreau's activities, see Moreau, *Mes souvenirs*, I, 57–63, and Dziembowski, "Les débuts d'un publiciste" (see Ch. 1, n.98); also Gembicki, *Histoire et politique* (see Ch. 2, n.22). The papers taken from Washington were published as [Moreau], *Mémoire*, and translated into English as *A Memorial, Containing a Summary View of Facts, with Their Authorities, in Answer to the Observations Sent by the English Ministry to the Courts of Europe* (Paris, 1757).

41. Séran de la Tour, x, says he based much of his account on Moreau's *Précis*. Compare Thomas, *Jumonville*, iii–xx, with *L'Observateur hollandois, ou seconde lettre*, 20–35. Thomas's epigraph from the *Aeneid* was quoted in Moreau's *Observateur hollandois, ou cinquième lettre*, 32. Also compare Moreau's *Observateur hollandois, ou deuxième lettre*, 37 ("Imputerai-je donc à toute la Nation angloise des forfaits qui ont fait honneur à des Peuples que les Européens traitent de Barbares?") with Lebrun, *Ode nationale*, 403 ("Au Huron qu'il dédaigne, et qu'il nomme barbare / Il apprend des Forfaits"), and the *Observateur hollandois, ou cinquième lettre*, 42 ("Chez les François, au contraire, la Patrie n'est point une idole pour laquelle on se passionne"), with *Considérations sur les différends*, 23 ("La Patrie est l'Idole, à laquelle les Anglois sacrifient tous les sentiments . . ."). This last piece may well be by Moreau himself, although it has never actually been attributed to him.

42. Among the other official propagandists was Edme-Jacques Genet, who cooperated with the anti-*philosophe* Palissot on yet another anti-English newspaper. See Dziembowski, *Un nouveau patriotisme*, 62–5, 177–82. On Lefebvre, see Bell, *Lawyers and Citizens* (see Ch. 1, n.12), 172, 184, 192. On Thomas, see Bonnet, *Naissance du Panthéon* (see Intro., n.43), 68; Etienne Micard, *Un écrivain académique au XVIIIe siècle: Antoine-Léonard Thomas (1732–1785)* (Paris, 1924), 23.

43. *Recueil général* . . . The volume included pieces by military officers and members of the King's bodyguard, as well as several odes by Voltaire and pieces previously published in periodicals. It also included several pieces in Provençal.

44. See Moreau, *Mes souvenirs,* I, 57–63.

45. Moreau, *L'Observateur hollandois, ou deuxième lettre,* 6.

46. Moreau, *Mes souvenirs,* I, 129; Jacob-Nicolas Moreau, *Lettre sur la paix, à M. le Comte de *** (Lyons, 1763).

47. These were the years of Moreau's famous anti-*philosophe* satire *Nouveau mémoire pour servir à l'histoire des Cacouacs* (Amsterdam, 1757), of Charles Palissot's *Les philosophes* (Paris, 1760), and many other anti-*philosophe* works, not to mention a hardening of censorship of the *philosophes* themselves. On the connection with the war, see Dziembowski, *Un nouveau patriotisme,* 119–30.

48. Dziembowski, esp. 298–311. For perceptions of English turbulence see Thomas, *Jumonville,* 5; *Considérations sur les différends,* 7; Lesuire, passim. On the importance of these perceptions in French political culture, see Baker, *Inventing the French Revolution* (see Intro., n.17), 173–85.

49. "Projet patriotique," in *Année littéraire,* 1756, VI, 43–4.

50. These gifts are described in Barbier, *Chronique de la Régence* (see Ch. 1, n.96), VII, 422–4. See also Dziembowski, *Un nouveau patriotisme,* 458–72.

51. *Lettres patentes du roi, Par lesquelles le Roi, en ordonnant que sa Vaisselle sera portée à l'Hôtel des Monnoies de Paris, pour y être convertie en Espèces, fixe le prix de celle qui y sera portée volontairement par les Particuliers* (Versailles, 1759). In Bibliothèque Nationale de France, F 21162, no. 111. Riley in *The Seven Years' War,* a study of French finances during the war, doesn't even mention these donations.

52. Barbier, VII, 199.

53. Bibliothèque de la Société de Port-Royal, Fonds Le Paige, 543 (unpaginated), letter from Decourtoux (?) to Le Paige. This volume of the Le Paige collection has considerable material on the "dons d'argenterie." My thanks to Mita Choudhury for the reference.

54. Jean de la Chapelle, *Lettres d'un Suisse, qui demeure en France, à un François, qui s'est retiré en Suisse, touchant l'éstat présent des affaires en Europe* (n.p., 1704). See also Klaits, *Printed Propaganda,* 113–70.

55. Klaits, 212–16; *Lettre du Roy a Mr. le Marquis d'Antin du 12. Juin 1709* (Paris, 1709). The letter was written by Torcy. See also André Corvisier, *L'armée française de la fin du XVIIè siècle au ministère de Choiseul: Le soldat,* 2 vols. (Paris, 1964), I, 105.

56. Moreau, *Mes souvenirs,* II, 559; Charles-Pierre Colardeau, *Le patriotisme, poëme* (Paris, 1762), 3; *Le patriotisme, poëme* [anonymous 1767 poem, not by Colardeau; see Ch. 1, n.86], 7.

57. De la Chapelle, *Lettre d'un Suisse,* "Quatrième lettre," E4v.

58. *Lettre du Roy,* 3.

59. See Etienne-François, duc de Choiseul, *Mémoire historique sur la négociation*

de la France et de l'Angleterre depuis le 26 mars 1761 jusqu'au 20 septembre de la même année, avec les pièces justificatives (Paris, 1761).

60. "Projet patriotique," 42.

61. Thomas, *Jumonville*, xvi, 18.

62. [Moreau], *L'Observateur hollandois, ou troisième lettre*, 3, 4, 12.

63. [Moreau], *L'Observateur hollandois, ou cinquième lettre* . . . , 6–8.

64. See, for instance, Moreau's disquisition on patriotism in ibid., 40–42, and the discussion in Chapter 1 above.

65. *Mémoires de Trévoux* (1756), II, 1750–1751.

66. [abbé Le Blanc], *Le patriote anglois, ou réflexions sur les Hostilités que la France reproche à l'Angleterre* (Geneva, 1756), ii. Le Blanc also wrote that "the hatred of the name Frenchman only blinds the vile populace."

67. *Journal encyclopédique*, 1756, I, Jan. 15, 30–31.

68. This suppleness would continue. See for instance Sobry, *Le mode françois* (see Ch. 1, n.63), 26–37. Sobry uses the word "nation" to describe England, France, and Spain, but "peuple" to describe other groups of Europeans.

69. Denis Diderot, "Eloge de Richardson," in *Oeuvres complètes* (Paris, 1951), 1063.

70. See, on this phenomenon, Grieder, *Anglomania*, and Acomb, *Anglophobia* (see Ch. 1, n.96). Both draw heavily on Georges Ascoli, *La Grande Bretagne devant l'opinion française au 18è siècle* (Paris, 1930).

71. Quoted in Greenfeld, *Nationalism* (see Intro., n.21), 156. Among the more famous examples of tracts against Anglomania is Louis Fougeret de Montbron, *Préservatif* (see Ch. 1, n.96).

72. Quoted in Dziembowski, *Un nouveau patriotisme*, 184.

73. Among the voluminous literature on the idea of Europe, see esp. René Pomeau, *L'Europe des lumières: Cosmopolitisme et unité européenne au dix-huitième siècle* (Paris, 1995 [1964]); Jean-Baptiste Duroselle, *L'idée d'Europe dans l'histoire* (Paris, 1965), 103–33; Derek Heater, *The Idea of European Unity* (New York, 1992), 61–90; Denis de Rougemont, *The Idea of Europe*, trans. Norbert Guterman (New York, 1966), 51–175. On precedents, see Denys Hay, *Europe: The Emergence of an Idea* (Edinburgh, 1957).

74. Voltaire, *Fontenoy*, "Discours préliminaire," unpaginated.

75. *Journal encyclopédique*, 1760, VIII, pt. II, 104. The anonymous writer also commented that "the Orientals themselves recognize the Europeans' mental superiority."

76. Quoted in de Rougemont, 150.

77. Rousseau, *Oeuvres complètes* (see Intro., n.42), III, 960. Cf. *Emile* (see Ch. 2, n.48), 593: "the original character of peoples is steadily being erased . . . As the races mix and the peoples blend, we see those national differences which once struck one at first glance, little by little disappearing."

78. One exception: The *Lettre d'un jeune homme* (see Intro., n.70), published in the War of American Independence, said that the English custom of having women retire early from the dinner table was worthy of "Africans or Orientals" (18).

79. Duchet, 32, and more generally, 25–136; Gilbert Chinard, *L'Amérique et le rêve exotique dans la littérature française au XVIIè et au XVIIIè siècles* (Paris, 1913); Geoffroy Atkinson, *Les relations de voyages du XVIIè siècle et l'évolution des idées: Contribution à l'étude de la formation de l'esprit du XVIIIè siècle* (Paris, 1927).

80. See also Karen Ordahl Kupperman, *America in European Consciousness, 1493–1750* (Chapel Hill, 1995), 1–24.

81. See Colley, *Britons,* 11–54.

82. For a brief summary of these works, see Henry Vyverberg, *Human Nature, Cultural Diversity, and the French Enlightenment* (New York, 1989), esp. 66–71. The arguments about temperate climate go back to Aristotle.

83. Rivarol, *L'universalité de la langue française* (Paris, 1991), 25.

84. D'Espiard, *L'esprit des nations,* 1753 Hague ed. (see Intro., n.38), II, 25.

85. Ibid., I, 145; II, 126.

86. [Thomas-Jean Pichon], *La physique de l'histoire, ou Considérations générales sur les Principes élémentaires du temperament et du Caractère naturel des Peuples* (The Hague, 1765), 262–3.

87. Cited in Kohn, *Prelude to Nation States* (see Ch. 2, n.15), 15.

88. On French notions of the *translatio studii,* spiritual counterpart to the *translatio imperii,* see Beaune, *Naissance* (see Intro., n.12), 405–9.

89. The most recent study of the "civilizing mission," Alice Conklin's *A Mission to Civilize: The Republican Idea of Empire in French West Africa, 1895–1930* (Stanford, 1997), acknowledges its Enlightenment origins without, however, discussing them in depth.

90. F. A. Isambert et al., *Recueil des anciennes lois françaises,* 18 vols. (Paris, 1821–33), XVI, 423. Colbert quoted in Axtell, *The Invasion Within* (see Ch. 1, n.113), 68. More generally, see Axtell, 43–127, and Cornelius J. Jaenen, "Characteristics of French-Amerindian Contact in New France," in Stanley H. Palmer and Dennis Reinharz, ed., *Essays on the History of North American Discovery and Exploration* (College Station, Tex., 1988), 79–101.

91. On the influence of the Jesuit *Relations* in particular, see Duchet, 76.

92. Thomas, *Jumonville,* 8.

93. Ibid., 44.

94. Lesuire, 61–62.

95. See the discussion in Duchet, 230–79. See also William B. Cohen, *The French Encounter with Africans: White Reponses to Blacks, 1530–1880* (Bloomington, 1980), 80.

96. Buirette de Belloy, *Le siège de Calais* (see Ch. 1, n.104), 32. See also, for example, Audibert, "Poëme," 47; Basset de la Marelle, *La différence* (see Ch. 2, n.41), 41; Lefebvre de Beauvray, *Adresse*, 9.

97. Lesuire, *Les sauvages de l'Europe*, 7.

98. Lefebvre de Beauvray, *Adresse*, 8.

99. Claude-Rigobert Lefebvre de Beauvray, *Le monde pacifié, poëme* (Paris, 1763), 6.

100. See Gilbert Chinard, *George Washington as the French Knew Him* (Princeton, 1940), 29. Chinard notes that during the War of American Independence, the French seem not to have drawn the connection between the young and middle-aged Washington. This was possibly as the result of the earlier confusion over Washington's name ("Washington / Wemcheston") and the failure of most French publicists—including Thomas—to use the name at all.

101. Quoted in Grieder, 108.

102. For a summary of this literature see Acomb, *Anglophobia*, 69–88. Lefebvre's work, a partial rewriting of his earlier *Adresse*, was published as Claude-Rigobert Lefebvre de Beauvray, "Fragments d'un opuscule en vers, intitulé *Hommages ou souhaits patriotiques à la France, par un citoyen*," in *Journal encyclopédique*, 1779, V, 105–9.

103. Labourdette, *Vergennes* (see Intro., n.70), 205; see also Edouard Dziembowski, "Traduction et propagande: Convergences franco-britanniques de la culture politique à la fin du dix-huitième siècle," in K. de Queiros Mattoso, ed., *L'Angleterre et le monde, XVIII–XXè siècle* (Paris, 1999), 81–111.

104. Labourdette, 206–7. See for example the coverage in *Annonces, affiches et avis divers . . .* 156 (1782), 1317–18; 157 (1782), 1326.

105. See Albert Mathiez, *La Révolution et les étrangers: Cosmopolitisme et défense nationale* (Paris, 1918), passim; Wahnich, *L'impossible citoyen*, 163–85.

106. Quoted in Mathiez, *La Révolution et les étrangers*, 56, and Georges Fournier, "Images du Midi dans l'idéologie révolutionnaire," in *Amiras: Repères occitans*, 15–16 (1987), 85.

107. On the shift, see Wahnich, *L'impossible citoyen*, 243–327.

108. Robespierre, in Alphonse Aulard, *La société des Jacobins: Recueil de documents pour l'histoire du club des Jacobins de Paris* (Paris, 1889–95), V, 634.

109. Wahnich, 301–25, quotation from 305, 323.

110. Barère, *Rapport*, 13.

111. Sophie Wahnich suggests that the shift in French sentiments towards England derived above all from the Jacobins' belief that in England, unlike in the other enemy nations, the people were sovereign, and thus responsible for their governments' actions. While this belief certainly helped shape revolutionary discourse on the subject, Wahnich overestimates its importance. The polemicists of the Seven Years' War employed similar rhetoric against the British without

ever invoking English national sovereignty. The willingness to make pejorative characterizations of the English as a people had far more to do with the proximity and perceived similarity between the two nations. See Wahnich, *L'impossible citoyen,* 281–327.

112. See the material quoted extensively in Wahnich, 252–80, 318–27. Wahnich's book, which draws heavily on the techniques of linguistic analysis devised by Jacques Guilhaumou, rarely strays beyond the legislative records of the revolutionary assemblies (the *Archives parlementaires*) for source material.

113. Quoted in Wahnich, 323, 326; Hampson, *Perfidy,* 150.

114. Barère, *Rapport sur les crimes de l'Angleterre,* 11, 12, 18.

115. Archives du Ministère des Affaires Étrangères, Mémoires et Documents: France, 651, fol. 239. I am grateful to Professor Thomas Kaiser, of the University of Arkansas, to whom I owe this citation, and who cited it in his paper "From the 'Austrian Committee' to the 'Foreign Plot': Marie-Antoinette, Austrophobia, and the Terror," Society for French Historical Studies, Scottsdale, March 2000.

116. Robespierre, in codicil to Barère, *Rapport,* 29. For examples of Vendéens described as barbarians and foreigners, see for instance Rivoire, *Le patriotisme* (see Ch. 1, n.40), 91.

117. De la Chapelle, *Lettres d'un Suisse . . . vingtième lettre,* (second pagination) S3r.

118. Quoted in Labourdette, 207.

119. See esp. Pallier, *Recherches sur l'imprimerie à Paris.*

120. [Antoine Arnaud], *Coppie de l'anti-espagnol, faict à Paris* (Paris, 1590), 12. In general, see Yardeni, *La conscience nationale* (see Intro., n.12), 270–77, also Mack P. Holt, "Burgundians into Frenchmen: Catholic Identity in Sixteenth-Century Burgundy," in Michael Wolfe, ed., *Changing Identities in Early Modern France* (Durham, 1997), 345–70.

121. Pagden, *Lords of All the World,* 24; Duchet, 210–11.

122. See Arthur Hertzberg, *The French Enlightenment and the Jews* (New York, 1968), 248–313. Barère is quoted in Wahnich, 318.

123. Elie Fréron, quoted in Dziembowski, *Un nouveau patriotisme,* 84.

124. This will be demonstrated in Chapter 4. And see above, note 7.

125. Which he actually spoke in Provençal: "Aquo es égaou, mori per la libertat." See Patrice Higonnet, "The Politics of Linguistic Terrorism and Grammatical Hegemony During the French Revolution," *Social History,* V/1 (1980), 57.

126. See for instance Pierre H. Boulle, "In Defense of Slavery: Eighteenth-Century Opposition to Abolition and the Origins of a Racist Ideology in France," in Frederick Krantz, ed., *History from Below: Studies in Popular Protest and Popular Ideology in Honour of George Rudé* (Montreal, 1985), 221–41; Laurent Versini, "Hommes des lumières et hommes de couleur," in Jean-Claude

Carpanin Marimoutou and Jean-Michel Racault, eds., *Metissages,* I (1992), 25–34; Béatrice Didier, "Le métissage de l'*Encyclopédie* à la Révolution: De l'anthropologie à la politique," in ibid., 13–24; Ivan Hannaford, *Race: The History of an Idea in the West* (Washington, 1996). Earlier literature on the same theme includes Duchet, *Anthropologie et histoire,* and Richard H. Popkin, "The Philosophical Basis of Eighteenth-Century Racism," in *Studies in Eighteenth-Century Culture,* III (1973), 245–62. See also Vyverberg, *Human Nature.* As intellectual background for the shift, the authors cite the weakening of Christian theology and its insistence on the common descent of the human race from Adam ("monogenesis"), and the increasing influence of the biological sciences with their penchant for classification and ranking.

127. See on this point Hannaford, *Race,* 235–76.

128. On the meanings of "race," see Boulle, "In Defense of Slavery," 222.

129. Pagden, "The 'Defence of Civilization'" (see Ch. 1, n.14), 40–44.

4. National Memory and the Canon

1. Antoine-Léonard Thomas, *Essai sur les éloges* (Paris, 1829), 40–41.

2. Bonnet, *Naissance du Panthéon* (see Intro., n.43). My differences with Bonnet's interpretation will become clear in the course of this chapter. In general on the phenomenon, see also Papenheim's important study, *Erinnerung und Unsterblichkeit* (see Intro., n.43), which Bonnet does not cite.

3. André Thevet, *Les vrais pourtraits et vies des hommes illustres* (Paris, 1584; repr. Delmar, NY, 1973). See also, for instance, Jean-Jacques Boissard, *Icones uirorvm illvstirvm, doctrina & eruditione praestantium contines* (Frankfurt, 1598).

4. Arlette Jouanna, *L'idée de race en France au XVIème siècle (1498–1614),* 3 vols. (Paris, 1976), I, 25.

5. Quoted in Peter Gay, *The Enlightenment: An Interpretation,* 2 vols. (New York, 1966), I, 47. See also Martha Waling Howard, *The Influence of Plutarch in the Major European Literatures of the Eighteenth Century* (Chapel Hill, 1970).

6. Margaret MacGowan, "Le phénomène de la galerie des portraits des illustres," in Roland Mousnier and Jean Mesnard, eds., *L'âge d'or du mécénat (1598–1661)* (Paris, 1985), 411–22, quote from 412.

7. Gabriel Michel de la Rochemaillet, *Pourtraictz de plvsievrs hommes illvstres qvi ont flory en France depvis l'an 1500 ivsques à present* (Paris, 1600) printed as a broadside (Bibliothèque Nationale, Cabinet des Estampes, Hennin 1200/G151576). Reprinted as *La vie des graves et illustres personnages qui ont diuersement excellee en ce Royaume, sous les règnes de Louys XII, François I, Henry II, François II, Charles IX, Henry III & Henry IIII heureusement regnant* (Rouen, 1609). Rev. ed.: C. Malingre, *Histoire chronologique de plusieurs*

grands capitaines, princes, seigneurs, magistrats, officiers de la couronne & autres hommes illustres qui ont paru en France depuis cent soixante & quinze ans iusques à present (Paris, 1617); Scaevole de Sainte-Marthe, *Gallorum doctrina illustrium, qui nostra patrumque memoria floruerunt, elogia* (Paris, 1602).

8. See Dowley, "D'Angiviller's *Grands Hommes*"; Silvestre de Sacy, *Le comte d'Angiviller;* Locquin, *La peinture d'histoire* (see Intro. n.48), 41–69; Marc Furcy-Raynaud, ed., "Correspondance de M. d'Angiviller avec Pierre," 2 vols., *Nouvelles archives de l'art français,* 3e série, vols. XXI–XXII (1905–6); Andrew McClellan, *Inventing the Louvre: Art, Politics and the Origins of the Modern Museum in Eighteenth-Century Paris* (Berkeley, 1994), 82–90; McClellan, "D'Angiviller's 'Great Men'" (see Intro., n.48); Thomas Crow, *Painters and Public Life in Eighteenth-Century Paris* (New Haven, 1985), 191–7. Crow points out that at the end of the 1770s, d'Angiviller started to put renewed emphasis on classical antiquity in his painting program. Still, French history paintings continued to appear, as did the sculpture program.

9. See especially Brenner, *L'histoire nationale* (see Ch. 2, n.61); Boës, *La lanterne magique* (see Intro., n.44).

10. These projects are discussed in Mona Ozouf, "Le Panthéon: L'école normale des morts," in Nora, ed., *Les lieux de mémoire* (see Intro., n.33), pt. I, 142–44; Papenheim, *Erinnerung,* 286–7; Bonnet, *Naissance,* 130–32; John McManners, *Death and the Enlightenment: Changing Attitudes to Death in Eighteenth-Century France* (Oxford, 1985), 330–33; Dominique Poulot, *Musée, nation, patrimoine, 1789–1815* (Paris, 1997), esp. 53, 122; McClellan, *Inventing,* 83. On Louis XV's approval, see Papenheim, *Erinnerung,* 181.

11. See Bonnet, *Naissance du Panthéon,* 55–66. In general, on the eulogy, see also Bonnet's pioneering article "Naissance du Panthéon," *Poétique* 33 (1978).

12. See Daniel Roche, *Le siècle des lumières en province: Académies et académiciens provinciaux, 1680–1789,* 2 vols. (Paris, 1978), I, 344.

13. Bonnet, *Naissance du Panthéon,* 111; Bonnet, "Naissance du Panthéon," 47.

14. Bonnet, *Naissance du Panthéon,* 67–82. On Thomas's friendship with d'Angiviller, see McClellan, *Inventing,* 83–9.

15. Schama, *Citizens* (see Ch. 2, n.60), 32. Schama suggests that the volume "broadened its criteria to include events and figures from civilian life" and soldiers who had risen from the ranks (33). Yet these aspects of the book also had long-standing precedents in the series. In fact, as will be seen below, in most respect the volume represented a step backwards to a noble, chivalric ideal. Schama is unaware that the work, published by Pierre Blin, is by the engraver Sergent. For attribution, see Colin and Charlotte Franklin, *A Catalogue of Early Colour Printing, From Chiaroscuro to Aquatint* (Oxford, 1977), 53. Schama does, however, recognize the importance of the printed collective bi-

ography. Bonnet does not mention the volumes; Papenheim, in *Erinnerung*, 127, alludes to them briefly.

16. On these galleries, see MacGowan, "Le phénomène de la galerie des portraits des illustres"; Gérard Sabatier, "Politique, histoire et mythologie: La galerie en France et en Italie pendant la premiere moitié du 17e siècle," in Jean Serroy, ed., *La France et l'Italie au temps de Mazarin* (Grenoble, 1986), pp. 283–301; and especially Christian Jouhaud, "L'énergie du pouvoir: le cas de Richelieu (1631–1642)," in Louis Cullen and Louis Bergeron (eds.), *Culture et pratiques politiques en France et en Irlande, XVIè–XVIIIè siècle* (Paris, 1991), 83–99.

17. See MacGowan, 416, also Griguette, *Eloges des hommes illustres*.

18. Subsequent references to the works by Griguette, Vulson, Perrault, Morvan, Du Castre d'Auvigny, Gautier Dagoty, Restout, Turpin, Sergent, and Manuel, and to the anonymous works entitled *Eloges, Mémoires, Nécrologe, Tablettes,* and *Faits et actions,* refer to the books listed in Table 3, page 113.

19. Perrault, *Les hommes illustres,* unpaginated preface.

20. See Darnton, *Literary Underground* (see Ch. 2, n.21), 1–40.

21. On Manuel, see Darnton, *Literary Underground,* 59–61, and Louis Michaud, ed., *Biographie universelle ancienne et moderne* (Paris, 1852), sv. Manuel; on Aublet de Maubuy, see Robert Darnton "Two Paths through the Social History of Ideas," in Haydn Mason, ed., *The Darnton Debate: Books and Revolution in the Eighteenth Century, Studies on Voltaire and the Eighteenth Century* 359 (1998), 262.

22. Locquin, 183.

23. For instance, Dominique-Joseph Garat's prize-winning *Eloge de Suger* (Paris, 1779) uses only facts found in, and often follows the structure of, the life of Suger in d'Auvigny's *Les vies des hommes illustres,* I, 1–71.

24. The work in question is Du Castre D'Auvigny, Perau and Turpin, *Les vies.* See above all Du Castre's fascinating prospectus, *Avis pour l'histoire des hommes illustres de la France* (Paris, 1741). Turpin's *La France illustre* and Restout's *Gallerie françoise* were also sold by subscription.

25. Du Castre d'Auvigny, *Les vies,* I, v.

26. *Procès-verbaux de l'Académie royale de Peinture et de Sculpture, 1684–1793* (Paris, 1888), VIII, 178; [Manson] (see Intro., n.50), 8–9.

27. Maille Dussausoy, *Le citoyen désinteressé, ou diverses idées patriotiques, concernant quelques établissemens et embellissemens utils à la ville de Paris,* 2 vols. (Paris, 1767), 141.

28. Charles-Irénée Castel de Saint-Pierre, *Discours sur les différences du grand homme et de l'homme illustre,* published in *Histoire d'Epaminondas pour servir de suite aux hommes illustres de Plutarque* (Paris, 1739), 36, quoted in Bonnet, *Naissance du Panthéon,* 34. See also Ozouf's discussion of the distinciton in "Le Panthéon," 143–4.

29. Manuel, I, v.

30. Dacier, ed., *Les vies des hommes illustres de Plutarque,* 10 vols. (Paris, 1778), I, 10.

31. Manuel, I, xv. See also Bernardin de Saint-Pierre's *Etudes sur la nature* (Paris, 1784), which proposes an "Elysée" of great men, for similar remarks; also the discussion in Ozouf, "Le Panthéon," 144. On court trials, see Maza, *Private Lives and Public Affairs* (see Ch. 2, n.18).

32. Particularly in Bonnet, *Naissance du Panthéon* and Ozouf, "Le Panthéon."

33. See, for instance, Turpin, *La France illustre;* Turpin, *Annales pittoresques;* [Sergent], *Portraits; Faits et actions héroïques des grands hommes.*

34. [Sergent], no. 14 (d'Aguesseau); for nos. 60 (Bayard) and 73 (Jeanne d'Arc), cf. Heince, Bignon and Vulson (1668 edition with red type on title page), 80, 134. Sergent seems to have borrowed most of his engravings from familiar sources, for instance Duguesclin's death (no. 77) is borrowed from the Brenet's 1776 painting "Trait de respect pour la vertu: Honneurs rendus au Connétable du Guesclin par la ville de Randon," commissioned by d'Angiviller. Louis XVI (no. 1) copies a state portrait by Duplessis.

35. Much of this material is available in the Bibliothèque Nationale de France under the *côte* Ln20. On eighteenth-century regionalism, see especially Revel, "La région" (see Ch. 2, n.105); Catherine Bertho, "L'invention de la Bretagne: Genèse social d'un stéréotype," *Actes de la recherche en sciences sociales,* 35 (1980), 45–62; Mona Ozouf, "La Révolution française et la perception de l'espace national: fédérations, fédéralisme et stéréotypes régionaux," in her *L'école de la France: Essais sur la Révolution, l'utopie et l'enseignement* (Paris, 1984), 27–54; Michel Vovelle, "La découverte en Provence, ou les primitifs de l'ethnographie provençale," in *De la cave au grenier: Un itinéraire en Provence au XVIIIè siècle* (Québec, 1980). On nineteenth-century regionalism, see particularly Anne-Marie Thiesse, *Ils apprenaient la France: L'exaltation des régions dans le discours patriotique* (Paris, 1997); Stéphane Gerson, "Parisian Litterateurs, Provincial Journeys and the Construction of National Unity in Post-revolutionary France," *Past and Present* 151 (1996), 141–73.

36. See Morrissey's excellent discussion in *L'empereur à la barbe fleurie* (see Ch. 1, n.11), 300–303.

37. Baumier, *Homage à la patrie* (Brussels, 1782), 61, 91.

38. Carl L. Becker, *The Heavenly City of the Eighteenth-Century Philosophers* (New Haven, 1932), 31. This is in part the approach taken by Bonnet in his initial article "Naissance du Panthéon," and also by Ozouf in "Le Panthéon."

39. The quote is from Bonnet, "Naissance du Panthéon," 47.

40. See Ozouf, *La fête révolutionnaire* (see Intro., n.81), esp. 447; and Albert Soboul, "Sentiment religieux et cultes populaires pendant la Révolution: Saints, patriotes et martyrs de la liberté," in *Annales historiques de la Révolution française,* 148 (1957), esp. 198.

41. They are collected in Antoine-Léonard Thomas, Oeuvres complètes (Paris, 1825).

42. See Heince, Bignon, and Vulson, *Les portraits,* 1668 ed., 80–94.

43. Aublet de Maubuy, *Les vies des femmes illustres,* I, 10. See also Gerd Krumeich, *Jeanne d'Arc à travers l'histoire,* trans. Josie Mély, Marie-Hélène Pateau and Lisette Rosenfeld (Paris, 1989).

44. Jean-François de La Harpe, *Eloge de Catinat* (Paris, 1775). See discussion in Bonnet, *Naissance du Panthéon,* 92–4.

45. Restout, *Galerie françoise,* iv.

46. Manuel, *L'année françoise,* I:v.

47. On the reception of Plutarch in Renaissance France, see Jouanna, *L'idée de race,* I:25.

48. See Bonnet, *Naissance du Panthéon,* 29–49.

49. Ibid., 111.

50. Ibid., 131–2.

51. Quoted in Brenner, *L'histoire nationale,* 197.

52. Buirette de Belloy, *Le siège de Calais* (see Ch. 1, n.104), vi–vii.

53. Lefebvre de Beauvray, *Dictionnaire* (see Ch. 1, n.103), 394–5, quoting Saint-Foix.

54. Turpin, *La France illustre, ou le Plutarque français.* See also Howard, 32.

55. Joachim Du Bellay, *Deffense et illustration de la langue françoise* (Paris, 1549).

56. François Charpentier, *Defense de la langue françoise pour l'inscription de l'Arc de Triomphe, dédiée au Roy par M. Charpentier, de l'Académie Françoise* (Paris, 1676). See Brunot et al., *Histoire de la langue française* (see Intro., n.30), V, 1–43; also Marc Fumaroli, "Le génie de la langue française," in Nora, ed., *Les lieux de mémoire,* pt. III, III, 911–73.

57. Quoted in Brunot, VII, 95.

58. Perrault, *Les hommes illustres,* unpaginated preface. On Perrault, see also Jay M. Smith, *The Culture of Merit: Nobility, Royal Service and the Making of Absolute Monarchy in France, 1600–1789* (Ann Arbor, 1996), 169–71.

59. Antoine-Léonard Thomas, "Eloge de Duguay-Trouin," in *Mémoires de M. Duguay-Trouin, Lieutenant Général des Armées Navales* (Rouen, 1785), 299. As for d'Angiviller's "Great Men," see the comments of McClellan, in "D'Angiviller's 'Great Men,'" 177: "But over and above brilliance and virtue, the common denominator linking the majority of the Great Men was loyal service to the Crown."

60. See McClellan, *Inventing the Louvre,* 83–89. The eulogist in question was the abbé Rémy. D'Angiviller, incidentally, warmly praised the address.

61. Sergent, *Portraits.*

62. See Papenheim, *Erinnerung,* 125–6.

63. Thomas, "Eloge de Duguay-Trouin," 275, 300, 276, 311.

64. See Peter Gay, *Voltaire's Politics: The Poet as Realist* (New York, 1965), esp.

309–33. For Thomas's relations with Voltaire, see Micard (see Ch. 3, n.42), 23–5, 57.

65. Thomas, "Eloge," 331.

66. Manuel, *L'année françoise,* I, 2.

67. Ibid., xv; See also Turpin, *Annales pittoresques,* 1782 edition, 20.

68. See Franco Venturi, "From Montesquieu to the Revolution," in *Utopia and Reform in the French Enlightenment* (Cambridge, 1971), 70–94; Johnson Kent Wright, *A Classical Republican in Eighteenth-Century France : The Political Thought of Mably* (Stanford, 1997); Keith Michael Baker, "Transformations of Classical Republicanism in Eighteenth-Century France," *The Journal of Modern History* LXXIII/I (2001), 32–53. In general on republicanism, see the classic work of Pocock, *The Machiavellian Moment* (see Ch. 1, n.83).

69. Montesquieu, *The Spirit of the Laws* (see Intro., n.41), 25–7.

70. See notably Landes, *Women and the Public Sphere* (see Intro., n.72); Hunt, *Family Romance* (see Intro., n.72); Sarah Maza, "Response to Daniel Gordon and David Bell" (see Intro., n.72).

71. The ARTFL database lists includes 1842 uses of the phrase "grand(s) homme(s)" for the eighteenth century, almost always in the sense of "great" rather than "tall" or "big." The only comparable female appellation is "femme illustre."

72. Maubuy, *Les vies des femmes illustres,* v–viii; quote from xviii.

73. The tradition extends back through Claude-Charles Guyonne de Vertron's *La Nouvelle Pandore* (Paris, 1703) to the works of Mlle. de Scudéry and the proto-feminist texts discussed by Carolyn Lougee in *Le paradis des femmes: Women, Salons and Social Stratification in Seventeenth-Century France* (Princeton, 1976). See also the fascinating discussion of the Chevalier d'Eon's library in Gary Kates, *Monsieur d'Eon Is a Woman: A Tale of Politique, Intrigue and Sexual Masquerade* (New York, 1995), 150–58.

74. The queens Fredegonde, Brunhilda, Bertrande, and Bathilde. See [Sergent], *Portraits.*

75. Aublet de Maubuy, x–xi.

76. See the lists in Bonnet, *Naissance du Panthéon,* 391–2, 395–6.

77. See the list of the collective biographies in Table 3, above.

78. See Furcy-Raynaud, ed., "Correspondance de M. d'Angiviller avec Pierre."

79. Morvan de Bellegarde, unpaginated preface.

80. Du Castre d'Auvigny, *Avis,* 9.

81. Turpin, *La France illustre,* 1782 edition, I, i.

82. See Colin Jones, "The Great Chain of Buying: Medical Advertisement, the Bourgeois Public Sphere, and the Origins of the French Revolution," *American Historical Review,* CI/1 (1996), 13–40.

83. See Tables 1 and 2, above.

84. On this subject, see particularly Gossman, *Medievalism* (see Ch. 1, n.116).

85. Gautier Dagoty and Restout, *Galerie Françoise* (see Table 3, above).

86. Turpin, *La France illustre*, I, 2.

87. Manuel, *L'année françoise*, I, viii.

88. Ibid., I:62–66, 135–40, III, 12–15.

89. Ibid., I, 99–120. On the earlier adoration of Charlemagne in the eighteenth century, see Morrissey, *L'empereur à la barbe fleurie*, 265–348.

90. This evidence therefore suggests, incidentally, that Robert Darnton and his critics have perhaps focused too intently on illegal productions in their debates over the existence, and potential radicalism, of Grub Street. See most recently Mason, ed., *The Darnton Debate*, esp. 105–88 and 251–94.

91. For an instance of plagiarism, these lines on the abbé Suger (I:53)—"Un homme simple porte à l'abbaye de Saint-Denis un enfant de neuf à dix ans, le pose sur l'autel, le consacre ou plutôt l'abandonne à Dieu, & se retire pour ne plus reparoître"—were taken verbatim from Dominique-Joseph Garat's *Eloge de Suger*, 8–9. Manuel, I, xi, admits some of his "borrowings."

92. See above all Papenheim, *Erinnerung*, 214–301; Bonnet, *Naissance du Panthéon*, 255–98.

93. [Thomas Rousseau, Léonard Bourdon et al.], *Recueil des actions héroiques et civiques des républicains français*, 5 issues (Paris, 1793–94). See Julia, *Les trois couleurs* (see Intro., n.11), 208–13. Julia calls the paper one of the rare instances "in which the Revolution was able to carry out decisions on a scale commensurate with its ambitions" (213).

94. This is the argument of Zizek's powerful "The Politics and Poetics of History" (see Ch. 2, n.107).

95. Turpin, *Histoire des illustres françois* (see Table 3).

96. See Ozouf, "Le Panthéon."

97. Quoted in ibid., 158.

98. See Bonnet, *Naissance du Panthéon*, 273–97, and Soboul, "Sentiment religieux"; more generally, Mathiez, *L'origine des cultes révolutionnaires* (see Intro., n.54).

5. National Character

1. Castilhon, *Considérations sur les causes physiques et morales* . . . Castilhon was not the only author to plagiarize d'Espiard. See Griffin, "Oliver Goldsmith" (see Intro., n.38).

2. See Michaud, *Biographie universelle*, s.v. d'Espiard. Espiard published his protests in the *Journal encyclopédique*, and Castilhon responded in the slightly revised 1770 edition of his book, which now admitted in the title to have been "taken in part from a book called *The Spirit of the Nations*," and defended himself against the charge of plagiarism (xv, xxi–xxvi).

3. [d'Espiard de la Borde], *L'esprit des nations* (The Hague, 1753 ed.), I, 144–45 (see Intro., n.38).

4. Castilhon (1770 ed.), I, 274.

5. D'Espiard, I, 238.

6. Castilhon II, 163.

7. D'Espiard, I, 155–56.

8. Castilhon, I, 295–96. By changing "société" to "brillante société," he altered its meaning from society as a whole to a single social class.

9. [d'Espiard de la Borde], *Essais sur le génie et le caractère des nations* (see Intro., n.37), II, bk IV, 41n.

10. Among the works of the major *philosophes*, Montesquieu's *L'esprit des lois*, Voltaire's *Essai sur les moeurs*, and Rousseau's *Considérations sur le gouvernement de Pologne* devoted particular attention to the question of national character. Among the books that directly focused on the question of national character, see particularly Louis Legendre, *Moeurs et coutumes des françois dans les differents temps de la monarchie* (Paris, 1712); Louis de Muralt's *Lettres sur les anglais et sur les français* (Zurich, 1725) and the anonymous reply *Apologie du caractère des anglois et des françois* (see Ch. 1, n.100); d'Espiard's works; Denesle, *Les préjugés du public, avec des observations, par M. Denesle* (Paris, 1747); [Pichon], *La physique de l'histoire* (see Ch. 3, n.86); Sébastien-Marie-Mathurin Gazon-Dourxigné, *Essai historique et philosophique sur les principaux ridicules des differentes nations* (Amsterdam, 1766); de Sacy, *L'honneur françois* (see Ch. 3, n.7); Johann Georg Zimmerman, *De l'orgueil national* (Paris, 1769), a translation of *Vom Nationalstolze* (see Ch. 1, n.111); James Rutledge [Rutlidge], *Essai sur le caractère et les moeurs des françois comparés à ceux des anglois* (London, 1776), a translation and adaptation of John Andrews, *An Account of the Character and Manners of the French* (London, 1770); *Lettre d'un jeune homme à son ami, sur les Français et les Anglais* (see Intro., n.70); Sobry, *Le mode françois* (see Ch. 1, n.63); Guiraudet, *Qu'est-ce que la nation et qu'est-ce que la France* (see Ch. 2, n.106); Joseph-Antoine-Joachim Cerutti, *Lettre sur les avantages et l'origine de la gaieté française* (Paris, 1762); Hugues Maret, *Mémoire dans lequel on cherche à déterminer quelle influence les moeurs des Français ont sur leur santé* (Paris, 1771). Periodicals that paid most attention to the subject were the *Journal encyclopédique*, the *Mémoires de Trévoux*, and the *Année littéraire*. On travel literature, see Mona Ozouf, "La Révolution française et la perception de l'espace national," and Bertho, "L'invention de la Bretagne" (see Ch. 4, n.35). On historical writing, see Blandine Barret-Kriegel, *Les historiens et la monarchie*, 4 vols. (Paris, 1989).

11. Ozouf, "La Révolution française et la formation de l'homme nouveau" (see Intro., n.4), 116.

12. Ozouf, in her otherwise marvellous essay, shifts back and forth between discussions of the "homme nouveau" and the "peuple neuf" or "peuple nouveau" as if the terms were equivalent.

13. For a summary of the debates, see Alex Inkeles, *National Character: A Psycho-Social Perspective* (New Brunswick, 1997).

14. Quoted in Julio Caro Baroja, *Le mythe du caractère national,* Jean-Paul Cortada, trans. (Lyon, 1975), 17. The book provides many more examples, as does Hale, *The Civilization of the Renaissance* (see Ch. 3, n.13), 51–66.

15. See esp. Jean Bodin, *Method for the Easy Comprehension of History,* trans. Beatrice Reynolds (New York, 1945). See in general Pagden, *The Fall of Natural Man* (see Ch. 3, n.35); also Shackleton, *Montesquieu* (see Intro., n.39); 302–19, and Vyverberg, *Human Nature, Cultural Diversity* (see Ch. 3, n.82).

16. François de la Mothe le Vayer, "Discours de la contrariété d'humeurs qui se trouve entre certaines nations, et singulièrement entre la françoise et l'espagnole," in *Oeuvres,* 7 vols. (Dresden, 1757), IV, pt. II, 311–86, quote from 324.

17. Rousseau, for instance, believed that *moeurs* and religion alike depended largely on the form of government. For Voltaire, in the *Essai sur les moeurs,* both were heavily influenced by the development of civilization.

18. Voltaire, *Essai sur les moeurs* (see Intro., n.41), VI, 230; Charles Duclos, *Considérations sur les moeurs de ce siécle* (Amsterdam, 1751), 16. Rousseau, *Emile* (see Ch. 2, n.48), 615.

19. D'Espiard, *Essai,* I, pt. I, 60, 87. D'Espiard's was the first to use the word "climate" for atmospheric conditions, as well as simply region. See Shackleton, 308–9.

20. For the evidence that Montesquieu read and was influenced by d'Espiard, see ibid.

21. Montesquieu, *The Spirit of the Laws* (see Intro. n.41), 231–35.

22. Quoted in Shackleton, 302.

23. See Duchet, *Anthropologie et histoire* (see Ch. 3, n.35); Anthony Pagden, *European Encounters with the New World: From Renaissance to Romanticism* (New Haven, 1993), 141–82. See also Robert Shackleton, "The Evolution of Montesquieu's Theory of Climate," *Revue internationale de philosophie* IX (1955), 317–29.

24. Montesquieu, 310.

25. *Journal encyclopédique,* 1757, III, pt. III, 38 (the observation came in a review of David Hume's essay on national character, which itself drew heavily on Montesquieu); Henri Gaillard, *Histoire de la rivalité de la France et de l'Angleterre,* 3 vols. (Paris, 1771), III, 285; Turpin, *Histoire des illustres françois sorti du ci-devant tiers-état* (see Ch. 4, table 3), I, 1.

26. Rousseau, *Confessions,* in *Oeuvres* (see Intro., n.42), I, 404.

27. Rousseau, *Considérations sur le gouvernement de la Pologne,* in ibid., III, 960. See also his *Projet de constitution pour la Corse.*

28. Thomas, *Essai sur les éloges* (see Ch. 4, n.1), 21; P.-J.-B. Chaussard, *La France régénérée* (Paris, 1791), 4.

29. Mirabeau, *L'ami des hommes* (see Ch. 1, n.90), 317.

30. Voltaire, *Essai.*

31. D'Espiard, *L'esprit des nations*, II, 207; Jacques-Antoine-Hippolyte de Guibert, *Le Connétable de Bourbon*, in *Oeuvres dramatiques de Guibert* (Paris, 1825), 22 (the heroine, Adélaïde, begins a line of verse by saying "Les hommes font les lois," and the hero, Bayard, completes it with the phrase "Les femmes font les moeurs"); Also Mignonneau, in *Réflexions politiques* (see Ch. 2, n.58), 22: "public *moeurs* in Europe, and especially in France, today depend solely on women."

32. Montesquieu, 310.

33. Jean-Jacques Rousseau, *Politics and the Arts: Letter to M. d'Alembert on the Theater*, trans. and ed. Allan Bloom (Ithaca, 1960), esp. 81–92, 100–113.

34. Voltaire, quoted in Gordon, *Citizens without Sovereignty* (see Ch. 1, n.15), 75; *Le Poëme sur la bataille de Fontenoy*, unpaginated; quoted in Goodman, *The Republic of Letters* (see Ch. 1, n.60), 50.

35. See for instance Muralt, passim; Zimmermann, *Vom Nationalstolze*, 201, 256; and the discussion of British views in Newman, *The Rise of English Nationalism* (see Intro., n.28), 74–84.

36. D'Holbach, quoted in Gordon, *Citizens without Sovereignty*, 76; See also, for instance, [Joseph Servan], *Le soldat citoyen, ou vues patriotiques sur la manière la plus avantageuse de pourvoir à la défense du royaume* ("Dans le pays de la liberté," 1780), 16, d'Espiard, *L'esprit des nations*, I, 62–64; Sobry, *Le mode françois*, 18.

37. On the history of notions of sociability in eighteenth-century France, see Gordon's fundamental *Citizens without Sovereignty*. On the issue of the French as a particularly sociable people, see esp. 75–77.

38. Montesquieu, *Lettres persanes* (Paris, 1964), 145–46; Diderot, quoted in Gordon, 29; Voltaire, Cerutti, and Duclos also called the French the most sociable of nations: Voltaire, discussed in Gordon, 75, and also in Claude-Gilbert Dubois, "Fonction des mythes d'origine dans le développement des idées nationalistes en France," *History of European Ideas*, XVI/4–6 (1993), 419; Duclos, *Considérations*, 171. On Cerutti, see Antoine de Baecque, *Les éclats du rire: La culture des rieurs au XVIIIᵉ siècle* (Paris, 2000), 158. I am indebted to Gordon's subtle and powerful analysis of *sociabilité* for much of this discussion.

39. See Louis-Charles Fougeret de Montbron, *Le cosmopolite ou le citoyen du monde* (London, 1753), 42; Favart, *L'anglois à Bordeaux* (see Ch. 1, n.96), esp. 17–19; and the material discussed in Grieder, *Anglomania* (see Intro., n.55), 61–62, 89.

40. Quoted in Gordon, 76.

41. Quoted in Dupront, "Du sentiment national" (see Intro., n.34), 1435.

42. D'Espiard, in his 1743 *Essai*, insisted that the "lightness of the nation" would have to be "corrected" for France to become a free state (II, bk. IV, 42). He returned to the theme often in *L'esprit des nations* (e.g. I, 62–64, 138, 154, 239). See also Mirabeau, *L'ami des hommes*, 250, 320; Louis-Sébastien Mercier, *Le tableau de Paris*, ed. Jean-Claude Bonnet, 2 vols. (Paris, 1994), I, 1474.

43. See, for instance, Montesquieu, *The Spirit of the Laws*, 310; Rivarol, *L'universalité* (see Ch. 3, n.83), 23; *Discours sur le patriotisme* (see Intro., n.56), 82. Cerutti is discussed in de Baecque, *Les éclats du rire*, 153–70.

44. Sobry, *Le mode françois*, 19; Perrin quoted in Grieder, *Anglomania*, 95–96. See also, for instance, the defense of *légereté* in *Apologie du caractère des anglois et des françois* (esp. 105), whose anonymous author claimed that it made the French more witty and adventurous.

45. For instance, "the most polite and civilized nation": Antoine Court, and Antonie Court de Gébelin, *Le patriote françois et impartial, ou réponse à la lettre de Mr. l'evêque d'Agen à Mr. le Contrôleur général, contre la Tolérance des Huguenots, en datte du 1 mai 1751*, 2 vols. (2d ed., "Villefranche," 1753), iv; "a spiritual, easy-going politeness" is one of the "traits which have made us famous": *Lettre d'un jeune homme à son ami*, 10; "the model of politeness": [Servan], *Le soldat citoyen*, 16; "French politeness . . . is an almost general quality in the Nation": d'Espiard, *L'esprit des nations*, I, 153.

46. Holbach, quoted in Gordon, 76; Servan, 16; Thomas, 333; d'Espiard, I, 153; Sobry, 379; Turgot, discussed in Febvre, "Civilisation" (see Ch. 1, n.14), 228.

47. See on this subject particularly Roger Chartier, "From Texts to Manners" (see Intro., n.18), and Gordon, *Citizens without Sovereignty*, 86–128.

48. See for instance Rivarol, *L'universalité de la langue française*, 25; d'Espiard, *L'esprit des nations*, II, 25; [Pichon], *La physique de l'histoire*, 262–63; Cerutti, quoted in de Baecque, *Les éclats du rire*, 160.

49. Montesquieu, 311–2; D'Espiard, *L'esprit des nations*, I, 153.

50. Gazon Dourxigné, *Essai*, 138.

51. Rivarol, 23.

52. D'Espiard, *L'esprit des nations*, I, vii.

53. He added that if Asians and Africans stopped keeping women in chains, "they would lose their cruelty, and grow civilized" like the French. *Lettre d'un jeune homme*, 16.

54. D'Espiard, *L'esprit des nations*, I, 153.

55. Gazon-Dourxigné, 138.

56. Rivarol, 23.

57. Rousseau, *Politics and the Arts*, 100.

58. Millot, *Discours sur le patriotisme françois* (see Ch. 2, n.41), 26, 35.

59. Brie-Serrant, *Ecrit adressé à l'Académie de Châlons-sur-Marne* (see Ch. 2, n.58), 15.

60. Thomas, *Essai*, 508.

61. See de Baecque, *The Body Politic* (see Ch. 2, n.102), 1–25, 133–56. See also on this subject Ozouf, "La formation de l'homme nouveau," and Zizek, "The Politics and Poetics of History" (see Ch. 2, n.107).

62. Dussausoy, *Le citoyen désinteressé* (see Ch. 4, n.27), 114.

63. Bouquier quoted in Ozouf, "L'homme nouveau," 134; Millot, *Discours sur le patriotisme*, 40; "Sur l'influence des mots et le pouvoir de l'usage," by "C. B., homme libre," in *Mercure national et révolutions de l'europe, journal démocratique*, 47 (Dec. 14, 1789), 1813; *Citoyens français*, quoted in de Baecque, 143; *De l'égalité des représentants, et de la forme des délibérations aux Etats-Généraux de 1789* (n.p., 1789), 3; Boissy d'Anglas, quoted in Elisabeth Liris, "Eduquer l'homme nouveau," in Boulad-Ayoub, ed., *Former un nouveau peuple?* (see Intro., n.11), 303.

64. Jean-Paul Rabaut de Saint-Etienne, *Précis historique de la Révolution française*, 5th ed. (Paris, 1809), 21.

65. Charles Chaisneau, *Le Panthéon français, ou discours sur les honneurs publics décernés par la nation à la mémoire des grands hommes* (Dijon, 1792), 6; See also *Citoyens français*, quoted in de Baecque, 143; Mercier, quoted in Zizek, 131; and other examples given by these two historians.

66. See for instance Guiraudet, *Qu'est-ce que la nation*, 63; prospectus to *La Feuille villageoise*, excerpted in Michel de Certeau, Dominique Julia, and Jacques Revel, *Une politique de la langue: La Révolution française et les patois* (Paris, 1975), 283; "Sur l'influence des mots," 1814.

67. Henri de Boulainvilliers, *Histoire de l'ancien gouvernement de France, avec XIV lettres historiques sur les parlements ou états généraux* (The Hague and Amsterdam, 1727), 69.

68. Laurent-Pierre Bérenger, *Porte-feuille d'un troubadour*, quoted in Gossman, *Medievalism* (see Ch. 1, n.116), 342. Gossman's work is fundamental on this subject.

69. Sacy, *L'honneur françois*.

70. See [Bachaumont, et al.], *Mémoires secrets* (see Ch. 2, n.64), VII, 182. On the fad for Renaissance clothing, see Clarence D. Brenner, "Henri IV on the French Stage" (see Ch. 1, n.40), esp. 544; and in general on Henri IV in the eighteenth century, Reinhard, *La légende de Henri IV* (see Ch. 1, n.38).

71. Quoted in de Baecque, *The Body Politic*, 140.

72. Quoted in ibid., 142.

73. Quoted in ibid.; *Le Moniteur*, August 17, 1793.

74. *Petition pour rendre à la France son véritable nom* (n.p., n.d.). The pamphet is signed "par Dupin et Lagrange, républicains gaulois." See Bibliothèque de la Société de Port-Royal, Fonds Révolution 120, no. 45.

75. On the uses of Hercules as a symbol of masculinity and strength, see Lynn

Hunt, *Politics, Culture, and Class in the French Revolution* (Berkeley, 1984), 94–116. On earlier French uses of Hercules, and the strong connection seen between him and the Gauls, see Michael Wintroub, "Civilizing the Savage and Making a King," *Sixteenth Century Journal*, XXIX/2 (1998), 467–96.

76. Pétion, quoted in De Baecque, 138–9; anonymous verse anthologized in *Poésies nationales de la Révolution française*, 18; Louis-Sébastien Mercier, *Adieux à l'année 1789* (n.p., n.d.), 3.

77. *La Passion, la mort, et la résurrection du peuple* ("Jérusalem," 1789), 5. On this general theme see especially Ozouf, "La formation de l'homme nouveau," 132–37. We will see many more examples in the next chapter.

78. Soanen, "Sur l'amour de la patrie" (see Intro., n.36), 1280. Similarly, the Jesuit teacher Jean-Baptiste Geoffroy, in his 1744 Latin oration *De amore patriae:* "we are born men and citizens," 6.

79. *Considérations sur les différends des couronnes* (see Ch. 3, n.21), 25.

80. Cerutti, *Discours qui a remporté le prix de l'éloquence* (see Ch. 2, n.41), 13–14.

81. Jean-Jacques Rousseau, *Oeuvres*, III, 364. This translation is Maurice Cranston's.

82. Rousseau, *Emile*, 38.

83. Quoted in Ozouf, *La fête révolutionnaire* (see Intro., n.81), 474.

84. See the discussion in Dupuy, "Genèse" (see Intro., n.33), 130.

85. *Discours sur le patriotisme*, 10–11.

86. Ibid., 82.

87. Ibid., 85.

88. Joseph-Antoine-Joachim Cerutti, *Mémoire pour le peuple* (Paris, 1788), 63; Rabaut quoted in Ozouf, "La formation," 125.

89. Quoted in Ozouf, *L'école*, 33; in Ozouf, "La formation," 133.

90. Robespierre, July 13, 1793, in James Guillaume, ed., *Procès-verbaux du Comité d'instruction publique de la Convention*, 6 vols. (Paris, 1891–1907), II, 35. This speech was given on the day of Marat's assassination.

91. Danton, quoted in Julia, *Les trois couleurs* (see Intro., n.11), 123. Recognizing the implications of his words, Danton continued: "No one respects nature more than I do. But the social interest demands that his loyalties lie there alone . . . you cannot remove your children from the national influence. And what should the reasoning of an individual matter to us in the face of the national reasoning?" Deputy Prieur de la Côte d'Or similarly told the French people that "your children belong less to you than to the *patrie*." Prieur de la Côte d'Or, *Adresse de la Convention Nationale au peuple français, 16 Prairial An II* (Paris, 1794), 3. Lepeletier's report is reproduced in Baczko, ed., *Une éducation pour la démocratie* (see Intro., n.11), 345–86.

92. *Réimpression de l'ancien Moniteur*, no. 192, 779.

93. Joseph Lavallée, *Manlius Torquatus, ou la discipline romaine* (Paris, 1794), 57.

94. Quoted in Rivoire, *Le patriotisme* (see Ch. 1, n.40), 145.

95. Lavallée, esp. 10–11; Maximilien Robespierre, *Rapport fait au nom du comité de Salut Public Sur les Rapports des idées religieuses et morales avec les principes républicains, et sur les fêtes nationales* (Paris, 1794), 4.

96. *Réimpression de l'ancien Moniteur,* XVIII, 351.

97. Gilles Boucher-Laricharderie, *De l'influence de la Révolution française sur le caractère national* (Paris, An VI), 2. My thanks to Sarah Maza for pointing this work out to me.

98. Ibid., 38–49, quotes from 45, 49.

99. Ibid., 51.

100. Ibid., 76–77.

101. Ozouf, "La formation de l'homme nouveau."

102. Quoted in Dupuy, "Genèse de la Patrie Moderne," 249–250.

103. On this literature, see Introduction, n.25, p. 222.

104. *Réimpression de l'ancien Moniteur,* Dec. 22, 1792, 803; quoted in Dupuy, "Genèse de la Patrie Moderne," 217. See also Albert Mathiez, *L'origine des cultes révolutionnaires, 1789–92* (Paris, 1904), 103.

105. Inevitably, in the remainder of this chapter, I will rely essentially on secondary sources. A comprehensive study of revolutionary cultural policies—at least one that takes into account recent research in revolutionary political culture—remains to be written. In the meantime, see the pioneering work of Hunt, *Politics, Culture and Class,* and Antoine de Baecque's well-informed survey of the eighteenth century in Antoine de Baecque and Françoise Mélonio, *Lumières et liberté,* III, 7–187, of Jean-Pierre Rioux and Jean-François Sirinelli, eds., *Histoire culturelle de la France,* 4 vols. (Paris, 1998).

106. The National Convention alone, in its Committee on Public Instruction, generated enough paper to fill the six massive volumes edited a century ago by James Guillaume. The standard works on the revolutionary education reforms are H. C. Barnard, *Education and the French Revolution* (Cambridge, 1969); Julia, *Les trois couleurs du tableau noir;* Baczko, ed., *Une éducation pour la démocratie;* R. R. Palmer, *The Improvement of Humanity: Education and the French Revolution* (Princeton, 1985); and Isser Woloch, *The New Regime: Transformations of the French Civic Order, 1789–1820's* (New York, 1993), 163–222. For a recent *mise à point,* see Boulad-Ayoub, ed., *Former un nouveau peuple?*

107. Quoted in Barnard, *Education,* 105.

108. "Moral education constituted the keystone of all the revolutionary projects": Julia, 194

109. *Réimpression de l'ancien Moniteur,* December 22, 1792, 802.

110. Ibid.

111. On the connections, see Julia, *Les trois couleurs,* 93, and 57–69. Jean-Louis

Labarrière, "De la vertu du citoyen éclairé" (see Intro., n.11), 66. Other important precedents included reports by the physicians Gilbert Romme and François-Xavier Lanthenas, also in Dec., 1792.

112. Lepeletier, in Baczko, ed., 352, 362.

113. Ibid., 351, 371.

114. This point was keenly observed by Georges Dumesnil, *La pédagogie révolutionnaire* (Paris, 1883), 220–21.

115. On the revolutionary theater, see Rivoire, *Le patriotisme;* Emmet Kennedy, ed., *Theaters, operas and audiences in Revolutionary France: Analysis and Repertory* (Westport, Conn., 1996); 76.

116. See Jeffrey S. Ravel, *The Contested Parterre: Public Theater and French Political Culture, 1680–1791* (Ithaca, 1999), esp. 191–97.

117. Louis-Sébastien Mercier, *Du théâtre, ou nouvel essai sur l'art dramatique* (Amsterdam, 1773). On Mercier's ideas, see Gregory S. Brown, "Scripting the Patriotic Playwright in Enlightenment-Era France: Louis-Sébastien Mercier's Self-Fashionings, between 'Court' and 'Public,'" *Historical Reflections / Réflexions historiques* 26/1 (2000), 1–27.

118. Edme-Nicolas Restif de la Bretonne, *La mimographe, ou idées d'un honnête femme pour la réformation du Théâtre National,* quoted in Boës, *La lanterne magique* (see Intro., n.44), 78. Other examples of calls for the theater to function as an *école des moeurs* can be found in Ravel, 191–97. See also the Chevalier d'Eon on the subject, quoted in Dziembowski, *Un nouveau patriotisme* (see Intro., n.33), 391.

119. These assertions are based on Gregory S. Brown, "Do Plays Make Revolutions?" paper presented to the Society for French Historical Studies, Washington, D.C., March, 1999.

120. L. W. B. Brockliss, *French Higher Education in the Seventeenth and Eighteenth Centuries: A Cultural History* (Oxford, 1987), 164, 166. The same was true of the ballets that accompanied the plays, and the long recited poems, called *sénatus-consultus,* which sometimes replaced them.

121. Titles included "La France victorieuse sous Louis le Grand," "Le grand monarque," "Le génie français ou les fêtes françaises," and "Le tableau de la gloire tracé d'après les fastes du peuple français." See the discussion in Boës, 26–44.

122. Melvin Edelstein, *La Feuille villageoise: Communication et modernisation dans les régions rurales pendant la Révolution* (Paris, 1977), 68, 74. In general on the revolutionary press, see the excellent synthesis of Jeremy Popkin, *Revolutionary News: The Press in France, 1789–1799* (Durham, N.C., 1990).

123. Edelstein, 74; see Cerutti's "Avis a tous les souscripteurs de 'La Feuille villageoise,'" reprinted in de Certeau et al., *Une politique de la langue,* 285–87.

124. Popkin, *Revolutionary News,* 150.

125. This description is taken from Schama, *Citizens* (see Ch. 2, n.60), 831–36. The fundamental work on the revolutionary festivals is Ozouf, *La fête révolutionnaire*. Condorcet is quoted in Labarrière, "De la vertu," 67.

126. *Reimpression de l'ancien Moniteur*, 803.

127. Ozouf, *La fête*, 446–53.

128. Ibid., 441–74.

6. National Language

1. On the *fête de la Fédération*, see Ozouf, *La fête révolutionnaire* (see Intro., n.81), 59–101.

2. Jean-Claude Meyer, *La vie religieuse en Haute-Garonne sous la Révolution (1789–1801)* (Toulouse, 1982), 59,77.

3. Antoine-Hyacinthe Sermet, *Discours prounounçat dabant la legiou de Sant-Ginest, Pel. R. P. Sermet, Exproubincial des Carmés Descaussés, Predicairé ourdinari del Rey, &c.* (Toulouse, 1790).

4. "Never forget, my children and good Comrades, to whom the Apostle Saint Paul, the greatest Preacher who has ever appeared on earth since the birth of Christianity, addressed this language. It was, so that you may know it, to our illustrious Ancestors, to the children of those Gauls, numbering more than a hundred and fifty thousand, who left this country some three thousand years ago to go beyond the seas, to the end of the known world of the time, to the depths of Asia to found the proud City of Ankara and to people the province which took their name and was called Galatia." Ibid., 1–2. The Galatians were indeed descended from Celts called Galatae.

5. The best scholarship on Villers-Cotterêts does not bear out the claims of linguistic imperialism. See Peyre, *La royauté*, 58–91; Trudeau, "L'ordonnance de Villers-Cotterêts" (see Intro., n.24). In the seventeenth and eighteenth centuries, the crown made several further attempts to impose the administrative use of French (edicts were issued for Béarn [1620], Flanders [1684], Alsace [1685], Roussillon [1700] and Lorraine [1748]). But these measures without exception applied only to areas recently annexed to France, where, unlike in Brittany and the Occitan regions, even the wealthier bourgeois and nobles generally did not speak French, thus making the new provinces seem far more "foreign" to their new rulers. See Brunot et al., *Histoire de la langue française* (see Intro., n.30), V and VII, passim; Peyre, 156; Emmanuel Le Roy Ladurie, "Les minorités périphériques: Intégration et conflits," in Revel and Burguière, eds., *Histoire de la France* (see Ch. 1, n.56), III, 455–630, esp. 623–27; A. Brun, *L'introduction de la langue française en Béarn et en Roussillon* (Paris, 1923). In Brittany, French had served as the official language since the eleventh century. Most recently, on the question of multilingualism in early

modern France, see the important work of Cohen, "Courtly French" (see Intro., n.24).

6. On Occitan, see Schneider, *Public Life in Toulouse, 1463–1789* (see Ch. 1, n.62); also Philippe Gardy, ed., *Pèire Godolin: Le Ramelet mondin et autres oeuvres* (Aix-en-Provence, 1984). The last old regime edition of Godolin's works was published in Toulouse in 1774 under the title *Las Obras de Pierre Goudelin.* On Alsatian publishing, see Franklin Ford, *Strasbourg in Transition, 1648–1789* (Cambridge, Mass., 1958), 207–34.

7. [Espiard de la Borde], *Essais* (see Intro., n.37), II, bk. V (separate pagination), 63.

8. Various examples are given by Hélène Merlin, "Langue et souveraineté en France au XVIIe siècle: La production autonome d'un *corps de langage,*" *Annales: Histoires, sciences sociales,* XLIX/2 (1994), 369–94, esp. 384–85.

9. I have found only two projects for linguistic unification before the late 1780s: one by the educational reformer Vallange, in *Nouveau système* (2nd vol. of *Nouveaux systèmes ou Nouveaux plans de méthode*) (Paris, 1719), 178–79, and one by Nicolas Legras, sponsor of a royal academy and *collège* in the town of Richelieu, in *Académie royale de Richelieu* (see Intro., n.20), 59, 77 (Legras was most concerned with the language of the nobility). Even treatment of peasant education rarely raised the linguistic question. See Harvey Chisick, *The Limits of Reform in the Enlightenment: Attitudes toward the Education of the Lower Classes in Eighteenth-Century France* (Princeton, 1981).

10. Quoted in Peyre, *La royauté,* 10. Similar views are quoted in Brunot, V, 176–81. By contrast, the Académie Française defined a "nation" (in which category it included France) as "the inhabitants of a common country, who live under the same laws, and use the same language. *Dictionnaire de l'Académie française,* 2 vols. (Paris, 1694), II, 110.

11. ". . . la causa damnada / de nosta lenga mesprezada . . . Cadun la leixa e desempara. / Tot lo mond l'apera barbara." Pey de Garros, *Poesias* (Toulouse, 1887), 299.

12. At least outside of German-speaking Alsace, whose thriving literary societies had recently embraced the *Sturm und Drang.* Alsace generally constitutes an exception to the French pattern in matters linguistic. See Paul Lévy, *Histoire linguistique d'Alsace et de Lorraine,* 2 vols. (Paris, 1929); Bell, "Nation-Building" (see Ch. 2, n.101).

13. Desgrouais, *Les gasconismes corrigés* (Toulouse, 1768, repr. 1812), viii.

14. On Occitan in the eighteenth century, see Henri Boyer, Georges Fournier, et al., *Le texte occitan de la période révolutionnaire: Inventaire, approches, lectures* (Montpellier, 1989), esp. Philippe Gardy. "Les modèles d'écriture: Ruptures et continuités" (473–516); René Merle, *L'écriture du provençal de 1775 à 1840,* 2 vols. (Beziers, 1990); Philippe Martel, ed., *L'invention du midi: Représentations*

du Sud pendant la période révolutionnaire, published as nos. 15–16 of *Amiras, repères occitans* (1987); Geneviève Vermès and Josiane Boutet, eds., *France, pays multilangue,* 2 vols. (Paris, 1987); Henri Boyer and Philippe Gardy, eds., *La question linguistique au sud au moment de la Révolution française,* published as *Lengas: Revue de sociolinguistique,* nos. 17–18 (1985); Maurice Agulhon, ed., *La Révolution vécue par la province: Mentalités et expressions populaires en Occitanie* (Beziers, 1990); *Cahiers critiques du patrimoine,* no. 2 (1986): *Révolution Contre-Révolution: Le texte dialectal de la période révolutionnaire: Provence, Bas-Languedoc oriental, Dauphiné.*

15. Which languages qualified as patois is not always clear—perhaps inherently so, given the dismissive meaning the word generally carried. Sometimes it covered non-French standard vernaculars, and sometimes not. On the etymology of patois, see Jacques Monfrin, "Les parlers en France," in François, ed., *La France et les français* (see Intro., n.34), 766. On eighteenth-century linguistic theory, see most recently Sophia A. Rosenfeld, "A Revolution in Language: Words, Gestures and the Politics of Signs in France, 1745–1804," Ph.D. diss., Harvard University (1995).

16. Obviously, only Romance-based patois could be fit into this particular mold. The best examples of the new attention to local languages are: Claude-François Achard, *Dictionnaire de la Provence et du comtat Venaissin,* 4 vols. (Marseille, 1785), Jérémie-Jacques Oberlin, *Essai sur le patois lorrain* (Strasbourg, 1775), and, in a more theoretical vein, Antoine Court de Gébelin, *Le Monde primitif analysé et comparé avec le monde moderne* (Paris, 1778). The older attitudes still prevailed in Rivarol's influential *De l'universalité de la langue française* (see Ch. 3, n.83), esp. 17, and in the *Encyclopédie* (see Pierre Achard, "Mise en ordre de la langue de raison: L'Etat et le français," in Max-Peter Gruenais, ed., *Etats de langue: Peut-on penser une politique linguistique?* [Paris, 1986], 51–83). On the general phenomenon, see Jacques Revel, "Forms of Expertise: Intellectuals and 'Popular' Culture in France (1650–1800)," in Steven L. Kaplan, ed., *Understanding Popular Culture: Europe from the Middle Ages to the 19th Century* (Berlin, 1984), 255–273, and Vovelle, "La découverte en Provence" (see Ch. 4, n.37).

17. *Réimpression de l'ancien Moniteur* (see Intro., n.3), August 25, 1790, 480. Many other similar examples could be adduced, most strikingly from the debates on the annexation of the (largely Occitan-speaking) French papal territories. See Brunot, IX, pt. I, 8.

18. Hyslop, *French Nationalism* (see Intro., n.22), 47–48.

19. "Sur l'influence des mots et le pouvoir de l'usage" (see Ch. 5, n.63), 1813–1818.

20. *Trois motions inconnues d'un député Gascon, ou Les Gasconnades patriotiques* (n.p. [1789–90]), 22.

21. For a detailed publishing history, see Boyer et al., *Le texte occitan* , 149–51.

22. On Sermet's literary abilities, see Timothy Jenkins, "Le père Sermet entre Godolin et l'abbé Grégoire," in Christian Anatole, ed., *Pèire Godolin, 1580–1649* (Toulouse, 1980), 215–23.

23. Daniel Bernard, "La révolution française et la langue bretonne," *Annales de Bretagne*, XXVIII (1912–13), 287–331. The laws mostly dealt with forest rights and tax collection.

24. Charles-François Bouche, *La constitution française, Traduite, conformément aux Decréts de l'Assémblée-nationale-constituante, en langue provençale, et présentée à l'Assemblée-nationale-législative* (Paris, 1792).

25. For instance de Certeau et al. (see Ch. 5, n.66), 280, for the club of Strasbourg; Brunot, IX, pt. I, 66, for the club of Apt; Merle, 295 for the club of Aix; Emile Coornaert, *La Flandre française de langue flamande* (Paris, 1969), 266, for clubs in Flanders.

26. For instance, see Garres, *Rasounomens, pensados & refflectious, d'un boun Pagès des embirouns de Toulouso* (Toulouse, 1791), 24; Claude Mauron and François-Xavier Emmanuelli, eds., *Textes politiques de l'époque révolutionnaire en langue provençale* (Saint-Rémy-de-Provence, 1986), 41–2, 64–71; Merle, 305; Georges Fournier, "La production toulousaine," in Boyer et al., *Le texte occitan*, 391–7. Although nearly all club registers are in French, and rarely refer to linguistic issues, there is evidence that the oral deliberations sometimes took place in the dialect. See for instance Dominique Villar to Grégoire, 7 Messidor II, Bibliothèque Nationale de France, Nouvelles Acquisitions Françaises (hereafter BN, NAF) 2798 (responses to the *enquête de Grégoire*), fol. 70r.

27. Admittedly, this amounted to less than one percent of total revolutionary production. For a general survey of patois literature in the Revolution, see Philippe Martel, "Les textes occitans de la période révolutionnaire: Un peu de géographie," in Boyer et al., 219–223. The Boyer volume contains (42–161) a detailed inventory of the Occitan texts. While some of the texts were apparently meant as "burlesque" amusement for French-speaking readers, many were clearly meant for reading aloud to largely illiterate, non-French speaking audiences.

28. Brunot, IX, pt. I, 48; Levy, passim. The newspaper, published by a fierce partisan of the German language named Andreas Ulrich, was entitled *Wöchentliche Nachrichten für die deutschsprechenden Einwohner Frankreichs, besonders aber für Handwerker und Bauer*. Fewer items appeared in other local languages.

29. The Assembly never allocated the necessary resources and personnel. However, officials in what would soon become the Ministry of Justice, unsure of how to proceed, did hire several volunteers (though deferring payment).

Brunot and other historians of revolutionary linguistic policies, perhaps placing too much faith in the efficacy of revolutionary government, thus argue
that the Assembly actively pursued a "politique des traductions." Yet the archival evidence makes clear that the initiative came almost entirely from
without. See Archives Nationales (Paris), AA 32, fols. 7, 15, 22, 24, 31. A volunteer named Dugas, an editor on Barère's *Le point du jour,* organized a
translation workshop for the Occitan dialects and produced many manuscript volumes, but ministry official found the project unsatisfactory, and the
collapse of the monarchy in any case rendered the documents obsolete before
they could be printed (AA 32, passim). In 1792, the Convention formed a
committee to study translations and confirmed the 1790 decree, but the practical result was again essential nil, although a few *représentants en mission* did
produce bilingual *affiches* on their own initiative. See Brunot, IX, pt. I, 155–
62; Dentzel, *Rapport et projet de décret faits au nom de la commission de
traduction, par le citoyen Dentzel, de Landau* (Paris, 1792).

30. Local languages were still spoken by the lower classes in many peripheral cities. However, as Mona Ozouf points out, eighteenth-century writers took for
granted that cities were a "crucible of homogeneity" and that "only in the
countryside did the relationship between men and the land fully express itself." Ozouf, *L'école de la France* (see Ch. 4, n.37), 29.

31. Grégoire's questionnaire is reprinted in de Certeau et al., *Une politique de la
langue,* 11–28. On the confusion between the *décrets* of the National Assembly and *décrets de prise de corps,* see *Moniteur,* February 9, 1790, 336. For later
pronouncements by Grégoire antedating his report to the Convention, see
Guillaume, ed., *Procès-verbaux du Comité d'Instruction publique* (see Ch. 5,
n.90), II, 177 (July 30, 1793); III, 368 (3 Pluviôse, II). For a legislative report
by Talleyrand that pays attention to language, see Jules Mavidal and Emile
Laurent, eds., *Archives parlementaires de 1787 à 1860,* 1st series, 82 vols.
(Paris, 1862–1913), XXX, 472 (September 10, 1791). The other major report,
by the Girondin Lanthenas, is discussed in Brunot, IX, pt. I, 135. In general,
for other legislative activity on language from this period, particularly in the
Convention's Comité d'Instruction, see Brunot, IX, pt. I, 135–48. Among
other revolutionary writings addressing the topic are *Adresse aux Communes
et aux sociétés populaires de la République . . . lue au Conseil Général de la
Commune de Paris* (Paris, 1792), 7 (Bibliothèque de la Société de Port-Royal,
hereafter B.S.P., Rév. 223, no. 14); Pierre-Vincent Chalvet, *Des qualités et des
devoirs d'un Instituteur publique* (Paris, 1793); the *Chronique de Paris* of November 10, 1792; the prospectus for the *Feuille villageoise,* the newspaper
aimed explicitly at the peasantry (reprinted in de Certeau et al., 283–85).

32. On the continuing need for translation, see de Certeau et al., 298–99;
Grégoire, in de Certeau et al., 310. Grégoire served on the Convention's com-

mittee on translations in 1793, and while in Nice as a *représentant en mission*, himself had proclamations translated into Italian. See Henri Grégoire et al., *Egualianza, libertà. Proclama. I commisari della Convenzione nazionale ai cittadini del dipartimento delle Alpi-Maritimi* (Nice, 1793). Even his report on the need to eradicate patois was translated into Italian, by the French government: Henri Grégoire, *Rapporto sulla necessità e sui mezzi d'abolire i Dialetti rozzi, e di rendere l'uso della Lingua Francese, universale* (Paris, 1794).

33. Barère's report is reprinted in de Certeau, et al., 292–99. Quote from 295.

34. Henri Grégoire, "Rapport sur la nécessité et les moyens d'anéantir les patois et d'universaliser l'usage de la langue française" (1794), reprinted in de Certeau et al., 300–317.

35. Ibid., 301, 316.

36. Alphonse Aulard, *Actes du Comité de Salut Publique*, XIII (Paris, 1900), 105; Brunot, IX, pt. I, 186. The Jacobin Prieur de la Côte d'Or delivered another scathing address on the subject entitled *Adresse de la Convention Nationale au Peuple Français. 16 Prairial II* (B.S.P., Rév. 223, no. 13).

37. F. C. Heitz, ed., *Les sociétés populaires de Strasbourg pendant les années 1790 à 1793: Extraits de leurs procès-verbaux* (Strasbourg, 1863), 252 and 346; Lévy, II, 22; R. R. Palmer, *Twelve Who Ruled* (Princeton, 1941), 190; Michel Brunet, *Le Roussillon: Une société contre l'état, 1780–1820* (Perpignan, 1990), 521. The principal evidence for a linguistic terror in Provence is effectively dismissed by Merle, 369–71.

38. Heitz, 64–5.

39. On these issues see Rosenfeld, "A Revolution in Language," 172–258.

40. Barère, in de Certeau et al., 291–2.

41. Grégoire, in de Certeau et al., 314.

42. See Weber, *Peasants into Frenchmen* (see Intro., n.28), 67–94, 312–13; Jean-François Chanet, *L'école républicaine et les petites patries* (Paris, 1996), 203–41.

43. See, for instance, Brunot, IX, pt. I; Weber, *Peasants into Frenchmen*, 67–94; Renzi, *La politica linguistica* (see Intro., n.63); R. D. Grillo, *Dominant Languages: Language and Hierarchy in Britain and France* (Cambridge, 1989). The literature on revolutionary language policies is immense. For summaries, see an earlier version of this chapter: David A. Bell, "Lingua Populi, Lingua Dei: Language, Religion and the Origins of French Revolutionary Nationalism," *American Historical Review*, C/5 (1995), 1403–37, esp. nn. 9, 32, and 43. Subsequent works include Rosenfeld, "A Revolution in Language"; Sophia A. Rosenfeld, "Universal Languages and National Consciousness during the French Revolution," in David A. Bell et al., eds., *Raison universelle et culture nationale au siècle des lumières* (Paris, 1999), 119–34; Brigitte Schlieben-Lange, *Idéologie, Révolution, et uniformité de la langue* (Liège, 1996).

44. Dentzel, *Rapport,* 2; Grégoire cited in de Certeau et al., 21; cited in Brunot, IX, pt. I, 142; Grégoire in Gazier, *Lettres* (see Intro., n.70), 293.

45. Grégoire, in de Certeau et al., 302.

46. To quote his report: "The vigorous accent of liberty and equality is the same, whether it comes out of the mouth of an inhabitant of the Alps or the Vosges, the Pyrenees or the Cantal, Mont-Blanc or Mont-Terrible." Barère, in de Certeau et al., 291.

47. Quoted in Wahnich, *L'impossible citoyen* (see Intro., n.33), 59.

48. *Réimpression de l'ancien Moniteur,* February 9, 1790, 336–37.

49. For the most recent studies of the disturbances, see Jean Boutier, *Campagnes en émoi: Révoltes et Révolution en Bas-Limousin, 1789–1800* (Treignac, 1987), and John Markoff, *The Abolition of Feudalism: Peasants, Lords and Legislators in the French Revolution* (University Park, Penn., 1996), esp. 203–426, 542–47. Boutier barely mentions the language issue and does not consider it an important cause of the revolts (see esp. 263–66). Markoff raises it only in passing, on 342. The reports of the deputies on the riots can be found in *Réimpression de l'ancien Moniteur,* February 9, 1790, 336–39.

50. Claire Asselin and Anne McLaughlin, in "Patois ou français la langue de la Nouvelle France au dix-septième siècle," *Langage et société,* 17 (1981), 3–57.

51. Yves Castan, "Les languedociens du 18e siècle et l'obstacle de la langue écrite," *96e Congrès national des Sociétés savantes, Toulouse, 1971: Section d'histoire moderne et contemporaine* (Paris, 1976), I, 73–84.

52. Grégoire is notably the most important eighteenth-century source for Weber's chapter on language in *Peasants into Frenchmen,* 67–94.

53. On these points see Louis-Jean Chalvet, *La sociolinguistique* (Paris, 1993); Pierre Bourdieu, *Language and Symbolic Power,* Gino Raymond and Matthew Adamson, trans. (Oxford, 1991).

54. See the works of Robert Lafont, beginning with *Lettre ouverte aux Français d'un Occitan* (Paris, 1973). As Maryon MacDonald has noted in *"We Are Not French!"* (see Intro., n.27), regionalist militants generally try to make their languages sound as un-French as possible.

55. Weber, 3–22.

56. Consider Weber, p. 76, where he quotes from "teachers and school inspectors" who "furnish useful information" in the 1870s. Might these teachers and inspectors have consciously or unconsciously exaggerated the height of the linguistic barriers between them and their pupils? See Lehning, *Peasant and French,* esp 144–45, and Ford, *Creating the Nation* (see Intro., n.28).

57. De Certeau et al, esp. 155–69. The same point of view is expressed more concisely in the classic essay of de Certeau, Julia, and Revel, "La beauté du mort," in Michel de Certeau, *La culture au pluriel* (Paris, 1978), 49–76.

58. See Rosenfeld, "A Revolution in Language."

59. Only two of the sixty correspondents who responded to Grégoire's *enquête* actively defended patois, and the many legislative reports on language aroused little resistance. See Brunot, IX, pt. I, 9. Correspondents who reported on their uses of patois included Auguste Rigaud of Montpellier (Gazier, 13), and Pierre Bernadau of Bordeaux (ibid., 128). Dithurbide of the Basque Country (ibid., 158–60) had previously volunteered as a French-Basque translator (Arch. Nat. AA 32, fol. 22r). The proposals to standardize the regional languages came from the Strasbourg professor Jérémie-Jacques Oberlin (BN NAF 2798, fol. 95), and the Montauban Protestant Antoine Gautier-Sauzin (Arch. Nat. F17 1309, reprinted in de Certeau et al., 259–63). Significantly, both were Protestants.

60. Both Brunot and Patrice Higonnet (in his excellent article "The Politics of Linguistic Terrorism"; see Ch. 3, n.125) see the language policies as products of the radical revolution.

61. On the attempt to create a new, uniform revolutionary culture, see Hunt, *Politics, Culture and Class* (see Ch. 5, n.75), esp. 52–86.

62. See esp. Grégoire, in de Certeau et al., 301, 306.

63. Grégoire, *Essai sur la régénération* (see Intro., n.61), 161.

64. See Talleyrand in *Archives parlementaires* XXX, 472.

65. Gellner, *Nations and Nationalism;* Anderson, *Imagined Communities* (see Intro., n.13).

66. Salivas, *Abis salutari de M. Salivas lou Xoubé al brabé moundé de las campagnos* (Albi, [1790 or 1791]) (Bibliothèque Municipale de Toulouse, hereafter B.M.T., Réserve C^xviii 151). Salivas identifies himself as a wool merchant on 12.

67. Ibid., 4–6. The awkward English sentence beginning "France will be the first" reads in the original: "La Franço sera la premeiro qu'en se randen libro respendra & proupagara la lei de nostré Seigné, & las Natieus de l'Europo que dexa bolou imita nostro Counstitutieu, espousaran tabé toute la puretat de l'Ebanxeli, & aital s'accoumplira lou desir de nostré Redemptiou."

68. Ibid., 7.

69. On the Civil Constitution, see the fundamental work of Timothy Tackett, *Religion, Revolution and Regional Culture in Eighteenth-Century France: The Ecclesiastical Oath of 1791* (Princeton, 1986).

70. Much larger even than in the provincial newspapers studied by Jeremy Popkin in "The Provincial Newspaper Press and Revolutionary Politics," *French Historical Studies,* XVIII/2 (1993), esp. 448–49. For the texts in Occitan, the largest part of the corpus, this conclusion was evident to the leading nineteenth-century specialist in the subject, Jean-Baptiste Noulet, in *Essai sur l'histoire littéraire des patois du midi de la France au xviiie siècle* (Paris, 1877), 137.

71. *Discour d'un péisan a sous councitouyens* (Montpellier, 1791), 9.

72. Compare Garres, *Rasounomens,* 20, and *Abis d'un boun pastou a sous parrouquias* (n.p., n.d.), 15 (B.M.T., Réserve D^{xviii} 756, no. 2).

73. Claude-François Marie Primat, *Herderlyken brief van Mr. den bisschop van het departement van het noorden* (Paris, 1791), 4 (B.S.P. Rév. 222, pp. 650–53). On the case of Flanders in general, see Cooraert, *La Flandre.*

74. In the absence of the necessary Breton language skills, I am forced here to rely on Bernard, "La Révolution française et la langue bretonne." One of the (bilingual) pamphlets in question is partially reproduced on pp. 301–9. The other is *Adresse de la Société des Amis de la Constitution, établie à Brest, aux habitants de la campagne* (Brest, 1791) (B.S.P. Rév. 222, pp. 643–49).

75. *Die neuesten Religionsbegebenheiten in Frankreich,* published in Strasbourg and cited in Popkin, "The Provincial Press," 449. As Popkin points out, there were also several provincial periodicals founded in French for the same purpose.

76. Contemporary historians of Occitan generally subscribe to this view. But these authors, who generally champion increased autonomy (at the least) for the modern Midi, have an ideological committment to excavate the remains of a complete Occitan civilization from under the oppressive structures of (northern) French domination, and it ill suits this purpose to give undue weight to religious uses of their language alone. See, for instance, Martel, "Les textes occitans," 232; Fournier, "La production toulousaine," 367, 391; Merle, 349. Regardless of their regionalist convictions, however, these scholars have produced serious and important work, informed by a deep knowledge of sociolinguistics and the history of their language.

77. The lion's share of these pamphlets can be found at the B.M.T. in the following *recueils:* Réserve D^{xviii} 243, 248, 756; Réserve D^{xix} 134. See also Fournier, "La production toulousaine," esp. 400, and Noulet, *Essai,* 137. For Sermet, see *Discours,* 18.

78. Boyer et al., *Le texte occitan,* 173. These figures leave out Occitan pamphlets published outside of the period 1789–1794 and undatable pamphlets. I am indebted to the meticulous and tireless authors of this book for locating much of the evidence discussed here.

79. Martel, "Les textes occitans," 239. Martel himself argues, somewhat bizarrely (232), that since the map of Occitan publications does not coincide with the map of religious conflict (measured by the percentage of priests who refused to swear allegiance to the Civil Constitution), the Civil Constitution cannot have been a crucial factor—as if regions of resistance such as the Massif central, which utterly lacked any serious tradition of publication in Occitan, would have matched Toulouse in their rates of publication!

80. Ibid., 225. The Toulouse newspaper was called *L'homé franc, Journal tout*

noubel én patois, Fait esprès per Toulouso, no. 1 (Feb. 8, 1791). Only one issue of this paper was printed. It was devoted in large part to the conflict over the Civil Constitution. On the rates of "juring" priests, see Tackett, 355, 373. On the religious situation in Toulouse, see Meyer, *La vie religieuse en Haute-Garonne.*

81. [Pierre Barrau], *Discours prounounçat, le décadi 30 Flouréal, deuxiemo annado de la Républiquo Franceso uno et indibisiblo, per Pierre Barrau, Agent natiounal proche le District de Rioux, imprimat d'aprex la déliberatiou de la Souciétat poupulario de Rioux, le premié Prairial de la memo annado* (Toulouse, 1794), pp. 6–7 (B.M.T. Réserve D^{xviii} 756, no. 12). See also, for instance, *Discours prounounçat par Pierre Barrau, jutgé dé pax dé la coumuno dé Rioux, departomen dé la Hauto-Garonoo, à l'ouccasiou dé la festo d'el 21 Janvié (estillé buffec), lé 10 Niboso (estillé sancer) al pé dé l'arbré dé la libertat* (Toulouse, 1794) (B.M.T. Réserve D^{xviii} 756, no. 14); [Jean-Philibert d'Auriol], *Tableau actuel de la situation publique & triomphante de la République française* (Toulouse, 1794) (B.M.T. Br. Fa. C. 1491). This last text consists of three "patriotic hymms" sung at the Temple of Reason.

82. Bernard, 324–30, 319–20.

83. J. Loth, quoted in Bernard, 295. Bernard himself comments (294): "The proclamations meant for the people of the countryside have the appearance of a sort of sermon, and their allure is much more familiar in the translation than in the [French] original."

84. Merle, 345.

85. Boyet et al., *Le texte occitan,* 42–161.

86. Mikel Bourrel, *Réflexious curiousos q'apprénen a estré cousténs; [constant} car tout passo, tout n'és qué béns, et y a d'annados malhurousos, mais apey bén lé boun téms* (Toulouse, 1790). On the carol, see Régis Bertrand, "Un prêtre provençaliste en Révolution, J. J.Tousaint Bonnet," in Agulhon, ed., *La Révolution vécue par la province,* 140.

87. On Grégoire, see Sepinwall, "Regenerating France" (see Ch. 1, n.91), and Rita Hermon-Belot, *L'abbé Grégoire: La politique et la vérité* (Paris, 2000).

88. Quoted in de Certeau et al., 21.

89. Reproduced in ibid., 13.

90. On the *visites,* see Marc Vénard and Dominique Julia, eds., *Répertoires des visites pastorales de la France,* 6 vols. (Paris, 1977–85). This comparison is also made by Michel Peronnet in "Réflexions sur 'une série de questions relatives aux patois et aux moeurs des gens de la campagne,' proposée par l'abbé Grégoire le 13 août 1790," in *Lengas,* 17 (1985), 79–96.

91. On the friendship, see letters between the men in B.M.T., Réserve D^{xix} 134, and B.S.P., Fonds Grégoire, Correspondence Sermet, as well as Henri Grégoire, *Oraison funèbre d'Antoine-Pascal-Hyacinthe Sermet, Ex-Provincial*

de l'Ordre des Carmes Déchaussés, Membre de l'Académie des Sciences de Toulouse, associé de celle de Montauban, ancien Evêque métropolitain du Sud, prononcé par M. Grégoire, ancien évêque de Blois, Sénateur (Toulouse, 1809).

92. Bernard, 291.

93. Coornaert, La Flandre française, 266.

94. Abbé Cambon to Grégoire, January 9, 1791, B.S.P. Rév. 222, p. 303. See other instances in Brunot, IX, pt. 1, 62–63; Merle, 297; Jean-Paul Damaggio, "La question religieuse à Montauban (1790–1793)," Lengas, 17 (1985), 145–155, esp. 148.

95. For instance, club of Amberieux (Ain) to Grégoire, Dec. 16 1790, BN NAF 2798, fol. 6r; unsigned and undated letter from Lorraine, BN NAF 2798, fol. 26v.; unsigned and undated response sent by the club of Auch, 1790, in Gazier, 100; François Chabot to Grégoire, Sept. 4, 1790, in Gazier, 78. On the professions of the correspondents, see de Certeau et al., 30.

96. Letter of May 11, 1792, Arch. Nat. AA 32, fol. 30ᵥ.

97. For instance, Rigaud to Grégoire, Jan. 28, 1791, in Gazier, 13; Chabot to Grégoire, Sept. 8, 1790, in Gazier, 57; Cambon to Grégoire, Jan. 9, 1791, in B.S.P. Rév. 222, p. 304.

98. Chabot to Grégoire, Sept. 4, 1790, in Gazier, 57; See also Club of Auch to Grégoire, undated, in Gazier, 103.

99. Barère, in de Certeau et al., 292–93. For his discussion of the Basques as a "new people" in danger of falling victim to priestly "fanaticism," see 294.

100. Ibid., 293.

101. Jacobin club of Auch to Grégoire (1790?), in Gazier, 89, 92. The author, by internal evidence, appears to have been a former military officer. Given the vagaries of Occitan orthography, (particularly eccentric for the Gascon dialects), and the inherent difficulty of d'Astros's verse, the bafflement of the peasantry is understandable.

102. As a Toulouse priest wrote in 1752, "Christian doctrine contains truths that are sublime by themselves, but to understand them demands much attention. It therefore only increases the dificulty when these truths are explained in a language unknown to most of those who have no contact with city dwellers." B.M.T. Ms. 892, "Catéchisme dogmatique et moral traduit en langue vulgaire de Toulouse" (1752), 450.

103. It was the clergy that had spurred the development of German in Charlemagne's Europe, and the Slavic languages in the high Middle Ages. In Western Europe, medieval church councils frequently urged priests to explain the mass, preach, and catechize in their parishioners' own language, and in 1562–63 the Council of Trent confirmed the principle See John Michael Wallace-Hadrill, The Frankish Church (Oxford, 1983); Francis Dvornik, Byzantine Missions among the Slavs: SS. Constantine-Cyril and Methodus (New Bruns-

wick, 1970). Early instances in Western Europe include Canon 17 of the Concile de Tours, held in 813. For the Tridentine decisions, see *Le Saint Concile de Trente, oecumenique et général, célébré sous Paul III, Jules III et Pie IV, Souverains Pontifes, nouvellement traduit par M. l'abbé Chanut,* 4th ed. (Rouen, 1705), 245 (Session XXII, ch. 8, Sept. 17, 1562) and 331 (Session XXIV, ch. 7, Nov. 11, 1563). A large section of the French clergy began following these decisions even before the (tardy) formal acceptance into France of Tridentine doctrine.

104. For a notable look at the African situation, see Lamin Sanneh, *Translating the Message: The Missionary Impact on Culture* (Maryknoll, NY, 1990).

105. On this subject, see most recently Margaret J. Leahey, "'Comment peut un muet prescher l'évangile?' Jesuit Missionaries and the Native Languages of New France," *French Historical Studies,* XIX/1 (1995), 105–32.

106. See Julien Maunoir, *Le Sacré Collège de Jesus divisé en cinq classes* (Quimper, 1659), 17–18. Some of Maunoir's missionaries were native Bretons, but most were not.

107. Quoted in Christian Anatole, "La Réforme tridentine et l'emploi de l'Occitan dans le pastorale," *Revue des langues romanes,* LXXVII (1967), 10.

108. Ibid. For many more similar examples of bishops urging their priests to preach and catechize "en langage vulgaire," see Brun, *Recherches historiques,* 433–79; Brunot, V, 25–50; VII, 66–76.

109. Croix (see Intro., n.25), 1207–10; Anatole, "La réforme tridentine," passim.

110. Le Roy Ladurie, "Les minorités périphériques," 608; Brun, *Recherches historiques,* 460.

111. Croix, 1207; Anatole, "La réforme tridentine," passim; Philippe Gardy. "Les modèles d'écriture," passim; R. Armogathe, "Les catéchismes et l'enseignement populaire en France au dix-huitième siècle," in Coulet, ed., *Images du peuple* (see Ch. 1, n.17), 102–21, esp. 114–15.

112. See on this subject Harvey Mitchell, "The World between the Literate and Oral Traditions in Eighteenth-Century France: Ecclesiastical Instructions and Popular Mentalities," in Roseann Runte, ed., *Studies in Eighteenth-Century Culture,* VIII (Madison, 1979), pp. 33–67.

113. See Brunot, VII, 19–25. On Occitan, see Noulet, 7–44. On Catalan, see Brun, *L'introduction du français,* 80.

114. On the debates over "dechristianization," see most recently Chartier, *Cultural Origins* (see Intro., n.32), 92–110. Alsace, again, is an exception to the rule here.

115. For instance, see the appendix to the report from the Club of Carcassonne in Gazier, 22–50; one of the reports from the Club of Auch in Gazier, 91; the report from Pierre Riou, on Brittany, of October 17, 1790, in Gazier, 282.

116. See Brunot, VII, 77–182.

117. Maunoir, *Le sacré collège*, 18.

118. Flemish, Catalan, German, and Italian were different matters, for obvious reasons. At least seven Breton works appeared: Pierre de Châlons, *Dictionnaire Breton-François du Diocèse de Vannes* (Vannes, 1723); Claude-Vincent Cillart de Kerampoul, *Dictionnaire françois-breton ou françois-celtique du dialecte de Vannes* (Leyden, 1744); Tanguy Grégoire de Rostrenen, *Dictionnaire françois-celtique ou françois-breton* (Rennes, 1732) and *Grammaire françoise-celtique ou françoise-bretonne* (Rennes, 1738); Maunoir, *Le sacré collège*; Louis Le Pelletier, *Dictionnaire de la langue bretonne*, 3 vols. (Paris, 1752); and Guillaume Quiquer, *Dictionnaire et colloques françois et breton* (Morlaix, 1626, 73 subsequent editions). The Occitan titles include Achard, *Dictionnaire de la Provence*; Jean Doujat, *Le dicciounari moundi, Dictionnaire de la langue toulousaine* (Toulouse, 1638); Jean-François Féraud, *Essais de grammaire et de glossaire de la langue provençale, pour servir d'introduction et de supplément au dictionnaire provençal* (Marseilles, 1787); Claude Odde de Triors, *Joyeuses recherches de la langue toulousaine* (Toulouse, 1578); Sauveur-André Pellas, *Dictionnaire provençal et françois dans lequel on trouvera les mots . . . et Proverbes expliqués en François* (Avignon, 1723); abbé Sauvages de la Croix, *Dictionnaire languedocien-françois* (Nîmes, 1756, repr. 1785).

119. The exception to this is the oft-reprinted Quiquer, not so much a dictionary or grammar as a bilingual conversation manual apparently designed for merchants operating in Breton-speaking areas. The clerical audience of the others is mentioned explicitly in the various titles, prefaces, and preambles. Given the lack of primary education in Breton, it is doubtful that native Breton-speakers could have used these dictionaries to learn French, and indeed two lacked Breton-French sections entirely (Cillart de Kérampoul and Grégoire de Rostrenen). On Maunoir's views, see *Le sacré collège*, 16. On Maunoir as the "father of modern Breton," see Yannick Pelletier, ed., *Histoire générale de la Bretagne et des Bretons*, 2 vols. (Paris, 1990), II, 508. As for the southern dictionaries, Pellas and Sauvages de la Croix were both priests. Achard was not, but still listed "priests charged with the instruction of the people" first among his potential clients *(Dictionnaire de la Provence*, xiii). Several more southern priests compiled large manuscript dictionaries of the local dialect that never reached a publisher.

120. See, for instance, Cillart de Kérampoul, 184, 189. Grégoire de Rostrenen has a similar definition on 508. French definitions are here given along with the Breton.

121. Castan, "Les languedociens du 18e siècle," 74n; Bernard, "La révolution française et la langue bretonne," 294; Merle, *L'écriture du provençal*, 345.

122. *La douctrino crestiano meso en rimos* (Toulouse, 1641), 5–6. A copy of this rare publication can be found in the B.M.T. Réserve D^xviii 371.

123. Further examples of such sessions can be found, for the Club of Aix, in Merle, 295, and for Strasbourg in de Certeau et al., 280. See also, in general, Brunot, IX, pt. 1, 62–3.

124. See Sepinwall, "Regenerating France," 51–58.

125. See Bell, "Nation-Building and Cultural Particularism," and Ford, *Strasbourg in Transition.*

126. Sepinwall, 35–50. quote from 36.

127. Oberlin, *Essai sur le patois lorrain.* The friendship is described in Sepinwall, 60–68.

128. Quoted in Sepinwall, 61. In French, the brothers were Jérémie-Jacques and Jean-Frédéric.

129. M. Grucker, "Le pasteur Oberlin," *Mémoires de l'Académie de Stanislas,* 5th ser., 4–6 (1888), xxxi–lvi, quote from lxii, quoted in Sepinwall, 66; in general on Oberlin, see Sepinwall, 62–66; Camille Leenhardt, *La vie de Jean-Frédéric Oberlin, 1740–1826* (Paris, 1911); Edmond Parisot, *Un éducateur moderne au XVIIIè siècle: Jean-Frédéric Oberlin (1740–1826)* (Paris, 1907); John W. Kurtz, *John Frederic Oberlin* (Boulder, CO, 1976). On both the Oberlins, I am also indebted here to David Troyansky's "Alsatian Knowledge and European Culture: Jérémie-Jacques Oberlin, Language, and the Protestant Gymnase in Revolutionary Strasbourg," *Francia* 27/2 (2000), 119–138.

130. Kurtz, 230–31, 276–77.

131. I am indebted to Alyssa Sepinwall for pointing me towards this conclusion.

132. See L. E. Schmidt, *Untersuchungen zur Entstehung und Struktur der neuhochdeutschen Schriftssprachen* (Cologne, 1966).

133. Jeremias-Jakob Oberlin to Grégoire in BN NAF 2798, fol. 95, Antoine Gautier-Sauzin in Arch. Nat. F17 1309, reprinted in de Certeau et al., 259–63.

134. See Victor E. Durkacz, *The Decline of the Celtic Languages: A Study of Linguistic and Cultural Conflict in Scotland, Wales and Ireland from the Reformation to the Twentieth Century* (Edinburgh, 1983), 2.

135. Quoted in ibid., 3–5. Similar legislation for Scotland dates from 1616.

136. For a summary of the existing literature, see Geoffrey Parker, "Success and Failure during the First Century of the Reformation," *Past and Present,* 136 (1992), 61–2.

137. Brunot, II, 21.

138. Brun, *Recherches historiques,* 426.

139. Queen Jeanne d'Albret had a Calvinist catechism and the psalms translated into Béarnais, and recruited Béarnais preachers. Though short-lived, her efforts so strengthened Béarnais that the kingdom, fully integrated into France in 1620, resisted French more fiercely than any other Occitan region (the Estates used a bastard Béarnais for their deliberations right down to 1789). See André Armengaud and Robert Lafont, eds., *Histoire de l'Occitanie* (Paris, 1979), 483–86; François Pic, "A propos de l'emploi de l'occitan par la

réforme: Le catéchisme bilingue français-béarnais de Jean-Raymond Merlin,"
*Bulletin de l'Association d'étude sur l'humanisme, la réforme et la renaissance
(France du centre et du sud-est)*, VI/11 (1980), 38–45; Brun, *L'introduction de
la langue française*, 28, 34.

140. After the fall of the Jacobins and the reestablishment of Catholicism,
Grégoire succeeded in getting a law passed to the effect that only the "sacra-
mental formulae" would remain in Latin. On this debate, and Grégoire's crucial role in it, see Brunot, IX, pt. I, 374–78, 396–97. At this date, of course, the
French constitutional church was disavowed by the Vatican.

141. See above all Van Kley, *Religious Origins* (see Intro., n.65).

142. Brunot, V, 25–28.

143. For a summary of these issues, see Sepinwall, 75–79.

144. Maza, *Private Lives and Public Affairs* (see Ch. 2, n.18), 85; cf. Marie-Hélène
Huet, *Rehearsing the Revolution: The Staging of Marat's Death, 1793–1797*,
trans. Robert Hurley (Berkeley, 1992), 49–58.

145. Carla Hesse, "La preuve par la lettre: Pratiques juridiques au tribunal
révolutionnaire de Paris (1793–1794)," *Annales: Histoire, Sciences Sociales*, LI/
3 (1996), 629–42.

146. Grégoire, in de Certeau et al, 303.

147. Chabot to Grégoire, Sept. 4, 1790, in Gazier, 73; Fonvielhe to Grégoire, undated, in BN NAF 2798, fol. 44v.

148. Quoted in Merle, 295.

Conclusion

1. See, for instance, Hobsbawm, *Nations and Nationalism* (see Intro., n.13), 44;
Hugh Seton-Watson, *Nation and States: An Enquiry into the Origins of Nations and the Politics of Nationalism* (New York, 1977), 107.

2. Results from Library of Congress Catalogue at catalog.loc.gov.

3. On the army as a "school of Jacobinism" and, *a fortiori*, of republican
Frenchness during Year II, see Jean-Paul Bertaud, *La Révolution armée: Les
soldats-citoyens et la Révolution française* (Paris, 1979), 194–229.

4. On the republican heritage in nineteenth- and twentieth-century French nationalism, and a comparison with Germany, see Rogers Brubaker, *Citizenship
and Nationhood in France and Germany* (Cambridge, Mass., 1992).

5. See Thiesse, *La création des identités nationales* (see Intro., n.14), which now
provides the best general guide to the phenomenon. Her work builds above
all on Eric Hobsbawm and Terence Ranger, eds., *The Invention of Tradition*
(Cambridge, 1983). On France, see also the work of Poulot, *Musée, nation,
patrimoine* (see Ch. 4, n.10).

6. See de Certeau et al. (see Ch. 5, n.66), esp. 160–69.

7. The crucial works here are Thiesse, *Ils apprenaient la France* (see Ch. 4, n.35), and Chanet, *L'école républicaine et les petites patries* (see Ch. 6, n.42).

8. See Zeev Sternhell, *Maurice Barrès et le nationalisme français* (Paris, 1972); Herman Lebovics, *True France: The Wars over Cultural Identity, 1900–1945* (Ithaca, 1992); and, for an example of Maurras's writings, Charles Maurras, *Maîtres et témoins de ma vie d'esprit: Barrès, Mistral, France, Verlaine, Moréas* (Paris, 1954).

9. Maurice Barrès, *Les déracinés* (Paris, 1911).

10. *Journal officiel de l'Etat français*, Dec. 27, 1941, quoted in Michel Baris, *Langue d'oïl contre langue d'oc de la prise de Montségur (1244) à la loi Deixonne (1951)* (Lyon, 1978), 98; cf. Chanet, 203–41.

11. See Yardeni, *La conscience nationale* (see Intro., n.12); R. Bütler, *Nationales und universales Denken im Werke Etienne Pasquiers* (Basel, 1948).

12. Jules Michelet, *Jeanne d'Arc* (Paris, 1879), and *Histoire de la Révolution française*, 2 vols. (Paris, 1852), I, 21–41.

13. Tallien quoted in Brubaker, 7. See also Jean-Pierre Gross, "La politique militaire française de l'An II et l'éveil du nationalisme," *History of European Ideas*, XV/1 (1992), 347–53.

14. See Wahnich, *L'impossible citoyen* (see Intro., n.33), 127–31.

15. For an extended treatment of this aspect of French nationalism and its comparison with German citizenship practices, see Brubaker, *Citizenship and Nationhood.*

16. On the situation of Alsace, see Bell, "Nation-Building and Cultural Particularism" (see Ch. 2, n.101).

17. Quoted in Albert Soboul, "La Révolution française: Problème national et réalités sociales," in Pierre Vilar, ed., *Actes du Colloque Patriotisme et Nationalisme en Europe à l'époque de la Révolution française et de Napoléon* (Paris, 1973), 29–58, at 34.

18. Ernest Renan, "What Is a Nation?" in Geoff Eley and Ronald Grigor Suny, eds., *Becoming National: A Reader* (Oxford, 1996), 42–55, quote from 53.

19. Many of them also cite Renan's stress on patrimony. See Jacques Chirac, speech to the Institut des Hautes Etudes de Défense Nationale, cited in *Le Monde*, May 31, 2000; also Interior Minister Jean-Pierre Chevènement in dialogue with German Foreign Minister Joschka Fischer, cited in *Le Monde*, June 21, 2000. In recent years in *Le Monde*, see also, for instance, the following articles: Roger-Pol Droit, "Questions de frontières," *Le Monde des Livres*, Sept. 16, 1996; Eric Melchior and Jérôme Sulim, "Thiers, Céline, Brasillach: non, nous n'assumons pas!" *Le Monde*, Feb. 15, 1997; Serina Guillaume, "Une réflexion nécessaire," *Le Monde*, Oct. 18, 1997; Albrecht Sonntag, "Le football: Ciment des nations," *Le Monde*, June 4, 1998; Alain Bergounioux et al., preliminary document of the Parti Socialiste on Europe, discussed in Michel Noblecourt,

"Le PS à la recherche d'une position equilibrée sur la construction européenne," *Le Monde,* Feb. 3, 1999; Jean-Philippe Vincent, "Renan et la Corse," *Le Monde,* June 4, 1999; Clément Jérôme, "France et Allemagne, demain," *Le Monde,* September 24, 1999; Cullin Michel, "Jörg Haider en quête d'une nouvelle identité nationale," *Le Monde,* Feb. 17, 2000.

20. *Réimpression de l'ancien Moniteur,* Dec. 22, 1792, 803.

21. Greenfeld, *Nationalism* (see Intro., n.21), 11, 89–188.

22. Here I take issue with Thiesse, especially in *La création des identités nationales* and her attempt to present French nationalism as fundamentally little different from other European varieties.

23. See Stuart J. Woolf, *Napoleon's Integration of Europe* (London, 1991).

24. See Weber, *Peasants into Frenchmen* (see Intro., n.28), 3–22, quote from 9. To be sure, these same bourgeois observers could also perceive the urban lower classes as dangerous and alien, but with the difference that the urban poor tended to be seen less as pure creatures of nature lacking in social organization, than as members of a corrupt, debauched form of society. In this sense, the distinction recapitulates the early modern distinction between "savages" and "barbarians." See the classic analysis of Louis Chevalier, *Classes laborieuses et classes dangereuses à Paris pendant la première moitié du XIXe siècle* (Paris, 1958).

25. See Woloch, *The New Regime* (see Ch. 5, n.106), 197–222.

26. Weber, 68, 303–38. See also Antoine Prost, *L'enseignement en France, 1800–1967* (Paris, 1968).

27. Quoted in Weber, 332–33.

28. See Jacques and Mona Ozouf, "La Tour de la France par deux enfants," and Pierre Nora, "Lavisse, instituteur national," in Nora, ed., *Les lieux de mémoire* (see Intro., n.33), I, 277–301 and 239–75.

29. See Chanet, esp. 216–23.

30. Most recently on this subject, see Alice Conklin, *A Mission to Civilize: The Republican Idea of Empire in France and West Arica, 1895–1930* (Stanford, 1997).

31. "Let us regard ourselves, you and I, in these cantons, as if we were in China or in Turkey, even though we are in the middle of Christianity, where one sees practically nought but pagans," a priest from the diocese of Nantes wrote to a colleague in 1731. Quoted in Chartier, *Cultural Origins* (see Intro., n.32), 104. For a sustained analysis of the comparison, see Dominique Deslandres, "Le modèle français d'intégration socio-religieuse, 1600–1650: Missions intérieures et premières missions canadiennes," Ph.D. diss., Université de Montréal (1990).

32. See Conklin, 102–4, 135–36.

33. See ibid., 142–173, 246–56.

34. On these points, see above all Gérard Noiriel, *The French Melting Pot: Immi-*

gration, Citizenship and National Identity, trans. Geoffroy de Laforcade (Minneapolis, 1996), esp. 1–90, 189–226. Nora's remarks quoted on 3. For some criticisms of Noiriel, see David A. Bell, "Forgotten Frenchmen," *Times Literary Supplement*, Jan. 24, 1997.

35. For a comparison of French and German citizenship laws, see Brubaker, *Citizenship and Nationhood*.

36. See Gérard Noiriel, "Français et étrangers," in Nora, ed., *Les lieux de mémoire*, pt. III, I, 275–76.

37. See esp. Richard Kuisel, *Seducing the French: The Dilemma of Americanization* (Berkeley, 1993). For commentary in the American media, see for instance Roger Cohen, "Lacking Barricades, France Is in a Funk," *The New York Times*, Dec. 29, 1996, sect. 4, p. 5; Howard LaFranchi, "The Two Faces of France," *The Christian Science Monitor*, July 25, 1994, 9; "The Declining Glory of France," cover story, *Newsweek*, European ed., May 9, 1994.

38. Nora. ed., *Les lieux de mémoire*. For comments on this work see Englund, "The Ghost of Nation Past" (see Intro., n.27), and Bell, "Paris Blues" (see Intro., n.27).

39. Paul Yonnet, *Voyage au centre du malaise français* (Paris, 1993).

40. Henri Mendras (with Alistair Cole), *Social Change in Modern France: Towards a Cultural Anthropology of the Fifth Republic* (Cambridge, 1991), 15.

41. Ibid., 16, and more generally 15–22. See also Henri Mendras, *La fin des paysans* (rev. ed. Paris, 1984).

42. The poll was cited in the *Toronto Star*, July 26, 1998. The figure of 38% was far higher than that in any other European country.

43. Quoted in *The Independent* (London), April 30, 1995, 17. The remark was made in 1991.

44. Pierre Nora, "De la République à la Nation" in *Les lieux de mémoire*, I, 559–67.

45. François Furet, *Interpreting the French Revolution*, Elborg Forster, trans. (Cambridge, 1981), 1–79; François Furet, Jacques Julliard, and Pierre Rosanvallon, *La République du centre: La fin de l'exception française* (Paris, 1988).

46. See Mendras, *Social Change*, 91–106.

47. See ibid., 226–46.

Note on Internet Appendices
and Bibliography

It is, regrettably, impossible to publish a full bibliography and extensive appendices in this book. However, the Internet has enabled scholars to provide longer appendices and bibliographies than were ever normally included in academic books, albeit at the cost of physically separating this material from the text of the book itself.

I have therefore placed the following material on my own permanent web site, www.davidbell.net:

French Quotations: The original French for all citations that appear in this book in translation.

Appendix I: Ten selected engravings of "illustrious Frenchmen" (including Joan of Arc and Marie de Medicis) done after paintings by Philippe Champaigne and Simon Vouët in the Palais Royal (now destroyed), initially published in Marc Vulson de la Colombière, *Les portraits des hommes illustres françois, Qui sont peints dans la galerie du Palais Cardinal de Richelieu, avec leurs principales Actions, Armes & Deuises* (Paris, 1668), discussed in Chapter 4.

Appendix II: The full text, including four engravings, of Antoine-Léonard Thomas, *Jumonville* (Paris, 1759), discussed in Chapter 3.

Appendix III. The full text and a translation into English of Antoine-Hyacinthe Sermet, *Discours prounounçat dabant la legiou de Sant-Ginest, Pel. R..P. Sermet, Exproubincial des Carmés Descaussés, Predicairé ourdinari del Rey, &c.* (Toulouse, 1790), discussed in Chapter 6.

Bibliography. A comprehensive guide to primary and secondary sources pertaining to patriotism and national identity in early modern and revolutionary France, and all other works cited in this volume.

Index